U0454011

美国《1996经济间谍法》
及配套法律中英文解析

Analysis of American " Economic Espionage Act of 1996"
and Related Laws in Chinese and English

侯仰坤　著

知识产权出版社

全国百佳图书出版单位

图书在版编目（CIP）数据

美国《1996 经济间谍法》及配套法律中英文解析／侯仰坤著．—北京：
知识产权出版社，2019.3
　　ISBN 978－7－5130－5832－2

　　Ⅰ.①美… Ⅱ.①侯… Ⅲ.①商业秘密—保密法—研究—美国 Ⅳ.①D971.234

中国版本图书馆 CIP 数据核字（2018）第 213495 号

责任编辑：齐梓伊		责任校对：王　岩	
执行编辑：凌艳怡		责任印制：刘译文	
封面设计：SUN 工作室　韩建文			

美国《1996 经济间谍法》及配套法律中英文解析

侯仰坤　著

出版发行：	知识产权出版社 有限责任公司	网　　址：	http：//www.ipph.cn
社　　址：	北京市海淀区气象路 50 号院	邮　　编：	100081
责编电话：	010－82000860 转 8176	责编邮箱：	qiziyi2004@qq.com
发行电话：	010－82000860 转 8101/8102	发行传真：	010－82000893/82005070/82000270
印　　刷：	北京嘉恒彩色印刷有限责任公司	经　　销：	各大网上书店、新华书店及相关专业书店
开　　本：	720mm×1000mm　1/16	印　　张：	21.75
版　　次：	2019 年 3 月第 1 版	印　　次：	2019 年 3 月第 1 次印刷
字　　数：	286 千字	定　　价：	86.00 元
ISBN 978－7－5130－5832－2			

自　序

　　美国作为世界上的超级大国,先进的科学技术是其立国之本,也是其重要的国家资源。为了有效地保护这种资源,美国已经采取了多种有效的保护措施,并且已经颁布了严密的法律规定,其中,对于涉嫌侵害这种资源中的商业秘密的人,或者认定为"盗窃商业秘密罪",或者认定为"经济间谍罪",同时追究刑事和民事法律责任,使其陷入痛苦而漫长的诉讼程序和牢狱之灾。对于涉嫌"经济间谍罪"的案件,主要由美国联邦调查局负责,他们使用国家权力和国家资源立案调查,其先进的侦查手段和强大的国家机器都是一般的刑事侦查难以比拟的。而且对于被调查者来说,在被逮捕之前往往并不知道自己早已处于被调查之中。

　　最近几年,已有许多位在美国长期从事科学研究的著名美籍华裔科学家,以及曾经在美国留学获得学位,后来又回国工作的中国籍专家学者被指控涉嫌"经济间谍罪",先后受到法律的追究。虽然其中有人确属被冤枉而最终获得无罪释放,但是其家庭和个人的身心都受到了极大的伤害。

　　现在,我国到美国进行留学、访学和技术交流的人员越来越多,参与国际商务活动和涉外工作的人员也越来越多,但是,通过官方的报道可以知道,在美国政府中也有个别的人士担忧我国的这些人员中会有不少潜在的"经济间谍"人员。这样,对于每一位留学生、访问学者、涉外工作人员和进行技术交流的专家学者来说,都有必要首先了解一下美国当前有关"经济间谍罪"的法律规定,避免在自己的留学、工作和技术交流过程中触犯这些法律规定,特别是避免由于自己的过失或者疏忽大意而导致这类行为的发生。

显然,通过正确的途径学习和了解国外的先进技术和科学知识非常重要。而且,我们也完全相信,对于我们中华民族来说,随着我国广大科技人员的不断努力和积极探索,在不远的将来,在一些科学领域,一定会有越来越多的科学技术和科学知识走到世界的前列,为人类社会的发展和进步作出我们中华民族的贡献!

为了保证所引用的美国法律的准确性,本书中所引用的全部美国法律分别来自美国国会的官方网站和美国政府提交给世界知识产权组织,由该组织官方网站发布的内容。

最后,由于作者水平和条件所限,本书中难免存在缺陷和不足之处,敬请各位读者批评指正。

侯仰坤

2018 年 8 月 16 日于北京

目 录
CONTENTS

第二篇　美国《1996 经济间谍法》及配套联邦商业秘密法律

第三篇 美国全国性适用的商业秘密保护示范法

第四篇　美国国会在审议的主要商业秘密立法草案

'01

第一篇
美国特殊的权力
分立与司法制度概况

第一章　美国特殊的权力分立制度

在世界各国中,美国可以说是一个比较特殊的国家。它不仅拥有世界上许多先进的科学技术,比较强大的军事力量和相当发达的经济实力,而且在国家权力的构成、权力的内部构造、权力的分配,以及权力的行使和制约上也有其鲜明的特点。

本书之所以要首先讨论这一问题,正是由于这种国家权力结构设计上的特殊性直接导致了美国司法机构、立法机构和执法机构的特殊性,以及本书中将要讨论的美国联邦知识产权法律的适用范围及其与各州保护知识产权法律的关系的问题。如果不了解这些内容,就难以正确地理解这些法律的相关规定和有些条款的具体含义,也就难以真正地掌握这些法律。正是基于这种原因,我们不得不首先了解和掌握这些与美国知识产权法律直接相关或者内在相关的背景知识。

第一节　国家权力分立的历史原因

一、13 个相互独立的州协商筹建了美国这个国家

众所周知,美国是一个通过独立战争(1775—1783 年)从英国殖民统治下独立出来的国家,而且这个国家就诞生在独立战争的战火中,是由当时仅有的13 个州的代表共同在费城举行的大陆会议上通过签署《独立宣言》宣告成立的,时间是 1776 年 7 月 4 日,这一天也就成了美国的诞生日。

在发生独立战争之前,甚至在已经发生了独立战争的 1775 年,"美利坚合众国"这个国家在世界上并未诞生,而且,在 1776 年 7 月 4 日建国时,

这个国家也只拥有 13 个州的疆域。现在的美国一共拥有 50 个州,后来增加的 37 个州都是在这个国家诞生以后分别通过战争、购买等方式拓展而来的。

在组建美国这个国家之前,这 13 个州都是英国的殖民地。由于没有统一的国家,这 13 个州虽然地域相连,他们居民的历史渊源也相近,除了当地的土著居民以外,外来移民主要来自英国和欧洲的其他国家,大家具有基本相同或者相近的文化传统和生活方式,但是,这 13 个州相互之间又是完全平等和相互独立的。基于对英国和欧洲其他国家的社会管理制度和管理方式的沿袭,当时各个州基本上都有自己相对独立的立法机构(议会),审判机构(法院)和行政管理机构。但是,在诸如地理气候条件、移民人口的状况、土著居民的传统文化和生活方式,以及其他政治经济文化等多种因素的影响下,各个州对于共同建立一个国家的具体期望和具体目标不可避免地存在着差异。在这种情况下,虽然 13 个州的代表存在着共同组建一个统一国家的愿望,并且在共同面临的英国殖民统治和英国军事进攻的压力下,代表们最终通过协商签署了著名的《独立宣言》,但是,相互之间仍然存在着一些问题需要协商。

在协商筹建美国这个国家时,各个州的代表们面临着需要共同解决下列问题:①这个国家成立以后,各个州的利益不能受到损害,各个州政府现有的权力也不能受到过多的影响和限制,这就要求这个国家的中央政府不能拥有太多的权力,而且应当明确地划分出中央政府与各州政府之间的权力界限,中央政府不得擅自超越这个界限行使权力。②既然成立的是一个国家,作为一个国家的中央政府,它应当享有在国际社会中一个中央政府应当拥有的基本权力,诸如国防、外交、统一货币、统一度量衡、统一国家税收等权力。③为了避免中央政府的权力不受约束,中央政府的权力被一分为三,即"立法权""行政权"和"司法权",分别由"美国国会""美国总统"和"美国联邦最高法院及其所属的各级联邦法院"来行使;同时要求在三类权力中,没有任何一类权力大于另外一类权力,也没有任何一类权力不受另外一类权力的约束,而是让每一类权力始终处于另外两类权力的制约和监督之下。④适当地把各州政府拥有的权力让渡给中央政府一部分,使其能够作为中央政府运行起来。⑤如何保障上述愿望得以实现和长久地保持不变。

二、权力分立与制衡在权力实施和权力监督中的渗透与多样化

在美国的权力结构中,实际上存在着三种不同的权力分立构造。第一类就是前文论述的中央政府与各州政府之间的权力分立与划分。第二类是各州之间的权力分立与划分。在统一的美国这个国家建立之前,13 个州都是英国统治的殖民地,它们之间处于相互"独立的状态",除了分别接受英国政府的领导和管理以外,对于自己有权力决定的事务,其他州是无权干涉和介入的,因此,各个州之间的法律地位是平等的。新的国家和中央政府诞生以后,各个州也都不愿意受到其他州的影响和介入,因此,也都不希望改变这种状况。第三类是中央政府和各州政府内部的权力分立与划分,在各个州政府的内部,也与中央政府相似,把政府的公权力全部划分给了州立法机关(州议会)、州司法机关(州高等法院或者州最高等法院指导下的各级州法院)和州行政机关(州长领导下的行政机构)。

对于美国社会来说,这种权力的分立和制衡还只是一个基本的框架,它们就像一台电脑的硬件。然而,能够使电脑产生工作效果的核心部件并不是这种硬件本身,而是安装在硬件上的各类软件。

如果进行综合的分析就能发现,对于美国社会来说,"权力的分立和制衡"并不简单地是指对已有公权力进行"分立和分化",以便让更多的主体分得权力,也不是简单地指对公权力进行外在的或者内在的"监督",它指的是一个系统性地由多种因素构成的相互交叉和相互影响的整体。

例如,对于中央政府权力的监督,如前所述,首先在中央政府内部将国家权力划分为三部分,使得三种权力之间相互制约和制衡。除此之外,分布在全国范围内的联邦法院也可以通过审理案件直接对美国总统颁布的行政命令是否合法进行审查和裁决,如果裁决其不符合美国《宪法》的规定,就可以否决总统作出的这一行政命令,而美国总统拥有的权力"开除"不了联邦法院的法官。这种对中央政府权力的制约就带有一定的广泛性,使得总统自己可能深感防不胜防。同样的道理,虽然各个州议会可以制定和颁布实施本州的法律,但是,如

果有的法律条款与美国《宪法》相冲突,美国联邦法院借助具体的案件也可以否定这一条款的法律效力,从而对各州立法实施监督。

在中央政府内部,对于美国国会审议通过的法案,美国总统享有一定的否决权。对于总统的这种否决权,在附加较高条件的情况下,美国国会又享有否决权的否决权。当美国总统任命自己属下的重要行政官员时,如"国防部长""司法部长"等,还需要美国国会的批准,否则无法任命。

除此之外,美国总统无权任命各州的州长,州长是由本州的社会公众选举产生的,这样,总统也无权领导各州的州长。与此相类似的是,在州以下的县(郡)和市政府中,"县长"和"市长"也不是由州长任命的,而是由所在地的社会公众选举产生的。因此,州长不能直接领导县长,县长不能直接领导市长,州长、县长和市长都无须对上级负责,只需要对自己所辖领域内的社会公众负责。如果表现不良,或者无所作为,在一般四年一届的选举中就可能被自己管辖的社会公众所抛弃,从而不再是"官"。

更突出的权力分立和权力制衡表现在对社会财产的管理权限上。对于美国总统,对中央政府中的行政机构正常运行所需要的年度资金都必须先进行年度预算,然后经过美国国会的批准,如果不能获得国会的批准,中央政府就无法自己运行,不得不关门。对于其他重要的资金也是如此。对于各个州的行政长官来说也是如此,州长、县长和市长都没有权力基于自己的判断签字批准使用社会公共的资金和资产,也没有权力随意地划拨土地和减免税收。这样,就把"公权力"自身限制在了一个他们认为合适的范围以内,不让"公权力"像野草一样,不受任何制约任意地疯长。

从科学的角度来说,控制人们不要在容易发生火灾的区域内随意地点火,比放纵人们随意地点火,然后再把工作重点放到筹建额外的消防队伍,训练消防队伍提高灭火技巧更科学;而控制人们不要在容易发生火灾的区域内随意地点火,又不如采取先进的技术措施把"容易发生火灾的区域"改造成"不容易发生火灾的区域"更加彻底和更加有效。很显然,在学术上,这是一种科学理念的讨论,而在现实中,在一定程度上,这却是真正地实现为民众服务,并且获取民众的理解和接受的两种不同的价值选择。

除了上述情形之外,对于直接执行公权力的机构和部门,如警察部门、检察部门和法院,以及其他的行政执法部门,对于它们的控制和影响也将直接影响着公权力的分立和制衡。在美国当前的社会中,在总统领导下的中央行政机关中没有像我国公安部这样统一领导全国警察的机构,也没有像我国最高人民检察院这样统一领导全国检察院的机构,以及像我国最高人民法院这样统一指导全国法院的机构。虽然美国也有全国最高法院,但是,美国的法院分为联邦法院和州法院两个相对独立的系统,全国最高法院属于联邦法院系统,对于各个州法院没有如我国最高法院对全国各级法院的指导关系。这样也就在一定程度上消减了总统的权力,也消减了这一系统中不同等级的长官的权力。

按照美国现有的管理模式,首先,他们直接省略了这些"公权力"中的一部分内容,特别是中间管理机构和管理环节中的权力;其次,把一部分"公权力"的决定权交给了各个公检法以及其他行政执法机构所在管辖地的社会公众,最终由当地的公众投票决定在这些机构中的部门负责人及其相关人员的去留,以及他们职位的留存;最后,还有一部分涉及公检法和其他行政执法的"公权力"的决定权交由美国国会或者中央行政机构中的具体部门负责。

这样,对于以美国总统为代表的各级行政机构中的领导们来说,第一,他们不能直接控制和支配财政;第二,他们不能直接决定重要的人事任免;第三,他们无权直接动用公检法机构和其他执法部门来实施自己的目的。

通过上述综合的设计,他们完成了对"公权力"比较彻底的"分立和制衡"。不难想象,在这种设计的土壤中,各种借助公权力进行腐败的种子恐怕都难以轻松地找到生根发芽的机会。

当然,对于管理社会的方式和方法问题,由于各个国家的具体国情不同,不可能简单地进行对比。同样,在一个国家行之有效的管理方式,在另一个国家可能并不会产生同样的社会效果。本书介绍上述内容的目的在于帮助读者能够对美国商业秘密法律中所包含的内容产生比较深入的了解和正确认识,除此之外,对于其他内容就不再进行讨论。

第二节 美国《宪法》对权力分立制度的固化与保障

一、美国《宪法》的基本宗旨和基本框架

(一)美国《宪法》的立法宗旨

美国《宪法》(本书中除了做特殊说明之处,《宪法》就是指美国《宪法》,不包括美国各个州的《宪法》)开篇即直接列出了立法的宗旨:我们美国人民,为了建立一个能够维护公平正义,确保国家安全和国内安宁,不断提高人民福利,确保我们自己以及子孙后代都能够享有自由和幸福的更加美好的联邦共和国,创建这部美国《宪法》。

我们从这一立法宗旨中可以认识到,作为一部法律,这一部《宪法》应当包含的基本内容,以及应当彰显的基本理念。

(二)美国《宪法》的签署与生效

在当前的美国社会中,《宪法》是一切国家权力的来源,以及判断除了《宪法》之外的所有美国法律是否合法的依据,因此,凡是被《宪法》明确确认的国家权力,都是合法性的权力;在此基础上,凡是由《宪法》明确授权行使某一类国家权力的主体都是合法的权力主体。在此情形下,为能够准确理解和掌握美国商业秘密法,就有必要对涉及联邦法律和州法律的《宪法》相关条款进行了解。

1787 年 9 月 17 日,包括在 1789 年当选第一届美国总统的华盛顿在内的来自 12 个州的 39 名代表在美国的费城市签署了美国的这一国家《宪法》(Constitution of the United States)。1788 年 6 月 21 日,经过 9 个州的投票批准以后,该《宪法》生效。

1787 年 9 月 17 日在《宪法》草案上签字的代表分别来自下列 12 个州:特拉华州、马里兰州、弗吉尼亚州、佐治亚州、北卡罗来纳州、南卡罗来纳州、新罕布什尔州、马萨诸塞州、康涅狄格州、纽约州、新泽西州、宾夕法尼亚州。

（三）美国《宪法》的基本框架

《宪法》包括正文（即未经过修改增加修正案的文本，也称为原始文本）的内容和修正案的内容两部分。

《宪法》正文共有 7 章 24 条。从 1789 年至 1992 年，又有 27 条修正案获得批准，作为《宪法》正文的附加条款。这些修正案都作为正文的附加条款附加在正文的后面，并未直接对正文本身进行修改，修正案与正文具有同等的法律效力。从 1992 年至今，没有新的修正案获得批准。值得说明的是，除了上述已经被批准的修正案以外，自《宪法》诞生以后，先后还有许多修正案未被批准。

因此，可以说，当今美国的《宪法》共包括 7 章 24 条的正文，以及 27 条的修正案。

《宪法》中七章正文所规定的主要事项分别为：①第一章是对美国国会相关事项的规定；②第二章是对总统有关事项的规定；③第三章是对美国司法制度，主要是联邦法院系统有关事项的规定；④第四章是有关各州之间，以及联邦政府与各州之间相互关系的规定；⑤第五章是有关修改《宪法》有关程序和条件的规定；⑥第六章是有关美国《宪法》和联邦法律与各个州的《宪法》及州的法律之间相互关系的规定；⑦第七章中规定《宪法》经过 9 个州批准后生效，并且在所批准的州中产生效力。

二、美国《宪法》中涉及权力分立的重要事项

美国《宪法》对国会、总统和联邦法院的权限及其选举制度进行了详细的规定，同时对国会的组成结构和修改《宪法》的程序也进行了规定。除此之外，其对各个州相互之间，以及各个州与联邦政府之间的权力关系和法律关系也进行了规定。

除了上述一般性的规定之外，还有一些具体的内容比较重要。

（一）总统与国会到底谁能最终决定一部联邦法律能否生效

按照《宪法》第一章第 7 条的规定，所有联邦法律都必须要先后经过众议院和参议院的表决通过，然后再提请总统批准以后，才能成为正式有效的国家法律。

从这一规定来看,虽然起草和审议通过一部联邦法律议案的权限在国会,但是,最终批准这一法律并使之生效的权限却在总统。由此可见,联邦法律立法的最终决定权在总统,而不在国会。

除此之外,在现实中,总统还可以通过发表国情咨文等方式建议国会对某些社会领域中的重要事项进行立法,或者修订那些已经与社会现实相脱节的现有法律。这样,总统还能在一定程度上参与或者影响某些立法活动。

从这两个方面来看,似乎对于国会的立法权来说,总统的行政权具有最终的决定权,其权力显然也大于立法权。但是,这只是问题的一个方面,因为如果真是这样,那就违背了三权分立和三权制衡的原则。

对此,《宪法》中又明确规定,如果总统未批准(包括否决)国会提交的法律议案,则需要按照下列三种不同的情形进行处理。

1. 总统直接否决了国会提请的法律议案

当国会把经过众议院和参议院分别表决通过的法律议案(bill)提请总统批准时,如果总统因为不同意该议案,而直接否决了该议案,那么,总统应当把该法律议案连同他的否决意见一起退回给国会,国会则把该法律议案及总统的否决意见一起退回给当初起草和提交审议该法律议案的众议院或者参议院。因为在国会中,无论众议院还是参议院都有自己的多个专门委员会,都能基于自己的调查和研究,起草和提交一项法律议案,然后由两院分别进行表决,两院一旦都表决通过以后就提请给总统批准。因此,被总统退回的法律议案既可能最终被退回到众议院,也可能最终被退回到参议院。

当初负责起草这一法律议案的众议院或者参议院收到被退回的材料后,该院可以重新对是否同意把该法律议案颁布为联邦法律进行表决,如果获得 2/3 以上的票数支持,则再提交给另一个议院(参议院或者众议院)进行表决,如果也获得了 2/3 以上的票数支持,则该法律议案直接生效为联邦法律(law),不再需要经过总统的批准。这样,也就实际否决了总统的决定,而且在程序上不再需要经过总统的审批,从而避免了陷入程序上的怪圈。通过这一程序,也体现出国会对总统享有的"立法决定权"的监督和制约。

当然,《宪法》中对于在这种情形下二次表决的程序做了限制性的规定,一是要求在二次表决时,不能先对已经遭到总统否决的法律议案本身的内容进行修改以后,然后再进行表决,只能是对原法律议案本身直接进行二次表决。二是表决时,可被选择的答案只能为"是否同意该法律议案成为联邦法律",议员们只能选择"是"或者"否",不能再有其他选项。三是要求把表决时各位议员作出的选项真实地记录下来,并且作为资料保存起来,用以证明表决结果的真实性,以及回应将来可能发生的复查活动。

在美国历史上,虽然议案因为遭到总统否决而未能成为法律的案例并不多,但是,也确实发生过一些案例。在被总统否决以后,又被国会实施"否决之否决",并且最终使得法律议案成为法律的案例,在最近几年中也发生过。例如,2016 年的一项联邦法律议案,当时就在总统奥巴马和国会之间经历了这样一种权力较量和权力制衡。

由美国民主党和共和党两党议员共同提交的法案——"9·11 受害者起诉沙特政府"法案,其主要内容是允许那些在美国本土遭受到恐怖袭击的受害者及其家属有权在美国的法院起诉涉嫌支持恐怖主义的外国政府(这里主要是指沙特政府)。该法案分别于 2016 年 5 月和 2016 年 9 月获得美国国会参议院和众议院的批准,但是在 2016 年 9 月 23 日,它却遭到总统奥巴马的否决,总统的理由是这一法案可能损害美国的安全利益。总统否决后,该法律议案连同总统的否决意见一起被退回了国会。2016 年 9 月 29 日,参议院以 97 票对 1 票,众议院以 348 票对 77 票的投票结果推翻了总统奥巴马对该法案的否决,使得该法案直接生效成为国家法律。当然,在美国历史上,出现这类能够顺利地否决总统已经作出的否决决定的情形比较少见。这是因为,最近几十年来,美国总统都是在"民主党"或者"共和党"之中产生,而众议院和参议院的议员也基本上来自上述两个党派,因此,国会在投票否决总统已经作出的决定时,往往会在一定程度上受到不同党派的影响,从而使在参众两院都能达到"2/3"以上多数票的可能性受到影响。本案中,国会两院的行为和表决结果直接彰显出对总统享有的"立法决定权"的约束①,也在现实中体现出三权分立和三权制衡的实际效果。

---

① 新华网:"奥巴马否决权首次被国会推翻",http://www.xinhuanet.com/world/2016 - 09/30/c_129307296.htm,访问日期:2018 年 3 月 28 日。

2. 总统 10 天未退回法律议案视为批准

《宪法》第一章第 7 条同时规定,如果国会把法律议案提交给总统,总统在收到后的 10 天内(周日除外)未退回,则视为总统已经批准了该法律议案。

3. 总统无法退回导致法律议案失效

《宪法》第一章第 7 条还同时规定,如果由于国会休会,导致总统不能按时把法律议案退回国会,将导致该法律议案失效,不能成为法律。

由此可见,根据美国《宪法》的上述规定,对于联邦法律的立法,最终的决定权应当在美国国会,而不是在总统,这也体现出国会对总统权力的一种总的制约和制衡。

需要说明的是,美国《宪法》第一章第 7 条还明确规定,除了联邦法律的立法程序需要严格按照上述规定办理以外,凡是需要经过国会的两院表决通过的任何规范社会事务的法规、命令等内容,也都需要经过总统批准,国会与总统对于这些法规和命令的权限及权限救济程序和法律议案审批的程序相同,即对于国会审议通过的法规和命令,最终的立法决定权仍然属于国会,而不属于总统。

另外,值得特别说明的是,根据美国《宪法》的规定,对于联邦的法律、法规和命令,无论是由总统批准生效的,还是由于未能获得总统的批准而最终是由国会批准生效的,这些已经生效的联邦法律、法规和命令最后都要受到联邦法院的监督和审查。联邦法院有权审查这些联邦法律、法规和命令是否存在违背《宪法》内容的情形,如果存在违反《宪法》内容的情形,则可以判决这些法律、法规和命令无效。

因此,可以说,从立法的程序上来说,国会对联邦法律、法规和命令能否生效享有最终的决定权,而对于已经生效的联邦法律、法规和命令来说,联邦法院则享有决定它们是否合法、是否能够存在和发生法律效力的最终决定权。这里的联邦法院不仅是指美国联邦最高法院,还包括众多联邦地区法院和联邦上诉法院。这一权力结构和运行模式再次体现出了美国立法、司法和行政三权分立,相互制衡的特色。

（二）联邦法院对于总统颁布实施的行政命令具有审查和否决权

根据美国《宪法》规定，除了国会可以起草、审议并向总统提交联邦法律、法规和命令以外，总统自己也有权力直接下达和实施一些行政命令，无须经过国会批准就能够直接生效，在全国行政机关内执行。但是，依据美国《宪法》规定，联邦法院同样有权对总统颁布实施的这些行政命令进行违宪审查，并且有权决定被审查的行政命令是否合法有效，以此直接决定这些行政命令能否存在和能否产生法律效力，这体现了司法权力对行政权力的最终监督权和决定权。

例如，美国总统特朗普于2017年1月27日签署了一份名为"阻止外国恐怖分子进入美国的国家保护计划"（以下简称旅行禁令）的行政命令。这份行政命令宣称，在未来90天内，禁止向伊拉克、叙利亚、伊朗、苏丹、索马里、也门和利比亚7个伊斯兰国家的普通公民发放签证，以防止从这些特朗普所称的"高危地区"输入恐怖主义。行政命令还指出，某些签证可以例外，如外交人员、持有北约成员签证的人员以及在联合国工作的员工可以免除相关要求。另外，特朗普还计划暂停原有的难民接纳项目120天，以便对难民进行充分背景核查；还要求无限期停止接收来自叙利亚的难民①。由于上述国家主要是以穆斯林为主要人口的国家，因此，特朗普总统的这一命令又被媒体称为"穆斯林禁令"。

2017年1月30日，美国华盛顿州总检察长鲍勃·弗格森（Bob Ferguson）宣布，他正在就总统特朗普禁止7国穆斯林入境美国的不合理的行政命令起诉特朗普。鲍勃·弗格森在新闻发布会上表示，如果起诉成功，这将令特朗普的这一不合法的行政命令在全美范围内失效。鲍勃·弗格森说："我们国家是基于宪法和法律存在的，在法庭上，并不是谁的声音最大谁就能胜诉，胜败应当由宪法决定。我们认为，总统的这一行政命令并不合法。"②

鲍勃·弗格森在提交给华盛顿州西雅图联邦地区法院的起诉状中称，"虽

① 观察者网："特朗普签署'穆斯林禁令'：停止向7个伊斯兰国家发签证拒绝叙利亚难民"，http://www.guancha.cn/global-news/2017_01_28_391747.shtml，访问日期：2017年1月28日。

② 中国新闻网："美国华盛顿州总检察长就'移民禁令'起诉特朗普"，https://news.qq.com/a/20170131/006678.htm，访问日期：2017年1月31日。

然旅行禁令中指出这样做是基于国家的起源或信仰,但是,这样做却违背了华盛顿州保护公民人权和宗教自由的历史","华盛顿州有责任去保护那些因为发生不合理的歧视行为而受到伤害的居民"。

2017 年 2 月 3 日,西雅图联邦地区法院的法官詹姆斯·罗巴特裁决在全国范围内暂停实施特朗普总统于 2017 年 1 月 27 日颁布的旅行禁令①。该裁决颁布以后,美国国务院和国土安全部称,作为对法院所作出禁令的回应,他们已经停止执行特朗普总统的行政命令。2 月 4 日,美国司法部针对西雅图联邦地区法院作出的这一裁决,依据法律程序,向位于加利福尼亚州旧金山市的美国联邦第九巡回上诉法院提起了上诉(按照美国法律规定,华盛顿州西雅图联邦地区法院审理的一审案件,由联邦第九巡回上诉法院负责二审),要求立即推翻一审法院的这一裁决②。

2017 年 2 月 5 日,美国联邦第九巡回上诉法院驳回了美国司法部的申请,拒绝立即恢复特朗普的旅行禁令。

随后,美国总统修改了其于 2017 年 1 月 27 日颁布的旅行禁令的内容,然后于 2017 年 3 月颁布了一个新的禁令,这一新的禁令同样遭遇到在其他联邦地区法院提起的诉讼,从而难以实施。总统不得不又于 2017 年 9 月颁布了另一个新的禁令。最后,美国联邦最高法院于 2017 年 12 月 4 日裁决总统特朗普于 2017 年 9 月颁布的最后这一旅行禁令可以在美国实施,但是,同时也指出,对于 2017 年 9 月最后颁布的这一旅行禁令,各地的联邦法院仍然享有审判权。当然,基于美国联邦最高法院的裁决,总统特朗普可以依据于 2017 年 9 月最后颁布的这一旅行禁令来禁止或者限制来自伊朗、利比亚、叙利亚、也门、索马里、乍得、朝鲜的公民,以及来自委内瑞拉的一些政府官员入境,哪怕他们有亲属在美国,或者是与美国机构有关联也难以豁免③。

至此,美国总统特朗普三易其稿以后的行政命令最后借助联邦最高法院的

---

① 搜狐网:"美国法官封杀特朗普'禁穆令'以禁令对禁令",http://news.sohu.com/20170204/n479880856.shtml,访问日期:2017 年 2 月 4 日。

② 凤凰网:"上诉法院驳回恢复移民禁令要求,特朗普首次面对联邦系统制约",http://news.ifeng.com/a/20170206/50655922_0.shtml,访问日期:2017 年 2 月 6 日。

③ 和讯新闻:"美国旅行禁令通过 联邦最高法院裁定特朗普早前签署的旅行禁令完全有效",http://www.news.hexun.com,访问日期:2017 年 12 月 5 日。

准许才最终得以实施。由此可见,对于美国总统颁布的行政命令,一位联邦地区法院的法官,相当于初审法院的法官,就能通过违宪审查直接裁决停止执行这一总统的命令,这一裁决一经作出立即生效,而且效力直接归属于总统领导的中央各行政部门,包括国务院、国土安全部等部门都不能再执行总统的这一命令。在这里,突出地彰显出司法裁决的效力大于行政权的效力,当然,也就是司法权对行政权的一种监督和制衡,明确地确认了司法权对行政权的最终决定权。

（三）联邦法律与各州法律的管辖领域不同

根据美国《宪法》第六章的规定,《宪法》、联邦法律,以及已经批准的国际条约在美国都属于最高的国家法律,全国所有的法官,无论是联邦法院的法官,还是各州法院的法官都必须遵从。对于属于州法院的法官来说,如果本州的《宪法》、州法律与美国《宪法》、联邦法律和国际条约发生冲突,则只能遵从法律效力高的美国《宪法》、联邦法律和国际条约,而不能适用本州的《宪法》、本州的法律。这一规定明确界定了国家级法律与各州法律之间的法律位阶和法律效力问题。

但是,需要说明的是,由于在国家权力分立中包含着中央政府与各州政府之间的权力分立和划分的问题,这样在社会事务中,也同样划分为专门由中央政府管辖的社会事务,以及专门由各州政府管辖的社会事务,两者相互独立,不发生交叉和重合。对于各自分管的社会事务,中央政府借助联邦法律和中央政府行政管理机构及其所属部门进行管理,各州政府借助本州的法律和本州政府行政管理机构及其下属部门进行管理,两者基本属于相互独立的两套体系。

在这种情况下,应该很少发生联邦法律与各州法律产生冲突的情况。当然,在具体的案件中,可能会发生有些权利属于州法律管辖,相关的另一些权利又属于联邦法律管辖,或者直接涉及是否违反《宪法》,是否涉及《宪法》中所规定的相关事项的问题。

由此可见,虽然在法律效力上可以笼统地说联邦法律的效力高于州法律的效力,但是,就两类法律对社会所产生的实际作用来说,这种比较更具有宣示国家主权和国家统一的性质,其内含的法律因素并不显著。

因此,从处理社会具体事务的角度来看,在多数情况下,应当并不经常体现出联邦法律高于州法律的问题。

三、美国《宪法》修正案中规定的公民基本权利

除了上述 7 章正文之外,在现有的 27 条修正案中,影响比较大的是从第 1 条到第 10 条的修正案,被人们习惯地称为"权利法案"(A Bill of Rights)。这一权利法案是从 1787 年到 1788 年的两年期间,当不同的州开始陆续批准这部《宪法》时就被作为条件提出来的。从马萨诸塞州开始,许多州都要求在这部《宪法》中增加一些公民应当享有的基本权利内容,这些权利内容在英国和当时的 13 个州的政治传统中都拥有核心的价值地位。《宪法》被批准生效后,根据《宪法》的规定立即成立了美国第一届国会,第一届国会成立后,立即批准了这一权利法案,即修正案的第 1 条到第 10 条,从 1791 年 12 月 15 日起生效。

这 10 条权利法案的基本内容为:

第 1 条:为保障基本人权禁止国会颁布相反法律的权利。

国会不得制定和颁布实施包含下列事项的法律:创建或者选择一种宗教为国教;禁止信教自由、言论自由、出版自由;取消人民享有的和平集会的权利,或者取消人民享有的向政府请愿或者申冤的权利。

第 2 条:保障民众拥有枪支的权利。

对于各州来说,纪律良好的民兵组织对于保护各州人民的安全十分重要,因此,人们合法地拥有武器的权利不可侵害。

值得说明的是,正是由于这一条款的存在,才使得美国当今社会有关取消私人拥有枪支的社会问题一直难以获得解决。因为按照美国《宪法》的规定,只要不修改或者废除这一条款,包括国会、总统和联邦最高法院在内的美国任何权力机构和任何个人都不得作出违背这一条款的规定和行为,否则就是违法。

而且,同样是根据美国《宪法》的规定,想要修订这一条款,必须启动严格的《宪法》修改和批准程序,而要启动和实现这一目的,由于当今社会中人们对

于这一问题的观点和立场还存在着很大的差异,因此,确实存在着许多难以克服的困难。

由此,也可以看出,为了保障这部《宪法》的稳定性和具有最高的法律效力,制宪者起草制定这部《宪法》时围绕这两个问题进行了比较精心的设计和安排。现在看来,这两个目标都圆满地实现了。现在人们想要轻易地避开其中的任何一道保护这种稳定性的"保险",会遇到难以逾越的困难。不过这也从另一个角度说明,对于一部法律来说,对启动修改程序设置严格和较高的条件,就像设置了一道比较复杂的密码一样,对于保障这部法律自身的稳定性还是很有作用的。

第 3 条:禁止军人私驻民宅的权利。

无论是在战争时期,还是在和平时期,除非法律有特殊的规定以外,未经房屋主人的同意,任何士兵都不准进驻私人的住宅。

第 4 条:保障公民基本人身安全的权利。

(1)公民享有人身不被逮捕,房屋、证件和财产不被搜查的权利;任何部门和个人都不得侵害这一权利,也不得指使或者授权他人侵害这一权利。

(2)只有依法履行了法定的手续以后,才能对法律明确规定的具体人员、地点和事物进行逮捕和搜查。

第 5 条:被告人在刑事诉讼中享有的权利和私有财产不被侵害的权利。

(1)(大陪审团的公诉审查权)除非被大陪审团批准同意进行公诉,任何人都不应当被法院判处死刑或者重罪。但是,当军人执行战时任务,或者民兵在国家处于危险状态执行本职任务时除外。

(2)(避免重复人身刑)基于同一犯罪行为,不得对任何被告判处两次人身刑,包括剥夺生命或者限制人身自由的惩罚。

(3)(不应自证有罪的权利)在任何刑事案件中,任何被告都不得被强迫证明自己有罪。

(4)(生命财产受法律保护的权利)未经法定的程序,任何人的生命、财产和自由都不得被剥夺。

(5)(私人财产不被充公的权利)没有公正合理的补偿,不得为了公共事务的目的而征用私人的财产。

值得讨论的是,在上述规定中,有些条款可能在一定的社会历史条件下是比较科学合理的,但是,当社会条件和社会的发展阶段已经发生了较大的变化以后,原有的一些法律规定可能就与现实的社会不再相融,甚至产生冲突,并且由此导致或者诱发可悲的社会结果。例如,对于第 5 条中的"被告的沉默权",如果站在犯罪嫌疑人的角度来说,可能会成为一把保护伞,助其尽量掩盖自己的罪行,逃避或者减轻法律的制裁。这样做,对应的另一种结果就是可能会给公检法机关查明案件事实增加很大的障碍和困难,从而导致犯罪嫌疑人不能得到应有的法律制裁,也使得受害人难以获得精神上的抚慰和经济上的救济,文明社会内含的公平和正义也得不到维护和彰显。显然,这不是法律所追求的目标,也不是社会公众和文明社会自身所希望看到的结局!因此,可以说,无论一些从事法学研究的专家学者们怎么基于自己的学术研究对于这一规定的合理性进行论述和解说,都无法改变这样的社会现实:即这种规定本质上是对社会公众利益的一种侵害,也在一定程度上是对犯罪行为的一种放纵,并且,这一规定在一定程度上加重了犯罪行为对社会公众心理的威吓程度,客观上帮助和协助了犯罪行为的实施、犯罪结果的延伸,以及犯罪危害性的扩大。

例如,2017 年 6 月 9 日,在美国发生的绑架中国公民章莹颖致死一案中,被告伊利诺伊大学香槟分校的在校博士生布伦特·A.克里斯滕森在被警方抓获后,一直拒绝说出章莹颖的下落。据媒体报道:"当地警方介绍,嫌疑人在受到询问时一直保持沉默,只是对于绑架章莹颖的指控予以否认。当警察数次询问他把章莹颖藏在哪里,嫌疑人都表示要找律师,并保持沉默。警方目前正在极力地搜集证据。"①这使警方不能及时地救出被害人章莹颖。甚至当此案已经被移交到美国联邦法院进行审理以后,被告仍然对于章莹颖的下落保持沉默,致使章莹颖失踪至今,一直没有被人们找到。

由此可见,在刑事案件中,设立和保护被告的沉默权,无论在法学理论上能够被论证得多么完整和完美,但是在社会现实中,对于被害人和社会公众来说,

---

① 新华网:"嫌犯拒不交代被绑架中国女留学生章莹颖下落",http://edu. sina. com. cn/a/2017 – 07 – 03/doc-ifyhrxsk1650950. shtml,访问日期:2017 年 7 月 3 日。

这种"沉默行为"的反复实施,可能都是一种新的不作为的犯罪行为,并由此造成新的伤害。

由此可见,任何一部法律的优劣,以及任何一项法律条款的优劣,都不能只看它是由谁起草的,是由什么机构颁布的,而应该审查这部法律和这一项条款本身是否能够公平合理地解决社会中的现实问题,这一标准应当作为评判的主要标准。

因此,对于本条款中的"被告的沉默权"这一规定,它是否符合社会的"公平正义"和"科学合理性"都是值得深入讨论的。

第 6 条:被告在刑事诉讼中享有的其他权利。

(1)在所有刑事诉讼中,只要案件发生地已经有明确的相关法律规定,被告就有权利获得由案件发生地的公正的陪审团进行及时公开审判的权利,并且应当被明确地告知所犯罪行的案由和犯罪类型。

(2)被告有对指认其构成犯罪的证人进行当面质证的权利。

(3)被告有利用司法途径获取对其有利证据的权利。

(4)被告有获得律师帮助辩护的权利。

第 7 条:获得陪审团参与审判的权利。

在依据普通法审理的案件中,只要诉争的标的超过 20 美元,就应当为当事人保留请求陪审团参与审判的权利,而且,凡是被陪审团认定的事实,其他所有的法院都不得再依据普通法的规定进行重复审理。

第 8 条:减免过度惩罚的权利。

对于被指控的人,应当采取适度的保证金、罚金和其他惩罚措施,不应当采用过度或者残忍的惩罚手段。

第 9 条:继续享有已有的权利。

《宪法》中虽然明确地列举了一些公民应当享有的具体权利,但是,这并不等于《宪法》否认或者忽视公民基于传统,以及原有的法律所已经享有的权利,人们仍然有权继续享有这些权利。

第 10 条：各州和民众分享的权利。

凡是国会没有授权给联邦政府，又没有明确禁止各州不能拥有的权力，都可以由各州和民众享有。

值得说明的是，上述 10 条修正案，即人们通常所说的"权利法案"在美国社会中一直发挥着重要的作用，对于美国民众的基本生活产生着重要的影响。

除了上述权利法案以外，其他的条款虽然也涉及一些社会的重要问题，但是总体来说关于总统和国会选举的内容居多，在此就不再详细地进行介绍和讨论。

第二章　美国特殊的司法制度

美国特殊的建国历史和建国方式,以及筹建这个国家的 13 个州的代表们通过协商所最终确立的国家权力划分、权力结构、权力构造和权力运行方式,使得美国这个国家的司法制度具有独特的特点,这种特点在法院系统、检察系统、警察系统和监狱系统中都有明显的体现。

第一节　联邦法院和州法院构成两套不同的法院系统

如前所述,在美国权力的划分中,包含着中央政府与各州政府之间的权力划分,在中央政府和各州政府的权力组成中,都分别包含着立法权、司法权和行政权,这样在中央政府和各州政府之间就不可避免地产生中央政府的法院(被称为联邦法院)和各州政府的法院(被称为州法院)两类不同的法院的划分。

美国的联邦法院和各州法院分别是相互独立的两个法院系统,分别独立地完成自己的案件受理和审判职能。但是,两个系统的内部又有着区别和不同,就整个国家来说,联邦法院自身是一个完整的法院系统,并且是一个全国统一的系统。而对于州法院系统来说情况则比较复杂,首先,各州之间的法院系统相互独立,各自独立地受理案件和完成自己的案件审判工作;其次,各个州的法院自身在法院总的层级设计,不同层级的法院名称,以及案件在二审后生效还是三审后生效等方面都各自为政,完全由各州自己决定和实施,呈现出一种多样性。特别是,各个州法院分别适用各个州自己的法律,两个州之间的法律不具有统一性。

显然,"州法院系统"只是一个法学术语和理论概念,在美国,每一个州的法院系统相对于联邦法院系统来说都可以被称为是一个"州法院系统"。可以说,50 个州存在着相互独立的 50 个州法院系统,每个州法院系统中各自存在着自己的初级法院、中级法院和高级法院,构成了一个个毫无关联的独立的系统。

对于各个州法院之间的相互关系,以及中央政府与各个州法院之间的关系,美国《宪法》中做了明确的规定:

(1)各个州之间应当相互尊重彼此独立的权力,尊重彼此的领土完整,各自的法律、法院判决、文化传统和行政措施,尊重各自公民所享有的权利,并且在跨州之间的贸易中不应当设置特别的贸易壁垒和关税等措施。

(2)在不违背美国《宪法》和联邦法律的前提下,中央政府应当尊重各个州已经存在的领土完整、州《宪法》、州法律、州议会、州法院、州行政机构,以及各个州的文化传统和贸易习惯。

以上内容都被规定在美国《宪法》及其修正案中。

值得注意的是,虽然在形式上全美范围内存在着联邦法院和州法院两个并列的系统,但是,由于两套法院系统的诞生方式不同,各个州的法院是在美国这个国家诞生以前,在各州已有法院的基础上发展演化而来的。虽然从一个国家的角度来说,这些州的法院统称为"州法院",但是,各个州的法院之间本身并不存在任何隶属关系和业务指导关系,它们完全是相互独立的不同的法院,只是在同一个州内部的上下级法院之间存在着审判业务的相关性。而整个联邦法院系统属于一个统一的法院系统,级别最高的法院是美国联邦最高法院,整个联邦法院系统都是在美国这个国家成立以后基于美国《宪法》创建出来的,因此,其中的任何一个法院也都是在建国以后基于美国《宪法》的规定诞生的。

因此,联邦法院系统和州法院系统属于完全不同的两类法院体系。

一、美国联邦最高法院及其指导下的联邦法院体系

根据美国《宪法》的规定,除了联邦最高法院以外,其他各级联邦法院都由美国国会批准组建。

在法院的设立上,联邦法院的设立由美国《宪法》规定,联邦法院系统包括三个等级,从低向高依次为:联邦地区法院(中文中也被翻译为联邦地方法院)

（U. S. Federal District Court）、联邦上诉法院（U. S. Courts of Appeal）和联邦最高法院（即全国最高法院，Federal Supreme Court）。

现在，美国联邦法院系统分别由 94 个联邦地区法院、13 个联邦上诉法院和一个最高法院组成。

（一）联邦地区法院

在联邦地区法院的设置上，首先，在每一个州至少都设立一个联邦地区法院；然后，根据各个州的区域面积，人口数量，社会经济发展情况，案件发生情况等综合因素，再在不同的州增加设立 1 至 3 个联邦地区法院。例如，在加利福尼亚州、纽约州和得克萨斯州都分别增加设立了 3 个联邦地区法院，使得它们州的联邦地区法院的数量都达到了 4 个。现在，美国 50 个州共设有 89 个地区法院，另外在哥伦比亚特区、波多黎各、美属维尔京群岛、关岛、北马里亚纳群岛也各设有一个地区法院，一共设立了 94 个联邦地方法院。

美国首都华盛顿的所在地——哥伦比亚特区（英文 Washington District of Columbia，简写为 Washington D. C.）是 1790 年美国为了建立首都专门设置的一个特殊行政区域，它不隶属于美国的任何一个州，而是由美国国会直接管辖的属于联邦政府的行政区域，在该行政区域内也专门设立了一个联邦地区法院。

联邦地区法院的法官都是由总统提名，然后经过国会参议院同意后任命，终身任职。联邦地区法官有权任命法院的书记官、执法官、法庭记录员等人员协助其工作。

联邦地区法院作为联邦法院系统中的一审法院，主要受理涉及联邦法律和《宪法》的案件。

对于美国的知识产权案件来说，例如，涉及专利、商标和著作权等方面纠纷的案件，由于这些知识产权法律都是由美国联邦法律规定的，因此，这类纠纷的案件都属于联邦地区法院管辖。对于商业秘密案件，由于一部分商业秘密法律属于联邦法律，另一部分商业秘密法律属于州法律，这样，凡是涉及联邦法律管辖的商业秘密纠纷案件都由联邦地区法院管辖，而涉及州法律管辖的商业秘密纠纷案件则由州法院管辖，这是知识产权案件中比较特殊的情形。

(二)联邦上诉法院

美国并没有在各个州(类似于我国的各个省、自治区或者直辖市)都设立联邦上诉法院。

美国在全国范围内设立了 11 个普通上诉审判区和 1 个哥伦比亚特区普通上诉审判区,以及 1 个联邦巡回上诉审判区,这样,在全国范围内,共设有 13 个不同类型的上诉审判区,即 12 个普通上诉审判区和 1 个巡回上诉审判区;然后,其在每一个上诉审判区中设立一个联邦上诉法院,这样就设立了 12 个属于普通上诉审判区的联邦上诉法院,和一个属于巡回上诉审判区的联邦巡回上诉法院。其中,11 个普通上诉审判区分布于全国各地,例如,联邦第九上诉法院(中文也翻译为联邦第九巡回上诉法院)就位于加利福尼亚州的旧金山市,而哥伦比亚特区联邦上诉审判区和联邦巡回上诉法院都位于首都所在区——哥伦比亚特区。

这 13 个联邦上诉法院共同负责办理全国范围内由 94 个联邦地区法院和特殊联邦法院审结的一审案件的二审工作。

其中,各类知识产权纠纷的上诉案件和有关税收等方面的上诉案件由联邦巡回上诉法院管辖。

对于另外的 11 个联邦上诉法院来说,它们都被指定了各自所管辖的地域范围,一般都管辖多个州,具体所管辖的州的数量也有所不同。例如,位于加利福尼亚的第九联邦上诉法院就管辖包括加利福尼亚州、内华达州、亚利桑那州、爱达荷州、蒙大拿州、俄勒冈州、华盛顿州、阿拉斯加州和夏威夷州 9 个州中所有联邦地区法院的上诉案件①。

联邦上诉法院一般只审理上诉案件,审理案件时一般由 3 名法官共同审理。按照美国《宪法》的规定,除了联邦最高法院以外,有关联邦上诉法院和联邦地区法院的数量,以及各个法院中联邦法官的数量等事项都由国会决定。联邦上诉法院的法官也都由总统提名,经过国会参议院举行听证后进行批准,也都为终身法官职位②。

---

① 马跃:《美国刑事司法制度》,中国政法出版社 2004 年版,第 250~251 页。
② 雾谷飞鸿:"美国驻华大使馆",http://blog.sina.com.cn/s/blog_67f297b00102v5tt.html,访问日期:2014 年 10 月 14 日。

除了上述联邦地区法院和联邦上诉法院以外,在美国联邦法院序列中还有两个特别的联邦法院,分别是国际贸易法院(U. S. Court of International Trade)和联邦索赔法院(U. S. Court of Federal Claims),它们与上述联邦地区法院和联邦上诉法院在案件的管辖权和案件的审级等方面都有所不同。

除了上述这两个特殊的联邦法院之外,在联邦法院序列中还有一个更加特殊的联邦法院,即联邦破产法院(U. S. Bankruptcy Court)。虽然它也属于联邦法院系统,但是它的法官并非由总统提名,任期也都有期限的限制,而非终身制,这使得它与其他联邦法院都有所不同,因此,可以说,它是联邦法院序列中最特别的一个联邦法院。

(三)联邦最高法院

美国联邦最高法院(Supreme Court of the United States)是基于1789年通过的《司法法案》,于1790年根据美国《宪法》建立的,属于美国联邦政府三权分立中的一支重要的国家权力机构[①]。

联邦最高法院有权受理上诉案件,也有权直接受理少数特别的一审案件。其直接受理的一审案件主要包括涉及大使、领事等外交纠纷的案件。对于上诉案件,可以受理各州高级法院(或者称为州最高法院)审理的案件,也可以受理经过联邦上诉法院审理的案件,这些案件应当涉及《宪法》中所规定的事项,或者是涉及联邦法律中的重要事项,或者是涉及审查某一州的法律是否合法等比较重要的事项。

联邦最高法院只有9名大法官,其中一名是首席大法官,这里的"首席大法官"不同于我国最高人民法院院长的行政职务,他在案件中与另外8位大法官享有相同的司法权力,他没有最终的行政决定权和司法决定权。在决定是否受理某一案件时,至少要有4名大法官同意,而且审理案件时,应当全体9名大法官全部出庭;对于案件的最终判决,实行表决制,每一位大法官都拥有平等的表决权,最终的判决结果依据"少数服从多数的原则"的表决结果确定。

大法官们也都由总统提名,由国会参议院批准后任命,实行终身制。

---

① Supreme Court of the United States:"History and Traditions", https://www. supremecourt. gov/, 访问日期:2018年4月22日。

二、各州相互独立的州法院体系

与联邦法院不同,各个州法院的成立和运行则完全由各个州的州宪法及州议会规定,而且,如前所述,各个州的法院往往比美国这个国家的历史还悠久,即在美国这个国家诞生之前,各个州的州法院就已经存在并担负起审判职能了。

另外,正如前文在介绍美国这个国家诞生的历史时所陈述的那样,当时是由 13 个州通过协商筹建的美国这个国家。也就是说,在美国这个国家成立时也只辖有 13 个州,现在所拥有的 50 个州中,除了原有的 13 个州以外,其余的 37 个州在美国这个国家诞生时并不属于美国,而是主要分别属于法国、墨西哥、俄国等国家,是美国通过购买和战争等方式先后获取的。这些州在归属美国之前,在其当时的所属国有的就是一个省,有的甚至是一个已经获得独立的国家。因此,它们具有自己本国的行政和司法管理体制,在归属美国之后,根据美国《宪法》的规定,逐步实施了相对统一的权力机构和管理模式。当然,由于各自的历史差异很大,因此,即使在当今的美国,不同州之间在州政府、县政府和市政府的权力行使,以及政治、经济、文化和传统生活上仍然存在着比较多的差异。

这一基本的社会特征决定了各个州法院不可避免地拥有一些自身的特点。

总体来说,各个州一般都把州法院系统分为州初级法院、州上诉法院和州高级法院(有的称为州最高法院)三个等级,也有的州把上诉阶段再区分为两个等级,形成两个层级的上诉法院,从而形成四个等级的州法院。

另外,不同的州对各个等级的州法院的称谓也不相同,甚至相互交叉和相互冲突。例如,在有些州把初级法院称为"最高法庭"(Supreme Court),而在有的州则把州上诉法院称为"最高法庭上诉法院"(Appellate Terms of the Supreme Court in the First and Second Departments);而在纽约州则把州最高法院反而称为上诉法院(Court of Appeals)。由此可见,由于各个州法院之间相互独立,在全国范围内没有统一的设计和管理,而各个州在历史和文化上又有较大的差异,从而导致了州法院在称谓上的混乱和矛盾①。

---

① 雾谷飞鸿:"美国驻华大使馆",http://blog.sina.com.cn/s/blog_67f297b00102v5tt.html,访问日期:2014 年 10 月 14 日。

除此之外,各个州法院的法官在选取和任命上也不尽相同。有些州的法官由州长提名,经过州议会批准后任命;而有些州的法官则直接经过选民投票产生;还有一些州则采用任命与选举相结合的方式进行。也有一些州则采取先由州长直接任命,在第一个任期结束时,再由选民投票决定是否留用的方式来选取和重新任命。在就职年限上也不相同,有的州的州法官的职位是终身的,而有的州则有年限的限制①。

第二节　联邦法律和州法律的主要权限范围

一、与知识产权相关的主要联邦法律的权限范围

美国《宪法》第一章第 8 条对联邦法律应当管辖的社会领域作出了明确的规定,其中,与知识产权相关的联邦法律主要包括下列两种类型。

(1)规范国际贸易和跨州贸易的联邦法律。美国《宪法》中规定美国国会应当制定用于规范国际贸易和跨州贸易的联邦法律,而那些用于规范在各个州范围内进行贸易的法律则由各个州制定州法律。

需要说明的是,在本书中所列出的保护商业秘密的各类联邦法律中,除了对经济间谍罪的规定以外,在法律的适用范围上,它们基本上都被限定在发生于"国际贸易"或者"不同州之间的州际贸易"中涉及的商业秘密纠纷或者侵害行为。如果某一贸易活动只发生在某一个州的领域之内,那么,即使在这一贸易活动中发生了侵害商业秘密的行为,原则上也只能适用该州法律中有关保护商业秘密的规定办理。

(2)专门保护知识产权的联邦法律。美国《宪法》中明确规定为了促进科学和有益的文学艺术的发展,国会应当颁布实施专门的联邦法律以便保护作者和发明者享有一定期限的专有权,借此来保护他们的创作或创造成果。

---

① 雾谷飞鸿:"美国驻华大使馆",http://blog. sina. com. cn/s/blog_67f297b00102v5tt. html,访问日期:2014 年 10 月 14 日。

实际上,也正是基于美国《宪法》中的这一规定,美国先后颁布实施并且不断地健全和完善了自身的知识产权法律体系,由此也决定了知识产权法律在美国属于联邦法律的属性。

现在,在美国的知识产权法律中,除了保护商业秘密的法律同时存在着联邦法律和各州法律以外,其他的知识产权法律都已经是完全的联邦法律,这些知识产权联邦法律分别是:①《美国版权法》(*Copyright Law of the United States and Related Laws*);②《美国专利法》(*Patent Law of the United States*);③《美国商标法》(*Trademark Law of the United States*);④《美国植物新品种保护法》(*Plant Variety Protection Act of the United States*);⑤《美国集成电路布图设计保护法》(*Semiconductor Chip Protection Act of* 1984);⑥《地理标志法规》(*Geographical Indications Laws and Regulations*)。

需要说明的是,根据美国《宪法》的规定,除了上述两类联邦法律以外,美国《宪法》中还明确规定了国会应当颁布实施的其他类型的联邦法律,由于它们与商业秘密保护没有关联性,笔者在本书中就不再一一地进行叙述,如果需要,可以阅读本书中所提供的美国《宪法》正文和 27 条修正案的英文原文。

由此可见,由于联邦政府的权力与各州政府的权力之间存在着不可逾越的界限,而这种权力的界限完全都被规定在《宪法》中,因此,只有在《宪法》中明确规定可以颁布实施联邦法律的领域和事项国会才有权力颁布实施联邦法律。相反,根据美国《宪法》的明确规定,凡是《宪法》中没有明确规定应当颁布实施联邦法律的领域和事项,都是属于各州权力管辖的范围,因此,都是不能颁布实施联邦法律的范围。也就是说,只有美国《宪法》中对联邦法律明确规定的范围才是其自身合法有效的范围。

二、各州法律的权限范围

(一)各州法律既相互独立又不相同

需要明确的是,这里的"州法律"是指美国各个州自己颁布实施的法律,在 50 个州中,各个州的法律并不相同,因此,"州法律"的确切含义应当是"50 个州的州法律的集合"。

如前所述,由于各个州的法律地位是相互平等的,因此,由各个州颁布的州法律的法律地位也是相互平等的,又由于根据美国《宪法》的规定,州法律属于各州权力覆盖的内容,联邦政府无权干涉,这样,就难以在全国范围内建立起统一的"州法律"。

在现实中,不同的州法律之间,或许在有些法律规定上具有一定的相似性,甚至有些相同,但是,在其他一些法律规定上就可能存在着很大的差异。

例如,美国的刑法主要属于州法律的范畴,除了少数犯罪行为属于联邦法律管辖的罪行以外,大部分违法犯罪行为都受州法律的管辖。然而,由于美国各个州的刑事法律并不完全相同,甚至存在着较大的差异,结果导致在有些州被视为犯罪的行为,在另外有的州则可能不被视为犯罪。

更有甚者,即使在同一个州内,虽然有关重罪的法律规定是统一的,但是,对于一些轻罪,如涉及赌博和酗酒等违法犯罪行为,同一个州内的不同县(郡)之间;甚至同一个县(郡)内的不同市之间,它们所颁布实施的当地的法律规定和执法政策也有差异,甚至可能大相径庭,在有关案件的起诉决定、辩诉交易、审判策略等方面都可能存在着不同的法律规定和执法政策。

很显然,这就不可避免地会导致相同或者相似的违法犯罪行为最终被认定的法律性质和法律结果可能完全不同的局面的出现,而且,有些在县级政府工作的地方检察官甚至还会拒绝执行那些在当地不受民众欢迎的某些州法律中的条款和规定①。

(二)州法律是美国社会中处理各类纠纷所广泛使用的法律

虽然各个州的法律之间相互独立,而且彼此之间还存在着一定的冲突和差异,并且在各州内部,各个县(郡)级和市级政府又会颁布一些只在当地实施的法律规定和执法政策,从而又导致各个州法律内部存在着内容上的多样性、冲突性和不协调性。但是,与联邦法律相比,各个州法律所管辖的领域和事项都与民众的基本工作、生活、财产、商业活动等事项相关,因此,对于民众来说,这些州法律才是与他们密切相关的重要法律。

另外,从法律的角度来说,不同州之间的州法律在客观上存在着一定的区别和差异,但是,这是对不同州法律进行比较的结果,对于那些生活和工作在其

---

① 何家弘:"论美国检察制度的特色",《外国法译评》1995 年第 4 期,第 35 ~ 36 页。

中任何一个州中的民众来说,当他们需要利用"法律"来维护自身的合法权益时,摆在他们面前的"法律"并不是多种多样甚至相互之间还存在着矛盾和冲突的。他们面前的法律只有一种,那就是在当地正在实施的被当地的人们视为合法有效的一种特定的法律规定。也许当地的很多民众只知道或者认为他们所知悉和应用的这一"法律"就是"正当的合适的法律",应该是全国法律的一部分,在这个国家内不应该也不会再有其他不同的法律规定。通过前文的讨论可知,如果站在整个国家的角度来说,他们所认识和认可的这种唯一的"法律规定"实际上只是他们所在的州,甚至是他们所在的县和市中实施的一种法律规定和执法政策,正是这些"法律规定和执法政策"的内容具有明显的地方特色,直接导致了不同州、同一州内不同县和市内的"法律规定和执法政策"的差异性。

因此,在现实中,虽然客观上存在着不同州之间的州法律的差异性和多样性,但是对于各州的民众来说,它们可能并没有感觉到这种差异性和多样性。显然,在这两者之间存在着一个理论分析和现实感受方面的差异,以及一个深层次的认识与一个表面生活上的相对肤浅的认识上的区别。

当然,在现实中,有些民众可能确实没有注意和意识到州法律之间的这种差异性,另外,也许有些民众已经意识到或者了解到了这种差异性,但是基于各种原因,或者由于各种条件的制约和限制,使其没有能力采取应对的办法和措施。

现实中,大量的一般性民事案件和刑事案件都是依据各个州的法律在各州法院审理终结的,就每年法院实际受理和审理的案件总数来说,各个州法院受理和审理的案件总数要远远大于联邦法院受理和审理的案件总数。如果进行分析就能发现,产生这种差距的主要原因就在于两类不同的法院系统,以及它们所适用的两类不同的法律体系所涉及的社会领域和事项本身存在着很大的差异。相对于那些归属于州法律和州法院管辖的发生在公民个人与个人之间,企业与企业之间,以及个人与企业之间的民事纠纷和各类一般的刑事案件来说,那些归属于联邦法律和联邦法院管辖的诸如涉及国防、外交、国家税收政策、法律条款是否违宪、州政府成为案件当事人,以及涉及专利、商标和著作权的案件,在案件数量上显然难以与州法律和州法院管辖的案件相比。当然,在案件的难易程度和对国家与社会可能产生的重大影响上,可能联邦法院管辖的案件要重要和突出一些。

因此,在一定程度上可以说,州法律对整个国家和社会作出了更多的法律贡献。

(三)州法律的权力界限具有宪法依据

如前所述,根据美国《宪法》修正案第 10 条的规定:凡是国会没有明确授权给联邦政府,又没有明确禁止各州不能拥有的权力,都可以由各州政府和民众享有。

基于这一《宪法》规定,各个州政府有权颁布实施州法律和州行政命令,这些州法律和州行政命令在本州范围内有效,由本州的州法院、州行政机关和执法机关组织实施。

因此,基于美国《宪法》的上述规定,州法律的权限范围如下:①联邦法律管辖范围以外的社会领域;②美国《宪法》未明确禁止的范围。

第三节　联邦法院与州法院的司法管辖权

一、两类法院司法管辖权的一般规定

在司法管辖上,基于联邦法律和州法律之间的界限和区别,联邦法院与州法院的管辖权也有一定的区别。例如,专利侵权纠纷案件,应当由联邦法院受理。由于联邦法律和州法律都涉及民事和刑事案件,因此,两类法院都能审理民事和刑事案件。

两类法院在司法管辖权上的基本界限是,凡是由联邦法律规范的法律纠纷都由联邦法院管辖,凡是由州法律规范的法律纠纷都由州法院管辖。

另外,虽然在一般情况下,两类法院的管辖权比较分明,但是,在有些情况下,由于同一案件涉及的法律问题比较复杂,可能同时包含着两类法院都能受理的部分内容,这样,就在客观上造成了管辖范围上的交叉。但是,由于同一案件又不能分别在两类法院同时受理,这就不可避免地发生了州法院同时审理了应当由联邦法院审理的内容,或者联邦法院同时审理了应当由州法院审理的事项。

除此之外,对于少数比较特殊的案件,虽然应当归属于联邦法院审理,有时候州法院也可以审理;而对于由州法院审理的可能涉及违宪的内容,联邦法院也可以对案件进行复议①。

由此可见,在现实中,联邦法院与州法院所实际受理的案件范围与联邦法律和州法律之间划分的权限范围可能并不完全一致。

二、美国《宪法》对联邦法院管辖范围的明确规定

美国《宪法》对联邦法院的管辖范围做了比较明确的规定,联邦法院主要审理涉及《宪法》的案件,涉及国际贸易及其相关事务的案件,涉及美国州与州之间发生的案件,以及涉及违反联邦法律的刑事案件;此外,破产案件、海事案件等也属于联邦法院的管辖范围;而州法院则主要负责审理发生在本州内的民事和刑事案件②。

美国《宪法》第三章第 2 条对联邦法院的司法管辖范围作了如下规定:

(1)联邦法院有权管辖所有涉及美国《宪法》和国际公约,以及由联邦法律所规范案件。

同时,其明确列举了下列具体事项:①所有涉及外交的案件,包括涉及大使、公使和领事的案件;②所有涉及海事和海事管辖权的案件;③所有把美国作为一方当事人的案件;④美国不同州政府之间发生的案件;⑤一个州的政府与另一个州的居民之间发生的案件;⑥不同州的居民之间发生的案件;⑦同一个州的居民之间就由其他的州政府批准的土地发生的纠纷案件;⑧一个州或者它的居民,与外国政府、外国居民、外国其他法律主体之间发生的案件。

(2)对于涉及外交的案件,以及美国作为一方当事人的案件,美国联邦最高法院具有一审管辖权;对于上述列举的其他案件,美国联邦最高法院在案件

---

① 马跃:《美国刑事司法制度》,中国政法大学出版社 2004 年版,第 246 页。

② 雾谷飞鸿:"美国驻华大使馆",http://blog.sina.com.cn/s/blog_67f297b00102v5tt.html,访问日期:2014 年 10 月 14 日。

事实和适用法律方面享有上诉管辖权,这些特殊的规定由国会另行颁布特殊的条例加以详细规范。

(3)根据美国《宪法》第11条修正案的规定,当另外一个州的居民,或者其他国家的公民或法律主体,利用普通法或者衡平法起诉美国的一个州政府时,该案件的司法管辖权属于州法院。

第四节　美国的警察系统、检察系统和监狱系统

一、美国不同等级政府中的行政权力

基于美国整个权力制度、立法制度和司法制度的特殊性,美国的警察系统、检察系统和监狱系统也有其自身的特殊性。

首先,美国当前的政府结构与我国的政府结构存在着很大的区别。众所周知,美国联邦政府(federal government)即中央政府(central government),由联邦立法机构(即美国国会)、联邦行政机构(即总统领导下的行政机构)和联邦司法机构(即联邦最高法院及全国所有的联邦法院)三部分组成。

从国家权力的结构上来说,在联邦政府之下是全国的州政府(state government),它在形式上是联邦政府的下一级政府,类似于我国的省一级政府,但是,它在与中央政府的实际权力关系上,与我国的省政府存在着根本的不同。在与联邦政府的权力关系方面,各州政府实际上只接受美国《宪法》、联邦法律和总统生效的行政命令的制约和约束,州政府的重要人事任免、州政府的财政、州法律、州法院、州警察、州检察机关、州行政执法部门和全州范围内的政治、经济、文化、科技政策等方面都基本不受联邦政府的管理和制约,享有高度的自治权。

在州政府这一级政府机构中,也类似于联邦政府的内部权力构造,把州政府的全部权力划分为既相互独立,又相互监督和制衡的三部分,即州立法权、州行政权和州司法权,对应的具体机构分别为州议会、州长领导的行政机构和州法院。

同样,在权力结构中,在州政府之下,是县一级的政府(中文中有的也把县翻译为郡)(county government),在县级政府之下是市级政府(city government),一个县往往管辖数个市,甚至十几个市。

　　在此值得说明的是,在美国行政结构中的"市"(city),与我国行政结构中的"市"的含义不同。在我国现阶段,"市政府"可以是省级的"直辖市政府",副省级的"较大市政府",地区一级的"市政府",以及县一级的"市政府"。即在我国"市级"的最低行政级别是"县级","市级政府"可以领导"县级政府",但是"县级政府"不能领导"市级政府"。这是我国的语言文化、生活习惯和政治术语所决定的。而在美国,它的"市政府"可能高于"县政府",也可能低于"县政府",这一点与我国不同。

　　其次,州政府、县政府、市政府相互之间的权力关系在很大程度上也是类似于州政府与联邦政府之间的形式上的隶属关系,并不像我国的省政府、较大市政府、地区级市政府(或者行政公署)、县政府(县级市政府)、乡政府相互之间存在的紧密的上下隶属权力关系。

　　在美国的各级政府中,最高行政长官分别是总统、州长、县长、市长,但是,这些行政长官都是由他们的行政权力所能发挥作用的范围内的选民选举产生的。因此,这些行政长官之间并不存在行政隶属关系,一般情况下,上级政府的行政长官不应当直接命令下级政府的行政长官开展工作。

　　例如,总统颁布了一项行政命令以后,在正常情况下,他可以命令直接归属于他所领导的联邦政府中的具体行政部门组织实施,但是,却不能命令某一州的州长组织实施这一命令;相反,如果某一州的州长不赞同总统的这一命令,他可以要求他所领导的本州的行政部门不执行这一命令,甚至通过本州的立法,明确禁止在本州范围内实施这一总统的命令。

　　对于从总统到市长的各级行政长官们来说,实际上,他们主要应当向两个不同的主体负责:①选举他们的选民。对于总统来说,他的选民是全国范围内具有选举权的所有美国公民,而对于州长、县长、市长们来说,则是他们所在的行政辖区内的全体选民。②《宪法》。对于总统来说,他还需要向美国《宪法》负责;而对于州长、县长、市长来说,他们则需要再向美国《宪法》,以及他们所在州的州《宪法》负责。

二、美国多种类不统一的警察系统

概括起来说,美国的警察系统具有以下特征:

(1)全国没有统一的警察管理机构。在美国联邦政府中,没有统一领导全国警察工作的中央一级的警察机构,如我国的公安部和安全部等部门,以此相对应,在各个州的政府中,也没有统一领导全州警察工作的管理机构。全国的警察机构分布于不同等级的政府中,不同的警察机构原则上只对领导其工作的政府负责,完成该政府所赋予他们的警察任务和职责,而不同的警察机构之间则一般没有隶属关系,存在着相互的独立性。

因此,在一定程度上可以说,美国的警察更像是一种社会职业和工作类别。

(2)美国的警察总体上可以分为联邦警察、州警察和地方警察三大类。隶属于联邦政府的警察属于联邦警察,隶属于州政府的警察属于州警察,隶属于县级政府和市级政府的警察属于地方警察。

归属于不同政府的警察之间没有隶属关系,联邦警察与各州警察之间,各州警察相互之间,以及州警察与地方警察之间都没有隶属关系①。

在联邦政府中,警察隶属于联邦政府的行政部门,在联邦政府众多的行政部门中,有些行政部门就领导和管理着隶属于本部门的具有专门执法职责的警察组织。目前,在美国联邦政府中,这类部门主要包括司法部、国土安全部以及财政部等部门。

三、美国的检察系统及检察官对案件处理的重要权限

首先,与我国不同的是,美国的检察机构属于政府行政机关,不属于司法机关,美国的司法机关只有法院系统。其次,美国检察机关包括两个相互独立的检察系统,分别是隶属于联邦政府的联邦检察系统,以及隶属于各州政府的州检察系统,两者相互独立,没有隶属关系。

美国的联邦检察系统是在独立战争以后建立的,美国建国之初,总统很需要一位法律顾问来帮助他处理各种法律事务。1789 年,国会在第一次会议上

---

① 马跃:《美国刑事司法制度》,中国政法大学出版社 2004 年版,第 152～160 页。

通过了一项法案,授权总统任命一名联邦检察长,其职权包括在联邦最高法院审理的刑事案件中提起公诉,参与联邦政府作为一方当事人的诉讼,以及应总统或者各部首长的要求提供法律咨询意见等①。

(一)联邦检察系统

整个联邦检察系统又由两部分组成,一部分是中央检察机构,包括联邦总检察长、副总检察长及相关辅助人员;另一部分是分布于全国各地的联邦地区检察官及其辅助人员。

1. 中央检察机构

与我国存在最高人民检察院这种独立的中央级的司法机构不同,美国没有独立的中央检察机构,在联邦政府中,它隶属于司法部,而且在司法部的机构中,也只设立有一个总检察长办公室(Office of the Attorney General),以此作为在联邦政府中检察系统的最高工作机构。其特别突出的一个特点还在于,联邦总检察长一职经常由司法部长兼任,然后再设立副总检察长。

2. 联邦地区检察官

联邦地区检察官的设立是由 1780 年的《司法法案》(中文也翻译为《司法条例》)(the Judiciary Act)规定的。地区检察官负责起诉那些应该由联邦法院管辖的违反联邦法律的犯罪案件,他们在自己的司法管辖区内享有独立的起诉权,这一权力不受任何外来力量的影响,联邦检察长与各地区的联邦检察官之间并没有行政上的隶属关系,一般情况下联邦检察长无权干涉各地区检察官的工作事务,但是,对于特殊的案件,联邦检察长具有指导和批准的权限②。

3. 联邦检察官的任命和工作分布

包括联邦总检察长和地区检察官在内的所有联邦检察官都由总统提名,经过国会参议院批准后任命。但是,与联邦法官不同的是,联邦法官的任命基本都是终身制,而联邦检察官的任期一般只有四年,在任期上与任命他们的总统的任期相吻合。

为了履行在联邦法院对违反联邦法律的违法犯罪行为提起公诉和完成

---

① 何家弘:"论美国检察制度的特点",载《外国法译评》1995 年第 4 期,第 33 页。
② 同上。

其他检察工作的职能,在全国范围内,与联邦法院的设置和地域分布相对应,美国政府设置了对应的联邦检察官办事处,每个办事处都由一名联邦检察官和若干名助理检察官组成,他们是联邦检察工作的主要力量。在一般的案件中,他们自行决定侦查和是否提起公诉,但要遵守总检察长制定的方针和政策;对于特殊的案件,需要得到联邦总检察长等上级领导的批准才能提起公诉①。

(二)州检察系统

美国的地方检察系统以州检察机构为主,人员一般由州检察长、州副检察长和州检察官组成,州检察官又分为县(郡)的州检察官和市(镇)的州检察官。

不同州之间,州检察官的名称极不统一,具体名称包括州检察官、地区检察官、县检察官、公诉律师、县公诉人、法务官、地区检察长等。州检察官领导的机构一般称为检察官办事处,主要负责调查和起诉违反本州法律的行为②。

另外,市镇检察机构是独立于州检察系统的地方检察机构,但是并非美国所有的市镇都有自己的检察机构。在有些州,市镇没有检察官员,全部检察工作都属于州检察官的职权。在那些有自己检察机构的市镇,检察官员无权起诉违反联邦或者州法律的行为,只能调查和起诉那些违反市镇法令的行为。这些违法行为称被为"微罪"或"轻罪",多与赌博、酗酒、交通、公共卫生等方面的事项有关。不过,市镇法令中有关"微罪"的规定与州法律中有关"轻罪"的规定有时会发生重合,市镇检察官的名称多为"市检察官"或者"自治体法律顾问"等。一般来说,他们的职责涉及广泛的法律事务,对各类违法行为的调查和起诉仅是其职能中的一小部分工作内容③。

州检察长一般都由本州公民直接选举产生。市镇检察官可以通过选举,被市长或者市议会任命,或者被市议会或市行政长官聘任这三种不同的方式产生,但是,不同的方式产生的法律效果不同。被任命者属于市政府的官员,而被聘任者则属于市政府的雇员④。

---

① 何家弘:"论美国检察制度的特色",载《外国法译评》1995 年第 4 期,第 25 页。
② 同上。
③ 同上。
④ 同上书,第 27 页。

（三）检察官对案件的重要决定权

美国实行检察官个人负责制为基础的检察制度,这一检察制度赋予了检察官两项重大的决定权:①决定是否把某一案件公诉到法院;②决定是否与被告人进行"辩诉交易"(plea bargaining)以结束这一案件。

检察官的这两项决定权原则上都不受司法审查,也即法院无权对这种决定的合法性进行司法审查,检察官本人作出决定后即产生法律效力。

很显然,在这种法律程序中检察官本人具有很大的司法裁量权,而且在客观上难以避免由于各种原因致使检察官本人决定不提起公诉,致使案件中的真正犯罪嫌疑人由于未被公诉到法院,因而逃脱了法律制裁的情形。因此,从维护公平正义的角度上来说,这一法律程序自身的合法性和合理性都值得进一步讨论。

所谓辩诉交易,是指检察官与被告人或其辩护律师经过谈判和讨价还价来达成由被告人认罪换取较轻的定罪或量刑的协议。检察官在决定对某人提起公诉之后有两条处理案件的途径:一条是提交法院进行审判,另一条就是进行辩诉交易。

检察官选择辩诉交易的主要理由有下列两点:①为了在对其他更严重的罪犯的起诉中获得该被告人的合作;②为了在有罪证据不够充分的情况下避免在法庭上败诉。

辩诉双方一旦达成辩诉协议之后,法院便不再对该案进行实质性的审判,而仅在形式上确认双方协议的内容,从而能够尽快地审结本案。而且按照法律规定,法官不得干涉辩诉交易。只要被告人的认罪是自愿的,而且他已经明确放弃依据美国《宪法》拥有的请求获得陪审团审判的权利,那么法官就不再进行法庭的调查和审判,直接根据检察官起诉的罪名进行判刑。这样做的结果实际上等于完全是由检察官直接决定被告人是否有罪,以及构成了何种罪,这也是美国检察制度的一个突出特点①。

（四）助理检察官是重要的检察力量

在检察机构中,除了联邦总检察长、副总检察长,以及州检察长和副检察

---

① 何家弘:"论美国检察制度的特色",载《外国法译评》1995 年第 4 期,第 38 页。

长及其辅助人员以外,各个联邦地区检察机构和州所属的地方检察机构,主要是由检察官、助理检察官和辅助检察人员组成,而真正负责办理调查和起诉工作的人员又主要是助理检察官。助理检察官是由其所在检察机构的检察官雇佣的工作人员,一般都会要求具有所在州的律师资格(美国的律师资格考试由各州独立举办,考试通过后一般在本州有效,没有全国统一的律师或者司法考试)。当然,其他具体条件各地可能有所不同①。

四、美国两套主要的相互独立的监狱系统

概括地说,当前美国的监狱系统总体上可以分为联邦监狱、州监狱和私营监狱三种类型。其中,联邦监狱是由联邦政府承办的监狱,分布在全国不同的州;州监狱是由各州政府及其所属的下级政府承办的监狱;私营监狱是从 20 世纪 80 年代以后,经过政府批准由私营公司承办的监狱。

当前,就全国范围来看,联邦监狱和州监狱是两套主要的监狱系统,私营监狱还不是重要的监狱系统。

目前,在全国范围内,无论是从羁押的罪犯总人数,还是从监狱的规模和数量上来看,州监狱都是最重要的力量。州监狱分布在各个州,监管那些因为违反各个州的法律,由各个州法院判决入狱的犯人。在联邦监狱中,监管的都是因为违背联邦法律,被联邦法院判决入狱的犯人。而私营监狱则是通过与政府签订合同承接而来的犯人。

当前,从对监狱监管的严厉程度和监狱保卫的等级来划分,全美的监狱可以划分为四个不同的等级,从高到低依次是超高级警戒度监狱、高级警戒度监狱、中等警戒度监狱和低等警戒度监狱。

除了上述正式的监狱以外,分布在各地的看守所一般负责监押刑期在一年以下的短期囚犯和尚未进行判决的未决犯,也在一定程度上承担着羁押犯人的工作。

---

① 何家弘:"论美国检察制度的特色",载《外国法译评》1995 年第 4 期,第 28 页。

第五节　美国司法部的组成及其特殊作用

一、美国司法部的诞生历程

美国司法部的英文名称为"The United States Department of Justice"。美国司法部与我国的司法部不同,我国的司法部隶属于国务院,其主要职能是管理全国的监狱工作、公证工作和律师工作,而美国司法部则不同,其职权范围要大得多。

美国司法部是依据 1789 年《司法法案》创建的。1789 年,美国国会在纽约市召开了第一次国会会议,目的是致力于为联邦政府的正常运营创建必要的基础和条件。这次会议几个月后,国会议员们立法通过了一项法案,称为《司法法案》,规定在新的联邦政府中设立司法部门的内容。该《司法法案》由国会通过以后,于 1789 年 9 月 24 日由第一任美国总统乔治·华盛顿签署后成为法律,从而使"司法部"这一联邦政府机构得以在美国诞生。并且该法案规定司法部长属于联邦政府中的内阁成员的职位,当时位居内阁成员中的第四位。

在司法部成立以后的很长一段时期内,其机构比较简单,在联邦政府中还不属于一个完全独立的政府机构,其职责更多的只是为总统和联邦政府的部门首长提供法律咨询和意见建议,在有些涉及联邦政府的案件中,代表联邦政府在联邦最高法院出庭。

这一状况在持续了八十多年。在美国南北战争以后,由于当时社会现实的需要,使得司法部的历史使命发生了彻底的改变。根据 1870 年法案(The 1870 Act)司法部不仅成了独立的联邦政府机构,而且组织结构和社会职责都得到了极大的扩充和拓展,最终使其成为美国联邦政府中非常重要的组成部门。现在,美国司法部基于在全国范围内开展工作的需要,已经雇用了近万名的律师开展司法工作,因此,在一定程度上,司法部也已经成了世界上最大的律师事务所和中央执行联邦法律的机构①。

美国建立司法部的宗旨在于：①执行法律，依法保护美国的国家利益；②反对来自国内外的各种威胁，确保公共安全；③为国家领导人提供阻止和控制各类犯罪的有效措施；④对违法犯罪行为作出公正的审判；⑤确保全体美国公民都能够享受到公平和公正的司法保障。

二、美国司法部的组织机构及其与"经济间谍罪"相关的机构

根据美国司法部官方网站公开的资料显示，截至 2018 年 3 月 29 日，美国司法部共有 62 个组织机构，已经覆盖了社会的多个重要领域。在这 62 个机构中，有 11 个机构属于专门规范司法部内部工作，以及专门为总统和联邦政府所属机构提供法律服务的机构。这些机构不直接对社会开展工作，属于内部性的机构。除了这 11 个机构以外，剩余的 51 个机构都属于国家级的联邦政府机构，都直接在全国范围内发挥作用，产生影响。对于其中的一些执法部门来说，它们都可以在全国范围内进行执法。

（一）美国司法部现有的组织机构名单

（1）反托拉斯局（Antitrust Division）

（2）非法资产没收管理办公室（Asset Forfeiture Program）

（3）酒精、烟草、枪支和炸药管理局——ATF（Bureau of Alcohol, Tobacco, Firearms and Explosives）

（4）司法援助局（Bureau of Justice Assistance）

（5）司法统计局（Bureau of Justice Statistics）

（6）保护联邦政府财产和信誉事务局（Civil Division）

（7）公民权利保护局（Civil Rights Division）

（8）扶持社区警务工作事务局——COPS（Community Oriented Policing Services）

（9）社区居民冲突调解服务办公室（Community Relations Service）

---

① The United States Department of Justice：Office of the Attorney General，https://www. justice. gov/ag/about-office，访问日期：2018 年 7 月 23 日。

（10）专门服务于联邦政府的刑事法律事务局（Criminal Division）

（11）司法部工作人员职业道德管理办公室（Departmental Ethics Office）

（12）药品监督管理局（Diversion Control Division）

（13）缉毒局——DEA（Drug Enforcement Administration）

（14）老人权益保护服务部（Elder Justice Initiative）

（15）环境和自然资源局（Environment and Natural Resources Division）

（16）移民审查行政办公室（Executive Office for Immigration Review）

（17）打击有组织毒品犯罪办公室（Executive Office for Organized Crime Drug Enforcement Task Forces）

（18）律师行政工作办公室（Executive Office for U. S. Attorneys）

（19）托管行为管理办公室（Executive Office for U. S. Trustees）

（20）联邦调查局——FBI（Federal Bureau of Investigation）

（21）联邦监狱管理局（Federal Bureau of Prisons）

（22）国民向外国政府索赔裁决委员会（Foreign Claims Settlement Commission）

（23）遏制知识产权犯罪工作办公室（Intellectual Property Task Force）

（24）国际刑警组织美国分局（INTERPOL Washington）

（25）司法部行政事务管理局（Justice Management Division）

（26）司法服务援助办公室（Legal Aid Interagency Round Table）

（27）刑事司法资料服务办公室（National Criminal Justice Reference Service）

（28）不良行为纠正研究所（National Institute of Corrections）

（29）司法研究所（National Institute of Justice）

（30）国家安全局（National Security Division-NSD）

（31）援助刑事受害者办公室（Office for Victims of Crime）

（32）律师招聘与管理办公室（Office of Attorney Recruitment & Management）

（33）信息政策管理指导办公室（Office of Information Policy）

（34）遏制犯罪司法协助办公室（Office of Justice Programs）

（35）关爱少年和犯罪预防办公室——OJJDP（Office of Juvenile Justice and Delinquency Prevention）

（36）法律顾问办公室（Office of Legal Counsel）

（37）法律政策办公室（Office of Legal Policy）

（38）法律事务联络办公室（Office of Legislative Affairs）

（39）公民隐私和自由保护办公室（Office of Privacy and Civil Liberties）

（40）律师和执法人员职业责任管理办公室（Office of Professional Responsibility）

（41）新闻工作办公室（Office of Public Affairs）

（42）性罪犯者信息登记和追踪服务办公室（Office of Sex Offender Sentencing, Monitoring, Apprehending, Registering, and Tracking）

（43）司法部长助理办公室（Office of the Associate Attorney General）

（44）司法部长办公室（Office of the Attorney General）

（45）司法部副部长办公室（Office of the Deputy Attorney General）

（46）司法部监察长办公室（Office of the Inspector General）

（47）联邦刑事犯罪赦免委员会律师办公室（Office of the Pardon Attorney）

（48）副检察长办公室（Office of the Solicitor General）

（49）部落事务司法办公室（Office of Tribal Justice）

（50）保护妇女免除暴力政策研究室（Office on Violence Against Women）

（51）工作透明与合作办公室（Open Government）

（52）律师职业责任咨询办公室（Professional Responsibility Advisory Office）

（53）保护儿童办公室（Project Safe Childhood）

（54）公职人员和退伍军人服务办公室（Servicemembers and Veterans Initiative）

（55）特别检察官办公室（Special Counsel's Office）

（56）税务部（Tax Division）

（57）保护部落公平与安全办公室（Tribal Justice and Safety）

（58）美国律师办公室（U. S. Attorneys）

（59）法警服务办公室（U. S. Marshals Service）

（60）假释委员会（U. S. Parole Commission）

（61）受托人计划工作办公室（U. S. Trustee Program）

（62）保护海外恐怖主义受害者特别工作组（U. S. Victims of Terrorism Abroad Task Force）①

需要说明的是,对于上述司法部组织机构名单的翻译,除了个别的名称以外,绝大多数名称都是采用的"意译",都是通过了解了这一机构的实际工作内容以后,结合中文的含义进行的翻译,不是直接采取字面含义的"直译"。

（二）专门为司法部或者联邦政府提供服务的司法部机构名单

在现有的司法部组织机构中,下列 11 个组织机构属于专门为司法部内部的工作,或者专门为总统或其他联邦政府部门提供法律咨询、法律意见和其他法律服务的机构。

（1）民事法律事务局

（2）刑事法律事务局

（3）司法部工作人员职业道德管理办公室

（4）司法部行政事务管理局

（5）律师招聘与管理办公室

（6）信息政策管理指导办公室

（7）法律顾问办公室

（8）法律政策办公室

（9）法律事务联络办公室

（10）律师和执法人员职业责任管理办公室

（11）司法部监察长办公室

（三）与"经济间谍罪"和"商业秘密罪"相关的司法部组织机构

在现有的司法部机构中,下列机构的工作内容都与本书讨论的"经济间谍罪""盗窃商业秘密罪",以及其他侵害商业秘密的违法活动有关。

（1）非法资产没收管理办公室

（2）联邦调查局——FBI

---

① The United States Department of Justice：" Alphabetical Listing of Components, Programs, & Initiatives", https://www. justice. gov/agencies/alphabetical-listing-components-programs-initiatives,访问日期:2018 年 4 月 26 日。

（3）联邦监狱管理局

（4）国民向外国政府索赔裁决委员会

（5）遏制知识产权犯罪工作办公室

（6）国际刑警组织美国分局

（7）司法服务援助办公室

（8）刑事司法资料服务办公室

（9）国家安全局

（10）援助刑事受害者办公室

（11）遏制犯罪司法协助办公室

（12）新闻工作办公室

（13）司法部长助理办公室

（14）司法部长办公室

（15）司法部副部长办公室

（16）副检察长办公室

（17）美国律师办公室

（18）法警服务办公室

通过以上所列出的组织机构可以看出,在美国司法部中包含着国家安全机关、侦查机关、检察机关、司法程序监督和管理机关、监狱管理机关、律师管理机关等国家重要部门。因此,它是一个非常具有实际权力和执行能力的政府部门。与我国相应的组织机构相比,美国司法部的职能大体上包括我国中央政法委、国家公安部、国家安全部、最高人民检察院、国家司法部等部门相关职能的总和,以及最高人民法院的部分职能。

三、惩办经济间谍罪完全由美国司法部统一领导和实施

从上述司法部的组织机构中可以看出,上述各个强力部门都是司法部的直属单位,在具体的工作中,在司法部的统一领导和协调下,这些部门之间能够相互协调和相互配合地开展各项工作。

例如,对于任何一起"经济间谍罪",在侦查阶段,美国联邦调查局和国家

安全局等部门不仅在全国范围内具有完全独立的调查权和采用各种先进技术手段的侦查权,而且还具有对各类嫌疑人采取必要措施的权力。

对于已经批准逮捕的各类嫌疑人员,包括总检察长(司法部长兼任)在内的隶属于司法部的联邦最高检察机构可以批准、监督或者协调全国范围内的联邦检察机构和联邦检察官对嫌疑人进行指控和公诉,然后交由具有管辖权的联邦法院进行审理。

在审判过程中,隶属于司法部的相关部门也有权力对于案件的相关事项进行协助,甚至监督。

当构成"经济间谍罪"的犯罪嫌疑人被判决入狱后,正常情况下应当由联邦监狱进行监管和收押,而司法部又主管着全国的联邦监狱工作。

由此可见,在美国司法部的统一领导和组织协调下,本书涉及的"经济间谍罪"和"盗窃商业秘密罪",除了审判环节由联邦法院办理,不隶属于司法部之外,整个案件的其他环节,从立案侦查,到审查起诉、审判监督,再到判决后的收监羁押,都完全处于司法部的掌控之中。显然,对于上述两类案件来说,司法部是最重要的联邦政府部门。

美国的这一特点与我国现阶段的政府部门和司法部门的组织结构很不相同。首先,在我国,没有"经济间谍罪"这一罪名,在美国能够构成"经济间谍罪"这一罪犯行为,在我国只能构成"侵害商业秘密罪",属于我国《刑法》中"侵害知识产权罪"的范畴。在整个《刑法》中最终也只被列为"破坏社会主义市场经济秩序罪"的范围,只是属于一般的经济类犯罪,并没有上升到能够严重危害国家安全带有一定政治内容的"间谍罪"的理论高度。在这种情况下,如果对本书后面所翻译和介绍的美国《1996 经济间谍法》中有关"经济间谍罪"的定义进行分析可能就会发现,把这类犯罪与一般的盗窃商业秘密犯罪区别开来还是更加科学合理的。

其次,众所周知,在我国的组织机构中,公安机关属于政府部门,检察院和法院属于司法部门,对于一般的刑事案件来说,三者分别承担着"立案和侦查""批准逮捕与起诉",以及"审理和判决"的不同使命。而且三者之间既要相互配合,更要相互监督。在这种体制下,虽然在党委机关设立了"政法委"这一机构来统一协调和组织三者之间的工作,但是,无论是公检法,还是领导监狱工作的司法部门,都在行政关系和业务关系上与政法委没有隶属关系,也就是说,政法委实际上对公安、检察、法院和司法部门没有最终的决定权。而且,最近几年来,我国的司法改革取向似乎正在向着把审判权更多地移交给审判案件的法官享有,并且由此要求他们对自己审理的案件承担终身责任的方向发展。

试想一下,如果在很多年以后,某一错误的案件终于获得纠正,按照上述要求应当追究当年这一错误案件审判法官的责任,问题在于这是否也在客观上存在着难以执行的难题。第一,这一法官无力承担这一责任;第二,对于这一法官来说,承担这一责任对其已经没有什么实际上影响和意义;第三,如果该法官不幸过世,当然也就无须承担这一责任。但是,不管怎样,对于这一错案的受害方来说,这种责任是不应当因为执行难而被放弃的。如果对上述问题进行进一步的分析就能发现,出现错案以后,对于受害方能承担责任的主体只能是国家,而不应当是承办案件的法官。因为"审判权"只能属于国家,而不能归属于个人,或者名义上属于国家,实际上由于国家疏于监管,而任由个人行使。

讨论上述问题的目的就在于把我国现在实施的司法实践取向与美国在"经济间谍罪"方面采取的组织管理和实践价值取向进行简单的对比,展示出两者之间存在的区别和差异。

美国司法部的这种组织模式在美国联邦调查局逮捕我国某大学教授张某一案中得到了充分的体现。

我国某大学的教授张某接到美方的邀请以后到美国参加学术会议,2015年5月16日,当他乘坐飞机从中国到达美国洛杉矶国际机场时遭到美国联邦调查局特工的逮捕。根据2015年5月19日美国司法部新闻工作办公室在司法部网站上发布的相关新闻介绍,包括张教授在内的6名中国人利用曾经在美国读书和工作的机会窃取了美国安华高科技公司(Avago Technologies)和思佳讯公司(Skyworks Solutions Inc.)的商业秘密,并把窃取的商业秘密用于某大学建设相关的高科技公司,依据美国《1996经济间谍法》涉嫌构成了"经济间谍罪""盗窃商业秘密罪""共谋经济间谍犯罪"和"共谋盗窃商业秘密犯罪"。2015年5月18日,该案件经过美国加利福尼亚州中心区联邦地区法院的初步审查后,决定将张教授押送到位于洛杉矶市和旧金山市之间的圣何塞市（San Jose City）关押，案件转到加利福尼亚州北部地区联邦地区法院做进一步的审理①。

在上述新闻中，也介绍了案件的调查和公诉经过。这一案件的侦查工作是由美国联邦调查局旧金山分局帕洛阿尔托市常驻机构的特工完成的。案件的公诉由加利福尼亚州北部区两名联邦助理检察官办理，并且他们要求就案件的相关问题与美国国家安全局反间谍部门进行协商。

值得注意的是，此案中，联邦调查局特工采取了诱捕的方法，即谎称邀请张教授到美国参加学术会议，并且发出了参加会议的邀请函。

在整个案件中，先由联邦调查局完成调查工作，并且采取灵活机动的诱捕措施实际抓捕了犯罪嫌疑人；然后，经由有管辖权的联邦地区法院初步审理后决定羁押；接下来，由联邦检察官决定向联邦地区法院提起公诉。

如果按照正常的法律程序进行下去，由联邦地区法院作出一审判决后，被告人如果不服还可以上诉，判决最终生效后，若判决有罪需要收监，将由联邦监狱收押。

在此值得说明是，涉及这一案件的三个重要单位——总检察长办公室（即司法部长办公室）、联邦调查局、国家安全局都是司法部的单位。

由此可见，在美国现有的司法体制下，对于涉及国家安全的刑事案件，特别是涉嫌间谍犯罪的案件，其基本的工作组织关系如图1所示。间谍案件的一般办案流程是：①第一步调查；②第二步准备起诉；③第三步在调查和起诉中与国家安全部门协商；④第四步联邦地区法院审理并作出判决；⑤第五步在联邦监狱执行生效的法院判决。

---

① The United States Department of Justice, Justice News, http://www. justice. gov/opa/pr/chinese-professors-among-six-defendants-charged-economic-espionage-and-theft-trade-secrets, 访问日期：2015 年 5 月 19 日。

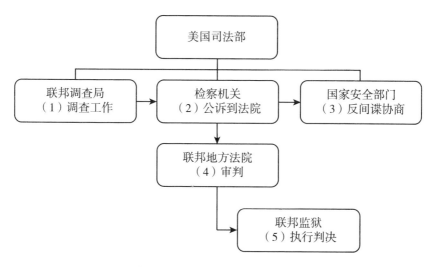

（在上述五个具体办案单位中，只有法院不隶属于司法部）

图1　美国司法部和联邦法院办理经济间谍罪程序

由此可见，司法部一旦启动调查某一经济间谍案件，在很大程度上，案件的最终结果就已经在其掌握之中。可以说，在很大程度上，对于这类案件的处理，是由一套相对闭合的内部程序来完成的。

另外，由于联邦调查局、国家安全局和检察机关等国家强力部门的介入，他们都能够充分地利用国家强力部门的各种资源和手段来获取证据，调查证人，抓捕嫌疑人，这些权力是一般国家机关所没有的。当然，从保护商业秘密的角度来说，这种保护手段也是最有效的。由此，也足以表明，美国政府对于商业秘密的保护，特别是对于打击"经济间谍罪"的态度是非常坚定的。

第六节　美国联邦调查局的工作任务和特点

在这里之所以要单独介绍美国联邦调查局（FBI）的基本情况，是由于在本书中所介绍的《1996 经济间谍法》中的"经济间谍罪"，主要是由美国联邦调查局主办的。因此，了解这一工作单位的基本情况，特别是其工作的职责和特点，对于更好地理解《1996 经济间谍法》的相关内容，以及涉及商业秘密保护的其他法律程序都是十分必要的。

需要再次明确的是,美国联邦调查局属于联邦政府中的行政机关,隶属于美国司法部。联邦局长由美国总统提名,由美国国会参议院批准后,由总统任命,每一届局长最长任期不得超过10年。

一、美国联邦调查局的诞生历程

美国联邦调查局诞生于1908年7月26日。据史料记载,促成这一行政机构诞生的直接原因有两个。一是当时的美国司法部长查尔斯·波拿巴(Charles J. Bonaparte)在1907年为了帮助所属检察官调查和处理一起案件,由于自己没有足够的具有丰富案件调查经验的调查人员,就从特勤局租用了9名专业调查人员帮助工作。可是,由于租金比较高,而且这些工作人员在完成调查工作后,不是直接向司法部长查尔斯·波拿巴汇报调查工作,而是直接向他们自己的局长汇报工作,致使查尔斯·波拿巴部长感到很沮丧,很想能够拥有一支自己的调查队伍。二是当查尔斯·波拿巴部长向国会反映这一难题希望获得国会支持时,国会反而决定联邦政府部门不得租用特勤局的工作人员从事调查工作。当时的美国总统是第26届总统西奥多·罗斯福(Theodore Roosevelt),在总统的支持下,查尔斯·波拿巴部长又把自己原先租借的9名调查人员找来,将他们与另外25名工作人员一起组成了一个34人的调查队。在1908年7月26日,查尔斯·波拿巴部长命令司法部内的有关部门把调查案件的工作全部移交给这支调查队统一负责,这一天也被认为是联邦调查局的诞生日。这支34人的调查队就是联邦调查局最早的工作人员。

到了1909年3月16日,查尔斯·波拿巴部长的继任者,司法部长乔治·威克沙姆给这个调查队起了另外一个名字——调查局,从此司法部内部的这一"调查队"变成了"调查局"。

起初,调查队的工作主要是调查有关白领犯罪和公民权利的案件,包括反托拉斯案件,以及土地欺诈、银行欺诈、入籍和侵害版权等案件。另外,它还处理一些涉及国家安全问题,包括叛国和一些无政府主义活动的案件。

1917年4月6日,美国国会批准参加第一次世界大战,自此以后,联邦调查局开始把反间谍工作作为重要的工作内容,同时也办理其他重要的侵害联邦法律的刑事案件。

到 2018 年,联邦调查局已经走过了 110 年的工作历程,其组织机构和工作范围都得到了很大的发展,它已经成为世界著名的调查机构。

当前,联邦调查局拥有 35 000 多名员工,其中包括情报分析员、语言专家、科学家和信息技术专家等特殊专家和出色的调查人员①。

二、美国联邦调查局的组织机构和工作特点

（一）美国联邦调查局的工作使命

美国联邦调查局的工作使命是保护美国人民,维护美国宪法。他们优先工作的事项:保护美国免遭恐怖袭击;保护美国免受外国情报行动和间谍活动的侵害;保护美国免受基于网络的攻击和高科技犯罪的危害;打击各级公共腐败;保护公民权利;打击实施跨国犯罪或国家犯罪的组织和企业;打击主要的白领犯罪;打击重大的暴力犯罪②。

（二）美国联邦调查局的组织机构

美国联邦调查局的组织机构分为内部处室和对外开展工作的部门③。

1. 对外开展工作的部门

（1）国家安全部门。具体包括下列六个部门:①执行助理总监;②反间谍工作部;③反恐工作部;④高价值被拘留者审讯组;⑤恐怖分子筛选中心;⑥大规模毁灭武器工作委员会。

（2）刑事、网络、响应和服务部门。具体包括下列六个部门:①执行助理主任;②刑事调查部;③重要事件响应小组;④网络工作部;⑤国际业务部;⑥受害者服务部。

---

① The Federal Bureau of Investigation, A Brief History, https://www.fbi.gov/history/brief-history, 访问日期:2018 年 5 月 8 日。

② 同上。

③ 同上。

(3)情报部门。具体包括下列四个部门：①执行助理主任；②情报总监；③合作伙伴关系办公室；④私营部门办公室。

(4)科学技术处。具体包括下列四个部门：①执行助理主任；②刑事司法信息服务部；③实验室工作部；④运营技术工作部。

(5)信息和技术处。具体包括下列四个部门：①执行助理总监；②IT 应用和数据部；③IT 企业服务部；④IT 基础设施部。

(6)人力资源处。具体包括下列四个部门：①执行助理总监；②人力资源部门；③安全部门；④培训处。

2. 内部工作科室

内部工作机构具体包括下列科室：①财务和设施部门；②检查部门；③首席信息官办公室；④国会事务办公室；⑤EEO 事务办公室；⑥总法律顾问办公室；⑦诚信与合规办公室；⑧监察专员办公室；⑨职业责任办公室；⑩公共事务办公室；⑪记录管理部门；⑫资源规划办公室。

(三)联邦调查局在世界范围内分布的办公地点

联邦调查局除了位于华盛顿特区的总部以外，在全美国主要城市设有 56 个分局，在全国各主要城镇设有 350 多个办事处，并且在美国驻外国大使馆设有 60 多个国际办事处，其调查人员称为法律专员。

通过上述介绍可以看出，美国联邦调查局具有完整的组织机构和先进的技术手段，对于调查经济间谍罪具有强大的工作能力和技术优势，因此，比较有利于对各类经济间谍案件的调查和侦破。

'02

第二篇

美国《1996经济间谍法》及配套联邦商业秘密法律

第一章 《1996 经济间谍法》

第一节 《1996 经济间谍法》简介

一、《1996 经济间谍法》的基本特征及修订版本

（一）生效时间

《1996 经济间谍法》由美国第 42 任总统克林顿批准后于 1996 年 10 月 11 日生效。

（二）法律分类和归属

由于《1996 经济间谍法》所规范的内容属于刑事范畴，所以被编入了《美国法典》的刑事部分，即《美国法典》的第 18 篇（刑事篇），列为第 90 章——"保护商业秘密"部分。

（三）修订历史和修订时间

《1996 经济间谍法》于 1996 年 10 月 11 日生效以后，至今（2018 年）已经先后经历了下列几次修订：

（1）2002 年对其中的第 1836 条进行了修订；

（2）2008 年对第 1834 条进行了修订；

（3）《2012 盗窃商业秘密罪扩大适用范围法》对其进行了修订；

（4）《2012 外国经济间谍罪加重处罚法》对其进行了修订；

（5）《2016 商业秘密保护法》对其进行了重大修订。

由此可见，《1996 经济间谍法》已经经历了五次修订，由于美国的立法特点和立法程序的限制，至今没有颁布一部经过全部修正以后的新的完整的《1996 经济间谍法》。因此，这部 1996 年 10 月 11 日生效的《1996 经济间谍法》仍然有效。但是，实际上其只是一部原始的法律版本，在面对现实中的具体法律问

题时,就不应当只依据这一原始版本中的法律条款来处理这些法律问题,而是应当依据修订后已经生效的法律规定来进行处理(可使用笔者整理的本篇第五章中的《1996 经济间谍法》修订综合版)。这也是这部原始版本在适用上应当受到的限制之处,否则,就不可避免地会出现适用法律错误的现象,显然,这是非常重要的问题,值得每一位读者重视和留意。

(四)主要特征

(1)《1996 经济间谍法》是美国历史上第一部专门保护商业秘密的联邦法律,也是美国历史上第一部保护商业秘密的联邦刑事法律。

(2)《1996 经济间谍法》把侵害商业秘密的犯罪行为区分为"经济间谍罪"和"盗窃商业秘密罪",在世界上属于首次,这不仅是立法条文和内容上的创新,也是知识产权理论的重大突破和创新。

二、《1996 经济间谍法》在适用上的版本限制和解决途径

由于经过五次修订,《1996 经济间谍法》不应当再单纯地适用。为此,本书专门综合整理出了上述五次修订后的综合版本,也可以称为综合修订版本,在此称为《1996 经济间谍法》修订综合版。这一综合版本是作者把《1996 经济间谍法》之外的三部法律中涉及《1996 经济间谍法》的全部条款添加到《1996 经济间谍法》之后所形成的综合性版本,包括中英文两种文本。

因此,读者现在如果想要了解和使用有关美国联邦商业秘密刑事保护及经济间谍的法律规定,就应当查找和使用这部《1996 经济间谍法》修订综合版中的规定和相关内容,而不应当只参照或使用包括《1996 经济间谍法》在内的上述四部单独的法律版本的规定。

第二节 《1996 经济间谍法》译文

《1996 经济间谍法》①

目 录

第 1831 条 经济间谍罪

任何单位或个人,如果为了使外国政府、外国政府的机构,或者外国政府的代理人受益,企图或者故意实施了下列行为,构成经济间谍罪;个人犯罪的,最高处罚 50 万美元,或者最高监禁 15 年,或者两者同时执行;单位犯罪的,最高处罚 1000 万美元。

(1)窃取,或者擅自占有、携带、运输、隐藏,或者通过欺诈、计谋、收买等非法手段获取商业秘密;

(2)擅自抄写、复印、记录、绘制、拍摄、下载、上传、修改、销毁、影印、根

---

① 1996 年 10 月 11 日生效,编入《美国法典》第 18 篇第 90 章"保护商业秘密"。

据知悉和记忆的内容重新制作、传输、传递、发送、邮寄、泄露,或者运送商业秘密;

(3)在知道商业秘密已经处于被盗窃、侵害、非法获取、非法传递的情况下,仍然接受、购买或者占有该商业秘密;

(4)企图实施上述(1)至(3)款中的任何一种犯罪行为的预备行为;

(5)与一个或者多个人共谋实施第(1)至(3)款中的任何一项所述的任何犯罪行为,以及其中的一名或者多名人员采取任何行动以促使共谋目的实用的行为。

第 1832 条　盗窃商业秘密罪

任何单位或个人,如果企图或者故意实施下列侵害他人商业秘密的行为,当这些商业秘密与用于国际贸易或者州际贸易的商品有关,或者包含于用在国际贸易或者州际贸易的商品中时,构成盗窃商业秘密罪。个人犯罪的,按照本法的规定处罚,或者最高监禁 10 年,或者同时实施罚款和监禁;单位犯罪的,最高罚款 500 万美元。

(1)窃取,或者擅自占有、携带、运输、隐藏,或者通过欺诈、计谋、收买等非法手段获取商业秘密;

(2)擅自抄写、复印、记录、绘制、拍摄、下载、上传、修改、销毁、影印、根据知悉和记忆的内容重新制作、传输、传递、发送、邮寄、泄露、运送商业秘密;

(3)在知道商业秘密已经处于被盗窃、侵害、非法获取、非法传递的情况下,仍然接受、购买或者占有该商业秘密;

(4)企图实施上述(1)至(3)款中的任何一种犯罪行为的预备行为;

(5)与一个或者多个人共谋实施第(1)至(3)款中的任何一项所述的任何犯罪行为,以及其中的一名或者多名人员采取任何行动以促使共谋目的实用的行为。

第 1833 条　禁止的例外情形

在本法中,下列行为属于合法行为:

(1)任何由美国联邦政府、各州政府,以及各州政府的分支机构决定实施的行为;

（2）向一个具有合法管辖权的联邦政府、州政府、州政府的分支机构报告涉嫌侵害商业秘密事务的行为。

第 1834 条　刑事没收

1. 对于实施本法犯罪的被告，法院在作出判决时，除了判处应有的刑罚以外，还应当罚没被告的下列财产：

（1）任何直接或者间接地借助犯罪行为所得的财产。

（2）任何人的财产，只要被用来或者企图被用来实施犯罪，或者为犯罪提供便利，无论被使用的方式和方法如何，法院在慎重考虑这些财产在犯罪中的性质，被使用的范围和比例以后决定没收的程度。

2. 对于应当没收的财产，在办理扣押和处置措施以及其他行政和司法手续时，应当按照 1970 年《综合药物滥用预防和控制法》（21 U. S. C 853）第 413 节的规定执行，但是其中的（d）和（j）款除外，不适用于本条的没收措施。

（注：美国国会于 2008 年对第 1834 条进行了修改，修改后增加的内容如下："第 1834 条刑事没收：除了依据本法提供的任何其他类似的救济以外，本法中所涉及的没收、销毁和归还措施都应当在《美国法典》第 2323 条的范围内实施。"）[①]

第 1835 条　司法程序中的保密令

在适用本法实施的任何刑事或者其他任何司法程序中，在符合联邦刑事和民事诉讼法、联邦证据法以及相关法律的前提下，法院应当颁布保密令并采取合理的必要措施保护商业秘密的秘密性。一审判决后，如果美国联邦政府提起上诉，则由联邦地区法院作出准予的决定或命令，并且授权或者指导对商业秘密的披露。

第 1836 条　禁止侵权的民事程序

1. 在民事诉讼中，对于本法中任何侵害商业秘密的行为，总检察长都有权力获取适当的禁令救济。

[①]　笔者通过查找和引用《美国法典》第 2323 条的规定，认为上述对第 1834 条的修改内容可以进一步解释为增加了下列内容："本法中，对于涉及侵害商业秘密的财产和非法收入采取没收、销毁、移交给商业秘密权利人等措施时，除了法律另有类似补偿的规定以外，应当依据《美国法典》第 2323 条的规定，由检察长在诉讼、执法和获得民事补偿等活动中依据自己的职责执行。"

2. 对于本条中的民事诉讼,联邦地区法院拥有一审案件的专属管辖权。

第 1837 条　对美国境外行为的效力

对于发生在美国境外侵害美国公司商业秘密的行为,如果存在下列情形之一的,也适用于本法:①美国公民;②在美国拥有永久居住权的外国人;③基于美国联邦政府、各州政府或者州政府所属的分支机构的法律法规所诞生的单位;④促使侵害行为发生的其他行为发生在美国。

第 1838 条　与其他法律的关系

本法的内容不影响和取代任何由美国联邦、州、领地、属地等政府机构颁布实施的法律法规中已有的对侵害商业秘密违法行为的民事或者刑事救济措施,也不影响任何政府雇员依据俗称"信息自由法"的《美国法典》第 5 篇第 552 条的规定合法披露信息的权利。

第 1839 条　相关术语的定义

本法中术语的含义如下:

(1)"外国政府的机构"是指本质上由外国政府所有、控制、指导、管理、掌握的各类政府所属的部、局、委员会、大学、研究机构,各类协会,各类法律、商业和企业组织,各类团体、公司和实体。

(2)"外国政府的代理人"是指外国政府的官员、雇员、代理机构、公务员、代表团成员、代表。

(3)"商业秘密"是指各种形式和类型的有关金融、商业、科学、技术、经济或者工程的各类信息。其包括式样、计划、资料汇编、程序设备、原理、设计、原型、方法、技术、工艺、程序或代码,无论是有形还是无形,也无论是以物理、电子、图形、照片或者书写的方式进行编撰和储存。同时,其还应当具有下列两项条件:①权利人已经对这一秘密信息采取了合理的保密措施;②由于这一秘密信息不被公众所知悉,也不易被他人轻易地通过合法手段所探知,因此,具有现实的或者潜在的经济价值。

(4)"商业秘密权利人"是指基于商业秘密公正地拥有合法权利的自然人或者经济实体。

(侯仰坤翻译,2018 年 1 月于北京)

第三节　对《1996 经济间谍法》的评析

一、《1996 经济间谍法》奠定了美国联邦政府保护商业秘密的刑事法律基础

《1996 经济间谍法》是美国联邦法律，也即国家级法律中第一部专门保护商业秘密的刑事类法律，既然属于国家级法律，因此，在美国全国范围内都有效。

在《1996 经济间谍法》颁布实施之前，美国对商业秘密的刑事保护，主要依据各个州自己颁布实施的各州的刑事法律执行，使用的罪名主要是盗窃罪。

如前所述，由于各个州相互之间是一种相互平等，相互独立的关系，而且对于那些属于州法律管辖范围内的事项，联邦法律又无管辖权。由此导致的另一种结果就是，对于归属于州法律管辖的事项，在全国范围内，缺少一种全国统一的立法标准和统一的法律规范，从而造成了各州法律的多样性和不一致性。

当前，面对这一难题，在商业秘密保护方面，目前在美国诞生了全国性的示范性法律，具体包括《统一商业秘密法》《侵权法重述》和《反不正当竞争法重述》。当然，这三类示范法的内容都属于民事侵权救济的范畴，不属于刑法范畴。而且目前只有《侵权法重述》被全国 50 个州全部采用，《统一商业秘密法》已经被绝大多数的州采用，而《反不正当竞争法重述》还很少被采用，有关这一方面的问题将在本书第三篇中做专门的介绍。

这样，当前在美国全国范围内，就出现了下列的局面：

（1）凡是在国际贸易和跨州贸易中发生了侵害他人商业秘密行为构成犯罪的，就适用《1996 经济间谍法》，具体适用该法中"经济间谍罪"或者"盗窃商业秘密罪"的条款进行处罚，由联邦法院管辖。

（2）凡是在同一个州内的贸易中发生了盗窃他人商业秘密犯罪行为的，就适用该州的法律，按照该州法律中有关商业秘密犯罪的条款处罚，并且由该州法院管辖。

不难想象,由于各个州法律的差异性,同样的犯罪行为,按照不同州的法律进行处理时,其法律结果可能会有不同,甚至存在比较大的差异。

由此可见,《1996 经济间谍法》的颁布实施,弥补了联邦法律中有关商业秘密刑事保护的空缺。另外,只有把它与各个州已有的有关保护商业秘密的刑事法律结合在一起,才能共同构成全国范围内保护商业秘密的刑事法律体系,这种法律体系如果用一个图示来表示就是如图 2 所示:

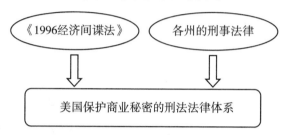

图 2　美国保护商业秘密的刑事法律构成

二、《1996 经济间谍法》在美国的适用范围

应该注意的是,对于盗窃商业秘密罪,各个州的刑事法律只能管辖其中的部分案件,即对于那些单纯地发生在本州贸易中的盗窃商业秘密案件进行管辖。与此相对应的是,《1996 经济间谍法》对于国际贸易和跨州贸易中盗窃商业秘密的犯罪行为进行管辖。

还应当注意的是,《1996 经济间谍法》中包含着两种不同的罪,一个是"盗窃商业秘密罪",另一个是"经济间谍罪"。上述管辖的划分只是针对"盗窃商业秘密罪"而言的,对于"经济间谍罪",各州的刑法都没有管辖权,这一犯罪行为的管辖权只属于联邦法院,具体只由《1996 经济间谍法》进行规范。同样,对于"经济间谍罪",无论是发生在国际贸易、跨州贸易,或者各州内部的贸易中,都归属于《1996 经济间谍法》规范,都只能按照"经济间谍罪"定罪处罚。

三、"经济间谍罪"在理论上突破了知识产权属于"民事权利"甚至"私权"的界限

长期以来,人们对于"知识产权"这类事物的认识一直处于探索之中。但是,在现有的探索成果中,人们在理论上基本把"知识产权"归属到了"民事权

利"的范畴,这一观点至少在我国已经成了通说,甚至在我国《民法通则》和《民法总则》中得到了确认。在这两部立法中,都把"知识产权"明确到了"民事权利"的范畴。另外,由于在 WTO 的《TRIPs 协议》[Agreement of the World Trade Organization on Trade-Related Aspects of Intellectual Property Rights (1994)]中有这样一句话,"Recognizing that intellectual property rights are private rights",在我们中文的译文,包括一些官方的译文中,基本上都把其翻译成"认识到知识产权是私权(或私有的权利)"。据此,我国的不少专家学者和法律工作者就以此作为主要的依据和理由,直接把知识产权定义为一种"私权"。

实际上,这种做法本身就是值得商榷的一种行为,虽然我们应当了解和遵从国际公约的相关规定。但是,毕竟"国际公约"本身并不等于"正确"和"真理",而且任何一部国际公约都会伴随着社会的发展不断地进行修订和完善。因此,不应当把"国际公约"中的具体条款和具体规定视为不可讨论和分析的内容。实际上,就绝大多数国际公约来说,特别是知识产权国际公约(包括条约、规定、协定等)都只是设立了基本原则、基本精神,需要规范的基本内容和基本规范的最低标准。没有,实际上也不可能对某一条款作出强制性的规定和要求。这是由于各个成员方的具体国情不同,而且作为国际公约,自身也没有这一"强制性的权力"。甚至,对于某些条款,考虑到不同成员方之间的国情差异,还允许成员方基于本国的国情自行决定具体的内容和选择。由此可见,国际公约中设立的内容,更多的是原则性的,示范性的,引导和启发性的,对于其中的任何规定,都是可以讨论的。

另外,还存在着一个问题就是,当人们所接受或者理解的理论指导与现实不一致,甚至发生冲突的时候,到底是应该严格地遵从书本上的理论或者法律中的条款来处理现实中存在的难题,还是应当基于实际情况努力寻找真正科学合理的办法来处理这种现实难题。如果我们仔细分析就能发现,表面上这只是一种对解决现实难题的不同办法进行选择的问题,实质上,这不仅是一种对这类问题的认识的事情,实际上涉及是否真正想要科学合理地解决这一现实中的难题的问题,也就是是否真正想对解决这一现实中的难题进行负责的问题。

之所以提出上述问题,是由于这一问题在理论上比较重要,属于知识产权根基性的问题,而在这一问题上当前又存在着认识上明显的差错,以及与社会现实明显不符之处。首先,在于无论是否知晓和了解《TRIPs 协议》中的上述内容,凡是熟悉我国知识产权法律的人们都应当知道,在我国想要获取专利权、商标权、植物新品种权、地理标志产品保护、集成电路布图设计专有权,都必须按照法律规定进行申请,等待审批。既然等待审批,客观上就存在着两种结果,获得批准,或者未获得批准,这是申请者个人难以决定的。其次,在通过批准,获取权利以后,对于有些已经获得的权利,还需要缴纳年费来维持这种权利的合法存在,而对于商标权来说,国家有关部门还在监督商标的使用,如果存在违法行为,则有权撤销已经存在的商标权等。由此说明,"知识产权"这类权利与一般民法中所界定的"私权"绝不是相同的事物,当然,如果认为即使再不相同,也要把这两类不同的事物归属于同一事物,这里就超越了一般的正常的逻辑范畴,发生了"指鹿为马"的行为。

笔者进行以上的分析只是想要说明,对于知识产权这类权利来说,简单地把其归属于民事权利,甚至私权,都是值得讨论的,在一定程度上来说,这种归属还存在着一些欠缺和不科学之处。

具体到"商业秘密"这一事物来说,首先,在世界范围内借助《保护工业产权巴黎公约》(以下简称《巴黎公约》)以及《TRIPs 协议》中对商业秘密保护的明确规定,商业秘密已经被明确地归属到了知识产权的范畴。

其次,目前世界各国对于保护商业秘密的国内立法不尽相同,而且有些差异还很显著,总体来说,在本国立法中颁布专门的商业秘密保护法律的国家很少。在这方面只有美国一个国家做得非常突出,不仅颁布了专门性的保护商业秘密的法律,而且已经形成了一个相对独立完整的法律体系。例如,美国的《1996 经济间谍法》和《2016 商业秘密保护法》,以及各州保护商业秘密的法律。在其他国家中,又以德国为代表,把"侵害商业秘密的行为"列为"不正当竞争的行为",因而利用制止不正当竞争行为的专门性或者相关的法律进行规制。而在商业性的生产经营中,"不正当竞争的行为"又有多种类型,"侵害商业秘密的行为"只是多种不同"不正当竞争的行为"中的一种,在利用专门性的法律规制"不正当竞争的行为"时,比较典型的专门性法律就是"反不正当竞争法"。这样一来,又以 1896 年德国颁布的世界上第一部《反不正当竞争法》为代表形成了对"商业秘密"这一类事物的另一种认识和法律规范,而且,这部法律已经影响了许多国家的国内立法,我国就是受其影响的国家之一。

除此之外,还有一些国家没有关于商业秘密的专门性立法,对于商业秘密的保护,借用合同法和其他法律,遵循公平合理的基本原则进行保护。

我国借鉴德国的立法模式和基本的立法理念,是以《反不正当竞争法》来对商业秘密进行保护的,在这种立法模式中,侵害他人商业秘密的行为被视为一种不正当的竞争行为,从逻辑上来说,它直接侵害的是"他人正当地从事生产经营的权利",也就是一种"经营权"。当然,结合商业秘密包含"技术秘密"和"经营秘密"这两类事物的这一特征,很显然,单纯地把商业秘密这类事物自身具有的社会功能和所能产生的社会作用都完全地界定为一种"经营权",这种界定本身是否科学与合理,也是值得讨论的问题。

我国在 1993 年颁布实施了《反不正当竞争法》之后,于 2017 年又对该法进行了修订和完善,但是在立法模式和立法理念上始终都没有超越德国反不正当竞争法的框架和范围,在理念上对于德国的反不正当竞争法是一种遵守和遵从的关系,这一特征比较明显。在这种框架下,虽然我国的现行立法中对于"经营权"是否完全属于"私权"这一问题没有进行明确的界定,而且我国的国有企业也存在着"经营权"的问题,并且这一"经营权"还受着政府权力的管理和约束。但是,总体上来说,在我国现行的知识产权法律中,由于受到《民法通则》和《民法总则》的影响,基本上还是把商业秘密归属于民事权利的范畴,甚至有些专家学者还是把其归属于"私权"的范畴。

在这种背景下,就能发现美国颁布实施《1996 经济间谍法》,特别是在该法中还把一部分"侵害商业秘密的行为"列为"经济间谍行为",这就极大地突破了商业秘密属于"民事权利和私权"的理论界限。因为"间谍罪"只能是一种涉及国家主权和国家公权力的犯罪行为,基于民事权利不可能涉及间谍罪的问题,这就涉及"民事权利"与"国家公权力",或者与国家"政治权力"之间的相互关系问题。基于社会常识,人们都知道,这是两类完全不同类型的权利与权力的关系,无论把"民事权利"或者"私权"进行怎样的扩大化解释,或者进行怎样的模糊化解释,都不可能延伸或者覆盖到"政治权力"或者"国家公权力"的领域中去。

因此,《1996 经济间谍法》把为了"外国政府的利益"而侵害"美国企业的商业秘密"的行为列为"经济间谍行为"是对知识产权理论的一大突破。当然,虽然在立法中做了这种规定,而且在现实中美国司法部门也根据这一法律办理了相关的重要案件,但是,对于这一问题在理论上进行更加深入的研究和论证仍然是十分必要的。这有利于推动人们对于"商业秘密",以及整个"知识产权"这一类事物的深入认识和了解,使其能够更好地为人类社会服务。

实际上,对于这一问题进行深入的分析可能就会发现,现在人们对于知识产权这类事物的认识可能还处于比较狭窄和肤浅的阶段。"知识产权"这类事物本身能够承担更多更重要的社会功能和作用,只是当前人们还没有这种全面和深刻的意识和了解。

四、把"犯罪动机"和"犯罪目的"作为划分"盗窃商业秘密罪"和"经济间谍罪"的依据

在《1996 经济间谍法》中,同时规定了两种罪,即在第 1831 条中规定的"经济间谍罪"和在第 1832 条中规定的"盗窃商业秘密罪"。

从立法条款中可以看出,两类罪名所对应的具体犯罪行为是完全相同的,具体行为都是五类行为。对于在第 1831 条和第 1832 条中所列举的五类行为,当存在下列三种状态之一时:企图实施,或者正在实施,或者已经实施,就构成了侵害商业秘密的犯罪,也就是说,区分这两类犯罪的依据不是犯罪行为本身。

在《1996 经济间谍法》中,也明确规定区分这两类犯罪的直接依据就是犯罪动机和犯罪目的,即如果犯罪动机和犯罪目的就是直接为了外国政府或者与外国政府相关者的利益,这种侵害商业秘密的犯罪就属于经济间谍罪,否则,就属于盗窃商业秘密罪。

当然,这种以犯罪动机和犯罪目的作为区分犯罪类型的做法本身有其一定的科学性和合理性,甚至,犯罪动机和犯罪目的也可以作为判断是否构成犯罪的条件之一。这里就在一定程度上涉及犯罪故意的问题,这属于刑法学研究和分析的问题,在此就不做深入的讨论和分析。现在需要讨论的另一个问题是,即使是为了外国政府或者与外国政府相关者的利益(以下统称为外国政府利

益)而实施了盗窃美国企业的商业秘密的行为,是否都应当被视为构成了"经济间谍罪"。如果进行分析就能发现,其中涉及下列五个方面的问题:

(1)是否行为人只要实施了第 1831 条中规定的五类行为中的任何一种具体的行为,他就直接构成了"经济间谍罪",而无须考虑实施这种行为的具体程度和持续的期限。

(2)是否需要评价被侵害的商业秘密自身的性质和其所能产生的社会作用,是否无论什么内容的商业秘密,只要属于商业秘密,一旦被符合"经济间谍罪"动机的行为所侵害都能直接构成"经济间谍罪"。

(3)是否需要考虑侵害行为所能产生的实际危害结果,或者已经产生的社会危害结果。

(4)此时的危害性,是以谁作为受害方作为参照依据,是以拥有该被侵害的商业秘密的权利人即美国企业作为唯一的受害人,还是增加美国政府,还是再增加美国社会或者整个人类社会。

(5)对于被涉嫌侵害的商业秘密本身来说,在侵害行为发生时,该商业秘密自身是否能够构成商业秘密,其是否存在,应当由谁作出评价和认定。

从上述问题的提出可以看出,在现有的《1996 经济间谍法》对于这些问题都没有作出明确的规定。这样,对于实际办理这类案件的司法部门来说,是否立案调查,以及是否对嫌疑人实施逮捕都具有很大的自由空间,具有很大的灵活性,当然也使此类司法活动具有比较大的随机性,这一特点和缺陷在已经发生的一些经济间谍案件中已经凸显了出来。

另外,由于这是直接涉及外国政府利益的案件,也就是说这类案件并不是单纯的一类刑事案件,也不是单纯的一类政治案件,而是既涉及经济、刑事、政治,又涉及国际社会不同政府间的案件。在这种情况下,为了科学合理以及公平公正地处理这类案件,避免产生国际纠纷,更应该对这类案件的立案标准,调查程序,审判程序和定罪量刑的标准具体化和明确化,并进行公开。

如果再进一步分析就能发现,在侵害商业秘密犯罪中之所以能够成立"间谍罪",在很大程度上是由于外国政府从中受益,从而使这一类案件具有了政治化的特征和属性,由此才能诞生和存在"间谍罪"的问题。

五、联邦法院拥有《1996 经济间谍法》中两类案件的一审专属管辖权

由于《1996 经济间谍法》属于联邦法律,按照联邦法院与各州法院的管辖权划分,各州法院管辖适用州法律的案件,联邦法院管辖适用联邦法律的案件,因此,适用《1996 经济间谍法》的案件都应当由联邦法院管辖。在具体的案件中,一审案件一般都由分布于各州的联邦地区法院受理,也即联邦法院的一审法院受理。

本章附录:《1996 经济间谍法》原文

ECONOMIC ESPIONAGE ACT OF 1996

PUBLIC LAW 104-294—OCT. 11, 1996

To amend title 18, United States Code,

to protect proprietary economic information, and for other purposes.

Be it enacted by the Senate and House of Representatives of the United States of America in Congress assembled,

SECTION 1. SHORT TITLE.

This Act may be cited as the "Economic Espionage Act of 1996".

TITLE I—PROTECTION OF TRADE SECRETS
CHAPTER 90—PROTECTION OF TRADE SECRETS

Sec.

§ 1831. Economic espionage

§ 1832. Theft of trade secrets

§ 1833. Exceptions to prohibitions

§ 1834. Criminal forfeiture

§ 1835. Orders to preserve confidentiality

§ 1836. Civil proceedings to enjoin violations

§ 1837. Applicability to conduct outside the United States

§ 1838. Construction with other laws

§ 1839. Definitions

§ 1831. Economic espionage

(a) IN GENERAL. —Whoever, intending or knowing that the offense will benefit any foreign government, foreign instrumentality, or foreign agent, knowingly—

(1) steals, or without authorization appropriates, takes, carries away, or conceals, or by fraud, artifice, or deception obtains a trade secret;

(2) without authorization copies, duplicates, sketches, draws, photographs, downloads, uploads, alters, destroys, photocopies, replicates, transmits, delivers, sends, mails, communicates, or conveys a trade secret;

(3) receives, buys, or possesses a trade secret, knowing the same to have been stolen or appropriated, obtained, or converted without authorization;

(4) attempts to commit any offense described in any of paragraphs (1) through (3); or

(5) conspires with one or more other persons to commit any offense described in any of paragraphs (1) through (3), and one or more of such persons do any act to effect the object of the conspiracy, shall, except as provided in subsection (b), be fined not more than $500,000 or imprisoned not more than 15 years, or both.

(b) ORGANIZATIONS.—Any organization that commits any offense described in subsection (a) shall be fined not more than $10,000,000.

§ 1832. Theft of trade secrets

(a) Whoever, with intent to convert a trade secret, that is related to or included in a product that is produced for or placed in interstate or foreign commerce, to the economic benefit of anyone other than the owner thereof, and intending or knowing that the offense will, injure any owner of that trade secret, knowingly—

(1) steals, or without authorization appropriates, takes, carries away, or conceals, or by fraud, artifice, or deception obtains such information;

(2) without authorization copies, duplicates, sketches, draws, photographs, downloads, uploads, alters, destroys, photocopies, replicates, transmits, delivers, sends, mails, communicates, or conveys such information;

（3）receives, buys, or possesses such information, knowing the same to have been stolen or appropriated, obtained, or converted without authorization;

（4）attempts to commit any offense described in paragraphs（1）through（3）; or

（5）conspires with one or more other persons to commit any offense described in paragraphs（1）through（3）, and one or more of such persons do any act to effect the object of the conspiracy, shall, except as provided in subsection（b）, be fined under this title or imprisoned not more than 10 years, or both.

（b）Any organization that commits any offense described in subsection（a）shall be fined not more than $5,000,000.

§ 1833. Exceptions to prohibitions

This chapter does not prohibit—

（1）any otherwise lawful activity conducted by a governmental entity of the United States, a State, or a political subdivision of a State; or

（2）the reporting of a suspected violation of law to any governmental entity of the United States, a State, or a political subdivision of a State, if such entity has lawful authority with respect to that violation.

§ 1834. Criminal forfeiture

（a）The court, in imposing sentence on a person for a violation of this chapter, shall order, in addition to any other sentence imposed, that the person forfeit to the United States—

（1）any property constituting, or derived from, any proceeds the person obtained, directly or indirectly, as the result of such violation; and

（2）any of the person's property used, or intended to be used, in any manner or part, to commit or facilitate the commission of such violation, if the court in its discretion so determines, taking into consideration the nature, scope, and proportionality of the use of the property in the offense.

（b）Property subject to forfeiture under this section, any seizure and disposition thereof, and any administrative or judicial proceeding in relation thereto, shall be governed by section 413 of the Comprehensive Drug Abuse Prevention and Control Act of 1970 (21 U. S. C. 853), except for subsections (d) and (j) of such section, which shall not apply to forfeitures under this section.

[Note: § 1834 was amended in 2008 as follows " § 1834. Criminal forfeiture: Forfeiture, destruction, and restitution relating to this chapter shall be subject to section 2323, to the extent provided in that section, in addition to any other similar remedies provided by law. "]

§ 1835. Orders to preserve confidentiality

In any prosecution or other proceeding under this chapter, the court shall enter such orders and take such other action as may be necessary and appropriate to preserve the confidentiality of trade secrets, consistent with the requirements of the Federal Rules of Criminal and Civil Procedure, the Federal Rules of Evidence, and all other applicable laws. An interlocutory appeal by the United States shall lie from a decision or order of a district court authorizing or directing the disclosure of any trade secret.

§ 1836. Civil proceedings to enjoin violations

(a) The Attorney General may, in a civil action, obtain appropriate injunctive relief against any violation of this section.

(b) The district courts of the United States shall have exclusive original jurisdiction of civil actions under this subsection.

§ 1837. Applicability to conduct outside the United States

This chapter also applies to conduct occurring outside the United States if—

(1) the offender is a natural person who is a citizen or permanent resident alien of the United States, or an organization organized under the laws of the United States or a State or political subdivision thereof; or

(2) an act in furtherance of the offense was committed in the United States.

§ 1838. Construction with other laws

This chapter shall not be construed to preempt or displace any other remedies, whether civil or criminal, provided by United States Federal, State, commonwealth, possession, or territory law for the misappropriation of a trade secret, or to affect the otherwise lawful disclosure of information by any Government employee under section 552 of title 5 (commonly known as the Freedom of Information Act).

§ 1839. Definitions

As used in this chapter—

(1) the term "foreign instrumentality" means any agency, bureau, ministry, component, institution, association, or any legal, commercial, or business organization, corporation, firm, or entity that is substantially owned, controlled, sponsored, commanded, managed, or dominated by a foreign government;

(2) the term "foreign agent" means any officer, employee, proxy, servant, delegate, or representative of a foreign government;

(3) the term "trade secret" means all forms and types of financial, business, scientific, technical, economic, or engineering information, including patterns, plans, compilations, program devices, formulas, designs, prototypes, methods, techniques, processes, procedures, programs, or codes, whether tangible or intangible, and whether or how stored, compiled, or memorialized physically, electronically, graphically, photographically, or in writing if—

(A) the owner thereof has taken reasonable measures to keep such information secret; and

(B) the information derives independent economic value, actual or potential, from not being generally known to, and not being readily ascertainable through proper means by, the public; and

(4) the term "owner", with respect to a trade secret, means the person or entity in whom or in which rightful legal or equitable title to, or license in, the trade secret is reposed.

第二章 《2012 盗窃商业秘密罪扩大适用范围法》

第一节 《2012 盗窃商业秘密罪扩大适用范围法》简介

一、《2012 盗窃商业秘密罪扩大适用范围法》的基本特征

（一）生效时间

《2012 盗窃商业秘密罪扩大适用范围法》由第 44 任美国总统奥巴马批准后于 2012 年 12 月 28 日生效。

（二）主要特征

《2012 盗窃商业秘密罪扩大适用范围法》是对《1996 经济间谍法》进行修改的一部法律，修改的内容也只是对《1996 经济间谍法》第 1832 条进行修改，具体修改的内容包括两点：①把法律规范的对象由"商品"扩展到"商品和服务"；②把实施行为由"用于"国际贸易和州际贸易扩展到"用于或者企图用于"国际贸易和州际贸易。

《2012 盗窃商业秘密罪扩大适用范围法》扩大了《1996 经济间谍法》的适用范围，也就扩大了这一法律的保护范围，从而增强了这一法律的保护力度，能够更加有效地保护商业秘密。

二、《2012 盗窃商业秘密罪扩大适用范围法》的适用

显然，虽然这是一部独立生效的法律，但是，由于其是对《1996 经济间谍法》某一条款内容的修订。因此，对其适用也就是直接对被其修改后的《1996 经济间谍法》的适用。

第二节　《2012 盗窃商业秘密罪扩大适用范围法》译文

第 1 条　本法名称

本法命名为:《2012 商业秘密盗窃罪扩大适用范围法》。

第 2 条　修订内容

在《美国法典》第 18 篇第 1832 条,即《1996 经济间谍法》第 1832 条第一段中删除"包含于用在国际贸易和或者州际贸易的商品中",修改为"包含于用在或者企图用在国际贸易或者州际贸易的商品或者服务中"。

(侯仰坤翻译,2018 年 2 月于北京)

本章附录:《2012 盗窃商业秘密罪扩大适用范围法》原文

Theft of Trade Secrets Clarification Act of 2012

126 STAT. 1627   PUBLIC LAW 112-236—DEC. 28, 2012

Public Law 112-236

112th Congress

An Act

To clarify the scope of the Economic Espionage Act of 1996.

Be it enacted by the Senate and House of Representatives of the United States of America in Congress assembled,

SECTION 1. SHORT TITLE.

This Act may be cited as the "Theft of Trade Secrets Clarification Act of 2012".

SEC. 2. AMENDMENT.

Section 1832(a) of title 18, United States Code, is amended in the matter preceding paragraph (1), by striking "or included in a product that is produced for or placed in" and inserting "a product or service used in or intended for use in".

Approved December 28, 2012.

第三章 《2012 外国经济间谍罪加重处罚法》

第一节 《2012 外国经济间谍罪加重处罚法》简介

一、《2012 外国经济间谍罪加重处罚法》的基本特征

（一）生效时间

《2012 外国经济间谍罪加重处罚法》由第 44 任美国总统奥巴马批准后于 2013 年 1 月 14 日生效。

（二）主要特征

该法主要包含两部分内容，一是对《1996 经济间谍法》第 1831 条的内容进行修订和补充，极大地提高了对被告的经济处罚力度；二是明确要求美国量刑委员会在制定有关商业秘密的定罪量刑条款时应当充分考虑在美国境外非法传递，或者企图为了外国政府的相关利益而非法传递美国商业秘密的各类行为。

这一法律比较明确地强调针对"外国经济间谍行为"，通过增加对这一类经济间谍行为的惩罚力度，以此来加强打击外国经济间谍行为的强度。

二、《2012 外国经济间谍罪加重处罚法》的适用

由于是对《1996 经济间谍法》某一条款内容的修订和补充，因此，对其适用的方式也就是对经过修改后的《1996 经济间谍法》的直接适用。

第二节 《2012 外国经济间谍罪加重处罚法》译文

第 1 条 ［本法的名称］本法命名为:《2012 外国经济间谍罪加重处罚法》。

第 2 条 ［保护美国商业及打击外国经济间谍］

1. 把《1996 经济间谍法》第 1831 条经济间谍罪中对个人的处罚数额由"最高 50 万美元"修改为"最高 500 万美元";

2. 把《1996 经济间谍法》第 1831 条经济间谍罪中对单位的处罚数额由"最高 1000 万美元"修改为"最高 1000 万美元;或者被侵害商业秘密价值的 3 倍,其中包括被告因利用间谍行为所节省的用于研发的费用,以及使用该商业秘密所应当支出的成本费用"。

第 3 条 ［美国量刑委员会的评议和审查职责］

1.［一般性规定］根据《美国法典》第 28 编第 994 条第 16 项(P 项)有关该量刑委员会职责的规定,美国量刑委员会应当审查并酌情修改联邦量刑准则和政策说明的内容,以便对经济间谍行为和在美国境外传递或者企图传递盗窃的美国商业秘密的行为进行恰当的定罪量刑,以彰显国会坚决惩罚这类罪行的意图,并且反映出这类罪行的严重性,以及这种罪行可能造成的实际的和潜在的危害性,并且提出能够有效打击这类犯罪行为的具有威慑力的惩罚措施。

2.［对美国量刑委员会的具体要求］为了实现上述目的,美国量刑委员会应当完成以下任务:

(1)在联邦量刑准则和政策说明中,应当比较准确地阐述简单地盗用商业秘密的客观危害性;

(2)考虑在联邦量刑准则和政策说明中是否需要额外地增加下列内容:①在美国境外传递或者企图传递盗窃美国商业秘密的行为;②为了外国政府、外国政府的机构,或者外国政府的代理人的利益,或者企图为了这些利益,而在美国境外传递或者企图传递盗窃的美国商业秘密的行为;

（3）确保在联邦量刑准则和政策说明中能够客观地反映出这些罪行的严重性和惩罚这些行为的必要性；

（4）确保使其能够与其他指令、其他联邦法规，以及联邦量刑准则和政策说明中的相关内容协调一致；

（5）对联邦量刑准则和政策说明作出必要的修改；

（6）确保量刑准则能够充分地符合《美国法典》第 18 篇第 3553 条第（1）款第（2）项中规定的量刑应当考虑的四项原则（即产生的社会危害性；对罪犯的威慑性；阻止犯罪行为的再犯性；为罪犯提供适当的教育和职业培训条件，并且保障他们能够获得基本的卫生和生活条件）。

3. ［应当开展的磋商活动］在执行上述所要求的审查时，量刑委员会应当与代表执法的个人或者团体，商业秘密的所有人，经济间谍活动的受害者，美国司法部，美国国土安全部，美国国务院和美国贸易代表办公室进行磋商。

4. ［完成评议和审查的期限］不迟于本法生效之日起的 180 天内，量刑委员会应当根据本法的要求完成上述审议和审查工作。

（侯仰坤翻译，2018 年 1 月于北京）

本章附录:《2012 外国经济间谍罪加重处罚法》原文

Foreign and Economic Espionage Penalty Enhancement Act of 2012

126 STAT. 2442   PUBLIC LAW 112-269—JAN. 14, 2013

Public Law 112-269 112th Congress

An Act

To amend title 18, United States Code, to provide for increased penalties for foreign and economic espionage, and for other purposes.

Be it enacted by the Senate and House of Representatives of the United States of America in Congress assembled,

SECTION 1. SHORT TITLE.

This Act may be cited as the "Foreign and Economic Espionage Penalty Enhancement Act of 2012".

SEC. 2. PROTECTING U. S. BUSINESSES FROM FOREIGN ESPIONAGE.

(a) FOR OFFENSES COMMITTED BY INDIVIDUALS. —Section 1831(a) of title 18, United States Code, is amended, in the matter after paragraph (5), by striking "not more than $500,000" and inserting "not more than $5,000,000".

(b) FOR OFFENSES COMMITTED BY ORGANIZATIONS. —Section 1831(b) of such title is amended by striking "not more than $10,000,000" and inserting "not more than the greater of $10,000,000 or 3 times the value of the stolen trade secret to the organization, including expenses for research and design and other costs of reproducing the trade secret that the organization has thereby avoided".

SEC. 3. REVIEW BY THE UNITED STATES SENTENCING COMM-ISSION.

（a）IN GENERAL. —Pursuant to its authority under section 994（p）of title 28, United States Code, the United States Sentencing Commission shall review and, if appropriate, amend the Federal sentencing guidelines and policy statements applicable to persons convicted of offenses relating to the transmission or attempted transmission of a stolen trade secret outside of the United States or economic espionage, in order to reflect the intent of Congress that penalties for such offenses under the Federal sentencing guidelines and policy statements appropriately, reflect the seriousness of these offenses, account for the potential and actual harm caused by these offenses, and provide adequate deterrence against such offenses.

（b）REQUIREMENTS. —In carrying out this section, the United States Sentencing Commission shall—

（1）consider the extent to which the Federal sentencing guidelines and policy statements appropriately account for the simple misappropriation of a trade secret, including the sufficiency of the existing enhancement for these offenses to address the seriousness of this conduct;

（2）consider whether additional enhancements in the Federal sentencing guidelines and policy statements are appropriate to account for—

（A）the transmission or attempted transmission of a stolen trade secret outside of the United States; and

（B）the transmission or attempted transmission of a stolen trade secret outside of the United States that is committed or attempted to be committed for the benefit of a foreign government, foreign instrumentality, or foreign agent;

（3）ensure the Federal sentencing guidelines and policy statements reflect the seriousness of these offenses and the need to deter such conduct;

（4）ensure reasonable consistency with other relevant directives, Federal sentencing guidelines and policy statements, and related Federal statutes;

（5）make any necessary conforming changes to the Federal sentencing guidelines and policy statements; and

(6) ensure that the Federal sentencing guidelines adequately meet the purposes of sentencing as set forth in section 3553(a)(2) of title 18, United States Code.

(c) CONSULTATION.—In carrying out the review required under this section, the Commission shall consult with individuals or groups representing law enforcement, owners of trade secrets, victims of economic espionage offenses, the United States Department of Justice, the United States Department of Homeland Security, the United States Department of State and the Office of the United States Trade Representative.

(d) REVIEW.—Not later than 180 days after the date of enactment of this Act, the Commission shall complete its consideration and review under this section.

Approved January 14, 2013.

Note: Additional annotation of 28 § 994(p) and 18 § 3553(a)(2), they are from the United States Code, which provided by Yangkun Hou on January 31, 2018. [①]

(a) § 994 of Title 28 – JUDICIARY AND JUDICIAL PROCEDURE

§ 994. Duties of the Commission

(p) The Commission, at or after the beginning of a regular session of Congress, but not later than the first day of May, may promulgate under subsection (a) of this section and submit to Congress amendments to the guidelines and modifications to previously submitted amendments that have not taken effect, including modifications to the effective dates of such amendments. Such an amendment or

---

① 下面所附的第 994 条的"(p)"款,以及第 335 条的"(a)"款都只是根据《2012 外国经济间谍罪加重处罚法》中涉及的内容摘取了对应法律条款中的部分内容,没有摘录全文。同时,由于这两项条款涉及的内容是美国量刑委员会在后续工作中需要参照的事项,不是《2012 外国经济间谍罪加重处罚法》中明文确定的法律规定,在此就没有把内容译出,列出原文是为了便于想要进一步研究这部分内容的读者参照使用。

modification shall be accompanied by a statement of the reasons therefor and shall take effect on a date specified by the Commission, which shall be no earlier than 180 days after being so submitted and no later than the first day of November of the calendar year in which the amendment or modification is submitted, except to the extent that the effective date is revised or the amendment is otherwise modified or disapproved by Act of Congress.

(b) § 3553 of Title 18 – CRIMES AND CRIMINAL PROCEDURE

§ 3553. Imposition of a sentence

(a) Factors To Be Considered in Imposing a Sentence. – The court shall impose a sentence sufficient, but not greater than necessary, to comply with the purposes set forth in paragraph (2) of this subsection. The court, in determining the particular sentence to be imposed, shall consider—

(1) the nature and circumstances of the offense and the history and characteristics of the defendant;

(2) the need for the sentence imposed—

(A) to reflect the seriousness of the offense, to promote respect for the law, and to provide just punishment for the offense;

(B) to afford adequate deterrence to criminal conduct;

(C) to protect the public from further crimes of the defendant; and

(D) to provide the defendant with needed educational or vocational training, medical care, or other correctional treatment in the most effective manner.

第四章 《2016商业秘密保护法》

第一节 《2016商业秘密保护法》简介

一、《2016商业秘密保护法》的基本特征

（一）生效时间

《2016商业秘密保护法》由美国第44任总统奥巴马批准后于2016年5月11日生效。

（二）主要特征

（1）《2016商业秘密保护法》是美国历史上第一部专门保护商业秘密的联邦民事法律。

（2）作为联邦法律，《2016商业秘密保护法》只适用于那些用于或者计划用于国际贸易或者美国不同州之间的贸易中的商品或服务中的商业秘密被侵害的情形；当存在于美国同一州内贸易中的商品或服务中的商业秘密被侵害时，适用各个州内的法律，当前对于美国绝大多数州来说，主要适用美国《侵权法重述》和《统一商业秘密法》。

（3）《2016商业秘密保护法》涉及多项对《1996经济间谍法》进行修改和补充的内容，而《1996经济间谍法》主要是刑事法律的内容，归属于《美国法典》第18篇（刑法篇）。可见，这部商业秘密民事保护法并不完全是对民事保护措施的设立和规范，还涉及部分刑事的内容。

（4）《2016商业秘密保护法》中的部分民事保护措施与美国《统一商业秘密保护法》中的内容相似或一致，基本包含了《统一商业秘密保护法》（1985）中的主要条款，因此，可以把本法看作是对《统一商业秘密保护法》的某种吸收。

（5）作为一部相对完善的第一部专门用于利用民事程序和民事法律责任保护商业秘密的联邦法律，虽然其中有些条款涉及《1996 经济间谍法》和《统一商业秘密保护法》中的内容，但是，另外还包含着一些上述两部法律不曾涉及的内容。因此，《2016 商业秘密保护法》仍然是一部具有创新内容比较重要的法律。

二、《2016 商业秘密保护法》适用范围的限制

《2016 商业秘密保护法》在适用上不受其他法律的制约和影响，完全可以独立地适用，只是在适用范围上仍然受到作为一部联邦法律应有的限制，即只能适用于发生在国际贸易或者美国不同州之间贸易中的涉及商业秘密纠纷案件。

第二节 《2016 商业秘密保护法》译文①

《2016 商业秘密保护法》

目 录

第一章 本法名称

第 1 条 本法命名为"2016 商业秘密民事保护法"。

第 2 条 当事人有权对侵害商业秘密的行为提起民事诉讼,本法中有关民事诉讼的内容添加到《1996 经济间谍法》第 1836 条中。

---

① 《2016 商业秘密保护法》的内容比较长,原文的格式比较烦琐,条款的排列格式与中国法律的一般排列格式差异很大,也与中文的阅读习惯有很大区别,不少条款存在前后交叉现象,而且相关条款之间穿插的其他内容比较多,容易引起读者的误解和混乱,为此,该译文按照中国法律的一般格式,在不增加、遗失或改动原文内容的前提下,把原文的部分条款位置和排列格式做了调整和重新归纳,以方便读者对整个法律规定和具体条文的正确理解和使用。

　　第 3 条　［民事诉讼的适用范围］当同时符合下列三项条件时,商业秘密权利人和其他适格的主体都可以依据本法对侵害商业秘密的行为提起民事诉讼:①商业秘密受到了侵害;②该商业秘密涉及一定的商品或服务;③该商品或服务用于或者计划用于国际贸易或者美国不同州之间的州际贸易。

第二章　民事诉讼程序的一般规定

第一节　民事扣押程序的一般规定

　　第 4 条　［实施扣押令的目的和基本程序］申请人依据本法规定申请扣押被申请人的财产时,应当提交扣押申请和本法规定的证据材料,并且应当办理相关的其他手续。

　　基于对申请人所提交申请材料的审查,对于符合条件的申请,结合具体的案情,为了阻止对商业秘密的散布和传播,法院应当签发命令扣押被申请人的必要财产。

　　第 5 条　［法院签发扣押令的必要条件］在具体案件中,只有当能够同时满足下列全部条件时,法院才能签发财产扣押令:

　　(1)依据《联邦民事程序法》第 65 条的规定,对被申请人发出禁令或者限制令以后,或者采用其他公平的救济措施以后,都不能充分有效地制止被申请人规避法律的行为,或者制止被申请人违反禁令或限制令的行为。

　　(2)如果不实施扣押令,无法避免的侵害行为就可能立刻发生。

　　(3)如果不实施扣押令,对申请人造成的危害将大于对被扣押者合法利益造成的损害,以及基本大于对任何第三方利益造成的损害。

　　(4)申请人应当提交下列证据材料:①证明商业秘密自身符合法律规定的材料。②证明被申请人具有下列行为之一的材料:(a)被申请人以不正当的手段盗用申请人的商业秘密;(b)或者共谋以不正当的手段盗用申请人的商业秘密。

　　(5)被申请人应当已经实际占有或者拥有下列事物:①涉案的商业秘密;②将被扣押的财产。

　　(6)在扣押申请书中应当合理地说明被扣押财产的特征,包括财产的合理范围、规模和程度,以及财产所在的具体地理位置。

（7）如果一旦申请人通知了被申请人，则被申请人或者其同谋者将会毁坏、转移、藏匿相关财产，使得法院难以查找和获得这些财产。

（8）申请人未对外公布申请的扣押事项。

第 6 条 ［扣押令中应当包含和涉及的具体事项］法院签发扣押令时，在扣押令中应当包含和涉及下列事项：

（1）明确列出签发扣押令所依据的事实和法律依据。

（2）在保障能够保护申请人合法利益的前提下，对必要的财产采取最低限度的扣押措施，并且尽量使得扣押行为最低限度地影响到其他第三人的商业活动，以及被申请人其他合法的商业活动。

（3）在扣押令中设置一项保护被扣押财产的专门性条款，禁止申请人和被申请人接触、披露、部分或者全部地复制财产信息，防止过度地破坏被申请人的财产，直到被申请人有机会参加法庭的听证为止。

经过法院批准后，申请人和被申请人可以接触被扣押的财产，但是，这种接触应当符合本法的规定。

（4）法院应当对执行扣押任务的执法人员进行指导，明确界定他们的权限范围，具体包括：①扣押令签发多少小时以后应当执行；②对于被锁住的房屋和区域是否准予使用强制手段进入。

（5）应当明确规定一个符合本法要求的尽早的听证日期，最晚不能迟于扣押令签发后的第七天，除非被申请人或者受到这一扣押令伤害的其他人同意超出上述日期举行听证。在申请人获得了扣押令以后，除了被申请人之外，其他任何被这一扣押令伤害的人都可以在任何时间，在向申请人发出通知之后，请求法院撤销或者修改扣押令。

（6）申请人应当按照法院规定的要求提供足额的担保金，用于赔偿由于错误的扣押或者错误的企图扣押，或者由于过度地扣押或者企图过度地扣押给他人合法利益造成的损失。

第 7 条 ［对扣押令的保密义务］法院应当采取合适的手段保护被执行扣押令的人免遭公开宣传，可以在扣押令中要求获得这一扣押令的人不得宣传这一扣押令和包含的事项。

第 8 条 ［对法院扣押材料的一般性规定］法院在审查和执行扣押令期间

所获取和扣押的全部资料都由法院保管,在整个扣押令实施期间和这些材料保管期间,法院应当确保这些材料能够通过物理方式或电子方式接触,并且按照下列要求执行:

(1)[对储存介质保密的要求]如果被扣押的材料中包含着储存商业秘密信息的介质,或者扣押的材料储存在介质上,在未经申请人和被申请人双方当事人一致同意之前,法院应当禁止把该介质连接到网络或者互联网上,直到依据本法的规定举行听证为止。

(2)[对非商业秘密材料的保密处理]法院应当采取合适的措施对依据本法规定扣押的不涉及商业秘密信息的材料进行保密,除非被申请人自己同意公开这些材料。

(3)[任命专门的保密负责人]法院可以任命一名法官作为专门的负责人来整理和保管被盗用的商业秘密信息,同时负责把不相关的被扣押的财产和资料返还给被申请人;这位专门负责人应当遵守法院批准的保密协议。

第 9 条　[扣押令的协助与执行]为申请人和执行活动提供服务及帮助的规定。

(1)法院应当制作一份扣押令的复制件,由联邦法律执行官送达到申请人,然后,由执行官执行扣押令。

(2)法院可以允许各个州以及当地的法律执行官参与扣押令的执行活动,但是不得允许申请人或者其代理人参与扣押活动。

(3)经过执行官的请求,法院可以准许与申请人及被申请人没有利益关联的技术专家协助扣押的执行,前提是技术专家必须遵守法院批准的保密协议,以及技术专家的参与能够帮助实际有效的执行和降低执行成本。

第 10 条　[有关扣押听证的规定]

(1)[确定听证日期]法院签发扣押令之后应当根据本法的规定确定一个举行听证的日期。

(2)[扣押申请人的举证责任]在举行听证时,已经获得了扣押令的申请人必须提供被申请人非法盗用了其商业秘密,以及应当采用扣押令的合理的证据和结论,否则,扣押令将被撤销或者被适当地修改。

(3)[对扣押令的撤销或者修改]被申请人以及任何受到扣押令损害的第

三人,在通知了申请人之后,在任何时间都可以请求法院撤销或者修改扣押令。

(4)[对听证期限的调整]当法院发现按照已有的期限举行听证可能达不到听证目的时,可以根据《联邦民事诉讼程序法》的规定调整听证的日期。

第11条 [对错误扣押所导致损害的赔偿]任何由于错误扣押或过度扣押遭受损害的人,都有权利向扣押令的申请人主张赔偿,赔偿的标准可以参照1946年《商标法》第34条第(4)款第(11)项[15 U. S. C. 1116(d)(11)]的规定执行。申请人依据本法规定向法院提供的保证金可以用于赔偿第三方由此受到的损失。

第12条 [请求对扣押物加密的提议]任何主张对扣押物存在利害关系的当事人或者第三人,在任何时候都可以请求法院对扣押物进行加密,法院经过单方面的听证后,可以对扣押的任何材料,包括存储在一定介质上的材料进行加密处理;请求人在提出请求时,应当尽可能地提供所希望的加密方法。

第二节 其他四类民事救济措施

第13条 [其他民事救济措施的类型]对于侵害商业秘密的行为,依据本法提起民事诉讼时,法院可以采取禁令、损害赔偿、惩罚性赔偿和承担律师费用等民事救济措施。

第14条 [对雇佣人员采取禁令]当有证据证明某一被雇佣人存在侵害商业秘密的危险时,这些证据不仅仅在于他已经知道了什么信息,而是在于他有侵害商业秘密的威胁性,此时,为了阻止现实的或者潜在的侵害商业秘密行为的发生,可以对该雇佣人员采取禁令措施。

此时的禁令不是直接禁止被雇佣人与雇佣人之间建立的劳动关系,而是禁止被雇佣人实施侵害商业秘密的行为,否则,这种禁令就可能与有些州法律规定的不准禁止他人从事合法的商业、贸易和职业活动的法令相冲突。

第15条 [对其他相关人员采取禁令]当法院认为有必要采取积极的措施来保护商业秘密时,可以对相关人员发出禁令。

第16条 [对禁令禁止下的商业秘密的特殊使用]在特殊情形下,被禁令禁止使用涉案商业秘密的人如果确实存在合理必要的理由需要继续使用该商业秘密时,他必须首先缴纳合理的特殊使用费,而且继续使用该商业秘密的期限不得超出该禁令的有效期间。

第17条　[损害赔偿的范围]损害赔偿的范围包括:①由侵害商业秘密行为造成的直接损失;②由侵害商业秘密行为导致的直接损失之外的间接损失。

第18条　[损失数额的估算]对于原告遭受的损失数额,可以参照转让或者许可使用该商业秘密时合理的费用标准来确定。

第19条　[惩罚性赔偿]如果侵害者以预谋或者恶意的方式侵害商业秘密,实行惩罚性赔偿,赔偿金的数额最高不超过正常赔偿金的2倍。

第20条　[律师费用的承担]如果有证据证明原告在缺乏诚信的情况下提起商业秘密侵权诉讼;原告或者被告在缺乏诚信的情况下请求终止禁令或者反对终止禁令;被告以预谋或者恶意的方式实施侵害行为。符合上述任何条件之一的,合理的律师费用由上述行为方承担。

第21条　[诉讼管辖权]对于本法中涉及的民事诉讼案件,联邦地区法院享有一审专属管辖权。

第22条　[诉讼时效]对于本法中的民事诉讼,诉讼时效为3年,自知道或者应当知道侵害行为发生之日起计算。本法中,连续实施的侵害行为可以作为同一侵害行为提起诉讼。

第三节　相关概念的含义

第23条　对《1996 经济间谍法》第1839条内容做如下修改:

(1)在第1839条第(3)项中删除"公众",添加"通过披露或者使用该信息能够获取经济利益的其他人",并且删除结尾处的"和";

(2)在第1839条第(4)项中删除结尾处的句号,添加一个分号,承接第(5)项;

(3)在第(4)项之后添加下列第24条、第25条和第26条的内容,共同作为《1996 经济间谍法》第1839条增加的内容。

第24条　[侵害行为]本法中侵害行为包括非法获取、非法使用和非法披露行为,具体包含下列行为:

(1)[非法获取行为]在知道或者应当知道第三方通过不正当的手段获取该商业秘密之后,仍然从第三方处获取该商业秘密。

（2）［非法获取后又擅自披露或者使用的行为］利用不正当的手段获取他人的商业秘密以后，又擅自披露或者使用该商业秘密。

（3）［对他人非法获取的商业秘密进行披露或者使用的行为］在知道或者应当知道该商业秘密是第三方利用不正当的手段获取的情况下，仍然擅自披露或者使用该商业秘密。

（4）［对他人违反保密或者限制使用义务获取的商业秘密进行披露或者使用的行为］在知道或者应当知道该商业秘密是第三方在违反自己承担的保密义务或者限制使用义务的情况下披露的，仍然擅自使用或者进一步披露该商业秘密。

（5）［对从被告处获取的商业秘密进行披露或者使用的行为］在知道或者应当知道该商业秘密是在第三方因为违反自己承担的保密义务或者限制使用义务已经被追究侵权责任的情况下泄露的，仍然擅自使用或者进一步披露该商业秘密。

（6）［对基于偶然或者错误原因获得的商业秘密进行披露或者使用的行为］在一个人的职位发生重要调整之前，基于偶然或者错误的原因使其获得了秘密信息，当他知道或者有理由知道这是一条商业秘密时，擅自使用或者披露该商业秘密。

第 25 条　［不正当手段］本法中"不正当行为"的是指下列行为：

（1）包括盗窃、贿赂、欺诈、违反保密义务，或者诱使他人违反保密义务，或者通过电子及其他手段实施的间谍行为。

（2）不包括通过反向工程、独立研发或者其他合法方式获得的相同的商业秘密。

第 26 条　本法中《1946 商标法》是指于 1946 年 7 月 5 日批准的，编号为 15 U. S. C. 1051 et seq. ，名称为"提供注册和保护用于商业活动的商标法"，以便落实相关国际公约的规定，以及实现保护商标的目的；该法一般称为"1946 商标法"，或者"兰哈姆法"。

第四节　其他规定

第 27 条　在《1996 经济间谍法》第 1833 条的前序中，在"禁止"之后添加

"或者设立一个个人诉讼的诉权"的内容。

第 28 条　［修改标题］把《1996 经济间谍法》第 1836 条的标题修改为"民事诉讼"；在《1996 经济间谍法》的条款目录中也把第 1836 条的标题修改为"民事诉讼"。

第 29 条　［生效日期］本法中修改的内容适用于所有的商业秘密侵害行为，侵害行为的含义和特征适用修改后的第 1839 条中的定义，任何发生在本法生效之日及其后的侵害行为都受本法约束。

第 30 条　［所修改内容的效力］本法中修改的内容并不影响在第 1838 条规定的与其他法律的关系，也不优先于任何其他法律。

第 31 条　［与其他知识产权法律的关系］本法是一部独立的法律，不从属于国会批准的其他知识产权法律。

第三章　对侵害商业秘密行为的其他保护规定

第一节　对《1996 经济间谍法》相关条款的修改

第 32 条　［对第 1832 条的修改］在《1996 经济间谍法》第 1832 条中，对于单位犯罪，把原最高处罚 5 000 000 美元，修改为"最高处罚 5 000 000 美元，或者处罚被盗窃商业秘密价值的 3 倍，其中包括被告单位因利用间谍行为所节省的用于研发的费用，以及正当地使用该商业秘密所应当支出的成本费用"。

第 33 条　［对第 1835 条的修改］对《1996 经济间谍法》第 1835 条作如下修改：

（1）删除原文中的"在任何司法程序"，添加"一般规定：在任何司法程序中"；

（2）在结尾处添加下列内容"商业秘密权利人拥有如下权利：

①当商业秘密的权利人主张某一信息属于他的商业秘密时，除非法院已经给他提供了机会，使他在提交给法院的密封的法律意见中阐述这些保密信息能够给他带来的利益，否则，法院不能授权或者指示披露这些信息。

②除非法律另有规定外，基于上述目的所提交的密封的法律意见不得被用于本法中的其他诉讼活动。

③按照法律规定向美国政府或受理案件的法院提交与商业秘密相关的信

息时,并不丧失对该商业秘密的保护;依据本法规定在司法程序中披露这些与商业秘密相关的信息时也不丧失对该商业秘密的保护,除非该商业秘密的权利人明确表示对该商业秘密放弃保护"。

第 34 条 ［对《美国法典》第 18 篇的其他修改］在第 1951 条之前,在第 1961 条的第(1)项中添加"第 1831 条和第 1832 条(关于经济间谍和盗窃商业秘密)"。

第二节 对发生在境外侵害商业秘密事件的报告

第 35 条 ［局长的含义］本法中"局长"是指美国专利及商标局的局长,其同时兼任主管知识产权事务的商务部副部长。

第 36 条 有关"外国政府的机构""外国政府的代理人"及"商业秘密"的含义参照《1996 经济间谍法》第 1839 条中有关上述术语的定义。

第 37 条 ［州的含义］本法中的"州"是指包括哥伦比亚特区在内的美国所有的州,领地和属地。

第 38 条 ［美国公司的含义］本法中"美国公司"是指依据美国联邦法律、州法律,或者州以下的政府分支机构所颁布的法律法规所成立的企业。

第 39 条 ［司法部长提交报告的制度］在不迟于本法生效后的一年的期限内,每半年实施一次下述制度:司法部长在与国家知识产权管理部门、执法部门的领导,以及其他相关组织的负责人协商后,应当向国会参众两院的司法委员会提交报告,并且应当在司法部网站上和总检察长认为的其他合适的方式向公众进行公开,报告应当包括下列内容:

(1)在美国境外发生的盗窃美国公司商业秘密的范围和程度。

(2)在发生于美国境外盗窃美国公司商业秘密的事件中,外国政府、外国政府的机构和外国政府的代理人参与的程度。

(3)在美国境外盗窃美国公司商业秘密所呈现出的威胁态势。

(4)在阻止境外盗窃他们的商业秘密方面,在追究境外盗窃者的法律责任方面,以及在阻止侵权产品进口到美国方面,作为商业秘密权利人的美国公司,都具有哪些权利和遭遇哪些限制。

(5)对于美国的贸易伙伴国来说,他们在保护美国公司的商业秘密方面都存在着哪些缺陷和不足,以及他们都做了哪些执法的努力和承诺;对于侵害美国公司商业秘密情形严重的国家应当单独列出一个国家名单,并且列出在这些国家中有关商业秘密盗窃的相关立法和相关执法情况。

(6)美国政府与外国政府通过合作对境外盗窃美国公司商业秘密的单位和个人进行调查、执行逮捕和进行追诉的案例。

(7)有关美国与相关国家在贸易协定和贸易条约方面的进展情况,包括外国政府为受到商业秘密盗窃侵害的美国公司实施补偿的措施。

(8)可能采取的立法和行政部门执法行动的建议,具体应当包含下列目的:①减少发生在美国境外盗窃美国公司商业秘密的行为,以及降低由此对经济造成的影响;②教育美国公司在境外遭遇商业秘密盗窃时应当如何应对这种威胁;③为在境外遭遇商业秘密盗窃的美国公司提供帮助,以降低它们丧失商业秘密的风险;④为美国公司建立一种可以值得它们信赖的机制,使得它们能够实名或者匿名地报告它们在境外遭受商业秘密盗窃的情况。

第三节　国会对侵害商业秘密行为的态度

第40条　国会对侵害商业秘密的行为持有如下的观点和态度:

(1)盗窃商业秘密的行为在包括美国在内的世界各地都会发生。

(2)商业秘密盗窃行为,无论发生在哪里,都会对商业秘密所属的公司及其公司的员工造成伤害。

(3)《1996经济间谍法》,也称《美国法典》第18篇第90章,对所有商业秘密盗窃行为都有约束力。

(4)在为了阻止商业秘密盗窃行为或者补偿盗窃行为造成的损失而获取相关的信息时,应当注意保护涉嫌实施侵害行为者所享有的合法利益以及其他第三方的利益不受侵害。

第四节　联邦司法中心的责任和义务

第41条　[保管和保密扣押的信息]自本法生效后的两年内,联邦司法中心应当利用现有的资源,建立一套最优的方案以实现下列目的:①有效地保管扣押信息和储存信息的媒介;②确保被扣押的信息和媒介不被泄密。

第42条　[信息的维护与更新]联邦司法中心应当对建立的最优方案及

其实施后的内容资料进行维护和更新。

第43条 ［向国会提交材料］联邦司法中心应当向国会参议院和众议院的司法委员会分别提交所建立的最优方案,以及实施该方案后所建立和更新的信息数据库的材料。

第五节　披露商业秘密责任的豁免和雇主的通知义务

第44条 把商业秘密披露给政府或者提交给法院归档不构成泄密行为。

第45条 ［对第1833条的修改］对《1996 经济间谍法》第1833条作如下修改:

(1)删除原文开头中的"本法",添加"第1项一般规定:本法"。

(2)删除原文第2款中的全部内容,然后在结尾处添加"按照下列第3款的规定披露商业秘密"。

(3)在随后添加下列内容"向政府或法院披露商业秘密的保密责任豁免",并且依次添加下列第44条、第45条、第46条、第47条、第48条、第49条、第50条和第51条的内容。

第46条 ［责任豁免的披露行为］实施下列披露行为,不承担任何由联邦或者州法律规定的擅自披露商业秘密应当承担的刑事责任和民事责任。

(1)［控告和诉讼中的披露行为］当披露商业秘密的行为属于对侵害商业秘密行为的控告,或者提交案件诉讼的材料,或者提交其他法定程序中规定的材料,而所提交的材料又都处于密封状态。

(2)［基于特定目的向特定人员的披露］①［特定的报告对象］秘密地直接或者间接地向联邦政府、州政府、地方政府的官员或者律师披露了商业秘密;②［特定的披露目的］披露商业秘密的目的只是为了控告或者调查涉嫌侵害商业秘密的行为。

(3)［在反报复性诉讼中使用商业秘密的特殊要求］如果雇主报告某雇员涉嫌侵害了其商业秘密,该雇员可以提起一件反报复的诉讼,可以向其聘请的律师披露该商业秘密,以及在法庭程序中使用该商业秘密的信息,但是,应当符合下列要求:①包含该商业秘密的材料被密封;②除非应法院的要求以外,不得主动披露该商业秘密。

第 47 条　[雇主对雇员的通知义务]雇主应当在与雇员签订的合同或者协议中,对那些管理使用商业秘密或者机密信息的雇员提供上述有关免责披露商业秘密行为的内容。

第 48 条　[对雇主通知雇员的要求]雇主对雇员提供的通知内容,应当能够使雇员知悉法定的免责披露行为,这种告知行为才符合本法要求。

第 49 条　[不遵守雇主通知义务的法律后果]如果雇主通知雇员的行为不符合本法的要求,当雇主依据《1996 经济间谍法》第 1836 条追诉雇员侵害其商业秘密时,不得享有获得惩罚性赔偿和由对方承担律师费的权利。

第 50 条　[适用范围]本法适用于自本法生效后雇主与雇员所签订或者更新的合同和协议。

第 51 条　[雇员的范围]本法中,"雇员"的范围包括任何为雇主从事工作的个人,包括承包人或者咨询顾问等。

第 52 条　[本法效力的界限]本法中,除了有明确的规定以外,任何条款都不得被解释为允许实施被法律所禁止的行为,或者免除这些行为的法律责任,例如,凡是以非法的方式接触他人商业秘密的行为都属于非法行为。

第 53 条　[对第 1838 条的修改]在《1996 经济间谍法》第 1838 条删除"本法",添加"除了第 1833 条第 2 款之外,本法"。

（侯仰坤翻译,2018 年 2 月于北京）

本章附录:《2016 商业秘密保护法》原文

DEFEND TRADE SECRETS ACT OF 2016

PUBLIC LAW 114-153—MAY 11, 2016

An Act

To amend chapter 90 of title 18, United States Code, to provide Federal jurisdiction for the theft of trade secrets, and for other purposes.

Be it enacted by the Senate and House of Representatives of the United States of America in Congress assembled,

SECTION 1. SHORT TITLE.

This Act may be cited as the "Defend Trade Secrets Act of 2016".

SEC. 2 FEDERAL JURISDICTION FOR THEFT OF TRADE SECRETS.

(a) IN GENERAL. —Section 1836 of title 18, United States Code, is amended by striking subsection (b) and inserting the following:

"(b) PRIVATE CIVIL ACTIONS. —

"(1) IN GENERAL. —An owner of a trade secret that is misappropriated may bring a civil action under this subsection if the trade secret is related to a product or service used in, or intended for use in, interstate or foreign commerce.

"(2) CIVIL SEIZURE. —

"(A) IN GENERAL. —

"(i) APPLICATION. —Based on an affidavit or verified complaint satisfying the requirements of this paragraph, the court may, upon ex parte application but only in extraordinary circumstances, issue an order providing for the seizure of property necessary to prevent the propagation or dissemination of the trade secret that is the subject of the action.

" (ii) REQUIREMENTS FOR ISSUING ORDER. —The court may not grant an application under clause (i) unless the court finds that it clearly appears from specific facts that—

" (I) an order issued pursuant to Rule 65 of the Federal Rules of Civil Procedure or another form of equitable relief would be inadequate to achieve the purpose of this paragraph because the party to which the order would be issued would evade, avoid, or otherwise not comply with such an order;

" (II) an immediate and irreparable injury will occur if such seizure is not ordered;

" (III) the harm to the applicant of denying the application outweighs the harm to the legitimate interests of the person against whom seizure would be ordered of granting the application and substantially outweighs the harm to any third parties who may be harmed by such seizure;

" (IV) the applicant is likely to succeed in showing that—

" (aa) the information is a trade secret; and

" (bb) the person against whom seizure would be ordered—

" (AA) misappropriated the trade secret of the applicant by improper means; or

" (BB) conspired to use improper means to misappropriate the trade secret of the applicant;

" (V) the person against whom seizure would be ordered has actual possession of—

" (aa) the trade secret; and

" (bb) any property to be seized;

" (VI) the application describes with reasonable particularity the matter to be seized and, to the extent reasonable under the circumstances, identifies the location where the matter is to be seized;

" (VII) the person against whom seizure would be ordered, or persons acting in concert with such person, would destroy, move, hide, or otherwise make such matter inaccessible to the court, if the applicant were to proceed on notice to such person; and

"(Ⅷ) the applicant has not publicized the requested seizure.

"(B) ELEMENTS OF ORDER. —If an order is issued under subparagraph (A), it shall—

"(i) set forth findings of fact and conclusions of law required for the order;

"(ii) provide for the narrowest seizure of property necessary to achieve the purpose of this paragraph and direct that the seizure be conducted in a manner that minimizes any interruption of the business operations of third parties and, to the extent possible, does not interrupt the legitimate business operations of the person accused of misappropriating the trade secret;

"(iii)(Ⅰ) be accompanied by an order protecting the seized property from disclosure by prohibiting access by the applicant or the person against whom the order is directed, and prohibiting any copies, in whole or in part, of the seized property, to prevent undue damage to the party against whom the order has issued or others, until such parties have an opportunity to be heard in court; and

"(Ⅱ) provide that if access is granted by the court to the applicant or the person against whom the order is directed, the access shall be consistent with subparagraph (D);

"(iv) provide guidance to the law enforcement officials executing the seizure that clearly delineates the scope of the authority of the officials, including—

"(Ⅰ) the hours during which the seizure may be executed; and

"(Ⅱ) whether force may be used to access locked areas;

"(v) set a date for a hearing described in subparagraph (F) at the earliest possible time, and not later than 7 days after the order has issued, unless the party against whom the order is directed and others harmed by the order consent to another date for the hearing, except that a party against whom the order has issued or any person harmed by the order may move the court at any time to dissolve or modify the order after giving notice to the applicant who obtained the order; and

"(vi) require the person obtaining the order to provide the security determined adequate by the court for the payment of the damages that any person may be entitled to recover as a result of a wrongful or excessive seizure or wrongful or excessive attempted seizure under this paragraph.

"(C) PROTECTION FROM PUBLICITY. —The court shall take appropriate action to protect the person against whom an order under this paragraph is directed from publicity, by or at the behest of the person obtaining the order, about such order and any seizure under such order.

"(D) MATERIALS IN CUSTODY OF COURT. —

"(i) IN GENERAL. —Any materials seized under this paragraph shall be taken into the custody of the court. The court shall secure the seized material from physical and electronic access during the seizure and while in the custody of the court.

"(ii) STORAGE MEDIUM. —If the seized material includes a storage medium, or if the seized material is stored on a storage medium, the court shall prohibit the medium from being connected to a network or the Internet without the consent of both parties, until the hearing required under subparagraph (B)(v) and described in subparagraph (F).

"(iii) PROTECTION OF CONFIDENTIALITY. —The court shall take appropriate measures to protect the confidentiality of seized materials that are unrelated to the trade secret information ordered seized pursuant to this paragraph unless the person against whom the order is entered consents to disclosure of the material.

"(iv) APPOINTMENT OF SPECIAL MASTER. —The court may appoint a special master to locate and isolate all misappropriated trade secret information and to facilitate the return of unrelated property and data to the person from whom the property was seized. The special master appointed by the court shall agree to be bound by a non-disclosure agreement approved by the court.

"(E) SERVICE OF ORDER. —The court shall order that service of a copy of the order under this paragraph, and the submissions of the applicant to obtain the order, shall be made by a Federal law enforcement officer who, upon making service, shall carry out the seizure under the order. The court may allow State or local law enforcement officials to participate, but may not permit the applicant or any agent of the applicant to participate in the seizure. At the request of law enforcement officials, the court may allow a technical expert who is unaffiliated with the applicant and who is bound by a court-approved non-disclosure agreement to participate in the seizure if the court determines that the participation of the expert will aid the efficient execution of and minimize the burden of the seizure.

"(F) SEIZURE HEARING. —

"(i) DATE. —A court that issues a seizure order shall hold a hearing on the date set by the court under subparagraph (B)(v).

"(ii) BURDEN OF PROOF. —At a hearing held under this subparagraph, the party who obtained the order under subparagraph (A) shall have the burden to prove the facts supporting the findings of fact and conclusions of law necessary to support the order. If the party fails to meet that burden, the seizure order shall be dissolved or modified appropriately.

"(iii) DISSOLUTION OR MODIFICATION OF ORDER. —A party against whom the order has been issued or any person harmed by the order may move the court at any time to dissolve or modify the order after giving notice to the party who obtained the order.

"(iv) DISCOVERY TIME LIMITS. —The court may make such orders modifying the time limits for discovery under the Federal Rules of Civil Procedure as may be necessary to prevent the frustration of the purposes of a hearing under this subparagraph.

"(G) ACTION FOR DAMAGE CAUSED BY WRONGFUL SEIZURE. —A person who suffers damage by reason of a wrongful or excessive seizure under this paragraph has a cause of action against the applicant for the order under which such seizure was made, and shall be entitled to the same relief as is provided under section 34(d)(11) of the Trade-mark Act of 1946 [15 U. S. C. 1116(d) (11)]. The security posted with the court under subparagraph (B)(vi) shall not limit the recovery of third parties for damages.

"(H) MOTION FOR ENCRYPTION. —A party or a person who claims to have an interest in the subject matter seized may make a motion at any time, which may be heard ex parte, to encrypt any material seized or to be seized under this paragraph that is stored on a storage medium. The motion shall include, when possible, the desired encryption method.

"(3) REMEDIES. —In a civil action brought under this subsection with respect to the misappropriation of a trade secret, a court may—

"(A) grant an injunction—

"(i) to prevent any actual or threatened misappropriation described in paragraph (1) on such terms as the court deems reasonable, provided the order does not—

"(Ⅰ) prevent a person from entering into an employment relationship, and that conditions placed on such employment shall be based on evidence of threatened misappropriation and not merely on the information the person knows; or

"(Ⅱ) otherwise conflict with an applicable State law prohibiting restraints on the practice of a lawful profession, trade, or business;

"(ii) if determined appropriate by the court, requiring affirmative actions to be taken to protect the trade secret; and

"(iii) in exceptional circumstances that render an injunction inequitable, that conditions future use of the trade secret upon payment of a reasonable royalty for no longer than the period of time for which such use could have been prohibited;

"(B) award—

"(i)(Ⅰ) damages for actual loss caused by the misappropriation of the trade secret; and

"(Ⅱ) damages for any unjust enrichment caused by the misappropriation of the trade secret that is not addressed in computing damages for actual loss; or

"(ii) in lieu of damages measured by any other methods, the damages caused by the misappropriation measured by imposition of liability for a reasonable royalty for the misappropriator's unauthorized disclosure or use of the trade secret;

"(C) if the trade secret is willfully and maliciously misappropriated, award exemplary damages in an amount not more than 2 times the amount of the damages awarded under subparagraph (B); and

"(D) if a claim of the misappropriation is made in bad faith, which may be established by circumstantial evidence, a motion to terminate an injunction is made or opposed in bad faith, or the trade secret was willfully and maliciously misappropriated, award reasonable attorney's fees to the prevailing party.

"(c) JURISDICTION. —The district courts of the United States shall have original jurisdiction of civil actions brought under this section.

"(d) PERIOD OF LIMITATIONS. —A civil action under subsection (b) may not be commenced later than 3 years after the date on which the misappropriation with respect to which the action would relate is discovered or by the exercise of reasonable diligence should have been discovered. For purposes of this subsection, a continuing misappropriation constitutes a single claim of misappropriation. ".

(b) DEFINITIONS. —Section 1839 of title 18, United States Code, is amended—

(1) in paragraph (3)—

(A) in subparagraph (B), by striking "the public" and inserting "another person who can obtain economic value from the disclosure or use of the information"; and

(B) by striking "and" at the end;

(2) in paragraph (4), by striking the period at the end and inserting a semicolon; and

(3) by adding at the end the following:

"(5) the term 'misappropriation' means—

"(A) acquisition of a trade secret of another by a person who knows or has reason to know that the trade secret was acquired by improper means; or

"(B) disclosure or use of a trade secret of another without express or implied consent by a person who—

"(i) used improper means to acquire knowledge of the trade secret;

"(ii) at the time of disclosure or use, knew or had reason to know that the knowledge of the trade secret was—

"(Ⅰ) derived from or through a person who had used improper means to acquire the trade secret;

"(Ⅱ) acquired under circumstances giving rise to a duty to maintain the secrecy of the trade secret or limit the use of the trade secret; or

"(Ⅲ) derived from or through a person who owed a duty to the person seeking relief to maintain the secrecy of the trade secret or limit the use of the trade secret; or

"(iii) before a material change of the position of the person, knew or had reason to know that—

"(Ⅰ) the trade secret was a trade secret; and

"(Ⅱ) knowledge of the trade secret had been acquired by accident or mistake;

"(6) the term 'improper means'—

"(A) includes theft, bribery, misrepresentation, breach or inducement of a breach of a duty to maintain secrecy, or espionage through electronic or other means; and

"(B) does not include reverse engineering, independent derivation, or any other lawful means of acquisition; and

"(7) the term 'Trademark Act of 1946' means the Act entitled 'An Act to provide for the registration and protection of trademarks used in commerce, to carry out the provisions of certain international conventions, and for other purposes, approved July 5, 1946 (15 U. S. C. 1051 et seq.) (commonly referred to as the "Trademark Act of 1946" or the "Lanham Act")'.".

(c) EXCEPTIONS TO PROHIBITION. —Section 1833 of title 18, United

States Code, is amended, in the matter preceding paragraph (1), by inserting "or create a private right of action for" after "prohibit".

(d) CONFORMING AMENDMENTS. —

(1) The section heading for section 1836 of title 18, United States Code, is amended to read as follows:

" § **1836. Civil proceedings**".

(2) The table of sections for chapter 90 of title 18, United States Code, is amended by striking the item relating to section 1836 and inserting the following:

"**1836. Civil proceedings.** ".

(e) EFFECTIVE DATE. —The amendments made by this section shall apply with respect to any misappropriation of a trade secret (as defined in section 1839 of title 18, United States Code, as amended by this section) for which any act occurs on or after the date of the enactment of this Act.

(f) RULE OF CONSTRUCTION. —Nothing in the amendments made by this section shall be construed to modify the rule of construction under section 1838 of title 18, United States Code, or to preempt any other provision of law.

(g) APPLICABILITY TO OTHER LAWS. —This section and the amendments made by this section shall not be construed to be a law pertaining to intellectual property for purposes of any other Act of Congress.

SEC. 3. TRADE SECRET THEFT ENFORCEMENT.

(a) IN GENERAL. —Chapter 90 of title 18, United States Code, is amended—

(1) in section 1832(b), by striking " $5,000,000" and inserting " the greater of $5,000,000 or 3 times the value of the stolen trade secret to the organization, including expenses for research and design and other costs of reproducing the trade secret that the organization has thereby avoided"; and

(2) in section 1835—

(A) by striking "In any prosecution" and inserting the following:

"（a）IN GENERAL. —In any prosecution"；and

（B）by adding at the end the following：

"（b）RIGHTS OF TRADE SECRET OWNERS. —The court may not author-ize or direct the disclosure of any information the owner asserts to be a trade secret unless the court allows the owner the opportunity to file a submission under seal that describes the interest of the owner in keeping the information confidential. No submission under seal made under this subsection may be used in a prosecution un-der this chapter for any purpose other than those set forth in this section, or other-wise required by law. The provision of information relating to a trade secret to the United States or the court in connection with a prosecution under this chapter shall not constitute a waiver of trade secret protection, and the disclosure of information relating to a trade secret in connection with a prosecution under this chapter shall not constitute a waiver of trade secret protection unless the trade secret owner ex-pressly consents to such waiver. ".

（b）RICO PREDICATE OFFENSES. —Section 1961（1）of title 18, United States Code, is amended by inserting "sections 1831 and 1832（relating to eco-nomic espionage and theft of trade secrets）," before "section 1951".

SEC. 4. REPORT ON THEFT OF TRADE SECRETS OCCURRING A-BROAD.

（a）DEFINITIONS. —In this section：

（1）DIRECTOR. —The term "Director" means the Under Secretary of Com-merce for Intellectual Property and Director of the United States Patent and Trade-mark Office.

（2）FOREIGN INSTRUMENTALITY, ETC. —The terms "foreign instru-mentality", "foreign agent", and "trade secret" have the meanings given those terms in section 1839 of title 18, United States Code.

（3）STATE. —The term "State" includes the District of Columbia and any commonwealth, territory, or possession of the United States.

（4）UNITED STATES COMPANY. —The term "United States company"

means an organization organized under the laws of the United States or a State or political subdivision thereof.

(b) REPORTS. —Not later than 1 year after the date of enactment of this Act, and biannually thereafter, the Attorney General, in consultation with the Intellectual Property Enforcement Coordinator, the Director, and the heads of other appropriate agencies, shall submit to the Committees on the Judiciary of the House of Representatives and the Senate, and make publicly available on the Web site of the Department of Justice and disseminate to the public through such other means as the Attorney General may identify, a report on the following:

(1) The scope and breadth of the theft of the trade secrets of United States companies occurring outside of the United States.

(2) The extent to which theft of trade secrets occurring outside of the United States is sponsored by foreign governments, foreign instrumentalities, or foreign agents.

(3) The threat posed by theft of trade secrets occurring outside of the United States.

(4) The ability and limitations of trade secret owners to prevent the misappropriation of trade secrets outside of the United States, to enforce any judgment against foreign entities for theft of trade secrets, and to prevent imports based on theft of trade secrets overseas.

(5) A breakdown of the trade secret protections afforded United States companies by each country that is a trading partner of the United States and enforcement efforts available and undertaken in each such country, including a list identifying specific countries where trade secret theft, laws, or enforcement is a significant problem for United States companies.

(6) Instances of the Federal Government working with foreign countries to investigate, arrest, and prosecute entities and individuals involved in the theft of trade secrets outside of the United States.

(7) Specific progress made under trade agreements and treaties, including

any new remedies enacted by foreign countries, to protect against theft of trade secrets of United States companies outside of the United States.

(8) Recommendations of legislative and executive branch actions that may be undertaken to—

(A) reduce the threat of and economic impact caused by the theft of the trade secrets of United States companies occurring outside of the United States;

(B) educate United States companies regarding the threats to their trade secrets when taken outside of the United States;

(C) provide assistance to United States companies to reduce the risk of loss of their trade secrets when taken outside of the United States; and

(D) provide a mechanism for United States companies to confidentially or anonymously report the theft of trade secrets occurring outside of the United States.

SEC. 5. SENSE OF CONGRESS.

It is the sense of Congress that—

(1) trade secret theft occurs in the United States and around the world;

(2) trade secret theft, wherever it occurs, harms the companies that own the trade secrets and the employees of the companies;

(3) chapter 90 of title 18, United States Code (commonly known as the "Economic Espionage Act of 1996"), applies broadly to protect trade secrets from theft; and

(4) it is important when seizing information to balance the need to prevent or remedy misappropriation with the need to avoid interrupting the—

(A) business of third parties; and

(B) legitimate interests of the party accused of wrongdoing.

SEC. 6. BEST PRACTICES.

(a) IN GENERAL. —Not later than 2 years after the date of enactment of this Act, the Federal Judicial Center, using existing sources, shall develop recommended best practices for—

(1) the seizure of information and media storing the information; and

(2) the securing of the information and media once seized.

(b) UPDATES. —The Federal Judicial Center shall update the recommended best practices developed under subsection (a) from time to time.

(c) CONGRESSIONAL SUBMISSIONS. —The Federal Judicial Center shall provide a copy of the recommendations developed under subsection (a), and any updates made under subsection (b), to the—

(1) Committee on the Judiciary of the Senate; and

(2) Committee on the Judiciary of the House of Representatives.

SEC. 7. IMMUNITY FROM LIABILITY FOR CONFIDENTIAL DISCLOSURE OF A TRADE SECRET TO THE GOVERNMENT OR IN A COURT FILING.

(a) AMENDMENT. —Section 1833 of title 18, United States Code, is amended—

(1) by striking "This chapter" and inserting "(a) IN GENERAL. —This chapter";

(2) in subsection (a)(2), as designated by paragraph (1), by striking "the reporting of a suspected violation of law to any governmental entity of the United States, a State, or a political subdivision of a State, if such entity has lawful authority with respect to that violation" and inserting "the disclosure of a trade secret in accordance with subsection (b)"; and

(3) by adding at the end the following:

"(b) IMMUNITY FROM LIABILITY FOR CONFIDENTIAL DISCLOSURE OF A TRADE SECRET TO THE GOVERNMENT OR IN A COURT FILING. —

"(1) IMMUNITY. —An individual shall not be held criminally or civilly liable under any Federal or State trade secret law for the disclosure of a trade secret that—

"(A) is made—

"(i) in confidence to a Federal, State, or local government official, either directly or indirectly, or to an attorney; and

"(ii) solely for the purpose of reporting or investigating a suspected violation of law; or

"(B) is made in a complaint or other document filed in a lawsuit or other proceeding, if such filing is made under seal.

"(2) USE OF TRADE SECRET INFORMATION IN ANTI-RETALIA-TION LAWSUIT. —An individual who files a lawsuit for retaliation by an employer for reporting a suspected violation of law may disclose the trade secret to the attorney of the individual and use the trade secret information in the court proceeding, if the individual—

"(A) files any document containing the trade secret under seal; and

"(B) does not disclose the trade secret, except pursuant to court order.

"(3) NOTICE. —

"(A) IN GENERAL. —An employer shall provide notice of the immunity set forth in this subsection in any contract or agreement with an employee that governs the use of a trade secret or other confidential information.

"(B) POLICY DOCUMENT. —An employer shall be considered to be in compliance with the notice requirement in subparagraph(A) if the employer provides a cross-reference to a policy document provided to the employee that sets forth the employer's reporting policy for a suspected violation of law.

"(C) NON-COMPLIANCE. —If an employer does not comply with the notice requirement in subparagraph (A), the employer may not be awarded exemplary damages or attorney fees under subparagraph (C) or (D) of section 1836 (b)(3) in an action against an employee to whom notice was not provided.

"(D) APPLICABILITY. —This paragraph shall apply to contracts and agreements that are entered into or updated after the date of enactment of this subsection.

"(4) EMPLOYEE DEFINED. —For purposes of this subsection, the term 'employee' includes any individual performing work as a contractor or consultant for an employer.

"(5) RULE OF CONSTRUCTION.—Except as expressly provided for under this subsection, nothing in this subsection shall be construed to authorize, or limit liability for, an act that is otherwise prohibited by law, such as the unlawful access of material by unauthorized means.".

(b) TECHNICAL AND CONFORMING AMENDMENT.—Section 1838 of title 18, United States Code, is amended by striking "This chapter" and inserting "Except as provided in section 1833(b), this chapter".

Approved May 11, 2016.

第五章 《1996 经济间谍法》修订综合版

第一节 《1996 经济间谍法》修订综合版简介

一、《1996 经济间谍法》修订综合版的基本内容和特征

（一）生效时间

这不是一部由美国国会和总统批准的单独的法律，而是由本书作者把现在生效的四部法律中相关内容汇集综合在一起所重构出来的一部法律，其内容包括《1996 经济间谍法》的内容，全部的《2012 盗窃商业秘密罪扩大适用范围法》的内容，全部的《2012 外国经济间谍罪加重处罚法》的全部内容，以及《2016 商业秘密保护法》的部分内容。

由于《2016 商业秘密保护法》自 2016 年 5 月 11 日生效，因此，可以说《1996 经济间谍法》修订综合版应当从 2016 年 5 月 11 日生效。因为，虽然另外三部法律的生效日期都早于这一时间，但是，《2016 商业秘密保护法》对《1996 经济间谍法》中的部分内容进行了修订和补充，从而使得自《2016 商业秘密保护法》生效之日起，《1996 经济间谍法》中涉及被修订的部分内容不再有效，必须按照《2016 商业秘密保护法》中所修订的内容实施。因此，确定《1996 经济间谍法》修订综合版自《2016 商业秘密保护法》生效之日起生效。

为了便于读者了解和掌握《1996 经济间谍法》《2012 盗窃商业秘密罪扩大适用范围法》《2012 外国经济间谍罪加重处罚法》《2016 商业秘密保护法》和《1996 经济间谍法》修订综合版五部法律之间的相互关系，列出图 3 来进行表示。

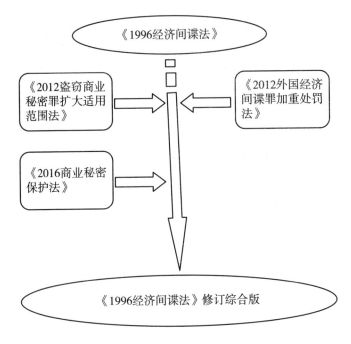

图 3　五部法律相互关系

（二）主要特征

（1）《1996 经济间谍法》修订综合版是《1996 经济间谍法》经过两次专门立法，以及《2016 商业秘密保护法》中设立修订补充内容以后所形成的立法内容。这是当前《1996 经济间谍法》相关内容的最终有效版本；就美国当前已经立法的内容，如果只使用《1996 经济间谍法》中的有关规定就是错误的。

（2）由于美国的立法特点，没有把《1996 经济间谍法》修订综合版这一最终版本再直接颁布为法律。因此，从形式上来说，由于其不是由美国国会正式颁布的版本，所以还不能把这一最终版本直接称为联邦法律的官方版本，但是就内容来说，它确实是这一法律相关内容的最终版本。

（3）在这里之所以要汇总和整理出《1996 经济间谍法》修订综合版，主要是出于有利于正确使用和掌握这些法律的目的。因为在涉及商业秘密的刑事案件需要适用这些相互交叉的联邦法律时，如果没有全面地了解和掌握已经颁布实施的四部法律的相互交叉和修改完善的关系，只适用《1996 经济间谍法》

《2012 盗窃商业秘密罪扩大适用范围法》《2012 外国经济间谍罪加重处罚法》，或者《2016 商业秘密保护法》中一部或部分法律的规定，不但都是片面的，而且涉及已经被后面的法律修改的内容时，如果还是适用未经修改的条款，则就是一种错误的适用。

因此，在这种情况下，就需要把这四部法律中相互交叉修改，以及补充调整的内容都归纳汇总到一起，这样能够使得人们避免自己查询核对的麻烦，并且尽可能地避免出现差错，这就是作者完成这部《1996 经济间谍法》修订综合版的初衷和目的。当然，在处理和研究美国有关的"经济间谍罪"和联邦法院管辖的"商业秘密盗窃罪"案件时，也只有使用这部《1996 经济间谍法》修订综合版的内容才是正确的。

二、《1996 经济间谍法》修订综合版适用的范围和受到的限制

（1）在美国凡是涉及经济间谍罪的案件都应当适用《1996 经济间谍法》修订综合版。

（2）凡是涉及国际贸易和不同州之间贸易中的商业秘密的刑事案件都应当适用《1996 经济间谍法》修订综合版。

（3）虽然在立法内容上《1996 经济间谍法》修订综合版与《2016 商业秘密保护法》存在着一定的交叉，但是，在具体法律适用上，凡是涉及由联邦法院管辖的商业秘密民事纠纷案件则都应当适用《2016 商业秘密保护法》，而涉及由联邦法院管辖的商业秘密刑事案件则都应当适用《1996 经济间谍法》修订综合版。

第二节 《1996 经济间谍法》修订综合版译文^①

《1996 经济间谍法》修订综合版

目 录

第 1831 条 经济间谍罪

任何单位或个人,如果为了使外国政府、外国政府的机构、外国政府的代理人受益,企图或者故意实施下列行为的,构成经济间谍罪。个人犯罪的,最高处罚 500 万美元,或者最高监禁 15 年,或者两者同时处罚。单位犯罪的,最高处罚 1000 万美元,或者被侵害商业秘密价值的 3 倍,其中包括被告单位因利用间谍行为所节省的用于研发的费用,以及正当地使用该商业秘密时所应当支出的成本费用。

(1)窃取,或者擅自占有、携带、运输、隐藏,或者通过欺诈、计谋、收买等非

---

① 由于中文和英文的语句顺序和表达法律的逻辑关系存在差异,在把具体的原文内容翻译成中文时,在保持原文含义不变的前提下,结合中国法律对应的表达格式和法律条款的一般表达方式对部分原文条款的排列方式进行了调整和重新组合。

法手段获取商业秘密；

（2）擅自抄写、复印、记录、绘制、拍摄、下载、上传、修改、销毁、影印、根据知悉和记忆的内容重新制作、传输、传递、发送、邮寄、泄露、运送商业秘密；

（3）在知道商业秘密已经处于被盗窃、侵害、非法获取、非法传递的情况下，仍然接受、购买或者占有该商业秘密；

（4）企图实施上述（1）至（3）款中的任何一种犯罪行为的预备行为；

（5）与一个或者多个人共谋实施第（1）至（3）款中的任何一项所述的任何犯罪行为，以及其中的一名或者多名人员采取任何行动以促使共谋目的实用的行为。

第 1832 条　盗窃商业秘密罪

任何单位或个人，如果企图或者故意实施下列侵害他人商业秘密的行为，当这些商业秘密包含于用在或者企图用在国际贸易或者州际贸易的商品或者服务中时，构成盗窃商业秘密罪。个人犯罪的，按照本法的规定处罚，或者最高监禁 10 年，或者同时处罚。单位犯罪的，最高处罚 500 万美元，或者被侵害商业秘密价值的 3 倍，其中包括被告因利用间谍行为所节省的用于研发和正当地使用该商业秘密时所应当支出的成本费用。

（1）窃取，或者擅自占有、携带、运输、隐藏，或者通过欺诈、计谋、收买等非法手段获取商业秘密；

（2）擅自抄写、复印、记录、绘制、拍摄、下载、上传、修改、销毁、影印、根据知悉和记忆的内容重新制作、传输、传递、发送、邮寄、泄露、运送商业秘密；

（3）在知道商业秘密已经处于被盗窃、侵害、非法获取、非法传递的情况下，仍然接受、购买或者占有该商业秘密；

（4）企图实施上述（1）至（3）款中的任何一种犯罪行为的预备行为；

（5）与一个或者多个人共谋实施第（1）至（3）款中的任何一项所述的任何犯罪行为，以及其中的一名或者多名人员采取任何行动以促使共谋目的实用的行为。

1833 条　禁止的例外情形

1833 - 1［基本规定］本法并不禁止政府和个人实施本条规定的下列行为，商业秘密权利人也不得对这些行为提起侵权诉讼。

1833-2［责任豁免的披露行为］实施下列披露行为，不承担任何由联邦或者州法律规定的擅自披露商业秘密应当承担的刑事责任和民事责任。

（1）［政府披露商业秘密的行为］任何由美国联邦政府、各州政府，以及各州政府的所属机构实施的商业秘密披露行为。

（2）［控告和诉讼中的披露行为］当披露商业秘密的行为属于对侵害商业秘密行为的控告，或者提交案件诉讼的材料，或者提交其他法定程序中规定的材料，而所提交的材料又都处于密封状态。

（3）［基于特定目的向特定人员的披露］①特定的报告对象：其秘密地直接或者间接地对联邦政府、州政府、地方政府的官员或者律师披露了商业秘密；②特定的披露目的：披露商业秘密的目的只是为了控告或者调查涉嫌侵害商业秘密的行为。

（4）［在反报复性诉讼中使用商业秘密的特殊要求］如果雇主报告某雇员涉嫌侵害了其商业秘密，该雇员可以提起一件反报复的诉讼，可以向其聘请的律师披露该商业秘密，以及在法庭程序中使用该商业秘密的信息，但是，应当符合下列要求：①包含该商业秘密的材料被密封；②除非应法院的要求以外，不得主动披露该商业秘密。

1833-3［雇主对雇员的通知义务］雇主应当在与雇员签订的合同或者协议中，对于那些管理使用商业秘密或者机密信息的雇员提供上述有关免责披露商业秘密行为的内容。

1833-4［对雇主通知雇员的要求］雇主对雇员提供的通知内容，应当能够使雇员知悉法定的免责披露行为，这种告知行为才符合本法要求。

1833-5［不遵守雇主通知义务的法律后果］如果雇主通知雇员的行为不符合本法的要求，当雇主依据《1996 经济间谍法》第 1836 条规定的民事程序追究雇员侵害其商业秘密的责任时，不得享有获得惩罚性赔偿和由对方承担律师费的权利。

1833-6［适用范围］本法适用于自本法生效后雇主与雇员所签订或者更新的合同和协议。

1833-7［雇员的范围］本法中，"雇员"的范围包括任何为雇主从事工作的个人，包括承包人或者咨询顾问等。

1833 -8[本法效力的界限]本法中,除了有明确的规定以外,任何条款都不得被解释为允许实施被法律所禁止的行为,或者免除这些行为的法律责任,例如,凡是以非法的方式接触他人商业秘密的行为都属于非法行为。

第 1834 条 刑事没收

1. 对于实施本法犯罪的被告,法院在作出判决时,除了判处应有的刑罚以外,还应当罚没被告的下列财产:

(1)任何直接或者间接地借助犯罪行为所得的财产;

(2)任何人的财产,只要被用来或者企图被用来实施犯罪,或者为犯罪提供便利,无论被使用的方式和方法如何,法院在慎重考虑这些财产在犯罪中的性质,被使用的范围和比例以后决定没收的程度。

2. 对于应当没收的财产,在办理扣押和处置措施以及其他行政和司法手续时,应当按照 1970 年《综合药物滥用预防和控制法》(21 USC 853)第 413 节的规定执行,但是其中的(d)和(j)款除外,不适用于本条的没收措施。

[注:美国国会于 2008 年对第 1834 条进行了修改,修改后增加的内容如下:"1834 条刑事没收:除了依据本法提供的任何其他类似的救济以外,本法中所涉及的没收、销毁和归还措施都应当在《美国法典》第 2323 条的范围内实施(由检察长在诉讼、执法和获得民事补偿等活动中依据自己的职责进行执行)。"]

第 1835 条 司法程序中的保密令

1835 -1[诉讼中的法院保密令]在适用本法实施的任何刑事或者其他任何司法程序中,在符合联邦刑事和民事诉讼法、联邦证据法以及相关法律的前提下,法院应当颁布保密令并采取合理的必要措施保护商业秘密的秘密性。一审判决后,如果美国联邦政府提起上诉,则由联邦地区法院作出准予的决定或命令,并且授权或者指导对商业秘密的披露。

1835 -2[诉讼中商业秘密权利人享有的特殊权利]

(1)当商业秘密的权利人主张某一信息属于他的商业秘密时,除非法院已经给他提供了机会,使他在提交给法院的密封的法律意见中阐述这些保密信息能够给他带来的利益,否则,法院不能授权或者指示披露这些信息。

(2)除非法律另有规定外,基于上述目的所提交的密封的法律意见不得被用于本法中的其他诉讼活动。

(3)按照法律规定向美国政府或受理案件的法院提交与商业秘密相关的信息时,并不丧失对该商业秘密的保护;依据本法规定在司法程序中披露这些与商业秘密相关的信息时也不丧失对该商业秘密的保护,除非该商业秘密的权利人明确表示对该商业秘密放弃保护。

1836 条　民事诉讼程序

1836 −1[总检察长提起民事诉讼]本法中,对于符合本法民事诉讼范围的商业秘密侵害案件,总检察长可以利用民事诉讼程序请求法院对侵害商业秘密的行为采取禁令措施。

1836 −2[权利人提起民事诉讼]本法中,对于符合本法民事诉讼范围的商业秘密侵害案件,该商业秘密的权利人可以依据本法提起民事诉讼。

1836 −3[民事诉讼的适用范围]当同时符合下列三项条件时,商业秘密权利人和其他适格的主体都可以依据本法对侵害商业秘密的行为提起民事诉讼:①商业秘密受到了侵害;②该商业秘密涉及一定的商品或服务;③该商品或服务用于或者计划用于国际贸易或者美国不同州之间的州际贸易。

1836 −4[实施扣押令的目的和基本程序]申请人依据本法规定申请扣押被申请人的财产时,应当提交扣押申请和本法规定的证据材料,并且应当办理相关的其他手续。

基于对申请人所提交申请材料的审查,对于符合条件的申请,结合具体的案情,为了阻止对商业秘密的散布和传播,法院应当签发命令扣押被申请人的必要财产。

1836 −5[法院签发扣押令的必要条件]在具体案件中,只有同时满足下列全部条件时,法院才能签发财产扣押令:

(1)依据《联邦民事程序法》第 65 条的规定,对被申请人发出禁令或者限制令以后,或者采用其他公平的救济措施以后,不能充分有效地制止被申请人规避法律的行为,或者制止被申请人违反禁令或限制令的行为;

(2)如果不实施扣押令,无法避免的侵害行为就可能立刻发生;

(3)如果不实施扣押令,对申请人造成的危害将大于对被扣押者合法利益

造成的损害,以及基本大于对任何第三方利益造成的损害;

(4)申请人应当提交下列证据材料:①证明商业秘密自身符合法律规定的材料;②证明被申请人具有下列行为之一的材料:被申请人以不正当的手段盗用申请人的商业秘密;或者共谋以不正当的手段盗用申请人的商业秘密;

(5)被申请人应当已经实际占有或者拥有下列事物:①涉案的商业秘密;②将被扣押的财产;

(6)在扣押申请书中应当合理地说明被扣押财产的特征,包括财产的合理范围、规模和程度,以及财产所在的具体地理位置;

(7)如果一旦申请人通知了被申请人,则被申请人或者其同谋者将会毁坏、转移、藏匿相关财产,使得法院难以查找和获得这些财产;

(8)申请人未对外公布申请的扣押事项。

1836 −6[扣押令中应当包含和涉及的具体事项]法院签发扣押令时,在扣押令中应当包含和涉及下列事项:

(1)明确列出签发扣押令所依据的事实和法律依据。

(2)在保障能够保护申请人合法利益的前提下,对必要的财产采取最低限度的扣押措施,并且尽量使得扣押行为最低限度地影响到其他第三人的商业活动,以及被申请人其他合法的商业活动。

(3)在扣押令中设置一项保护被扣押财产的专门性条款,禁止申请人和被申请人接触、披露,部分或者全部地复制财产信息,防止过度地破坏被申请人的财产,直到被申请人有机会参加法庭的听证为止。

经过法院批准后,申请人和被申请人可以接触被扣押的财产,但是,这种接触应当符合本法的规定。

(4)法院应当对执行扣押任务的执法人员进行指导,明确界定他们的权限范围,具体包括:①扣押令签发多少小时以后应当执行;②对于被锁住的房屋和区域是否准予使用强制手段进入。

(5)应当明确规定一个符合本法要求的尽早的听证日期,最晚不能迟于扣押令签发后的第七天,除非被申请人或者受到这一扣押令伤害的其他人同意超出上述日期举行听证。在申请人获得了扣押令以后,除了被申请人之外,其他任何被这一扣押令伤害的人都可以在任何时间,在向申请人发出通知之后,请求法院撤销或者修改扣押令。

（6）申请人应当按照法院规定的要求提供足额的担保金，用于赔偿由于错误的扣押或者错误的企图扣押，或者由于过度地扣押或者企图过度地扣押给他人合法利益造成的损失。

1836－7［对扣押令的保密义务］法院应当采取合适的手段保护被执行扣押令的人免遭公开宣传，可以在扣押令中要求获得这一扣押令的人不得宣传这一扣押令和包含的事项。

1836－8［对法院扣押材料的一般性规定］法院在审查和执行扣押令期间所获取和扣押的全部资料都由法院保管，在整个扣押令实施期间和这些材料保管期间，法院应当确保这些材料能够通过物理方式或电子方式接触，并且按照下列要求执行：

（1）［对储存介质保密的要求］如果被扣押的材料中包含着储存商业秘密信息的介质，或者扣押的材料储存在介质上，在未经申请人和被申请人双方当事人一致同意之前，法院应当禁止把该介质连接到网络或者互联网上，直到依据本法的规定举行听证为止。

（2）［对非商业秘密材料的保密处理］法院应当采取合适的措施对依据本法规定扣押的不涉及商业秘密信息的材料进行保密，除非被申请人自己同意公开这些材料。

（3）［任命专门的保密负责人］法院可以任命一名法官作为专门的负责人来整理和保管被盗用的商业秘密信息，同时负责把不相关的被扣押的财产和资料返还给被申请人；这位专门负责人应当遵守法院批准的保密协议。

1836－9［扣押令的协助与执行］为申请人和执行活动提供服务及帮助的规定。

（1）法院应当制作一份扣押令的复制件，由联邦法律执行官送达到申请人，然后，由执行官执行扣押令。

（2）法院可以允许各个州以及当地的法律执行官参与扣押令的执行活动，但是不得允许申请人或者其代理人参与扣押活动。

（3）经过执行官的请求，法院可以准许与申请人及被申请人没有利益关联的技术专家协助扣押的执行，前提是技术专家必须遵守法院批准的保密协议，以及技术专家的参与能够实际帮助有效的执行和降低执行成本。

1836 -10[有关扣押听证的规定]

(1)[确定听证日期]法院签发扣押令之后应当根据本法的规定确定一个举行听证的日期。

(2)[扣押申请人的举证责任]在举行听证时,已经获得了扣押令的申请人必须提供被申请人非法盗用了其商业秘密,以及应当采用扣押令的合理的证据和结论,否则,扣押令将被撤销或者被适当地修改。

(3)[对扣押令的撤销或者修改]被申请人以及任何受到扣押令损害的第三人,在通知了申请人之后,在任何时间都可以请求法院撤销或者修改扣押令。

(4)[对听证期限的调整]当法院发现按照已有的期限举行听证可能达不到听证目的时,可以根据《联邦民事诉讼程序法》的规定调整听证的日期。

1836 -11[对错误扣押所导致损害的赔偿]任何由于错误扣押或过度扣押遭受损害的人,都有权利向扣押令的申请人主张赔偿,赔偿的标准可以参照1946 年《商标法》第 34 条第(4)款第(11)项[15 U. S. C. 1116(d)(11)]的规定执行。申请人依据本法规定向法院提供的保证金可以用于赔偿第三方由此受到的损失。

1836 -12[请求对扣押物加密的提议]任何主张对扣押物存在利害关系的当事人或者第三人,在任何时候都可以请求法院对扣押物进行加密,法院经过单方面的听证后,可以对扣押的任何材料,包括存储在一定介质上的材料进行加密处理;请求人在提出请求时,应当尽可能地提供所希望的加密方法。

1836 -13[其他民事救济措施的类型]对于侵害商业秘密的行为,依据本法提起民事诉讼时,法院可以采取禁令、损害赔偿、惩罚性赔偿和承担律师费用等民事救济措施。

1836 -14[对雇佣人员采取禁令]当有证据证明某一被雇佣人存在侵害商业秘密的危险时,这些证据应不仅仅能证明他已经知道了什么信息,而应能证明他有侵害商业秘密的威胁性,此时,为了阻止现实的或者潜在的侵害商业秘密行为的发生,可以对该雇佣人员采取禁令措施。

此时的禁令不是直接禁止被雇佣人与雇佣人之间建立的劳动关系,而是禁止被雇佣人实施侵害商业秘密的行为,否则,这种禁令就可能与有些州法律规定的不准禁止他人从事合法的商业、贸易和职业活动的法令相冲突。

1836 –15［对其他相关人员采取禁令］当法院认为有必要采取积极的措施来保护商业秘密时，可以对相关人员发出禁令。

1836 –16［对禁令禁止下的商业秘密的特殊使用］在特殊情形下，被禁令禁止使用涉案商业秘密的人如果确实存在合理必要的理由需要继续使用该商业秘密时，他必须首先缴纳合理的特殊使用费，而且继续使用该商业秘密的期限不得超出该禁令的有效期间。

1836 –17［损害赔偿的范围］损害赔偿的范围包括：①由侵害商业秘密行为造成的直接损失；②由侵害商业秘密行为导致的直接损失之外的间接损失。

1836 –18［损失数额的估算］对于原告遭受的损失数额，可以参照转让或者许可使用该商业秘密时合理的费用标准来确定。

1836 –19［惩罚性赔偿］如果侵害者以预谋或者恶意的方式侵害商业秘密，实行惩罚性赔偿，赔偿金的数额最高不超过正常赔偿金的 2 倍。

1836 –20［律师费用的承担］如果有证据证明：原告在缺乏诚信的情况下提起商业秘密侵权诉讼；原告或者被告在缺乏诚信的情况下请求终止禁令或者反对终止禁令；被告以预谋或者恶意的方式实施侵害行为，那么符合上述任何条件之一的，合理的律师费用由实施上述行为的一方承担。

1836 –21［诉讼管辖权］对于本法中涉及的民事诉讼案件，联邦地区法院享有一审专属管辖权。

1836 –22［诉讼时效］对于本法中的民事诉讼，诉讼时效为 3 年，自知道或者应当知道侵害行为发生之日起计算。本法中，连续实施的侵害行为可以作为同一侵害行为提起诉讼。

第 1837 条　对美国境外行为的效力

对于发生在美国境外侵害美国公司商业秘密的行为，如果行为者符合下列情形之一的，也适用于本法：①美国公民；②在美国拥有永久居住权的外国人；③基于美国联邦政府、各州政府或者州政府所属的分支机构的法律法规所诞生的单位；④促使侵害行为发生的其他行为发生在美国。

第 1838 条　与其他法律的关系

除了本法第 1833 条中有关"向一个具有合法管辖权的联邦政府、州政府、州政府的分支机构报告涉嫌侵害商业秘密事务的行为"属于合法行为的规定之外,本法的内容不影响和取代任何由美国联邦、州、领地、属地等政府机构颁布实施的法律法规中已有的对侵害商业秘密违法行为的民事或者刑事救济措施,也不影响任何政府雇员依据俗称"信息自由法"的《美国法典》第5篇第552条的规定合法披露信息的权利。

第 1839 条　相关术语的定义

1839 −1[外国政府的机构]是指本质上由外国政府所有、控制、指导、管理、掌握的各类政府所属的部、局、委员会、大学、研究机构,各类协会,各类法律、商业和企业组织,各类团体、公司和实体。

1839 −2[外国政府的代理人]是指外国政府的官员、雇员、代理机构、公务员、代表团成员、代表。

1839 −3[商业秘密]是指各种形式和类型的有关金融、商业、科学、技术、经济或者工程的各类信息,包括式样、计划、资料汇编、程序设备、原理、设计、原型、方法、技术、工艺、程序或代码,无论是有形还是无形,也无论是以物理、电子、图形、照片或者书写的方式进行编撰和储存。同时,还应当具有下列两项条件:①权利人已经对这一秘密信息采取了合理的保密措施;②由于这一秘密信息不被通过披露或者使用该信息能够获取经济利益的其他人所知悉,也不易被他人轻易地通过合法手段所探知,因此,具有现实的或者潜在的经济价值。

1839 −4[商业秘密权利人]是指基于商业秘密公正地拥有合法权利的自然人或者经济实体。

1839 −5[侵害行为]本法中侵害行为包括非法获取、非法使用和非法披露行为,具体包含下列行为:

（1）[非法获取行为]在知道或者应当知道第三方通过不正当的手段获取该商业秘密之后,仍然从第三方处获取该商业秘密。

（2）[非法获取后又擅自披露或者使用的行为]利用不正当的手段获取他人的商业秘密以后,又擅自披露或者使用该商业秘密。

（3）[对他人非法获取的商业秘密进行披露或者使用的行为]在知道或者应当知道该商业秘密是第三方利用不正当的手段获取的情况下,仍然擅自披露或者使用该商业秘密。

(4)[对他人违反保密或者限制使用义务获取的商业秘密进行披露或者使用的行为]在知道或者应当知道该商业秘密是第三方在违反自己承担的保密义务或者限制使用义务的情况下披露的,仍然擅自使用或者进一步披露该商业秘密。

(5)[对从被告处获取的商业秘密进行披露或者使用的行为]在知道或者应当知道该商业秘密是在第三方因为违反自己承担的保密义务或者限制使用义务已经被追究侵权责任的情况下泄露的,仍然擅自使用或者进一步披露该商业秘密。

(6)[对基于偶然或者错误原因获得的商业秘密进行披露或者使用的行为]在一个人的职位发生重要调整之前,基于偶然或者错误的原因使其获得了秘密信息,当他知道或者有理由知道这是一条商业秘密时,擅自使用或者披露该商业秘密。

1839 -6[不正当手段]本法中"不正当行为"的是指下列行为:

(1)包括盗窃、贿赂、欺诈、违反保密义务,或者诱使他人违反保密义务,或者通过电子及其他手段实施的间谍行为。

(2)不包括通过反向工程、独立研发或者其他合法方式获得的相同的商业秘密。

1839 -7[参照的 1946 商标法]本法中《1946 商标法》是指于 1946 年 7 月 5 日批准的,编号为 15 U. S. C. 1051 et seq. ,名称为"提供注册和保护用于商业活动的商标法",以便落实相关国际公约的规定,以及实现保护商标的目的;该法一般称为"1946 商标法",或者"兰哈姆法"。

1839 -8[本法的附则]

(1)条款的修订:美国法典第 18 篇第一部分的章节通过在第 89 章的条款之后插入以下内容进行修正:"90:保护商业秘密……1831"。

(2)有关报告的规定:本法生效后的 2 年和 4 年内,总检察长应当向国会报告依据本法规定收取的罚金数额,以及分配交存于根据 1984 年"犯罪受害者法"第 1402 条设立的犯罪受害者基金中的金额。

(侯仰坤整理并翻译,2018 年 2 月于北京)

本章附录:《1996 经济间谍法》修订综合版原文

ECONOMIC ESPIONAGE ACT OF 1996

(consolidated version in 2018)

SECTION 1. SHORT TITLE.

TITLE I—PROTECTION OF TRADESECRETS

CHAPTER 90—PROTECTION OF TRADE SECRETS

Sec.

§ 1831. Economic espionage.

§ 1832. Theft of trade secrets.

§ 1833. Exceptions to prohibitions.

§ 1834. Criminal forfeiture.

§ 1835. Orders to preserve confidentiality.

§ 1836. Civil proceedings.

§ 1837. Applicability to conduct outside the United States.

§ 1838. Construction with other laws.

§ 1839. Definitions.

§ 1831. Economic espionage

(a) IN GENERAL. —Whoever, intending or knowing that the offense will benefit any foreign government, foreign instrumentality, or foreign agent, know-ingly—

shall, except as provided in subsection (b), be fined not more than $ 5,000,000 or imprisoned not more than 15 years, or both.

(b) ORGANIZATIONS. —Any organization that commits any offense described in subsection (a) shall be fined not more than the greater of $ 10,000,000 or 3 times the value of the stolen trade secret to the organization, including expenses for research and design and other costs of reproducing the trade secret that the organization has thereby avoided.

(1) steals, or without authorization appropriates, takes, carries away, or conceals, or by fraud, artifice, or deception obtains a trade secret;

(2) without authorization copies, duplicates, sketches, draws, photographs, downloads, uploads, alters, destroys, photocopies, replicates, transmits, delivers, sends, mails, communicates, or conveys a trade secret;

(3) receives, buys, or possesses a trade secret, knowing the same to have been stolen or appropriated, obtained, or converted without authorization;

(4) attempts to commit any offense described in any of paragraphs (1) through (3); or

(5) conspires with one or more other persons to commit any offense described in any of paragraphs (1) through (3), and one or more of such persons do any act to effect the object of the conspiracy.

§ 1832. Theft of trade secrets

(a) Whoever, with intent to convert a trade secret, that is related to a product or service used in or intended for use in interstate or foreign commerce, to the economic benefit of anyone other than the owner thereof, and intending or knowing that the offense will, injure any owner of that trade secret, knowingly—

shall, except as provided in subsection (b), be fined under this title or imprisoned not more than 10 years, or both.

(b) the greater of $5,000,000 or 3 times the value of the stolen trade secret to the organization, including expenses for research and design and other costs of reproducing the trade secret that the organization has thereby avoided.

§ 1833. Exceptions to prohibitions

(a) IN GENERAL. —This chapter does not prohibit or create a private right of action for—

(1) any otherwise lawful activity conducted by a governmental entity of the United States, a State, or a political subdivision of a State; or

(2) the disclosure of a trade secret in accordance with subsection (b); and

(b) IMMUNITY FROM LIABILITY FOR CONFIDENTIAL DISCLOSURE OF A TRADE SECRET TO THE GOVERNMENT OR IN A COURT FILING. —

(1) IMMUNITY. —An individual shall not be held criminally or civilly liable under any Federal or State trade secret law for the disclosure of a trade secret that—

(A) is made—

(i) in confidence to a Federal, State, or local government official, either directly or indirectly, or to an attorney; and

(ii) solely for the purpose of reporting or investigating a suspected violation of law; or

(B) is made in a complaint or other document filed in a lawsuit or other proceeding, if such filing is made under seal.

(2) USE OF TRADE SECRET INFORMATION IN ANTI-RETALIA-TION LAWSUIT. —An individual who files a lawsuit for retaliation by an employer for reporting a suspected violation of law may disclose the trade secret to the attorney of the individual and use the trade secret information in the court proceeding, if the individual—

(A) files any document containing the trade secret under seal; and

(B) does not disclose the trade secret, except pursuant to court order.

(3) NOTICE. —

(A) IN GENERAL. —An employer shall provide notice of the immunity set forth in this subsection in any contract or agreement with an employee that governs the use of a trade secret or other confidential information.

(B) POLICY DOCUMENT. —An employer shall be considered to be in compliance with the notice requirement in subparagraph (A) if the employer provides a cross-reference to a policy document provided to the employee that sets forth the employer's reporting policy for a suspected violation of law.

(C) NON-COMPLIANCE. —If an employer does not comply with the notice requirement in subparagraph (A), the employer may not be awarded exemplary damages or attorney fees under subparagraph (C) or (D) of section 1836(b)(3) in an action against an employee to whom notice was not provided.

(D) APPLICABILITY. —This paragraph shall apply to contracts and agreements that are entered into or updated after the date of enactment of this subsection.

(4) EMPLOYEE DEFINED. —For purposes of this subsection, the term "employee" includes any individual performing work as a contractor or consultant for an employer.

(5) RULE OF CONSTRUCTION. —Except as expressly provided for under this subsection, nothing in this subsection shall be construed to authorize, or limit liability for, an act that is otherwise prohibited by law, such as the unlawful access of material by unauthorized means.

§ 1834. Criminal forfeiture

(a) The court, in imposing sentence on a person for a violation of this chapter, shall order, in addition to any other sentence imposed, that the person forfeit to the United States—

(1) any property constituting, or derived from, any proceeds the person obtained, directly or indirectly, as the result of such violation; and

(2) any of the person's property used, or intended to be used, in any manner or part, to commit or facilitate the commission of such violation, if the court in its discretion so determines, taking into consideration the nature, scope, and proportionality of the use of the property in the offense.

(b) Property subject to forfeiture under this section, any seizure and disposition thereof, and any administrative or judicial proceeding in relation thereto, shall be governed by section 413 of the Comprehensive Drug Abuse Prevention and Control Act of 1970 (21 U. S. C. 853), except for subsections (d) and (j) of such section, which shall not apply to forfeitures under this section.

[Note: § 1834 was amended in 2008 as follows " § 1834. Criminal forfeiture: Forfeiture, destruction, and restitution relating to this chapter shall be subject to section 2323, to the extent provided in that section, in addition to any other similar remedies provided by law. "]

§ 1835. Orders to preserve confidentiality

(a) IN GENERAL. —In any prosecutionor other proceeding under this chapter, the court shall enter such orders and take such other action as may be necessary and appropriate to preserve the confidentiality of trade secrets, consistent with the requirements of the Federal Rules of Criminal and Civil Procedure, the Federal Rules of Evidence, and all other applicable laws. An interlocutory appeal by the United States shall lie from a decision or order of a district court authorizing or directing the disclosure of any trade secret.

(b) RIGHTS OF TRADE SECRET OWNERS. —The court may not authorize or direct the disclosure of any information the owner asserts to be a trade secret unless the court allows the owner the opportunity to file a submission under seal that describes the interest of the owner in keeping the information confidential.

No submission under seal made under this subsection may be used in a prosecution under this chapter for any purpose other than those set forth in this section, or otherwise required by law.

The provision of information relating to a trade secret to the United States or the court in connection with a prosecution under this chapter shall not constitute a waiver of trade secret protection, and the disclosure of information relating to a trade secret in connection with a prosecution under this chapter shall not constitute a waiver of trade secret protection unless the trade secret owner expressly consents to such waiver.

§ 1836. Civil proceedings

(a) The Attorney General may, in a civil action, obtain appropriate injunctive relief against any violation of this chapter.

(b) PRIVATE CIVIL ACTIONS. —

(1) IN GENERAL. —An owner of a trade secret that is misappropriated may bring a civil action under this subsection if the trade secret is related to a product or service used in, or intended for use in, interstate or foreign commerce.

(2) CIVIL SEIZURE. —

（A）IN GENERAL. —

（i）APPLICATION. —Based on an affidavit or verified complaint satisfying the requirements of this paragraph, the court may, upon ex parte application but only in extraordinary circumstances, issue an order providing for the seizure of property necessary to prevent the propagation or dissemination of the trade secret that is the subject of the action.

（ii）REQUIREMENTS FOR ISSUING ORDER. —The court may not grant an application under clause（i）unless the court finds that it clearly appears from specific facts that—

（Ⅰ）an order issued pursuant to Rule 65 of the Federal Rules of Civil Procedure or another form of equitable relief would be inadequate to achieve the purpose of this paragraph because the party to which the order would be issued would evade, avoid, or otherwise not comply with such an order;

（Ⅱ）an immediate and irreparable injury will occur if such seizure is not ordered;

（Ⅲ）the harm to the applicant of denying the application outweighs the harm to the legitimate interests of the person against whom seizure would be ordered of granting the application and substantially outweighs the harm to any third parties who may be harmed by such seizure;

（Ⅳ）the applicant is likely to succeed in showing that—

（aa）the information is a trade secret; and

（bb）the person against whom seizure would be ordered—

（AA）misappropriated the trade secret of the applicant by improper means; or

（BB）conspired to use improper means to misappropriate the trade secret of the applicant;

（Ⅴ）the person against whom seizure would be ordered has actual possession of—

（aa）the trade secret; and

（bb）any property to be seized;

（Ⅵ）the application describes with reasonable particularity the matter to be seized and, to the extent reasonable under the circumstances, identifies the location where the matter is to be seized;

(Ⅶ) the person against whom seizure would be ordered, or persons acting in concert with such person, would destroy, move, hide, or otherwise make such matter inaccessible to the court, if the applicant were to proceed on notice to such person; and

(Ⅷ) the applicant has not publicized the requested seizure.

(B) ELEMENTS OF ORDER. —If an order is issued under subparagraph (A), it shall—

(ⅰ) set forth findings of fact and conclusions of law required for the order;

(ⅱ) provide for the narrowest seizure of property necessary to achieve the purpose of this paragraph and direct that the seizure be conducted in a manner that minimizes any interruption of the business operations of third parties and, to the extent possible, does not interrupt the legitimate business operations of the person accused of misappropriating the trade secret;

(ⅲ)(Ⅰ) be accompanied by an order protecting the seized property from disclosure by prohibiting access by the applicant or the person against whom the order is directed, and prohibiting any copies, in whole or in part, of the seized property, to prevent undue damage to the party against whom the order has issued or others, until such parties have an opportunity to be heard in court; and

(Ⅱ) provide that if access is granted by the court to the applicant or the person against whom the order is directed, the access shall be consistent with subparagraph (D);

(ⅳ) provide guidance to the law enforcement officials executing the seizure that clearly delineates the scope of the authority of the officials, including—

(Ⅰ) the hours during which the seizure may be executed; and

(Ⅱ) whether force may be used to access locked areas;

(ⅴ) set a date for a hearing described in subparagraph (F) at the earliest possible time, and not later than 7 days after the order has issued, unless the party against whom the order is directed and others harmed by the order consent to another date for the hearing, except that a party against whom the order has issued or any person harmed by the order may move the court at any time to dissolve or modify the order after giving notice to the applicant who obtained the order; and

(ⅵ) require the person obtaining the order to provide the security determined adequate by the court for the payment of the damages that any person may be entitled to recover as a result of a wrongful or excessive seizure or wrongful or excessive attempted seizure under this paragraph.

(C) PROTECTION FROM PUBLICITY. —The court shall take appropriate action to protect the person against whom an order under this paragraph is directed from publicity, by or at the behest of the person obtaining the order, about such order and any seizure under such order.

(D) MATERIALS IN CUSTODY OF COURT. —

(ⅰ) IN GENERAL. —Any materials seized under this paragraph shall be taken into the custody of the court. The court shall secure the seized material from physical and electronic access during the seizure and while in the custody of the court.

(ⅱ) STORAGE MEDIUM. —If the seized material includes a storage medium, or if the seized material is stored on a storage medium, the court shall prohibit the medium from being connected to a network or the Internet without the consent of both parties, until the hearing required under subparagraph (B)(ⅴ) and described in subparagraph (F).

(ⅲ) PROTECTION OF CONFIDENTIALITY. —The court shall take appropriate measures to protect the confidentiality of seized materials that are unrelated to the trade secret information ordered seized pursuant to this paragraph unless the person against whom the order is entered consents to disclosure of the material.

(ⅳ) APPOINTMENT OF SPECIAL MASTER. —The court may appoint a special master to locate and isolate all misappropriated trade secret information and to facilitate the return of unrelated property and data to the person from whom the property was seized. The special master appointed by the court shall agree to be bound by a non-disclosure agreement approved by the court.

(E) SERVICE OF ORDER. —The court shall order that service of a copy of the order under this paragraph, and the submissions of the applicant to obtain the order, shall be made by a Federal law enforcement officer who, upon making service, shall carry out the seizure under the order. The court may allow State or local law enforcement officials to participate, but may not permit the applicant or any agent of the applicant to participate in the seizure. At the request of law enforcement officials, the court may allow a technical expert who is unaffiliated with the applicant and who is bound by a court-approved non-disclosure agreement to participate in the seizure if the court determines that the participation of the expert will aid the efficient execution of and minimize the burden of the seizure.

(F) SEIZURE HEARING. —

(i) DATE. —A court that issues a seizure order shall hold a hearing on the date set by the court under subparagraph (B)(v).

(ii) BURDEN OF PROOF. —At a hearing held under this subparagraph, the party who obtained the order under subparagraph (A) shall have the burden to prove the facts supporting the findings of fact and conclusions of law necessary to support the order. If the party fails to meet that burden, the seizure order shall be dissolved or modified appropriately.

(iii) DISSOLUTION OR MODIFICATION OF ORDER. —

A party against whom the order has been issued or any person harmed by the order may move the court at any time to dissolve or modify the order after giving notice to the party who obtained the order.

(iv) DISCOVERY TIME LIMITS. —The court may make such orders modifying the time limits for discovery under the Federal Rules of Civil Procedure asmay be necessary to prevent the frustration of the purposes of a hearing under this subparagraph.

(G) ACTION FOR DAMAGE CAUSED BY WRONGFUL SEIZURE. —A person who suffers damage by reason of a wrongful or excessive seizure under this paragraph has a cause of action against the applicant for the order under which such seizure was made, and shall be entitled to the same relief as is provided under section 34(d)(11) of the Trade-mark Act of 1946 [15 U. S. C. 1116(d)

(11)]. The security posted with the court under subparagraph (B)(vi) shall not limit the recovery of third parties for damages.

(H) MOTION FOR ENCRYPTION. —A party or a person who claims to have an interest in the subject matter seized may make a motion at any time, which may be heard exparte, to encrypt any material seized or to be seized under this paragraph that is stored on a storage medium. The motion shall include, when possible, the desired encryption method.

(3) REMEDIES. —In a civil action brought under this subsection with respect to the misappropriation of a trade secret, a court may—

(A) grant an injunction—

(i) to prevent any actual or threatened misappropriation described in paragraph (1) on such terms as the court deems reasonable, provided the order does not—

(I) prevent a person from entering into an employment relationship, and that conditions placed on such employment shall be based on evidence of threatened misappropriation and not merely on the information the person knows; or

(II) otherwise conflict with an applicable State law prohibiting restraints on the practice of a lawful profession, trade, or business;

(ii) if determined appropriate by the court, requiring affirmative actions to be taken to protect the trade secret; and

(iii) in exceptional circumstances that render an injunction inequitable, that conditions future use of the trade secret upon payment of a reasonable royalty for no longer than the period of time for which such use could have been prohibited;

(B) award—

(i)(I) damages for actual loss caused by the misappropriation of the trade secret; and

(II) damages for any unjust enrichment caused by the misappropriation of the trade secret that is not addressed in computing damages for actual loss; or

(ii) in lieu of damages measured by any other methods, the damages caused by the misappropriation measured by imposition of liability for a reasonable royalty for the misappropriator's unauthorized disclosure or use of the trade secret;

（C）if the trade secret is willfully and maliciously misappropriated, award exemplary damages in an amount not more than 2 times the amount of the damages awarded under subparagraph（B）; and

（D）if a claim of the misappropriation is made in bad faith, which may be established by circumstantial evidence, a motion to terminate an injunction is made or opposed in bad faith, or the trade secret was willfully and maliciously misappropriated, award reasonable attorney's fees to the prevailing party.

（c）JURISDICTION. —The district courts of the United States shall have original jurisdiction of civil actions brought under this section.

（d）PERIOD OF LIMITATIONS. —A civil action under subsection（b）may not be commenced later than 3 years after the date on which the misappropriation with respect to which the action would relate is discovered or by the exercise of reasonable diligence should have been discovered. For purposes of this subsection, a continuing misappropriation constitutes a single claim of misappropriation.

§ 1837. Applicability to conduct outside the United States

This chapter also applies to conduct occurring outside the United States if—

（1）the offender is a natural person who is a citizen or permanent resident alien of the United States, or an organization organized under the laws of the United States or a State or political subdivision thereof; or

（2）an act in furtherance of the offense was committed in the United States.

§ 1838. Construction with other laws

Except as provided in section 1833（b）, this chapter shall not be construed to preempt or displace any other remedies, whether civil or criminal, provided by United States Federal, State, commonwealth, possession, or territory law for the misappropriation of a trade secret, or to affect the otherwise lawful disclosure of information by any Government employee under section 552 of title 5（commonly known as the Freedom of Information Act）.

§ 1839. Definitions

As used in this chapter—

(1) the term "foreign instrumentality" means any agency, bureau, ministry, component, institution, association, or any legal, commercial, or business organization, corporation, firm, or entity that is substantially owned, controlled, sponsored, commanded, managed, or dominated by a foreign government;

(2) the term "foreign agent" means any officer, employee, proxy, servant, delegate, or representative of a foreign government;

(3) the term "trade secret" means all forms and types of financial, business, scientific, technical, economic, or engineering information, including patterns, plans, compilations, program devices, formulas, designs, prototypes, methods, techniques, processes, procedures, programs, or codes, whether tangible or intangible, and whether or how stored, compiled, or memorialized physically, electronically, graphically, photographically, or in writing if—

(A) the owner thereof has taken reasonable measures to keep such information secret; and

(B) the information derives independent economic value, actual or potential, from not being generally known to, and not being readily ascertainable through proper means by another person who can obtain economic value from the disclosure or use of the information.

(4) the term "owner", with respect to a trade secret, means the person or entity in whom or in which rightful legal or equitable title to, or license in, the trade secret is reposed.

(5) the term "misappropriation" means—

(A) acquisition of a trade secret of another by a person who knows or has reason to know that the trade secret was acquired by improper means; or

(B) disclosure or use of a trade secret of another without express or implied consent by a person who—

(i) used improper means to acquire knowledge of the trade secret;

(ii) at the time of disclosure or use, knew or had reason to know that the knowledge of the trade secret was—

(I) derived from or through a person who had used improper means to acquire the trade secret;

（Ⅱ）acquired under circumstances giving rise to a duty to maintain the secrecy of the trade secret or limit the use of the trade secret; or

（Ⅲ）derived from or through a person who owed a duty to the person seeking relief to maintain the secrecy of the trade secret or limit the use of the trade secret; or

（iii）before a material change of the position of the person, knew or had reason to know that—

（Ⅰ）the trade secret was a trade secret; and

（Ⅱ）knowledge of the trade secret had been acquired by accident or mistake;

（6）the term "improper means"—

（A）includes theft, bribery, misrepresentation, breach or inducement of a breach of a duty to maintain secrecy, or espionage through electronic or other means; and

（B）does not include reverse engineering, independent derivation, or any other lawful means of acquisition; and

（7）the term "Trademark Act of 1946" means the Act entitled "An Act to provide for the registration and protection of trademarks used in commerce, to carry out the provisions of certain international conventions, and for other purposes, approved July 5, 1946（15 U. S. C. 1051 et seq.）（commonly referred to as the 'Trademark Act of 1946' or the 'Lanham Act'）".

（b）CLERICAL AMENDMENT. —The table of chapters at the beginning part I of title 18, United States Code, is amended by inserting after the item relating to chapter 89 the following:

90. Protection of trade secrets...........................1831.

（c）REPORTS. —Not later than 2 years and 4 years after the date of the enactment of this Act, the Attorney General shall report to Congress on the amounts received and distributed from fines for offenses under this chapter deposited in the Crime Victims Fund established by section 1402 of the Victims of Crime Act of 1984（42 U. S. C. 10601）.

（Consolidated version completed by Yangkun Hou in February 2018, Beijing）

'03

美国全国性适用的
商业秘密保护示范法

第一章 《侵权法重述》(节选)

第一节 《侵权法重述》简介

一、《侵权法重述》的基本特征

(1)《侵权法重述》是由美国法学会编撰的一部法律文献,供美国的法官、律师、教师和其他法律工作者适用、理解、应用和学习研究法律时使用,作为一部法律文献,其自身不具有法律效力。但是,按照美国的立法传统,各个州的议会可以把这些法律文献的内容列入本州的立法中,从而使这些法律文献的内容成为本州的法律内容得以作为法律进行应用和实施。

(2)美国法学会成立于1923年,由一批著名的美国法官、律师和教师组成,目的是作为一个长期的组织促进美国法律的完善和进步①。长期以来,美国法学会围绕美国现有的法律体系,已经编撰了多种不同的法律文献,范围涉及美国印第安人法、仲裁、商业组织和公司法、集体诉讼、商法、竞争法、合同法、刑法、选举法、就业和劳动法、伦理法、外交关系法、保险法、知识产权法、侵权法、诉讼法等众多法律领域②,在编撰过程中对于相关的法律进行学理性分析和解释,以及对于应用中的疑难问题进行分析和界定,以便于公众理解和把握。

美国法学会建立了自己的官方网站,在其官方网站上公开出售自己所编纂的各类法律文献,也对自己的工作成果,即所编纂的法律文件进行介绍和展示,其网址是"https://www. ali. org/"。

---

① The American Law Institute, Creation, https://www. ali. org/about-ali/creation/,访问日期:2018年5月6日。

② The American Law Institute, Areas of Law, https://www. ali. org/about-ali/creation/,访问日期:2018年5月6日。

（3）本书所收录的是这种法律文献中，属于侵权法范围内的涉及商业秘密侵权责任的一个具体的条款，即《侵权法重述》（第一次）这一法律文献中的第757 条。

美国法学会对各种不同法律的重述不仅构成了一个重述的系列，而且就是对于"侵权法"的重述，即《侵权法重述》自身也已经构成了一个重述的系列，这一系列由两部分构成，一部分是时间序列构成的重述系列，至今已经有了第一次重述，第二次重述和第三次重述。在第三次重述中又涉及对多种法律责任的重述，即由对于不同法律内容的重述所构成的重述系列，例如，《侵权法重述》（第二次）的编纂内容是"侵权行为"，而《侵权法重述》（第三次）中则包含有较多的内容，形成了多个独立的文本，它们分别是：①《侵权法重述》（第三次），侵权责任：分摊责任；②《侵权法重述》（第三次），侵权责任：经济损害责任；③《侵权法重述》（第三次），侵权责任：身体和情感伤害的责任；④《侵权法重述》（第三次），侵权责任：产品责任；⑤《侵权法重述》（第三次），侵权责任：对人故意侵权的责任①。

本书涉及的文献属于第一次编纂的文献中的内容，因此，笔者称其为《侵权法重述》（第一次）第 757 条，该条款的具体内容是关于擅自披露或者使用他人商业秘密的一般责任的规定，该法律文献发表于 1939 年 5 月 13 日，也被称为 1939 年文本。

二、通过各州立法方式适用《侵权法重述》的各州名单

表 1　利用本州法律通过立法保护商业秘密的各州名单②

编号	中文州名	英文州名	各州保护商业秘密的 州法律名称和立法日期
1	亚拉巴马州	Alabama	Ala. Code 1975，§§ 8 - 27 - 1 to 8 - 27 - 6（1993）

---

① The American Law Institute：All Restatements，https：//www. ali. org/publications/#publication-type-restatements/，访问日期：2018 年 5 月 6 日。

② WIPO：WIPO Lex，http：//www. wipo. int/wipolex/en/，访问日期：2018 年 2 月 7 日。

续表

编号	中文州名	英文州名	各州保护商业秘密的州法律名称和立法日期
2	阿拉斯加州	Alaska	Alaska Stat. §§ 45. 50. 910 to 45. 50. 945（1994）
3	亚利桑那州	Arizona	Ariz. Rev. Stat. Ann. §§ 44 – 401 to 44 – 407（1994）
4	阿肯色州	Arkansas	Ark. Code Ann. §§ 4 – 75 – 601 to 4 – 75 – 607（Michie 1993）
5	加利福尼亚州	California	Cal. Civ. Code §§ 3426 to 3426. 10.（West 1995）
6	科罗拉多州	Colorado	Col. Rev. Stat. §§ 7 – 74 – 101 to 7 – 74 – 110（1986）
7	康涅狄格州	Connecticut	Conn. Gen. Stat. §§ 35 – 50 to 35 – 58（1987）
8	特拉华州	Delaware	6Del. Cod. Ann. §§ 2001 to 2009（1993）
9	哥伦比亚特区	District of Colombia	D. C. Code 1981，§§ 48 – 501 to 48 – 510（1995）
10	佛罗里达州	Florida	Fla. Stat. ch. §§ 688.001 to 688.009（1994）
11	佐治亚州	Georgia	Ga. Code Ann. §§ 10 – 1 – 760 et seq
12	夏威夷州	Hawaii	Hawaii Rev. Stat. §§ 482B – 1 to 482B – 9（1992）
13	爱达荷州	Idaho	Idaho Code §§ 48 – 801 to 48 – 807（1994）
14	伊利诺伊州	Illinois	Ill. Rev. Stat. ch. §§ 1065/1 to 1065/9（1993）
15	印第安纳州	Indiana	Ind. Code. §§ 24 – 2 – 3 – 1 to 1257 24 – 2 – 3 – 8（1994）
16	艾奥瓦州	Iowa	Iowa Code. §§ 550.1 to 550.8（1994）
17	堪萨斯州	Kansas	Kan. Stat. Ann. §§ 60 – 3320 to 60 – 3330（1994）

续表

编号	中文州名	英文州名	各州保护商业秘密的州法律名称和立法日期
18	肯塔基州	Kentucky	Ky. Rev. Stat. Ann. §§ 365. 880 to 365. 900（Michie/Bobbs-Merrill1994）
19	路易斯安那州	Louisiana	La. Rev. Stat. Ann. §§ 51：1431 to 51：1439（West 1987 and Supp. 1995）
20	缅因州	Maine	Me. Rev. Stat. Ann. tit. 10 §§ 1541 to 1548（West 1994）
21	马里兰州	Maryland	Md. Code Ann. Com. Law II §§ 11 – 1201 to 11 – 1209（1990）
22	马萨诸塞州	Massachusetts	Mass. Gen. Laws ch. 93 §§ 42 – 42A（1993）
23	密歇根州	Michigan	Provided through common law
24	明尼苏达州	Minnesota	Minn. Stat. §§ 75 – 26 – 1 to 75 – 26 – 19（1992）
25	密西西比州	Mississippi	Miss. Code. Ann. §§ 325C. 01 to 325C. 08（1993）
26	密苏里州	Missouri	Provided through common law
27	蒙大拿州	Montana	Mont. Code §§ 30 – 12 – 401 to 30 – 14 – 409（1993）
28	内布拉斯加州	Nebraska	Neb. Rev. Stat. §§ 87 – 501 et seq
29	内华达州	Nevada	Nev. Rev. Stat. §§ 600A. 010 to 600A. 100（1991）
30	新罕布什尔州	New Hampshire	N. H. Rev. Stat. Ann. §§ 350 – B：1 to 350 – B：9（1994）
31	新泽西州	New Jersey	Provided through common law
32	新墨西哥州	New Mexico	N. M. Stat. Ann. §§ 57 – 3A – 1 to 57 – 3A – 7（Michie 1994）
33	纽约州	New York	Provided through common law
34	北卡罗来纳州	North Carolina	N. C. Gen. Stat. §§ 66 – 152 to 66 – 157（1994）
35	北达科他州	North Dakota	N. D. Cent. Code §§ 47 – 25. 1 – 01 to 47 – 25. 1 – 08（1993）

续表

编号	中文州名	英文州名	各州保护商业秘密的 州法律名称和立法日期
36	俄亥俄州	Ohio	Ohio Rev. Code Ann. §§ 1333. 61 to 1333. 69（1994）
37	俄克拉荷马州	Oklahoma	Okla. Stat. Tit. 78 §§ 85 to 94（1991）
38	俄勒冈州	Oregon	Or. Rev. Stat. §§ 646. 461 to 646. 475（1993）
39	宾夕法尼亚州	Pennsylvania	Provided through common law
40	罗得岛州	Rhode Island	R. I. Gen. Laws §§ 6 – 41 – 1 to 6 – 41 – 11（1992）
41	南卡罗来纳州	South Carolina	S. C. Code Ann. §§ 39 – 8 – 1 to 39 – 8 – 11（1993）
42	南达科他州	South Dakota	S. D. Codified Laws 37 – 29 – 1 to 37 – 29 – 11（1994）
43	田纳西州	Tennessee	Provided through common law
44	得克萨斯州	Texas	Provided through common law; see also, Tex. Penal Code Ann. , 167. 31. 05
45	犹他州	Utah	Utah Code Ann. §§ 13 – 24 – 1 to 13 – 24 – 9（1992）
46	佛蒙特州	Vermont	Provided through common law
47	弗吉尼亚州	Virginia	Va. Code Ann. §§ 59. 1 – 336 to 59. 1 – 343（Michie 1986）
48	华盛顿州	Washington	Wash. Rev. Code §§ 19. 108. 010 to 19. 108. 940（1993）
49	西弗吉尼亚州	West Virginia	W. Va. Code §§ 47 – 22 – 1 to 47 – 22 – 10（1992）
50	威斯康星州	Wisconsin	Wis. Stat. Ann. §§ 134. 90（West 1989）
51	怀俄明州	Wyoming	Provided through common law

（注：其中包括哥伦比亚特区，其被视为一个州。）

第二节 《侵权法重述》(节选)译文

《侵权法重述》(第一次)(节选第 757 条)

(第九篇 对商业关系的干扰,第一部分 贸易惯例,

第 36 章 一般事务的贸易惯例)

第 757 条 对擅自披露或者使用他人商业秘密法律责任的一般规定

任何人,在未获得合法许可的情况下,擅自实施下列行为,披露或者使用他人的商业秘密,应当对该商业秘密权利人承担责任。

(1)通过不正当的手段发现了他人的商业秘密;

(2)商业秘密权利人基于对他的信任把该商业秘密告知了他,但是,他却违背这种信任擅自使用或者对外披露该商业秘密;

(3)当他从第三方获悉该商业秘密时就已经发现这是一件商业秘密,并且发现该第三方是利用不正当的手段获知的该商业秘密,或者发现该第三方对外披露该商业秘密的行为违背了其所承担的保密责任;

(4)当他获知该商业秘密时就已经发现这是一件商业秘密,而且发现是由于出现了差错才把这一商业秘密错误地告知了他。

(侯仰坤翻译,2018 年 3 月于北京)

本章附录:《侵权法重述》(节选)原文

Restatement of the Law-Torts

Restatement (First) of Torts

Division 9. Interference With Business Relations

Part 1. By Trade Practices

Chapter 36. Miscellaneous Trade Practices

§ 757. Liability for Disclosure or Use of Another's Trade Secret —General Principle

One who discloses or uses another's trade secret, without a privilege to do so, is liable to the other if

(a) he discovered the secret by improper means, or

(b) his disclosure or use constitutes a breach of confidence reposed in him by the other in disclosing the secret to him, or

(c) he learned the secret from a third person with notice of the facts that it was a secret and that the third person discovered it by improper means or that the third person's disclosure of it was otherwise a breach of his duty to the other, or

(d) he learned the secret with notice of the facts that it was a secret and that its disclosure was made to him by mistake.

第二章　《统一商业秘密法》

第一节　《统一商业秘密法》简介

一、《统一商业秘密法》的基本内容和特征

（一）生效时间

（1）《统一商业秘密法》于 1979 年 8 月 9 日经过美国全国统一州法律委员会批准后生效；然后又对其进行了一次修订，现在适用的是 1985 年修订版本，这一修订版本由美国全国统一州法律委员会起草，于 1985 年 8 月 2 日至 9 日在美国明尼苏达州的明尼阿波利斯市召开的第 94 届美国全国统一州法律委员会年会上获得批准。

（2）《统一商业秘密法》（1985 年修订版本）中所附的前言和对每一条款的诠释由美国律师协会完成，并于 1986 年 2 月 11 日在马里兰州的巴尔德摩市批准生效。

（二）主要特征

（1）《统一商业秘密法》既不是由美国国会和总统批准生效的联邦法律，也不是由州议会和州长批准生效的州法律，而是由美国全国统一州法律委员会起草并批准的一部准法律，其基本特征类似于《侵权法重述》，都属于示范法。

（2）《统一商业秘密法》在内容上涉及的都是有关商业秘密保护的民事措施和相关规定，没有涉及商业秘密刑事保护的问题。

（3）由于有关《统一商业秘密法》的起草和审查批准经过了比较长期的调查和论证，具有比较高的理论和实践基础，并且是由美国全国统一州法律委员会负责起草并批准的，因此其内容比较科学合理，具有比较强的实用性，而且具有全国性的可适用性。

二、《统一商业秘密法》的适用方式和特点

（1）由于其自身不是一部具有强制力的法律,因此,美国全国统一州法律委员会批准后是向全国所有的州进行推荐实施,而不是直接命令各州实施。

（2）截至 2018 年 7 月,在美国全国 50 个州中,已经有 47 个州,以及哥伦比亚特区、波多黎各和维尔京群岛立法适用了《统一商业秘密法》。只有马萨诸塞州（Massachusetts）,北卡罗来纳州（North Carolina）和纽约州（New York）三个州还没有专门立法适用《统一商业秘密法》①。

（3）虽然自 2016 年 5 月 11 日起,《2016 商业秘密保护法》开始生效,但是,由于《2016 商业秘密保护法》主要涉及国际贸易和不同州之间的贸易中的商业秘密民事纠纷问题,而在各个州内部的大量贸易中的商业秘密民事纠纷问题则仍然需要参照或者适用《统一商业秘密法》,如前所述,这是由联邦和各州之间拥有不同的立法权所导致的局面。当然,随着《2016 商业秘密保护法》的颁布和实施,由于《2016 商业秘密保护法》在内容上比《统一商业秘密法》更加丰富和完整,当州法院在面对复杂的商业秘密纠纷案件时,如果在《统一商业秘密法》中缺失相应规定时,州法院的法官应当有权参照甚至适用《2016 商业秘密保护法》中的相关规定。

三、通过各州立法方式适用《统一商业秘密法》的中英文名单②

表 2　适用《统一商业秘密法》1979 年文本的州

编号	中文州名	英文州名
1	阿肯色州	Arkansas
2	加利福尼亚州	California
3	康涅狄格州	Connecticut

---

① The National Conference of Commissioners on Uniform State Laws, Legislative Fact Sheet-Trade Secrets Act, http://www. uniformlaws. org/LegislativeFactSheet. aspx？ title = Trade% 20Secrets% 20Act, 访问日期:2018 年 7 月 16 日。

② WIPO, WIPO LEX, http://www. wipo. int/wipolex/en/, 访问日期:2018 年 3 月 14 日。

编号	中文州名	英文州名
4	印第安纳州	Indiana
5	路易斯安那州	Louisiana
6	罗得岛州	Rhode Island
7	华盛顿州	Washington

表3 适用《统一商业秘密法》1985 年文本的州

编号	中文州名	英文州名
1	亚拉巴马州	Alabama
2	阿拉斯加州	Alaska
3	亚利桑那州	Arizona
4	科罗拉多州	Colorado
5	特拉华州	Delaware
6	哥伦比亚特区	District of Columbia
7	佛罗里达州	Florida
8	佐治亚州	Georgia
9	夏威夷州	Hawaii
10	爱达荷州	Idaho
11	伊利诺伊州	Illinois
12	艾奥瓦州	Iowa
13	堪萨斯州	Kansas
14	肯塔基州	Kentucky
15	缅因州	Maine
16	马里兰州	Maryland
17	密歇根州	Michigan
18	明尼苏达州	Minnesota
19	密西西比州	Mississippi
20	密苏里州	Missouri

编号	中文州名	英文州名
21	蒙大拿州	Montana
22	内布拉斯加州	Nebraska
23	内华达州	Nevada
24	新罕布什尔州	New Hampshire
25	新墨西哥州	New Mexico
26	北达科他州	North Dakota
27	俄亥俄州	Ohio
28	俄克拉荷马州	Oklahoma
29	俄勒冈州	Oregon
30	宾夕法尼亚州	Pennsylvania
31	南卡罗来纳州	South Carolina
32	南达科他州	South Dakota
33	田纳西州	Tennessee
34	美属维尔京群岛	U. S. Virgin Islands
35	犹他州	Utah
36	佛蒙特州	Vermont
37	弗吉尼亚州	Virginia
38	西弗吉尼亚州	West Virginia
39	威斯康星州	Wisconsin
40	怀俄明州	Wyoming
41	新泽西州	New Jersey
42	得克萨斯州	Texas

表4　2010年参照适用《统一商业秘密法》的州

编号	中文州名	英文州名
1	马萨诸塞州	Massachusetts
2	纽约州	New York

第二节 《统一商业秘密法》诞生过程译文

序　言

一、在美国建立全国统一的商业秘密保护法的必要性①

作为对发明者向公众公开其发明创造的一种交换,联邦专利法授予发明者有效期为 17 年的发明专有权。但是,一旦这一专利权被法院认定为无效,这一发明的内容就等于向竞争对手无条件地进行了公开。鉴于大量的专利权被法院认定为无效,现在,许多企业选择利用保护商业秘密的州法律来保护其具有商业价值的信息。编号为 416 U. S. 470(1974)的 *Kewanee Oil Co. v*(诉). *Bicron Corp.* 一案宣示了下列一种理念,即由于无论是美国的宪法,还是美国的联邦专利法,都没有对利用各州的法律来保护商业秘密作出规定,因此可以得出这样的结论:无论是可专利性的内容还是不可专利性的内容都能够借助商业秘密获得保护。这种立法局面在客观上提高了利用商业秘密保护有价值的信息的影响力。

编号为 99 S. Ct. 1096,201 USPQ 1(1979)的 *Aronson v. Quick Point Pencil Co* 案件中重申了 *Kewanee Oil Co. v. Bicron Corp.* 一案中的理念,即联邦专利法并不影响商业秘密的保护和使用,通过合同约定,一方可以通过支付许可使用费的方式来使用另一方的商业秘密。

尽管各个州的商业秘密法对不同州之间的州际商业贸易具有重要的引导作用,但是,由于各个州是相互独立平等的法律实体,因此,任何一个州的法律都不能对州际贸易拥有管辖权。而且,各个州的商业秘密保护法本身都还有许多值得完善之处。这是因为各个州的商业秘密保护法是相互独立的,而且基于各个州的不同和差异,导致各个州的法律发展不平衡。首先,在商业比较发达的州,其商业秘密保护法就相对比较完善,而在那些人口较少,或者以农业为主

---

① 基于中国法律的习惯,为了便于读者理解下文中的含义,在此添加了本标题。

的州中商业秘密的保护则比较差。其次,即使在那些已经发生过重要的商业秘密诉讼案件的一些州中,也存在着一些对商业秘密保护极度不确定的因素,以及对损害赔偿十分不合理的情况。显然,这些因素都严重地制约着对商业秘密的合理保护。

一位评论者对于"对盗窃商业秘密的行为应当制定法定的解决方案"评论道:"在经济和技术的压力下,尽管现有的普通法和损害赔偿的法律措施处于令人难以满意和比较混乱的状态,工商业界仍然在积极地寻求利用商业秘密来获得保护,因此,非常需要尽快制定出科学合理的全国统一的商业秘密法。"[120 U. Pa. L. Rev. 378,380-81(1971)]。

然而,尽管存在着社会的这种客观需求,但是在商业秘密保护中最被人们广泛接受的保护规则,即《侵权法重述》第757条中的内容,却从《侵权法重述》中被删除(见[2d(1978)])。

现在,在《统一商业秘密法》中编纂了普通法中有关商业秘密保护的基本原则,并且保留了与专利法的基本区别。例如,按照《统一商业秘密法》和普通法的规定,对于同一信息,多个人有权同时分别对其主张商业秘密权利和主张法律保护;对合法获得的产品利用反向工程的手段从中获取商业秘密属于合法行为。

对于《统一商业秘密法》中确定的商业秘密侵害行为,在编号为187 USPQ 47,48(D. Md. 1975)的 *Miller v. Owens-Illinois, Inc.* 一案中,以及编号为182 USPQ 135,144-45,(N. D. Ill. 1974)的 *Wesley-Jessen, Inc., v. Reynolds* 一案中都列举了免责的情形。

《统一商业秘密法》中确定的商业秘密侵害行为是指在知道或者应当知道属于他人商业秘密的情况下,使用不正当的手段获取这一秘密信息,或者未经授权擅自披露或使用这一秘密信息的行为。但是在上述两个案件中,法官确认了两种例外情形:①被告在先独立地发现了相同的秘密信息,可以免除被告侵害原告商业秘密的责任;②原告正常地生产销售自己的产品以后,被告通过反向工程获取了其中的商业秘密时,被告不承担侵害原告商业秘密的责任。

在《统一商业秘密法》中,承担侵害商业秘密责任的条件是:①商业秘密本身必须存在;②他人采用本法规定的不正当手段获取,或者使用,或者披露了商业秘密。

如果仅仅是对未获得批准的专利的条目进行复制则不构成侵害商业秘密的行为。

正如传统的有关保护商业秘密的相关规定,在《统一商业秘密法》中也包含了一般性的概念。《统一商业秘密法》的主要贡献在于:①统一确立了"商业秘密"和"商业秘密侵害行为"的含义;②对各种类型的财产合同和准合同关系,以及在普通法中适用的侵害信托关系的非合同责任都规定了统一的时效制度;③借鉴了那些能够合理地处理商业秘密侵害补偿问题的相关案件的有益成果。

二、《统一商业秘密法》的诞生历史和发展经过

(一)"统一商业秘密法特别委员会"的诞生和发展历史

1968 年 2 月 17 日,美国律师协会的小组委员会向大会的执行委员会提交了一份报告,报告的内容是关于"建立统一商业秘密保护法"的建议。

具体的建议内容如下:"这一法案由美国律师协会主席皮尔斯,委员乔尔纳和艾力森·邓汉姆起草,由美国律师协会专利法委员会递交给小组委员会。这件事反映出早在 1966 年美国律师协会专利法委员会就曾经广泛地讨论过下列问题:美国律师协会支持建立一部统一的用以保护商业秘密的州法律,用以制止非法披露或盗用商业秘密、技巧以及被他人进行过保密处理的其他信息的行为。"专利法委员会决定先不对这一法案进行投票表决,而是由专利法委员会对相关问题进行进一步的研究,同时向大会建议应当考虑如下的几个问题:①当前,无论是联邦性的法律还是各州的法律,都在不断地发展和完善之中。②但是,在专利和商业秘密之间还有一个基本性的政策冲突没有解决,即当前的州法律在保护商业秘密时倾向于对创新性技术秘密的保护,而联邦的专利政策则是鼓励人们公开他们的创新性技术。解决这种冲突的方法就是要在这一冲突之间设计一种比较合理的折中方案,这就需要联邦政府和州政府都要为此努力进行一定的立法改革。③对于这种折中方案,专利委员会还没有明确的方案。同时为了调查和起草保护商业秘密的统一法案,建议设立一个专门的委员会,并且与美国律师协会的专利委员会、公司银行和商业委员会,以及反不正当竞争法委员会建立联系。

大会执行委员会收到小组委员会提交的建议案以后,随后在这次于 1968

年 2 月 17 日和 18 日,在伊利诺伊州的芝加哥市召开的年中会议上对这一议案进行了投票表决。经过表决,决定批准成立一个有关统一商业秘密保护法案的专门委员会,以便调查解决起草这一法案时所可能遇到的问题,并指导建立与美国律师协会的专利委员会、公司银行和商业委员会、反不正当竞争法委员会的联系。这一专门委员会成立时,聘请了理查德教授,他来自华盛顿州的西雅图市所属的科士威,现在他是唯一的一位仍然在这一专门委员会工作的原始委员。在随后的时间中,专门委员会的委员不断地发生更替,除了理查德教授以外,后来加入专门委员会的另一位委员,是来自艾奥瓦州艾奥瓦市的年轻的理查德福·道尔教授,自从加入专门委员会以后他也一直工作至今。

(二)《统一商业秘密法》的表决通过

专门委员会成立以后,各项工作一直在进行中,并且完成了"统一商业秘密保护法案"的草案。全国统一州法委员会委员会议在 1972 年 8 月 10 日的周四下午召开,"统一商业秘密保护法案"被作为第一读的三个法案之一进行了一读。然而,随后由于一系列的原因,专门委员会的工作处于停滞状态,更加遗憾的是,专门委员会的原始主席于 1974 年 12 月 7 日过世。到了 1976 年,专门委员会的工作又活跃起来,又对草案进行了多次修改和完善,并且在 1978 年召开的全国统一州法委员会年度委员会议上提交了比较完善的草案第五稿作为立法建议稿。

尽管"统一商业秘密保护法案"已经在 1972 年的大会上进行了一读,但是,专门委员会建议,由于时间间隔比较长,主张把这次在 1978 年年会上的讨论作为一读。大会同意了这一建议,这一立法建议稿将在 1979 年年会上进行产生效力的二读,其如果通过将颁布实施。

1979 年 8 月 9 日,《统一商业秘密法》获得批准并被推荐给美国所有的州参照实施。随后,经过律师和法官们的广泛讨论,专门委员会建议对 1979 年的版本进行修订,修订其中第 2 条的第 2 项,第 3 条的第 1 项,第 7 条,第 11 条,明确界定这一法案的立法目的。

1985 年 8 月 8 日,上述 4 条修改建议获得批准,诞生了《统一商业秘密法》(1985 年版本),并被推荐给美国所有的州参照实施。

（三）具体起草专家名单、批准时间和联系方式的附录

（1）《统一商业秘密法》由全国统一州法律委员会起草，于 1985 年 8 月 2 日至 9 日在明尼苏达州的明尼阿波利斯市召开的第 94 届年会上获得批准，并推荐在全国各州实施。

本法中所附的序言和对每一条款的诠释由美国律师协会于 1986 年 2 月 11 日在马里兰州的巴尔德摩市批准。

（2）参与《统一商业秘密法》（1985 年修订文本）起草工作的委员会专家共有六人，他们分别是林得思·冠恩（委员会主席）、托马斯·卡文迪、罗伯特·康奈尔、理查德·科士威、理查德·杜勒、卡莱尔·瑞恩和威廉姆·皮尔斯（委员会办公室执行主任）。

最后，被批准的正式文本的复印件都可以从全国统一州法律委员会获取，地址是美国伊利诺伊州芝加哥市 645 北密歇根大街 510 号，全国统一州法律委员会；邮编：60611；电话：（312）321 - 9710。

（侯仰坤翻译，2018 年 3 月于北京）

第三节　《统一商业秘密法》正文及诠释的译文①

《统一商业秘密法》
（1985 年修订版本）

第 1 条　定义

除非另有规定以外,本法中的下列术语含义如下:

1.1［不正当手段］不正当手段包括盗窃、贿赂、欺诈、违反保密义务,或者诱使他人违反保密义务,或者通过电子及其他手段实施的间谍行为。

1.2［侵害行为］侵害行为包括非法获取、使用和披露行为,本法中具体包含下列行为:

（1）［非法获取行为］在知道或者应当知道第三方通过不正当的手段获取该商业秘密之后,仍然从第三方处获取该商业秘密。

（2）［非法获取后又擅自披露或者使用的行为］利用不正当的手段获取他人的商业秘密以后,又擅自披露或者使用该商业秘密。

（3）［对他人非法获取的商业秘密进行披露或者使用的行为］在知道或者应当知道该商业秘密是第三方利用不正当的手段获取的情况下,仍然擅自披露或者使用该商业秘密。

（4）［对他人违反保密或者限制使用义务获取的商业秘密进行披露或者使用的行为］在知道或者应当知道该商业秘密是第三方在违反自己承担的保密义务或者限制使用义务的情况下披露的,仍然擅自使用或者进一步披露该商业秘密。

（5）［对从被告处获取的商业秘密进行披露或者使用的行为］在知道或者应当知道该商业秘密是在第三方因为违反自己承担的保密义务或者限制使用

---

① 《统一商业秘密法》的原文标题中没有"诠释"的字样,但在原文正文中附带了对条款的诠释,为了准确地标出条文中所实际包含的内容,在译文的标题中添加了"诠释"字样。另外,基于中国法律的逻辑关系和法律条文的格式习惯,在保持原文内容不变的前提下,在译文中对原文中的部分格式和条款顺序做了调整。

义务已经被追究侵权责任的情况下泄露的,仍然擅自使用或者进一步披露该商业秘密。

(6)[对基于偶然或者错误获得的商业秘密进行披露或者使用的行为]在一个人的职位发生重要调整之前,基于偶然或者错误的原因使其获得了秘密信息,当他知道或者有理由知道这是一条商业秘密时,擅自地使用或者披露该商业秘密。

1.3[人的含义]本法中"人"是指自然人、公司、商业信托机构、房地产公司、信托基金、合伙机构、协会、合资企业、政府、政府部门或机构,或者任何其他法律的或者商业的实体。

1.4[商业秘密]本法中"商业秘密"是指包括配方、模型、材料汇编、程序、设计、方法、技术或工艺在内的各类信息;这些信息同时具有下列特征:①自身具有现实的或者潜在的经济价值,而且属于秘密信息;②对于那些能够利用它们获取经济利益的人来说,采取正常的获取方式难以获取或者知悉它的内容;③权利人已经采取了合理的保密措施。

对第 1 条的诠释

商业秘密法所内含的基本精神就是"从事商业活动要保持和遵守基本的商业道德准则"。在编号为 416 U. S. 470(1974)的 *Kewanee Oil Co. v. Bicron Corp.* 一案中就体现着这种原则。在《侵权法重述》第 757 条的评述中总结出如下结论:"对所有的不正当行为进行统一的汇总和分类是不可能的。"因此,在本法第 1 条的 1.1 中只是列举了其中的部分类型。

为了更好地认识和判断不正当行为,也可以从正当行为的角度入手加以分析,下面将讨论与商业秘密有关的主要的正当行为。

1. 正当地获取受保护的商业秘密的行为主要包括下列五种行为:

(1)通过独立研发获得了该商业秘密,实际上是获得了与该商业秘密内容相同的信息。

(2)通过"反向工程"获得了该商业秘密。"反向工程"就是对已有的产品通过采用反向拆解和分析的方式破解其中内涵的技术、工艺和原理的方法。值得说明的是,用于"反向工程"的产品本身必须是合法产品,即应当是通过公平合理及合法的方式获得的产品,如是在公开的市场上以合理的价格购买的。

（3）在获得商业秘密所有人的许可使用以后，从而获知了该商业秘密。

（4）通过对公开使用或者公开展览中的产品及相关材料的观察研究，从中获知了该商业秘密。

（5）从公开发表的文献资料中获知了该商业秘密。

2. 在不正当的行为中包含着一些自身属于合法行为的行为类型，只是在特定的环境下，这些行为的结果侵害了他人的商业秘密，其才被视为"不正当的行为"。例如，当一家企业正在建造自己的工厂时，它的竞争对手为了获取工厂的布局就故意地派出飞机从正在建造的工厂上空飞越和侦查，这种行为显然属于不正当的行为。当然，如果不涉及侦查的目的，飞机单纯地飞越某一企业工厂上空的行为应当属于合法行为。参见编号为 431 F. 2d 1012（CA5，1970），cert. den. 400 U. S. 1024（1970）的 *E. I. du Pont de Nemours & Co. , Inc. v. Christopher* 案件。另外，由于商业秘密一经公开，其秘密性就将被破坏，也就不再属于商业秘密。因此，擅自披露他人商业秘密的行为属于侵害行为。

对于商业秘密权利人来说，如果他所实施的保密措施是合理的，调整某人的职务也是合理的。但是，某人由于职务的变动却偶然地或者错误地获知了商业秘密，显然，在这一过程中商业秘密权利人自身并没有过错，在这种情况下，如果这一被调整职务的人再擅自地使用或者披露该商业秘密就明确地构成了侵害行为。

本法中的商业秘密概念摆脱了《侵权法重述》（第一次）中要求商业秘密必须在企业中"连续使用"的条件限制，显然这样有利于对那些还没有机会，或者还没有能力实施其商业秘密的权利人的保护。另外，商业秘密还包括那些来自失败教训中但是具有商业价值的信息，例如，通过一项花费了较长时间和较高成本的研究结果证明某一工艺不具有可行性，那么，这一信息对于竞争对手来说就很有价值。

参见编号为 510 F. 2d 894（CA10，1975），Per curiam，cert. dismissed 423 U. S. 802（1975）的 *Telex Corp. v. IBM Corp.* 一案。在此案中，被告的侵权产品虽然未销售，但是原告主张被告应当支付其所节省的研发成本。虽然任何人都可以通过自己独立的研发活动获取与他人内容相同的商业秘密，并以此合法地对自己的商业秘密独立地享有权利，但是，通过非法地获取他人的商业秘密并进行使用就节省了应当支出的研发成本。

本法中"方法和技术"的概念中包含着"诀窍"的意思。

"不为一般的人利用正当的方式所获悉或者容易地探知",这一要求并不是指只有当商业秘密被社会公众所知悉以后,该商业秘密才不复存在,而是指只要那些能够利用该商业秘密获取经济利益的人已经普遍地知悉了它,该商业秘密就已经被破坏,不再属于商业秘密。例如,铸造金属的方法并不为社会公众所知悉,从社会公众的角度而言其似乎属于一种技术秘密,但是,对于铸造行业的技术人员来说则容易知悉和掌握,因此,这一技术并不属于商业秘密。

如果某一信息在商业期刊、参考书籍或者出版发行的材料中出现,该信息就比较容易被知悉和了解。通常情况下,某一产品一旦在市场上被销售,它的特性也就容易被了解。另外,如果某一反向工程需要花费较长的时间和较高的成本,完成这一反向工程的人就可以享有其所获取的商业秘密的权利。

最后,通过合理的手段来保护商业秘密的行为还包括明确地告知员工哪些事项属于商业秘密,并且规定除了"基于工作需要必须知道"的情形以外,禁止人们接触商业秘密;未经允许禁止他人进入工厂等。然而,通过产品展览,出版发行商业期刊,对外广告以及其他不谨慎的行为向公众展示相关信息的做法都会影响到对商业秘密的保护。

保护商业秘密的合理性标准是"具体环境下的合理性",法院并不要求原告采取过分昂贵的程序来防止现实中存在的经济间谍行为。可以参见前面所述的 *E. I. du Pont de Nemours & Co. , Inc. v. Christopher* 案件。另外,在商业秘密使用中,合理的标准包括禁止向一般的员工披露商业秘密,在许可他人使用时也应当要求被许可人符合一定的保密要求。

第 2 条 禁令救济

2.1［禁令的一般规定］凡是对商业秘密存在现实或者潜在侵害的行为都应当被禁止。商业秘密终止后,应当事人的申请,法院可以终止禁令。但是,为了消除侵害行为给被告带来的非法商业优势,可以合理地延长禁令的期限。

2.2［利用许可使用费换取禁令下的继续使用］在特殊情况下,可以允许被告通过支付合理使用费的方式来换取其继续使用该商业秘密,但是,继续使用的期限不得超过禁令的有效期限。特殊情况包括但不限于,在被告知道或者应当知道侵害行为之前,已经发生了重要事项,导致再实施禁令不够公平。

2.3[法院主动颁布禁令]在合适的情况下,基于保护商业秘密的需要,法院可以主动地颁布禁令。

对第2条的诠释

利用禁令来禁止被告对商业秘密的进一步使用或者披露已经成为常用的救济方式。从时间上来说,禁令分为惩罚性的无期限的禁令和有期限的禁令两种类型。法院颁布实施的无期限的禁令,如编号为494 S. W. 2d 204(Tex. Civ. App. 1973)的 *Elcor Chemical Corp. v. Agri-Sul*, *Inc.* 一案。有期限的禁令就是具有一定有效期间的禁令措施,除了禁止被告继续使用或者披露商业秘密以外,还在于消除被告基于侵害行为所获取的竞争优势,这类禁令措施可以参见编号为506 F. 2d 471(CA9, 1974)的 *K-2 Ski Co. v. Head Ski Co.*, *Inc.* 一案。

无论是哪一类禁令措施,禁令的最长期限都不得超过被告通过独立研发或者合法的反向工程手段获得该商业秘密时的期间。

禁令的有效期应当尽可能地延长,直到将被告基于侵害行为所获得的商业优势和领先使用时间全部消除以后才是合理的结束时间,这是有关禁令合理期限的一般性原则。

当为了消除被告的"领先使用优势"而延长禁令期限时,如果该商业秘密已经被善意的竞争者们普遍地知悉,或者已经被人们通过合法地使用产品时借助反向工程所获悉,那么,此时禁令措施应当终止。

例如,假如 A 拥有一项具有经济价值的商业秘密,同一行业的 B 和 C 并不知悉。如果后来 B 侵害了该商业秘密并被禁止使用,后来 C 通过合法的反向工程获取了该商业秘密,在此情况下,对 B 实施的禁令措施延续到 B 非法获取的领先优势被完全消除时为止。此时,原商业秘密已经不再是商业秘密,任何人都可以利用它获取经济利益。当 B 的非法优势被消除因而禁令措施也终止的情况下,可以继续利用反不正当竞争措施限制 B 对原商业秘密的使用。

如果侵害人并没有从侵害行为中获得领先优势,或者在法院判决时诚实的竞争者已经赶上了侵害人的生产经营状态,在这种情况下,如果继续披露或者使用该商业秘密已经不会再对商业秘密权利人造成损害,因此,无须实施禁令措施。[参见编号为 484 F. 2d 1057(CA7, 1973)的 *Northern Petrochemical Co. v. Tomlinson* 一案]此案中,审判法院不同意颁布初步禁令的部分原因在于侵害人自己工厂的爆炸阻止了其基于侵害行为获取领先优势的可能性。在编号为[185 USPQ 391(Mich. App. 1974)]的 *Kubik, Inc. v. Hull* 一案中,确认利用合法的反向工程破译原告商业秘密的行为,一般只对禁令措施的有效期限产生影响,而不对损害赔偿产生影响。

本条 2.2 款涉及处理特殊情形下的禁令问题,在有些特殊情形下,虽然允许被告继续非法使用商业秘密将进一步损害商业秘密权利人的利益,但是,如果利用禁令禁止被告继续使用将会产生新的不公平。

这里的特殊情形包括下列两类事项:①重要的公共利益需要被告继续使用该商业秘密;②个人在未知商业秘密被侵害的情况下善意地获取了该商业秘密,如果被禁止使用将会损害其合法权益。在编号为 152 USPQ 830(N. Y. Sup. Ct. 1967)的 *Republic Aviation Corp. v. Schenk* 一案中,阐述了基于公共利益免予发出禁令的理由。法院认为,禁止被告向美国提供飞机武器控制系统会给在越南的军事人员带来危险。

基于上述第二种特殊情形,法院虽然可以不对善意地获取商业秘密的被告颁发禁令,但是,在此情况下,商业秘密权利人可以通知被告该商业秘密已经处于被侵害的状态,而且自被告收到该通知之日起,被告就成为实际侵害该商业秘密的侵害人。

在衡量受害人的利益与已经善意地利用自己的能力使用该商业秘密的被告的利益的基础上,法院可能决定善意的被告可以继续使用该商业秘密。

对于那些善意地获得被侵害商业秘密的被告来说,本法中 2.2 款的规定与《侵权法重述》(第一次)中第 758 条第 2 项的原则一致;但是两种法律又有所不同,《侵权法重述》对所有的基于善意地购买或者使用该商业秘密而向其他侵害该商业秘密的人支出过合理费用的人实施完全彻底的禁令豁免,但是,本法则未作出这类规定。

本法 2.2 款的原则受到编号为 452 F. 2d 621 (CA7, 1971)的 *Forest Laboratories, Inc. v. Pillsbury Co.* 一案的支持,在此案件中,被告因为收购一个

公司的资产,而在此资产中包含着一项已经被秘密地非法泄露的商业机密,此时,该被告不能因为在收购资产时已经支付了合理的对价而免除其基于侵害商业秘密的禁令。

适用2.2款时,法院有权慎重地决定让侵害者支付一定数额的合理使用费然后继续使用被侵害的商业秘密。同时,正如所有的禁令救济措施一样,只有当侵害者通过实施侵害行为获得了竞争优势,并且基于这一竞争优势的存续期间来决定禁令的有效期限才是合适的。

在有些情况下,对于有些善意地购买了已被他人侵害的商业秘密的购买者,法院一旦认为不应当对该购买者颁布禁令时,基于同样的考虑,也就无须颁布缴纳使用费以后有条件地进行使用的禁令(利用使用费折抵禁令)。此时可以参照编号为 198 USPQ 618(N. J. Super. Ct. 1976)的 *Prince Manufacturing, Inc. v. Automatic Partner, Inc.* 一案。在此案中,在商业秘密被通过产品销售的方式公开泄露以后,购买者从侵害者的资产管理人处购买了侵害者的资产,在这种情况下,购买者无须对商业秘密的泄露承担法律责任。

在2.2款"利用许可使用费换取禁令下的继续使用"中提出的"合理使用费"与在下面第3条中提出的"合理赔偿费用"是不同的,"合理赔偿费用"将在下面对第3条的诠释中进行讨论。

基于2.3款的规定,法院可以颁布强制性的禁令要求侵害者把侵害所得的成果归还给受害人,例如,窃取的图纸、照片和资料等。

如果基于某一内容相同的商业秘密同时存在着多位不同的所有人,那么,只有商业秘密遭到侵害的这一权利人才有权利主张侵害救济。

第3条　损害赔偿

3.1[经济赔偿额的计算]除非在知道或者应当知道由他人造成的侵害行为发生之前,由于存在重要的情形致使被告承担经济补偿明显不公平之外,受害人都有权向被告主张经济赔偿,经济赔偿包括实际损失和未被实际损失包含的被告的不当得利两部分,当赔偿损失的数额难以计算时,可以把合理的许可使用费数额作为参照依据。

3.2[惩罚性赔偿]如果存在故意和恶意的侵害,法院可以作出惩罚性赔偿,数额不超过一般赔偿额的两倍。

对第 3 条的诠释

正如对禁令措施的一般性要求一样,经济赔偿一般的合理期限也应当限定于商业秘密的有效期限以内;除此之外,如果侵害者基于侵害行为比那些未实施侵害行为的诚实的竞争者获取了一定的非法竞争优势,那么,经济赔偿的合理期限则可以延长到这一竞争优势被完全消除之日;计算受害人的实际损失或者侵害者的不当得利时都应当以这一期限为准。可以参照编号为 172 F. 2d 150 (CA2,1949)的 *Conmar Products Corp. v. Universal Slide Fastener Co.* 一案,在此案中,法院认为如果把商业秘密申请了专利,自在专利中被公开之日期起,不得再作为计算商业秘密经济损失的期限。但是,在编号为 454 S. W. 2d 540(Mo. 1970)的 *Carboline Co. v. Jarboe* 一案中,法院认为经济赔偿的合理期间截至被告通过合法途径获取了该商业秘密时为止。

原告可以同时向法院提出损害赔偿请求和禁令请求,其中,损害赔偿包括原告的实际损失和被告的非法净利润(不当得利)。但是,值得注意的是,一旦两种请求都被法院批准,那么通常情况下,在核算损害赔偿的有效期限时,由于在禁令期限内被告的侵害行为被禁止,因此就应当扣除禁令的有效期限这一时间阶段。

根据 3.1 款确定的原则,只要没有重复计算,原告的损害赔偿总额应当包括原告的实际损失和被告的不当得利。例如,在编号为 525 F. 2d 432(CA9, 1975)的 *Tri-Tron International v. Velto* 一案中,法院就把原告的损失与被告的非法收益合并计算并以此作为原告的损害金额进行赔偿。

在有些案件中,由于应当对被告实施惩罚性赔偿措施,因而可以把原告的损失与被告的不当得利进行重复计算,以达到双倍赔偿这一惩罚的目的。例如,在编号为 510 F. 2d 894(CA10, 1975)(per curiam), cert. dismissed, 423 U. S. 802(1975)的案件中,对于侵害者利用其侵害的商业秘密所生产的产品占有原告产品市场的行为,法官在计算原告的损失总额时采取了一种大体性的总体计算的方式进行估算,其中包括了被告基于侵害行为所节省的研发成本的费用。但是,在该案中法官也明确表示不采用惩罚性赔偿,即对同一费用不在原告的损失和被告的不当得利之中重复计算。

原告也可以借助许可使用费的金额作为依据来主张损害赔偿的数额,利用这种方式进行主张时,原告应当提供有关该许可使用费的合理有效的证据材料。

值得注意的是,这里依据许可使用费计算损害赔偿额的方法与第 2 条 2.2 款"利用许可使用费换取禁令下的继续使用"中对已经被实施禁令以后,再通过缴纳许可使用费来换取继续使用该商业秘密的方法是两类完全不同的方法。

首先,这种借助许可使用费来计算损害赔偿额的方法是可以经常使用的一类计算方法,而在 2.2 款"利用许可使用费换取禁令下的继续使用"中所做的规定只能适用于特殊情形中,一般情况下不能适用。

其次,两者对应的不是同一行为,损害赔偿是对过去已经发生的侵害行为所造成的损失进行的赔偿,而在 2.2 款"利用许可使用费换取禁令下的继续使用"中规定的则是对未来实施行为所预先缴纳的许可使用费。

最后,如果被告符合 2.2 款"利用许可使用费换取禁令下的继续使用"的条件,那么,对于他被通知该商业秘密属于被侵害的商业秘密之前所实施的行为,也不再承担损害赔偿责任。

除此之外,损害赔偿和禁令救济是两类不同的法律责任救济措施,因此,无论禁令救济是否获得批准,都不影响法院实施损害赔偿措施。对于被告来说,如果他是在不知道该商业秘密已经被他人侵害的情况下善意地获得了该商业秘密,而且存在着重要的特殊情形,那么,他既可以请求法院免除对其实施禁令措施,也可以请求法院免除其承担损害赔偿的责任。可以参见编号为 172 F. 2d 1950(CA2,1949)的 *Conmar Products Corp. v. Universal Slide Fastener Co.* 一案,在此案中,雇员违背了其与前雇主签订的保守前雇主商业秘密的义务,但是,因为新雇主在接到该雇员实施侵害前雇主商业秘密的通知之前已经真诚地承诺将支出 4 万美元用于研发该商业秘密,因此,新雇主对于雇员侵害其前雇主的商业秘密行为不承担法律责任。

对于故意或者恶意实施的侵害行为,3.2 款授权法院可以实施惩罚性赔偿,除了实际损失以外,再给予不超过实际损失两倍的赔偿。这条规定的依据是联邦专利法的内容,即使可能有陪审团参加案件的审理,法官也有权力自由地裁定三倍的赔偿额。对此,可以参考《美国法典》(1976)第 35 篇第 284 条的相关规定。

同样的要求是,即使对于内容相同的商业秘密分别存在着多位不同的权利人,但是,也只有实际遭受到侵害的那位权利人有权获得赔偿。

第 4 条　律师费用的承担

存在下列行为之一的,法院责令其承担对方合理的律师费用:①故意和恶意地实施侵害他人商业秘密的行为;②恶意地主张取消法院颁布的禁令,或者抵制禁令;③恶意地提起商业秘密侵权诉讼。

对第 4 条的诠释

第 4 条允许法院在下列特定的情形下判令败诉方承担胜诉方合理的律师费用,这些特定的行为包括:恶意地提起侵权诉讼;恶意地主张终止法院颁布的禁令措施;故意和恶意地实施侵害他人商业秘密的行为。

对于故意和恶意地实施的侵害行为,法院在决定让其承担合理的律师费用之后,还应当考虑使其承担惩罚性赔偿的幅度。另外,根据专利法的规定,即使是有陪审团参与审理的案件,法院也可以考虑让败诉方承担胜诉方的合理的律师费的问题,这一规定在商业秘密侵权案件中同样可以适用,可以参考《美国法典》(1976)第 35 篇第 285 条的相关规定。

第 5 条　保持商业秘密的秘密性

在诉讼期间,法院应当采取合理的方式保护涉案商业秘密的秘密性,具体可以采取下列措施:①对展示商业秘密的程序颁布保密令;②采取不公开的(秘密性的)听证程序;③对司法程序中记录的所有材料都进行签字密封;④命令参与诉讼的任何人,未经法院的事先批准都不得擅自披露该商业秘密。

对第 5 条的诠释

如果没有有效的保密措施做保障,原本值得人们信赖的商业秘密侵权诉讼活动就会丧失信誉,甚至导致新的危害后果。在制定保密措施时,法院应当确保为答辩人提供充分的案件材料以便使其能够合理地为自己进行辩护,并且应当为案件事实充分地提供已经掌握的材料以便查明案情。除了法律中规定的应当说明的技术内容以外,在这些案件中,法院应当限制向双方的律师及其助手披露商业秘密,可以任命一位与双方当事人都无利害关系的专家作为特别第三方来了解原告的商业秘密的内容,并且与被告涉嫌的信息内容进行比对,然后把比对的结果向法官进行汇报。

第6条　诉讼时效

自知道或者应当知道侵害行为发生之日起3年内,应当提起侵权诉讼。本法中持续进行的侵害行为属于一项侵害行为。

对第6条的诠释

目前,存在的争议焦点是商业秘密侵害行为是否属于一个持续的侵害行为。在编号为407 F. 2d 288(CA9, 1969)的 *Monolith Portland Midwest Co. v. Kaiser Aluminum & Chemical Corp.* 一案中,根据加利福尼亚州的法律规定,本案不是持续的侵害行为,本案中的时效期限最早可以从侵害行为最初发生之日起开始计算。在编号为371 F. 2d 950(CADC, 1966), cert. den., 386 U. S. 911(1967)的 *Underwater Storage, Inc. v. U. S. Rubber Co.* 一案中,法院认为属于持续侵害行为,根据持续侵害行为的一般规则,具体到其中的某一具体侵害行为时,它的时效期限最早从这一侵害行为实际发生之日起计算。

本法中并不把一个持续存在的侵害行为的持续存在时间列为诉讼时效时间,而是把受害人知道或者有合理的理由应当知道该侵害行为存在时的时间作为诉讼时效的开始时间。如果客观上已经把发生侵害行为的通知送达受害人,那么,从通知送达之日起,就应当开始计算诉讼时效,在此之后的3年期限内,受害人应当有充足的时间依法保护自己的合法权利。

第7条　与其他法律的关系

7.1[本法与各州法的关系]除了下列7.2款中的特殊规定以外,凡是在各州法律中对于侵害商业秘密的民事救济措施所规定的侵权救济、返还原主救济和其他法律规定与本法的规定相冲突的,都以本法的规定为准。

7.2[不属于本法规范的事项]下列事项不属于本法规范的范围:①无论是否基于侵害商业秘密的行为而产生的合同赔偿;②基于侵害商业秘密行为之外的其他民事行为而导致的民事赔偿;③无论是否基于侵害商业秘密的行为而产生的刑事赔偿。

对第 7 条的诠释

本法不涉及由于侵害商业秘密而导致的刑事赔偿问题,也不包含所有的民事赔偿问题,本法的立法目的就在于保护那些具有一定竞争意义的秘密信息。例如,本法不适用那些基于明示或者暗示的合同条款所自愿约定的权利义务,即使在这类合同条款中涉及不得泄露商业秘密或者不得实施竞业竞争等行为的内容,这类合同纠纷也由其他法律管辖,而不是由本法管辖。当然,本法更不适用于与商业秘密无关的民事纠纷,例如,代理人与委托人之间的委托合同纠纷等。

第 8 条　构建全国各州统一的法律

本法的目的在于在全国范围的各个州内通过各州的立法建立起一套在各州之间内容相同的保护商业秘密的民事法律救济制度。

第 9 条　本法的名称

本法命名为"统一商业秘密法"。

第 10 条　条款的相对独立性

如果本法中的任一条款,或者某些条款对某一人或者某一情形的实施出现不合法的情况,这些条款并不影响其他条款或者实施的有效性,基于此,本法的条款之间存在一定的相对独立性。

第 11 条　本法的溯及力

本法于 1985 年 8 月 9 日由全国统一州法律委员会批准生效。本法不具有溯及力。对于本法生效前已经发生的侵害行为不具有效力;对于本法生效前已经发生,并且延续到本法生效后的侵害行为也不具有效力。

对第 11 条的诠释

本法只对其生效之后发生的商业秘密侵害行为有效。对于本法生效之前发生并且已经结束的侵害行为,以及在本法生效之前已经发生,但是一直持续到本法生效之后的侵害行为,本法都不发生效力。

第 12 条　废止(以后的内容废止)。

(侯仰坤翻译,2018 年 3 月于北京)

本章附录一:《统一商业秘密法》诞生过程原文

UNIFORM TRADE SECRETS ACT

WITH 1985 AMENDMENTS

PREFATORY NOTE

A valid patent provides a legal monopoly for seventeen years in exchange for public disclosure of an invention. If, however, the courts ultimately decide that the Patent Office improperly issued a patent, an invention will have been disclosed to competitors with no corresponding benefit. In view of the substantial number of patents that are invalidated by the courts, many businesses now elect to protect commercially valuable information through reliance upon the state law of trade secret protection. Kewanee Oil Co. v. Bicron Corp., 416 U. S. 470 (1974), which establishes that neither the Patent Clause of the United States Constitution nor the federal patent laws pre-empt state trade secret protection for patentable or unpatentable information, may well have increased the extent of this reliance.

The recent decision in Aronson v. Quick Point Pencil Co. ,99 S. Ct. 1096, 201 USPQ 1 (1979) reaffirmed Kewanee and held that federal patent law is not a barrier to a contract in which someone agrees to pay a continuing royalty in exchange for the disclosure of trade secrets concerning a product.

Notwithstanding the commercial importance of state trade secret law to interstate business, this law has not developed satisfactorily. In the first place, its development is uneven. Although there typically are a substantial number of reported decisions in states that are commercial centers, this is not the case in less populous and more agricultural jurisdictions. Secondly, even in states in which there has been significant litigation, there is undue uncertainty concerning the parameters of trade secret protection, and the appropriate remedies for misappropriation of a trade secret. One commentator observed:

"Under technological and economic pressures, industry continues to rely on trade secret protection despite the doubtful and confused status of both common law and statutory remedies. Clear, uniform trade secret protection is urgently needed...."

Comment, "Theft of Trade Secrets: The Need for a Statutory Solution", 120 U. Pa. L. Rev. 378, 380 – 81 (1971).

In spite of this need, the most widely accepted rules of trade secret law, § 757 of the Restatement of Torts, were among the sections omitted from the Restatement of Torts, 2d (1978).

The Uniform Act codifies the basic principles of common law trade secret protection, preserving its essential distinctions from patent law. Under both the Act and common law principles, for example, more than one person can be entitled to trade secret protection with respect to the same information, and analysis involving the "reverse engineering" of a lawfully obtained product in order to discover a trade secret is permissible. Compare Uniform Act, Section 1 (2) (misappropriation means acquisition of a trade secret by means that should be known to be improper and unauthorized disclosure or use of information that one should know is the trade secret of another) with Miller v. Owens-Illinois, Inc. , 187 USPQ 47,48 (D. Md. 1975) (alternative holding) (prior, independent discovery a complete defense to liability for misappropriation) and Wesley-Jessen, Inc. , v. Reynolds,182 USPQ 135,144 – 45, (N. D. Ill. 1974) (alternative holding) (unrestricted sale and lease of camera that could be reversed engineered in several days to reveal alleged trade secrets preclude relief for misappropriation).

For liability to exist under this Act, a Section 1 (4) trade secret must exist and either a person's acquisition of the trade secret, disclosure of the trade secret to others, or use of the trade secret must be improper under Section 1 (2). The mere copying of an unpatented item is not actionable.

Like traditional trade secret law, the Uniform Act contains general concepts. The contribution of the Uniform Act is substitution of unitary definitions of trade secret and trade secret misappropriation, and a single statute of limitations for the various property, quasicontractual, and violation of fiduciary relationship theories of noncontractual liability utilized at common law. The Uniform Act also codifies the results of the better reasoned cases concerning the remedies for trade secret misappropriation.

The History of the Special Committee on the Uniform Trade Secrets Act

On February 17, 1968, the Conference's subcommittee on Scope and Program reported to the Conference's Executive Committee as follows:

"14. Uniform Trade Secrets Protection Act.

This matter came to the subcommittee from the Patent Law Section of the American Bar Association from President Pierce, Commissioner Joiner and Allison Dunham. It appears that in 1966 the Patent Section of the American Bar Association extensively discussed a resolution to the effect that 'the ABA favors the enactment of a uniform state law to protect against the wrongful disclosure or wrongful appropriation of trade secrets, know-how or other information maintained in confidence by another.' It was decided, however, not to put such a resolution to a vote at that time but that the appropriate Patent Section Committee would further consider the problem. In determining what would be appropriate for the Conference to do at this juncture, the following points should be considered:

(1) At the present much is going on by way of statutory development, both federally and in the states.

(2) There is a fundamental policy conflict still unresolved in that the current state statutes that protect trade secrets tend to keep innovations secret, while our federal patent policy is generally designed to encourage public disclosure of innovations. It may be possible to devise a sensible compromise between these two basic policies that will work, but to do so demands coordination of the statutory reform efforts of both the federal government and the states.

（3）The Section on Patents, the ABA group that is closest to this problem, is not yet ready to take a definite position.

It is recommended that a special committee be appointed to investigate the question of the drafting of a uniform act relating to trade secret protection and to establish liaison with the Patent Law Section, the Corporation, Banking and Business Law Section, and the Antitrust Law Section of the American Bar Association. "

The Executive Committee, at its Midyear Meeting held February 17 and 18, 1968, in Chicago, Illinois, "voted to authorize the appointment of a Special Committee on Uniform Trade Secrets Protection Act to investigate the question of drafting an act on the subject with instructions to establish liaison with the Patent Law Section, the Corporation, Banking and Business Law Section, and the Antitrust Law Section of the American Bar Association. " Pursuant to that action, a Special Committee was appointed, which included Professor Richard Cosway of Seattle, Washington, who is the only original Committee member to serve to the present day. The following year saw substantial changes in the membership of the Committee. Professor Richard F. Dole, Jr. ,of Iowa City,Iowa,became a member then and has served as a member ever since.

The work of the Committee went before the Conference first on Thursday afternoon, August 10, 1972, when it was one of three Acts considered on first reading. Thereafter, for a variety of reasons, the Committee became inactive, and, regrettably, its original Chairman died on December 7, 1974. In 1976, the Committee became active again and presented a Fifth Tentative Draft of its proposed bill at the 1978 Annual Meeting of the National Conference of Commissioners on Uniform State Laws.

Despite the fact that there had previously been a first reading, the Committee was of the opinion that, because of the lapse of time, the 1978 presentation should also be considered a first reading. The Conference concurred, and the bill was proposed for final reading and adoption at the 1979 Annual Meeting.

On August 9,1979, the Act was approved and recommended for enactment in all the states. Following discussions with members of the bar and bench, the Special Committee proposed amendments to Sections 2(b), 3(a), 7 and 11 that clarified the intent of the 1979 Official Text. On August 8, 1985, these four clarifying amendments were approved and recommended for enactment in all the states.

Appendix

UNIFORM TRADE SECRETS ACT

WITH 1985 AMENDMENTS

Drafted by the

NATIONAL CONFERENCE OF COMMISSIONERS

ON UNIFORM STATE LAWS

and by it

Approved and Recommended for Enactment

in All the States

At its

ANNUAL CONFERENCE

MEETING IN ITS NINETY-FOURTH YEAR

IN MINNEAPOLIS, MINNESOTA

AUGUST 2 – 9, 1985

With Prefatory Note and Comments

Approved by the American Bar Association

Baltimore, Maryland, February 11, 1986

UNIFORM TRADE SECRETS ACT

WITH 1985 AMENDMENTS

The Committee that acted for the National Conference of Commissioners on Uniform State Laws in preparing the Uniform Trade Secrets Act with 1985 Amendments was as follows:

LINDSEY COWEN, 24 Ridgewood Drive, Cartersville, GA 30120, Chairman

THOMAS E. CAVENDISH, 31st Floor, 41 South High Street, Columbus, OH 43215

ROBERT H. CORNELL, 25th Floor, 50 California Street, San Francisco, CA 94111

RICHARD COSWAY, University of Washington, School of Law, Seattle, WA 98105

RICHARD F. DOLE, JR., University of Houston, Law Center, 4800 Calhoun, Houston, TX 77004

CARLYLE C. RING, JR., Room 322 – D, 5390 Cherokee Avenue, Alexandria, VA 22312, President(Member Ex Officio)

WILLIAM J. PIERCE, University of Michigan, School of Law, Ann Arbor, MI 48109, Executive Director

Final, approved copies of all Uniform and Model Acts and other printed matter issued by the Conference may be obtained from:

NATIONAL CONFERENCE OF COMMISSIONERS

ON UNIFORM STATE LAWS

645 North Michigan Avenue, Suite 510

Chicago, Illinois 60611

(312)321 – 9710

本章附录二:《统一商业秘密法》正文及诠释的原文

UNIFORM TRADE SECRETS ACT
WITH 1985 AMENDMENTS
（The 1985 Amendments are Indicated by Underscore and Strikeout）

TABLE OF CONTENTS

SECTION 1. DEFINITIONS.

As used in this［Act］, unless the context requires otherwise：

（1）"Improper means" includes theft, bribery, misrepresentation, breach or inducement of a breach of a duty to maintain secrecy, or espionage through electronic or other means；

(2)"Misappropriation" means:

(i) acquisition of a trade secret of another by a person who knows or has reason to know that the trade secret was acquired by improper means; or

(ii) disclosure or use of a trade secret of another without express or implied consent by a person who

(A) used improper means to acquire knowledge of the trade secret; or

(B) at the time of disclosure or use, knew or had reason to know that his knowledge of the trade secret was

(I) derived from or through a person who had utilized improper means to acquire it;

(II) acquired under circumstances giving rise to a duty to maintain its secrecy or limit its use; or

(III) derived from or through a person who owed a duty to the person seeking relief to maintain its secrecy or limit its use; or

(C) before a material change of his [or her] position, knew or had reason to know that it was a trade secret and that knowledge of it had been acquired by accident or mistake.

(3) "Person" means a natural person, corporation, business trust, estate, trust, partnership, association, joint venture, government, governmental subdivision or agency, or any other legal or commercial entity.

(4) "Trade secret" means information, including a formula, pattern, compilation, program, device, method, technique, or process, that:

(i) derives independent economic value, actual or potential, from not being generally known to, and not being readily ascertainable by proper means by, other persons who can obtain economic value from its disclosure or use, and

(ii) is the subject of efforts that are reasonable under the circumstances to maintain its secrecy.

COMMENT

One of the broadly stated policies behind trade secret law is "the maintenance of standards of commercial ethics. " Kewanee Oil Co. v. Bicron Corp. , 416 U. S. 470(1974). The Restatement of Torts, Section 757, Comment(f), notes: "A complete catalogue of improper means is not possible," but Section 1(1) includes a partial listing.

Proper means include:

1. Discovery by independent invention;

2. Discovery by "reverse engineering", that is, by starting with the known product and working backward to find the method by which it was developed. The acquisition of the known product must, of course, also be by a fair and honest means, such as purchase of the item on the open market for reverse engineering to be lawful;

3. Discovery under a license from the owner of the trade secret;

4. Observation of the item in public use or on public display;

5. Obtaining the trade secret from published literature.

Improper means could include otherwise lawful conduct which is improper under the circumstances; e. g. , an airplane overflight used as aerial reconnaissance to determine the competitor's plant layout during construction of the plant. E. I. du Pont de Nemours & Co. , Inc. v. Christopher, 431 F. 2d 1012(CA5, 1970), cert. den. 400 U. S. 1024(1970). Because the trade secret can be destroyed through public knowledge, the unauthorized disclosure of a trade secrets also a misappropriation.

The type of accident or mistake that can result in a misappropriation under Section 1(2)(ii)(C) involves conduct by a person seeking relief that does not constitute a failure of efforts that are reasonable under the circumstances to maintain its secrecy under Section 1(4)(ii).

The definition of "trade secret" contains a reasonable departure from the Restatement of Torts(First) definition which required that a trade secret be "continuously used in one's business. " The broader definition in the proposed Act extends protection to a plaintiff who has not yet had an opportunity or acquired the means to put a trade secret to use. The definition includes information that has commercial value from a negative viewpoint, for example the results of lengthy and expensive research which proves that a certain process will not work could be of great value to a competitor.

Cf. Telex Corp. v. IBM Corp., 510 F. 2d 894 (CA10, 1975) per curiam, cert. dismissed 423 U. S. 802 (1975) (liability imposed for developmental cost savings with respect to product not marketed). Because a trade secret need not be exclusive to confer a competitive advantage, different independent developers can acquire rights in the same trade secret.

The words "method, technique" are intended to include the concept of "know-how."

The language "not being generally known to and not being readily ascertainable by proper means by other persons" does not require that information be generally known to the public for trade secret rights to be lost. If the principal persons who can obtain economic benefit from information are aware of it, there is no trade secret. A method of casting metal, for example, may be unknown to the general public but readily known within the foundry industry.

Information is readily ascertainable if it is available in trade journals, reference books, or published materials. Often, the nature of a product lends itself to being readily copied as soon as it is available on the market. On the other hand, if reverse engineering is lengthy and expensive, a person who discovers the trade secret through reverse engineering can have a trade secret in the information obtained from reverse engineering.

Finally, reasonable efforts to maintain secrecy have been held to include advising employees of the existence of a trade secret, limiting access to a trade secret on "need to know basis", and controlling plant access. On the other hand, public disclosure of information through display, trade journal publications, advertising, or other carelessness can preclude protection.

The efforts required to maintain secrecy are those "reasonable under the circumstances. " The courts do not require that extreme and unduly expensive proce-dures be taken to protect trade secrets against flagrant industrial espionage. See *E. I. du Pont de Nemours & Co. , Inc. v. Christopher, supra* . It follows that rea-sonable use of a trade secret including controlled disclosure to employees and li-censees is consistent with the requirement of relative secrecy.

SECTION 2. INJUNCTIVE RELIEF.

(a) Actual or threatened misappropriation may be enjoined. Upon application to the court, an injunction shall be terminated when the trade secret has ceased to exist, but the injunction may be continued for an additional reasonable period of time in order to eliminate commercial advantage that otherwise would be derived from the misappropriation.

(b) In exceptional circumstances, an injunction may condition future use up-on payment of a reasonable royalty for no longer than the period of time for which use could have been prohibited. Exceptional circumstances include, but are not limited to, a material and prejudicial change of position prior to acquiring knowl-edge or reason to know of misappropriation that renders a prohibitive injunction in-equitable.

(c) In appropriate circumstances, affirmative acts to protect a trade secret may be compelled by court order.

COMMENT

Injunctions restraining future use and disclosure of misappropriated trade se-crets frequently are sought. Although punitive perpetual injunctions have been granted, e. g. , *Elcor Chemical Corp. v. Agri-Sul, Inc. ,* 494 S. W. 2d 204 (Tex. Civ. App. 1973) , Section 2 (a) of this Act adopts the position of the trend of au-thority limiting the duration of injunctive relief to the extent of the temporal advan-tage over good faith competitors gained by a misappropriator. See, e. g. , *K – 2 Ski Co. v. Head Ski Co. ,Inc.* ,506 F. 2d 471 (CA9 , 1974) (maximum appropriate duration of both temporary and permanent injunctive relief is period of time it would have taken defendant to discover trade secrets lawfully through either independent development or reverse engineering of plaintiff's products).

The general principle of Section 2(a) and (b) is that an injunction should last for as long as is necessary, but no longer than is necessary, to eliminate the commercial advantage or "lead time" with respect to good faith competitors that a person has obtained through misappropriation. Subject to any additional period of restraint necessary to negate lead time, an injunction accordingly should terminate when a former trade secret becomes either generally known to good faith competitors or generally knowable to them because of the lawful availability of products that can be reverse engineered to reveal a trade secret.

For example, assume that A has a valuable trade secret of which B and C, the other industry members, are originally unaware. If B subsequently misappropriates the trade secret and is enjoined from use, but C later lawfully reverse engineers the trade secret, the injunction restraining B is subject to termination as soon as B's lead time has been dissipated. All of the persons who could derive economic value from use of the information are now aware of it, and there is no longer a trade secret under Section 1(4). It would be anti-competitive to continue to restrain B after any lead time that B had derived from misappropriation had been removed.

If a misappropriator either has not taken advantage of lead time or good faith competitors already have caught up with a misappropriator at the time that a case is decided, future disclosure and use of a former trade secret by a misappropriator will not damage a trade secret owner and no injunctive restraint of future disclosure and use is appropriate. See, e. g. , *Northern Petrochemical Co. v. Tomlinson* , 484 F. 2d 1057(CA7, 1973)(affirming trial court's denial of preliminary injunction in part because an explosion at its plant prevented an alleged misappropriator from taking advantage of lead time); *Kubik, Inc. v. Hull* , 185 USPQ 391 (Mich. App. 1974)(discoverability of trade secret by lawful reverse engineering made by injunctive relief punitive rather than compensatory).

Section 2(b) deals with the special situation in which future use by a misappropriator will damage a trade secret owner but an injunction against future use nevertheless is inappropriate due to exceptional circumstances. Exceptional circumstances include the existence of an overriding public interest which requires the denial of a prohibitory injunction against future damaging use and a person's reasonable reliance upon acquisition of a misappropriated trade secret in good faith and without reason to know of its prior misappropriation that would be prejudiced by a prohibitory injunction against future damaging use. *Republic Aviation Corp. v. Schenk* ,152 USPQ 830(N. Y. Sup. Ct. 1967)illustrates the public interest justification for withholding prohibitory injunctive relief. The court considered that enjoining a misappropriator from supplying the U. S. with an aircraft weapons control system would have endangered military personnel in Viet Nam. The prejudice to a good faith third party justification for withholding prohibitory injunctive relief can arise upon a trade secret owner's notification to a good faith third party that the third party has knowledge of a trade secret as a result of misappropriation by another. This notice suffices to make the third party a misappropriator thereafter under Section 1(2)(ii)(B)(I). In weighing an aggrieved person's interests and the interests of a third party who has relied in good faith upon his or her ability to utilize information, a court may conclude that restraining future use of the information by the third party is unwarranted. With respect to innocent acquirers of misappropriated trade secrets, Section 2(b) is consistent with the principle of 4 Restatement Torts(First) § 758(b)(1939), but rejects the Restatement's literal conferral of absolute immunity upon all third parties who have paid value in good faith for a trade secret misappropriated by another. The position taken by the Uniform Act is supported by Forest Laboratories, Inc. v. Pillsbury Co. , 452 F. 2d 621 (CA7, 1971)in which a defendant's purchase of assets of a corporation to which a trade secret had been disclosed in confidence was not considered to confer immunity upon the defendant.

When Section 2(b) applies, a court has discretion to substitute an injunction conditioning future use upon payment of a reasonable royalty for an injunction prohibiting future use. Like all injunctive relief for misappropriation, a royalty order injunction is appropriate only if a misappropriator has obtained a competitive advantage through misappropriation and only for the duration of that competitive advantage. In some situations, typically those involving good faith acquirers of trade secrets misappropriated by others, a court may conclude that the same considerations that render a prohibitory injunction against future use inappropriate also render a royalty order injunction inappropriate. See, generally, *Prince Manufacturing*, *Inc. v. Automatic Partner, Inc.*, 198 USPQ 618 (N. J. Super. Ct. 1976) (purchaser of misappropriator's assets from receiver after trade secret disclosed to public through sale of product not subject to liability for misappropriation).

A royalty order injunction under Section 2 (b) should be distinguished from a reasonable royalty alternative measure of damages under Section 3 (a). See the Comment to Section 3 for discussion of the differences in the remedies.

Section 2 (c) authorizes mandatory injunctions requiring that a misappropriator return the fruits of misappropriation to an aggrieved person, e. g. , the return of stolen blueprints or the surrender of surreptitious photographs or recordings.

Where more than one person is entitled to trade secret protection with respect to the same information, only that one from whom misappropriation occurred is entitled to a remedy.

SECTION 3. DAMAGES.

(a) Except to the extent that a material and prejudicial change of position prior to acquiring knowledge or reason to know of misappropriation renders a monetary recovery inequitable, a complainant is entitled to recover damages for misappropriation. Damages can include both the actual loss caused by misappropriation and the unjust enrichment caused by misappropriation that is not taken into account in computing actual loss. In lieu of damages measured by any other methods, the damages caused by misappropriation may be measured by imposition of liability for a reasonable royalty for a misappropriator's unauthorized disclosure or use of a trade secret.

(b) If willful and malicious misappropriation exists, the court may award exemplary damages in an amount not exceeding twice any award made under subsection(a).

COMMENT

Like injunctive relief, a monetary recovery for trade secret misappropriation is appropriate only for the period in which information is entitled to protection as a trade secret, plus the additional period, if any, in which a misappropriator retains an advantage over good faith competitors because of misappropriation. Actual damage to a complainant and unjust benefit to a misappropriator are caused by misappropriation during this time alone. See *Conmar Products Corp. v. Universal Slide Fastener Co.*, 172 F. 2d 150(CA2, 1949)(no remedy for period subsequent to disclosure of trade secret by issued patent); *Carboline Co. v. Jarboe*, 454 S. W. 2d 540 (Mo. 1970) (recoverable monetary relief limited to period that it would have taken misappropriator to discover trade secret without misappropriation). A claim for actual damages and net profits can be combined with a claim for injunctive relief, but, if both claims are granted, the injunctive relief ordinarily will preclude a monetary award for a period in which the injunction is effective.

As long as there is no double counting, Section 3(a) adopts the principle of the recent cases allowing recovery of both a complainant's actual losses and a misappropriator's unjust benefit that are caused by misappropriation. E. g. , *Tri-Tron International v. Velto*, 525 F. 2d 432(CA9, 1975)(complainant's loss and misappropriator's benefit can be combined). Because certain cases may have sanctioned double counting in a combined award of losses and unjust benefit, e. g. , *Telex Corp. v. IBM Corp.*, 510 F. 2d 894(CA10, 1975)(per curiam), cert. dismissed, 423 U. S. 802(1975)(IBM recovered rentals lost due to displacement by misappropriator's products without deduction for expenses saved by displacement; as a result of rough approximations adopted by the trial judge, IBM also may have recovered developmental costs saved by misappropriator through misappropriation with respect to the same customers), the Act adopts an express prohibition upon the counting of the same item as both a loss to a complainant and an unjust benefit to a misappropriator.

As an alternative to all other methods of measuring damages caused by a misappropriator's past conduct, a complainant can request that damages be based upon a demonstrably reasonable royalty for a misappropriator's unauthorized disclosure or use of a trade secret. In order to justify this alternative measure of damages, there must be competent evidence of the amount of a reasonable royalty.

The reasonable royalty alternative measure of damages for a misappropriator's past conduct under Section 3 (a) is readily distinguishable from a Section 2 (b) royalty order injunction, which conditions a misappropriator's future ability to use a trade secret upon payment of a reasonable royalty. A Section 2 (b) royalty order injunction is appropriate only in exceptional circumstances; whereas a reasonable royalty measure of damages is a general option. Because Section 3 (a) damages are awarded for a misappropriator's past conduct and a Section 2 (b) royalty order injunction regulates a misappropriator's future conduct, both remedies cannot be awarded for the same conduct. If a royalty order injunction is appropriate because of a person's material and prejudicial change of position prior to having reason to know that a trade secret has been acquired from a misappropriator, damages, moreover, should not be awarded for past conduct that occurred prior to notice that a misappropriated trade secret has been acquired.

Monetary relief can be appropriate whether or not injunctive relief is granted under Section 2. If a person charged with misappropriation has materially and prejudicially changed position in reliance upon knowledge of a trade secret acquired in good faith and without reason to know of its misappropriation by another, however, the same considerations that can justify denial of all injunctive relief also can justify denial of all monetary relief. See *Conmar Products Corp. v. Universal Slide Fastener Co.*, 172 F. 2d 1950 (CA2, 1949) (no relief against new employer of employee subject to contractual obligation not to disclose former employer's trade secrets where new employer innocently had committed ＄40,000 to develop the trade secrets prior to notice of misappropriation).

If willful and malicious misappropriation is found to exist, Section 3(b) authorizes the court to award a complainant exemplary damages in addition to the actual recovery under Section 3(a) an amount not exceeding twice that recovery. This provision follows federal patent law in leaving discretionary trebling to the judge even though there may be a jury, compare 35 U. S. C. Section 284(1976).

Whenever more than one person is entitled to trade secret protection with respect to the same information, only that one from whom misappropriation occurred is entitled to a remedy.

SECTION 4. ATTORNEY'S FEES.

If (i) a claim of misappropriation is made in bad faith, (ii) a motion to terminate an injunction is made or resisted in bad faith, or (iii) willful and malicious misappropriation exists, the court may award reasonable attorney's fees to the prevailing party.

COMMENT

Section 4 allows a court to award reasonable attorney fees to a prevailing party in specified circumstances as a deterrent to specious claims of misappropriation, to specious efforts by a misappropriator to terminate injunctive relief, and to willful and malicious misappropriation. In the latter situation, the court should take into consideration the extent to which a complainant will recover exemplary damages in determining whether additional attorney's fees should be awarded. Again, patent law is followed in allowing the judge to determine whether attorney's fees should be awarded even if there is a jury, compare 35 U. S. C. Section 285(1976).

SECTION 5. PRESERVATION OF SECRECY.

In an action under this [Act], a court shall preserve the secrecy of an alleged trade secret by reasonable means, which may include granting protective orders in connection with discovery proceedings, holding in-camera hearings, sealing the records of the action, and ordering any person involved in the litigation not to disclose an alleged trade secret without prior court approval.

COMMENT

If reasonable assurances of maintenance of secrecy could not be given, meritorious trade secret litigation would be chilled. In fashioning safeguards of confidentiality, a court must ensure that a respondent is provided sufficient information to present a defense and a trier of fact sufficient information to resolve the merits. In addition to the illustrative techniques specified in the statute, courts have protected secrecy in these cases by restricting disclosures to a party's counsel and his or her assistants and by appointing a disinterested expert as a special master to hear secret information and report conclusions to the court.

SECTION 6. STATUTE OF LIMITATIONS.

An action for misappropriation must be brought within 3 years after the misappropriation is discovered or by the exercise of reasonable diligence should have been discovered. For the purposes of this section, a continuing misappropriation constitutes a single claim.

COMMENT

There presently is a conflict of authority as to whether trade secret misappropriation is a continuing wrong. Compare *Monolith Portland Midwest Co. v. Kaiser Aluminum & Chemical Corp.*, 407 F. 2d 288 (CA9, 1969) (not a continuing wrong under California law-limitation period upon all recovery begins upon initial misappropriation) with *Underwater Storage, Inc. v. U. S. Rubber Co.*, 371 F. 2d 950 (CADC, 1966), cert. den., 386 U. S. 911 (1967) (continuing wrong under general principles-limitation period with respect to a specific act of misappropriation begins at the time that the act of misappropriation occurs).

This Act rejects a continuing wrong approach to the statute of limitations but delays the commencement of the limitation period until an aggrieved person discovers or reasonably should have discovered the existence of misappropriation. If objectively reasonable notice of misappropriation exists, three years is sufficient time to vindicate one's legal rights.

SECTION 7. EFFECT ON OTHER LAW.

(a) Except as provided in subsection (b), this [Act] displaces conflicting tort, restitutionary, and other law of this State providing civil remedies for misappropriation of a trade secret.

(b) This [Act] does not affect:

(1) contractual remedies, whether or not based upon misappropriation of a trade secret;

(2) other civil remedies that are not based upon misappropriation of a trade secret; or

(3) criminal remedies, whether or not based upon misappropriation of a trade secret.

COMMENT

This Act does not deal with criminal remedies for trade secret misappropriation and is not a comprehensive statement of civil remedies. It applies to a duty to protect competitively significant secret information that is imposed by law. It does not apply to a duty voluntarily assumed through an express or an implied-in-fact contract. The enforceability of covenants not to disclose trade secrets and covenants not to compete that are intended to protect trade secrets, for example, is governed by other law. The Act also does not apply to a duty imposed by law that is not dependent upon the existence of competitively significant secret information, like an agent's duty of loyalty to his or her principal.

SECTION 8. UNIFORMITYOF APPLICATIONAND CONSTRUCTION.

This [Act] shall be applied and construed to effectuate its general purpose to make uniform the law with respect to the subject of this [Act] among states enacting it.

SECTION 9. SHORT TITLE.

This [Act] may be cited as the Uniform Trade Secrets Act.

SECTION 10. SEVERABILITY.

If any provision of this [Act] or its application to any person or circumstances is held invalid, the invalidity does not affect other provisions or applications of the [Act] which can be given effect without the invalid provision or application, and to this end the provisions of this [Act] are severable.

SECTION 11. TIME OF TAKING EFFECT.

This [Act] takes effect on August 2 – 9, 1985, and does not apply to misappropriation occurring prior to the effective date. With respect to a continuing misappropriation that began prior to the effective date, the [Act] also does not apply to the continuing misappropriation that occurs after the effective date.

COMMENT

The Act applies exclusively to misappropriation that begins after its effective date. Neither misappropriation that began and ended before the effective date nor misappropriation that began before the effective date and continued thereafter is subject to the Act.

SECTION 12. REPEAL.

The following Acts and parts of Acts are repealed:

(1)

(2)

(3)

第三章 《反不正当竞争法重述》(节选)

第一节 《反不正当竞争法重述》简介

《反不正当竞争法重述》是由美国法学会完成并发布的法律文献,本书收录的内容是其中的部分节选,具体包括第 39 条到第 45 条共 7 条的内容,全部是关于商业秘密保护的条款,包括每一条款的正文和对该条款内容的详细诠释。

由于这是法律文献,只能作为一种示范法,因此,其自身不具有强制力,只有被各个州的法律采用以后才能在该州产生法律效力。

与前文中的《侵权法重述》和《统一商业秘密法》两部示范法相比,该重述中对于商业秘密的含义和特征、侵害行为及其救济问题的介绍和分析更加细致和全面,是深入了解和认识美国商业秘密制度的非常重要的法律文献。

下文中的文本是 1995 年发表的《反不正当竞争法重述》。

第二节 《反不正当竞争法重述》(节选)译文①

目 录

第 39 条 商业秘密的定义

商业秘密是指能够在生产经营中得以利用的任何信息。由于其自身具有一定的经济价值并且处于秘密状态,因此,可以为权利人带来实际的或者潜在的经济优势。

对第 39 条的诠释

一、保护商业秘密的基本原理

在历史上,保护商业性的秘密信息的规定最早可以追溯到罗马法,在罗马

---

① 为了用适合中国法律逻辑关系和语言习惯表述原文的含义,在保持原文含义不变的请提下,对原文中的一些标题、顺序做了调整。

法中,如果有人诱使别人的雇员泄露其雇主有关商业活动的秘密事项,他就应当对这个雇主承担救济损失的责任。19世纪初期,在英国开始出现有关商业秘密保护的现代法律规定,目的在于应对在工业革命进程中如何保护不断积累起来的各种技术诀窍,以及如何处理由于雇员的不断流动而对原雇主有价值的秘密信息进行有效保护的问题。到了19世纪中期,美国在普通法中也已经开始认识到应当合理有效地保护商业秘密的问题。到了19世纪末期,有效保护商业秘密的基本法律规则已经初步建立起来。

商业秘密可以给权利人带来多种利益。早期的商业秘密案例主要强调通过侵害他人的商业秘密,侵权人能够从中获取不正当的竞争优势,即主要强调侵权行为能够导致不公平的竞争优势。与此相对应,立法的重点也主要在于消除侵权人的非法竞争优势,以及剥夺侵权人基于侵权所获得的非法收益,并且将其直接列为侵权人的侵权责任。随着侵害商业秘密案件的增多,这种理念就逐渐构成了维护商业公平竞争原则的一部分内容。

近年来,随着科技的发展和社会的进步,保护商业秘密的目的在维护商业公平竞争的基础上又增添了保障和促进科技研发投入的功能,方法是通过对商业秘密的有效保护,可以使得人们从成功的发明创造中获取应有的回报,从而鼓励人们开展进一步的研发活动。

除此之外,通过有效地保护商业秘密可以促使人们充分利用商业秘密,避免把商业秘密包含的知识因为无效的囤积而造成浪费,原理是通过对商业秘密提供切实可行的保护可以消除人们对侵害商业秘密的担忧,这样他们可以积极地把商业秘密提供给自己的雇员、代理机构、被许可人或者其他能够合理使用该商业秘密的人加以使用。

最后,借助对商业秘密的保护,通过对违反诚实信用的行为以及非法获取他人秘密信息的行为的制止和惩罚,也有利于保护个人的隐私。

值得注意的是,商业秘密保护的主题和范围不可避免地要受到社会公众希望自由地获取有价值的信息的合理需求的限制。对于那些不受专利权、版权、商标权和其他知识产权以及其他法律保护的信息来说,在市场竞争中人们可以自由地进行获取、复制和使用,但是,通过这种方式获取、复制和使用的信息显然不能包括那些通过非法手段获得的信息。

因此,可以把侵害商业秘密的行为主要归纳为违反诚信,以及非法地获取、使用或披露他人商业秘密的行为。

二、保护商业秘密学说的发展

在早期的商业秘密案件中,人们普遍地认为因为商业秘密是一类有经济价值的信息,因此,它应当属于一类社会财富,商业秘密权利人应当属于财产权利人。这样,凡是违反诚实信用原则侵害他人商业秘密的行为,实际上也就是侵害他人财产权的行为,因而人们就普遍地适用衡平法的司法原则,采用禁令救济的措施来保护商业秘密权利人即财产权人的利益,这一理念和做法在当前的商业秘密侵权案件判决中仍有体现。

对于财产权理论来说,最重要的是被保护的对象自身应当具备"财产"的基本属性,因此,对于商业秘密来说,关键强调的是被保护的"信息"自身应当同时满足"价值性"和"秘密性"两个条件。对于具体的商业秘密侵权案件来说,除了审查商业秘密自身是否具有上述两个条件以外,还应当审查被告所实施行为是否具有正当性,这是判断被告的行为是否构成侵权的基本条件,也是商业秘密侵权纠纷案件一直遵从的基本规则。

需要说明的是,在商业秘密侵权纠纷案件中,只有当被告以不正当的手段使用、获取或者披露了原告的秘密信息时,审查和判断该秘密信息是否构成商业秘密才有价值,反之,如果被告未实施侵权行为,则在这一案件中认定原告的秘密信息是否构成商业秘密,或者是否具有财产属性都没有具体意义。

另外,在有些商业秘密侵权纠纷案件中,有些人可能会从法学理论上明确地否认商业秘密属于财产权的客体,进而否认基于商业秘密能够产生财产权。但是,这些观点和主张并不影响法院通过审查被告是否实施了违背诚实信用原则的行为,或者对原告的商业秘密实施了其他不正当的行为从而认定被告是否侵害了原告的商业秘密。

对于商业秘密的财产属性问题,虽然《侵权法重述》(1939)第 757 条中提到"财产的概念常常处于变化之中,没有统一的确定的含义",并且由此得出一般的责任理论应当是"凡是违背诚信者都应当承担责任"。但是,基于《侵权法重述》(1939)和现实中的案例,对于那些已经获得法院支持和保护的商业秘密来说,仍然都是基于财产权的理论首先要求诉争的商业秘密自身应当符合财产的基本条件,即应当同时具备适格的"财产性"和"秘密性"两项条件,否则不能受到法律的保护。

实际上,对于商业秘密本身是否属于财产权范畴的争论并没有多少实际的价值和意义,对于构建和完善商业秘密的侵权责任也只起到有限的作用。在实际的诉讼案件中,法院要求原告举证的证据主要包括首先证明自己的秘密信息符合商业秘密的构成条件,其次证明被告实施了侵权行为,一般情况下,法院通过对这些证据的审查就能基本判断被告是否已经实施了侵权行为。在许多商业秘密侵权纠纷案件中,被告与原告之间还都存在着一定的竞争关系。

除此之外,如前所述,商业秘密在法律上客观地存在着下列多项权利:①商业秘密权利人对于被告实施的违背诚实信用的行为和不正当的行为享有的诉权,以及对损失的救济请求权;②利用商业秘密参与竞争的权利;③许可他人使用该商业秘密的权利;④借助商业秘密的回报和收益鼓励和实施创新的权利;⑤确保利用该商业秘密从竞争中获取收益的权利。由此可见,商业秘密自身所拥有的权利与一般的财产权利有所不同。

1979年,美国全国统一州法律委员会颁布了《统一商业秘密法》,在该法的序言中明确地指出"把普通法的基本原则作为保护商业秘密的统一准则"。现在,《统一商业秘密法》的1979年版本或者1985年修订版本都已经被美国的绝大多数州转换为本州的法律进行适用,因此,除了作出特别提示以外,在本法中有关商业秘密保护的基本原则都采用《统一商业秘密法》中所主张的普通法中的一般原则。

除此之外,在美国有些州还专门制定了打击侵害商业秘密犯罪的刑事法律,而在另一些州,则把已有的一般的刑法条款拓展适用于侵害商业秘密的犯罪行为。当然,在有些情况下也会发生犯罪竞合的情形,例如,一个侵害商业秘密的行为可能还会同时侵害《联邦资讯和邮件欺诈法》[见《美国法典》刑法篇(第18篇)第1341和1343条]中规定的行为,以及在《联邦盗窃财产法》[见《美国法典》刑法篇(第18篇)第2314条]中规定的行为。

需要说明的是,本法中有关商业秘密的定义只适用于本法的条文,只对应于本法规定的民事责任。这一定义不适合于刑法,以及那些对于商业秘密侵害行为未规定民事责任的法律,如《自由信息法》(见《美国法典》第 5 篇第 552 条),在该法中也规定了禁止非法披露商业秘密的行为。

三、与专利法和著作权法的关系

美国联邦专利法规定对"任何新的有用的方法、设备、产品或者组合物提供保护"(参见《美国法典注解》第 35 篇第 101 条)。但是,如果该发明被创造出来时在其所属的技术领域中已经明显地属于常见技术时,则该发明创造不能受到专利法的保护(参见《美国法典注解》第 35 篇第 103 条)。联邦的设计专利保护那些具有"新颖性、原创性的对产品的装饰性设计",同时还应当符合"非显而易见性"(即具有一定的技术设计创新水平)的要求(参见《美国法典注解》第 35 篇第 135 条)。

显然,专利权与基于商业秘密获得的权利不同,基于商业秘密获得的权利是一种受到限制的权利,同一时间可以相互独立地存在着多个内容相同的商业秘密,这些相同的商业秘密都可以分别合法地受到保护,也可以同时被不同的主体所拥有;因此,任何一位商业秘密权利人都不能利用自己的权利来限制其他人合法地获取和拥有内容相同的商业秘密,也无权限制他人合法地利用或者披露他人的商业秘密,权利人只能依据被告对自己所拥有的商业秘密实施的不正当行为来主张权利并制止这种侵权行为。

而专利权则是一种排他性的权利,专利权人不仅有权禁止他人擅自利用自己的专利发明来制造、使用或者销售产品,而且有权禁止他人利用那些完全来自于自己的独立研发或者反向工程获得的与其专利发明相同的技术(参见《美国法典注解》第 35 篇第 271 条)。

当然,专利权享有比商业秘密权利更高的法律效力,也需要承担更高的要求和条件。一份发明申请书应当包含专门性的内容,其中应当包括"一份书面的介绍和说明该专利技术内容的材料,以及如何使用该专利技术的说明材料;特别是需要包含一份发明人自己认为的实施该专利技术的最优的技术方案,即制造和使用该专利的最佳方案"(参见《美国法典注解》第 35 篇第 111 条和第 112 条)。而且,国家专利部门受理专利申请材料以后还应当向社会公开,当专利被公开以后,专利申请书中所填写的专门性技术和其他材料都将向公众展示,接受公众的审查,当然,对于商业秘密来说,没有这些条件和要求。

另外,所有在专利审查中被公开的资料都不可能再作为商业秘密进行保护,即使该专利申请最终未获得专利权,或者获得专利权以后又被宣告无效(参见《联邦条例法典》第37篇第1.11条)。当然,如果提交专利申请以后,在被依法公布之前,申请人主动地撤回申请或者放弃申请,由于此时申请内容还未对社会公布(参见《美国法典注解》第35篇第111条和第122条,以及《联邦条例法典》第37篇第1.14条),在此情况下,仍然可以把这些用于专利申请的资料作为商业秘密加以保护。

在编号为416 U. S. 470, 94 S. Ct. 1879, 40 L. Ed. 2d 315(1974)的 *Kewanee Oil Co. v. Bicron Corp.* 一案中,美国联邦最高法院就曾指出,当一件信息既可以作为商业秘密进行保护,又可以申请专利进行保护时,联邦专利法并不享有优先于各州商业秘密保护法的权利和法律效力。联邦最高法院也同时指出,正是由于商业秘密保护法要求信息必须具有秘密性才能获得保护,从而使得商业秘密与通过专利公布而处于公共状态的专利信息之间界限分明,避免了两者之间产生冲突。联邦最高法院又进一步地指出,商业秘密保护法对秘密性的条件要求与专利法中所主张的利用向公众公开专利信息来换取专利权的理念是完全不同的,这种差异将在很大程度上制约着人们借助商业秘密保护法来保护那些能够申请专利的信息资料。

然而,出于对公共利益的考量,以及对公众有权自由地获取和使用公共信息的保护,在编号为489 U. S. 141, 109 S. Ct. 971, 103 L. Ed. 2d 118(1989)的 *Bonito Boats, Inc. v. Thunder Craft Boats, Inc.* 一案中,联邦最高法院强调如果州法律的规则明显地干涉人们利用那些已经公开披露的信息,或者那些有明显的证据证明来自于公共资源的信息,这种干涉行为就是一种不合法的行为,从而为商业秘密与公共信息之间划出了界限。

与专利法和商业秘密不同的是,联邦版权法保护那些"由作者原创的并且已经固定在可见的媒介上的作品"(参见《美国法典注解》第17篇第111条和

第 102 条第 1 款)。利用版权可以制止未经授权的复制,制作衍生作品,以及对作品的发行、公开表演和公开展示等行为(参见《美国法典注解》第 17 篇第 106 条)。

然而,版权的保护范围也同样受到一定的限制,当作品完全是由"想法、程序、过程、系统、方法、概念、原理或发现"等内容构成时,该作品不能享有版权(参见《美国法典注解》第 17 篇第 102 条第 1 款)。另外,版权以能够受到保护的作品的存在为基础,与该作品是否已经在公众中进行了披露或者传播无关,即使从未发表过的作品仍然能够获得版权保护(参见《美国法典注解》第 17 篇第 302 条)。

如果一篇作品中包含了一件商业秘密,则在该作品被公开之前,相关文件对该作品既可以主张版权,也可以利用商业秘密法对该商业秘密进行保护。

虽然在《著作权法》第 301 条"优于其他法律"中规定凡是属于《著作权法》保护范围内的作品优先获得著作权,并且在此作品上不应当再依据其他法律诞生其他权利。但是,本法第 40 条中规定的基于商业秘密获得的权利不在这一版权限制的范围之内,也就是当作品的内容属于商业秘密时,可以先主张商业秘密保护。

获得版权保护并不需要进行版权登记和办理其他手续(参见《美国法典注解》第 17 篇第 408 条)。当然,根据自己保护版权的需要,可以另行办理版权登记,但是版权登记不是获得版权的条件。如果把一件还未发表的作品进行版权登记,则需要把该完整的作品都提交登记机关保存(参见《美国法典注解》第 17 篇第 408 条第 2 款第 1 项),然后这一作品将向公众开放接受公众的监督和检查(参见《美国法典注解》第 17 篇第 705 条)。由此可见,办理版权登记后的作品将被公开。

但是,法律也同时规定对于计算机软件程序的版权登记,版权登记办公室应当准许版权登记申请人删除那些属于商业秘密的计算机软件程序内容,而且对于由于版权登记工作所造成的侵权行为应当给予特别的救济。

如果一件作品的内容包含着商业秘密,当该作品进行版权登记时应当遵守保护商业秘密的一般要求,具体规定内容在本条的第 6 款解释中进行陈述。

四、商业秘密包含的主题事项

商业秘密可以由方案、样品、数据汇编、计算机程序、设备、方法、技术、工艺流程或者其他形式的有价值的信息组成。

商业秘密可以涉及技术问题，例如，产品的结构或者设计，制造方法或者实施特定操作或者服务所需的技术诀窍等。商业秘密也可以涉及商业经营方面的事项，例如，有关产品的定价、产品的营销、客户名单和客户的需求等内容。

尽管通常情况下都是由从事生产经营活动的企业和其他从事商业性活动的经济实体主张享有商业秘密，但是，诸如慈善机构、教育机构、政府机构、兄弟组织和宗教组织等这些非营利的机构也可以对自己拥有的具有经济价值的信息提出商业秘密保护，例如，潜在的成员或者捐助者的名单等。

首先，有关商业秘密保护的早期立法中曾经把商业秘密限制在"能够连续地在商业活动中使用"的范围以内，从而把那些与单独事件关联的商业秘密排除在了受保护的范围以外，这类商业秘密诸如秘密投标的内容，即将发布的商业公告的内容，以及那些一经商业性地使用自身的"秘密性"就将立即被破坏秘密信息等。

然而，虽然在早期的立法中把这类与单独事件关联的商业秘密排除在了立法保护之外，但是在具体的实践中，无论是在判例法中，还是早期的立法中，都禁止利用不正当的手段获取这类短期的有价值的信息，虽然未把它们列入商业秘密的范畴，但是实际上仍然对这类信息参照商业秘密进行了保护。

其次，本法中对于代理机构在代理关系中涉及的"商业秘密"和"其他类似的秘密事项"都给予保护，并且禁止代理机构在代理关系终结以后未经授权使用或者披露这类信息。

与早期立法不同的是，在《统一商业秘密法》中就去除了"能够连续地在商业活动中使用"这一要求和条件，对于商业秘密被使用的情况以及商业秘密能够存在的时间长短都没有做任何要求（参见《统一商业秘密法》第 1 条第 4 款及其对应的评论）。本法中也采用了《统一商业秘密法》中的规定。

在诉讼中，需要由法院审查和确认商业秘密是否存在，以及侵权行为是否存在，这都是原告的举证责任。如果商业秘密涉及的是技术类信息，一般应当通过向法院展示包含该商业秘密的特定产品、工艺流程，或者实体模型来说明该商业秘密。当然,如果某一商业秘密能够被清晰地通过相关材料阐述清楚,那就无须再提供包含着该商业秘密的有形的实体材料来进行说明。

在有的案件中,有时需要由原告承担的证明程度与应当考虑的被告的合法利益相关,例如,当原告所主张保护的商业秘密是一种与前雇员适当保留的一般技能和专业知识紧密结合的信息时,法院可能就需要原告提交更多的证据材料。

当事人之间如果在协议中将特定的信息界定为"商业机密",这一约定对于法院认定该信息是否属于商业秘密很重要,然而,这并不是决定性的因素。但是,如果在协议中又规定了防止披露该信息的条款,那么,这一条款就能证明该信息具有价值和秘密性,这样也就进一步证明该信息应当属于商业秘密。而且这一保密条款还在当事人之间建立起了保密义务。

但是,对于当事人之间的这种约定,由于还不能排除这一信息本身是属于公共领域中的信息,或者是来自于公共领域中的信息,因此,这一协议还无法排除被告对这一信息本身是否符合商业秘密条件的质疑,因此,最终还需要对该信息本身进行审查。

很显然,在现实中,如果想要制定出一套用于判断某一信息自身是否符合商业秘密条件的详细标准几乎是不可能的。

当法院审查确认一件信息是否符合商业秘密条件时,需要对相关的多项内容进行比较、评估和判断,包括该信息的价值、秘密性,作为一件信息的确定性,以及被告实施的不当行为的情况等因素。

五、认定信息具有价值的证据

商业秘密自身应当具有一定的经济价值,这种经济价值使得商业秘密的权利人在生产经营活动中能够基于该商业秘密比那些未拥有这一商业秘密的经营者更加具备现实的或者潜在的经济优势。

但是,这种经济优势并不一定是巨大的。这种经济优势体现在对于商业秘密权利人来说,与自己原有的状况相比确实诞生了一种优势。另外,虽然商业秘密也可以由能够申请专利的技术发明组成,但是,商业秘密并不要求这一技术发明必须达到联邦专利法中所规定的获得专利的技术标准和技术高度。

被认为属于商业秘密的信息其自身的价值可以用直接的或者间接的证据

来证明。直接证据包括秘密的内容,以及它在直接相关的生产经营活动中所能产生的作用。信息具有价值的间接证据包括原告为了研究获得该信息所投入资源的价值、为了保持该信息的秘密性所采取的保密措施的成本价值,以及许可他人使用时的许可使用费用。

原告在生产经营中使用该商业秘密这一行为本身就是证明这一秘密信息具有价值的一种证据;如果商业秘密权利人能够区分出通过利用该商业秘密所对应产生的特别收益,则这种特别收益也是该秘密信息具有价值的一种证据。

在一些早期的案件中,对商业秘密的“使用”被商业秘密权利人赋予了特殊的使命,认为自己对商业秘密的实际使用是起诉被告侵害商业秘密的前提条件之一。但是,这种把“使用”的含义定义为“商业秘密权利人已经实际利用了该商业秘密”这种概念上的做法,实际上是不合理地限制了对该商业秘密进行有效保护的范围。一方面这样做把开发研究这一商业秘密的过程排除在了保护范围之外(因为此时商业秘密还未诞生,也就不存在商业秘密权利人实际利用该商业秘密的行为);另一方面如果商业秘密权利人自身没有利用该商业秘密的能力,也就不存在该商业秘密权利人已经实际利用了该商业秘密的行为。

另外,这种“使用”的定义也使得那些包含着消极的内容但是自身具有价值的信息难以受到保护。这类信息的价值在于它们能够提示人们哪些信息、资料、程序或者技术不适合在某些生产经营中使用,从而避免人们遭受损失。

因此,在当前许多商业秘密侵权诉讼案件中,商业秘密权利人都放弃了把“使用”作为保护商业秘密的前提条件。在《统一商业秘密法》中也反对把“使用”设立为获得保护的前置条件,本法中也不接受这种前置条件。

六、认定信息具有秘密性的证据

要成为商业秘密,该信息必须具有秘密性。同时,秘密性又不是一种绝对性的概念。本法中秘密性的作用只需信息能够为权利人提供实际的或者潜在的经济优势即可。在形式上,如果想要通过独立研发获得它的人必须面对很多困难,或者必须付出较高的成本才能达到目的,或者只有借助不正当的手段来获取它,那么这条信息在法律上就具有秘密性。

另外,对于构成商业秘密的信息来说,也不需要其具有专利法中的“新颖性”。虽然在有些商业秘密案件中也宣告构成商业秘密的信息自身需要具备一定的"新颖性",但是这里的"新颖性"本质上就是指向本法中的"秘密性"和"价值性"。实际上,这种不同的说法只是换了一种词语来观察和定义这类信息,因为一直真正处于"秘密"状态的信息自然地应当具备"新颖性"的基本特征。

信息被商业秘密权利人以外的第三方知悉以后,如果该第三方也能够继续保护该信息的秘密性,此时,对于那些还未知悉这一信息的其他人来说,这一信息仍然属于秘密信息,仍然具有潜在的经济价值,因此,此时这一信息仍然可以被视为商业秘密。

如果商业秘密权利人之外的第三方通过自己的独立研发获得了这一商业秘密,但是他也对这一商业秘密进行了保密,此时这一商业秘密仍然属于合法有效的商业秘密,因此仍然受到法律的保护。与此相似的是,基于工作需要把商业秘密披露给自己的雇员使用,或者通过许可使用合同允许被许可人知悉并使用,或者合法地允许其他人知悉等行为都不破坏该商业秘密的合法有效性。甚至在发生了有限范围的泄密事件以后,也并不必然地导致该商业秘密的有效性终结。例如,如果通过非法泄密途径知悉该秘密信息的人又对该信息采取了保密措施,在此情况下,这一信息仍然属于有效的商业秘密。

但是,构成商业秘密的信息一旦被那些想利用它获取经济收益的人通过合法的途径比较方便地获得或者确认时,该信息就不再属于商业秘密。例如,一些自身可能具有经济价值的信息通过专利或者其他公开出版的材料进行了公开,那么这些信息就不再属于商业秘密的范畴。与此类似的是,如果一条信息能够被人们从公开销售或者展示的产品中轻易地破解出来,那么它也不再是商业秘密。那些通过对已经存在并且被人们普遍知悉的工艺流程、程序、方法等进行简单的修改或者技术置换所得到的信息,由于自身缺乏必要的秘密性,因而也不属于商业秘密。

值得说明的是,商业秘密中信息的"秘密性"是针对构成这一商业秘密的整条信息来说的,如果整条信息是由多条子信息构成的,而子信息中又有一部分甚至全部都是众所周知的信息,那么,只要通过对这些子信息进行不同的组合、编撰或者结合,最终所形成的整体信息自身可能是一条独特的新信息,不为公众所知悉,因而具有秘密性;如果其再具有一定的经济价值,那么就能构成一件商业秘密。

另外,第三方通过合法的理论研究掌握某一商业秘密信息的行为并不必然地破坏与其内容相同的已经存在的商业秘密的有效性;只有当第三方通过简单的研究就能掌握这一信息时,该商业秘密的秘密性才被破坏,该商业秘密才被终结。

与此相似的是,如果第三方不是以侵害商业秘密为目的,通过研究那些实际包含了某一商业秘密信息的零碎内容的公开材料,或者通过对其他公开材料的研究分析,从而最终掌握了这一商业秘密的信息,显然,该第三方并不需要承担任何侵害商业秘密的责任。此时,虽然该第三方已经知悉了该商业秘密的内容,但是,这并不影响该商业秘密权利人对那些已经对其商业秘密实施了侵权行为的人提起侵权诉讼并追究侵权责任。

对于能够用来证明"秘密性"的证据,如果他人利用合法购买的产品来破解其中的商业秘密是困难的、昂贵的,甚至是旷日持久的,那么,这一商业秘密就具有有效的"秘密性"。当然,任何通过合法的反向工程的方式获得商业秘密的行为都是合法行为。

除此之外,还可以利用间接证据来证明秘密性,可以利用间接证据来证明该商业秘密通过合法手段是难以获取的,由此证明该商业秘密的有效性。例如,原告为了保护信息的秘密性而采取的保密措施;签署的许可使用协议;被告未获得成功的侵权行为;其他人以合法方式复制该信息;被告以非法方式获取该信息等行为都可以作为秘密性有效的间接证据。当被告利用各种非法途径想要获得某一商业秘密时,也从反面说明该商业秘密具有秘密性,并且更值得受到法律的保护。

在现实中,虽然法院不会承认来自公共领域中的信息享有商业秘密权,但是,如果被告基于合法的信赖关系获得某一商业秘密后,又非法地使用或者披露了该商业秘密,在这种情况下就不属于该商业秘密来自于公共领域的情形。那么,从被告获知到披露这一商业秘密的这一期间内,法院应当认可该商业秘密秘密性的有效性。

另外,有观点主张应当对"可信赖的披露"的义务范围作出更多的限制,即商业秘密一旦失去了"秘密性",原告也就不再享有追诉被告侵权行为,即非法使用或者披露其商业秘密的权利。然而,在很多案件中,法院并没有把丧失

"秘密性"作为一个法律问题进行考虑。实际上,当被告非法地使用或者披露原告的商业秘密时,需要判断此时该信息是否能够从公共领域中比较容易地获得和确认,对于被告的非法披露行为来说,如果原告的商业秘密被公开从而丧失了"秘密性",这可能正是被告的非法披露这一侵权行为导致的结果,因此不能免除侵权责任;对于非法使用来说,原告的商业秘密丧失"秘密性"也可能是其非法使用直接或者间接导致的结果,因此,在这种情况下,应当公正地由被告承担侵权责任。

当然,当一条信息的秘密性不再符合商业秘密的要求时,使用该信息也就无须承担侵害商业秘密的法律责任。

一旦信息在公共领域中能够比较容易地获得,该信息也就难以再给其权利人带来重要的利益,而且失去了秘密性,因此也就不再属于商业秘密。即使是那些很少考虑秘密性丧失问题的法院,当法院最终查明被告实际上是通过对公共领域中的相关信息进行研究后获得该信息时,都会宣布被告不承担侵害原告商业秘密的责任。

然而值得讨论的是,基于保护公众利益的需要,往往就会支持这样的结论:构成商业秘密的信息一旦丧失秘密性,该商业秘密将不再受到保护,使用该信息也就不应受到限制。但是应当明确的是,在商业秘密丧失其秘密性之前,被告实施的任何非法使用或者披露行为都应当承担侵权责任。《统一商业秘密法》对这一原则作出了规定。在《统一商业秘密法》中把"侵害行为"定义为利用不正当的手段获取、披露或者使用他人商业秘密的行为。同时在商业秘密范围中排除那些"一般性常识"和"通过合法的方式容易确定的信息"。

最后,商业秘密权利的有效期间应当截至该信息丧失秘密性时为止;对于丧失秘密性之前发生的侵权行为所实施的禁令措施和经济赔偿要求,除了特殊情况外,其期限也应当到秘密性丧失时为止。

七、为保密所采取的预防措施的证据

为了保持信息的秘密性而采取的保密措施是决定该信息是否构成商业秘密的条件之一。

保密措施可以有下列多种不同的形式:①通过物理隔离手段防止他人接触该秘密信息;②对必须知悉该信息的人只限制其了解其需要了解的部分,如果没有必要,就不让其知悉信息的全部内容;③对接受信息者强调保密的重要性,与其签署专门的保密协议,设置保密提示标志,限制有关该信息消息的传播。

上述保密措施可以作为该信息具有经济价值和秘密性的证据。在《侵权法重述》(1939 年)中也把这种保密措施认为是构成商业秘密的重要条件之一。

在《统一商业秘密法》中规定商业秘密应当被合理地采取了"保密措施"。无论是把这种保密措施单独地作为构成商业秘密的必要条件,还是把它与其他条件一起共同地作为构成商业秘密成立的条件,信息的权利人对该信息采取了保密措施这一行为都有助于证明该信息自身具有经济价值和秘密性。当然,如果该信息自身的经济价值和秘密性已经明确,则就无须再利用该保密措施来进行证明。

在侵权诉讼中,商业秘密权利人已经采取了保密措施的证据还有下列相关的作用:①由于采取了保密措施,可以从另一个角度证明当商业秘密权利人把该商业秘密披露给自己的雇员或者其他人时,都是权利人基于对这些人的信任而自愿披露的行为,这种行为有助于证明被告是否已经实际掌握了该商业秘密的内容,以及被告应当对原告承担诚实信用和忠诚的义务;②决定被告通过其他特殊方式获得该商业秘密的行为是否属于不正当行为;③决定由于差错而意外地披露了该商业秘密的行为能否导致该商业秘密无效。

八、"创意规则"

在有些案件中涉及雇员、消费者、发明者或者其他人向企业提出的一些创意、建议、要求和想法,其中有些内容可以用于生产经营实践。对于这些案件,有时需要按照"创意规则"单独地进行分析。

这类案件经常涉及对一些产品或者项目提出的一些新方案或者改善产品的新想法,也有一些想法是有关娱乐行业的事项。在这类案件中,原告基于这些创意和想法(统称为创意)向被告主张损害赔偿的理由主要是根据许可使用合同,在这些合同中一般都明确或者默示地承诺接受这些创意的人应当为此支付报酬。但是,在有些案件中,原告也会基于侵权损害或者归还原主的原则主张赔偿。

在缺少合同约定的情况下,法院一般都会按照审查商业秘密的一般规则对这些创意的性质以及当时提交这些内容时的相关情形进行分析,在有些审查结论中明确地将有些创意归于商业秘密的范畴之中。为了支持原告的主张,将侵害创意的行为认定为侵害商业秘密的行为,为此,绝大多数法院都会对这些创意设置几项获得保护的前置条件和要求:①这些创意必须具有新颖性,不能是已经被人们普遍知悉的内容;②这些创意的内容必须具体和明确,能够使人们评估它的价值;③这些创意已经被接受者所使用;④创意的提供者与接受者之间有关保密义务的约定情况,两者之间的相互关系,两者之间处理这类事务的先例,这一行业的习惯,接受者履行保守秘密的信誉情况。

当然,如果基于《统一商业秘密法》和本法的规定,并不要求商业秘密的权利人实际使用了涉案的创意,只要创意作为一类信息本身符合商业秘密对经济价值和秘密性的要求,而且权利人又采取了保密措施,就应当被视为商业秘密,这些创意也就可以直接被作为商业秘密进行保护。

对于那些缺乏明示或者默示合同的案件,由于创意的提供者与接受者之间关于保密的约定还不明确,因此,对于这类案件可以把本法中针对商业秘密保护设立的有关规则作为一般性的规则加以适用,适用范围包括侵害商业秘密的案件,以及原告直接或者类似的主张侵害创意的案件。

另外,基于对社会公共利益以及对公众自由地获取公共领域中信息权利的保护,对于创意本身的内容是否属于公共领域中的信息需要审查和判断,实际上,这种审查也有助于审理那些存在合同关系的保护创意的案件。对在合同中明示或者默示地约定应当对创意支付费用的内容,许多法院也要求首先证明创意的"新颖性"和确切的内容。因此,本法中建立的规则也有助于分析有关创意的合同责任问题。

第 40 条　侵害商业秘密的行为

如果实施了下列行为,就应当承担侵害商业秘密的侵权责任。

1. 在行为人知道或者应当知道属于他人商业秘密的情况下,仍然使用不正当的手段获取该商业秘密;

2. 在未获得商业秘密权利人同意的情况下,擅自使用或者披露该商业秘密,同时存在下列情形之一的:

(1)行为人知道或者应当知道该信息是商业秘密,他是在违背信任关系的情况下获取的该商业秘密。

（2）行为人知道或者应当知道该信息是商业秘密，但是他却采用不正当的手段获取该商业秘密。

（3）行为人知道或者应当知道该信息是商业秘密，某人向他提供了该商业秘密，但是，该提供者又是通过不正当的手段从第三人处获得的该商业秘密；或者该提供者向行为人披露该商业秘密的行为违背了自己承担的保密义务。

（4）行为人知道或者应当知道该信息是商业秘密，他是通过偶然或者错误的行为获得了该商业秘密；除非导致这种结果是由于商业秘密权利人未能采取合理的保密措施造成的。

对第 40 条的诠释

一、商业秘密案件适用范围和原告的举证责任

本法适用于普通法中有关商业秘密侵权和损害赔偿的诉讼活动，这里的"侵权行为"包括那些可能被分别称为"侵害""侵权"，或者"转换"商业秘密的各种能够危害他人商业秘密的非法行为，以及基于侵害商业秘密所产生的"不当得利"和"违反保密义务"的法律纠纷。

除了上述规定以外，本法也适用《统一商业秘密法》中所规定的各种侵权行为。

本法不适用于与商业秘密无关的下列事项：①侵害与商业秘密无关的其他合同利益的行为；②雇主对雇员或者其他机构的欠款纠纷；③违反不涉及商业秘密的其他保密义务的纠纷。

本法也不适用于下列违反合同义务的纠纷：①违反不适用或者不涉及商业秘密的合同纠纷；②违反不涉及与商业秘密权利人进行商业竞争的合同纠纷。

这些合同纠纷一般适用于有关合同成立和合同履行的规定，包括为了限制某些商业活动而限制合同履行的规定［见重述中说明的第二部分，合同第186－188 条（1981 年）］。然而，本法中所规定的规则可以在这些合同纠纷中作为一般性的原则参照适用。根据本法规定，如果存在一个保护商业秘密的明示或者暗示的合同，就属于本法管辖的商业秘密侵权纠纷的范围。在这类合同中可能涉及多项法律问题，包括合同中约定的商业秘密自身是否适格，以及承担保密义务的问题。

在商业秘密侵权诉讼中,在商业秘密已经成立的前提下,原告一般还需要承担下列举证责任:①如果受保护的商业秘密未受到侵害,原告所能获得的收益,即证明原告的损失;②被告对该商业秘密所实施的侵权行为,包括非法获取、使用、披露的行为。

在本法中,基于自己独立研发获取的商业秘密,或者通过合法行为获得的他人的商业秘密,都是合法地拥有商业秘密的行为,也都能获取合法的收益。关于雇员所创造发现的商业秘密,以及基于这类商业秘密在雇主与雇员之间的权利义务关系将在本法第 42 条中进行讨论。

另外,在审查某一信息是否符合商业秘密的条件时,并不要求该信息必须具有"新颖性"和"绝对的秘密性",因此,当不同的人各自分别独立地研发出内容相同的信息时,如果该信息能够符合商业秘密的条件,他们每个人都是自己信息的商业秘密权利人,因此也都有权利基于自己的商业秘密获取合法的收益。

二、通过不正当手段获得商业秘密

在有关商业秘密保护的早期立法中,只对非法使用或者非法披露他人商业秘密的行为设立了侵权责任,未对非法获取商业秘密的行为规定专门的法律责任[参见《侵权法重述》(1939 年)第 757 条]。

当然,在判例法中,非法使用或者非法披露的行为也是提起商业秘密侵权诉讼的常见性案由。在这类案件中,原告需要证明被告实施了非法使用或者非法披露的行为。比较典型的类型是被告通过合法的途径从商业秘密权利人那里获得了该商业秘密,因此,其获得商业秘密的行为是合法的,只是随后被告违反自己承担的保密义务,非法地进行了使用或者披露,显然,这类行为构成了非法行为。对于这类案件,法院通常认为只要被告存在实施非法使用或者非法披露该商业秘密的可能性,无论被告是否已经实际实施了这些侵权行为,原告都可以按照被告已经实际实施这些侵权行为时所可能获得的非法收益来主张赔偿。

如果有证据证明被告曾经主动地通过非法手段去获取原告的商业秘密,那么,这些证据同时也能够用来证明被告即将非法地使用或者披露原告的商业秘密。

本法采用了《统一商业秘密法》中的相关规定,把非法获取他人商业秘密的行为也规定为侵权行为。一个人通过窃听的方式,或者通过引诱他人泄露的方式获取第三人的商业秘密,或者在违背诚实信用的原则下故意地接受他人披露的第三人的商业秘密等,这些行为都属于侵权行为。如果在非法获取商业秘密之后再进行非法地使用或者披露,则是更进一步的侵权行为。当然,一旦被告在非法获取商业秘密之后又进行了非法的使用或者非法地泄露时,原告将能够享有更多的救济措施。

三、非法的使用或披露

本法中,对于构成"使用"的行为没有任何技术上的限制和要求。

本法中,基于社会常识,凡是利用商业秘密可能导致对该商业秘密权利人造成损害,或者可能使得被告从中获得收益的行为都属于"使用"行为。因而,凡是销售含有商业秘密的商品,利用商业秘密进行生产或者制造,依赖商业秘密帮助或者促进研究和开发,或者利用商业秘密拓展客户等行为都属于"使用"行为。

当然,所有的非法使用行为都将涉及承担侵权责任的问题。

另外,对于商业秘密的非法使用并不要求涉及商业秘密的全部内容或者全部特征,只要使用了商业秘密的重要部分就构成了非法使用。与此类似的是,被告可能并不以原有的使用方式使用该商业秘密,甚至在使用中会独立地对使用方式或者商业秘密自身进行一些修改或者完善,但是,只要使用的结果主要是由该商业秘密决定的,就属于使用该商业秘密的行为。然而,基于被告所独立进行的修改和完善可能会为被告带来一定的收益,因此,在计算被告的非法收益时应当考虑到这一部分的收益问题。当然,如果商业秘密只对被告的产品或者生产起到轻微的作用,被告的生产或者产品主要依靠了其他的信息或者自己独立研发的信息,在这种情况下,被告将不承担侵害原告商业秘密的责任。

在侵权案件中,商业秘密权利人承担着证明被告非法使用该商业秘密,被告知悉该商业秘密,以及被告与商业秘密权利人双方在产品和生产上存在着本质上相似的义务。

非常显然的事实是,当商业秘密被非法使用和披露以后,将侵害商业秘密权利人的利益。披露行为可以分为向公众披露和私下在小范围内进行披露两种,向公众披露将破坏该商业秘密的秘密性,从而终结该商业秘密;私下小范围内的披露可能并不破坏该商业秘密的秘密性,但是将增加非法使用和进一步披露的可能性。因此,无论是公开披露还是私下小范围内的披露都属于非法披露行为,都应当承担侵权责任。

披露行为并不要求必须要有"表达"行为,本法中任何能够使得他人知悉该商业秘密的行为都属于披露行为,包括销售或者转让商品以及其他可见物体的行为,只要他人能够从这些物品中获知该商业秘密,就属于披露该商业秘密的行为,非法披露者就应当承担侵权责任。

接受非法披露商业秘密的客户通常有两种,一种是与商业秘密权利人存在竞争关系的人,他们通过获取和利用该商业秘密的商业价值来提高自身的竞争力;第二类人是那些潜在的想要利用该商业秘密的人。

在普通法和《统一商业秘密法》中,对于那些并非为了商业利用而披露他人商业秘密的行为的法律责任问题并未进行明确的规定。如果行为人披露他人商业秘密的目的主要在于给该商业秘密的权利人造成伤害,那么,即使该披露行为不是为了商业利用,法院也将判决行为人承担侵权责任。同样的道理,如果一个雇员为了报复雇主与其终止了雇佣关系而公开披露该雇主的商业秘密,也应当承担侵权责任。

然而,在有些情况下,行为人并非为了商业利益,而是为了重要的公共利益,或者是在必须说明该商业秘密的特殊情形下披露该商业秘密。例如,在司法程序中,依据法律规定证人必须如实地披露他人的商业秘密,此时该证人无须承担任何法律责任。

在有些特殊情况下,某些主体依据特权也可以披露他人的商业秘密,但是应当说明所要披露的信息的性质,披露的目的,以及获得该信息的方式。这里的特权主要涉及下列行为:披露行为涉及公共健康和安全,涉及追究犯罪或者侵权的司法行为,或者其他受公众关注的重要事项。

四、非法占有的责任

依据本法的规定,只有当被告知道或者应当知道使用或者披露他人的商业秘密属于非法的前提下仍然使用或者披露该商业秘密时,被告才承担相应的侵权责任。

如果被告从第三人处获得了某一商业秘密,当他得知该第三人是通过非法的手段获得的该商业秘密,在此情况下,如果被告仍然使用或者披露该商业秘密则构成侵权行为。当然,如果被告直接以非法的方式获取某一商业秘密,如采用引诱的方式,再使用或者披露该商业秘密,则属于侵权行为。

然而,如果被告从第三方获得了该商业秘密,但是,该第三方并未告知被告自己是以违反保密义务,通过不正当的手段获取的该商业秘密,此时,被告对自己使用或者披露该商业秘密的行为不承担侵权责任;但是,如果被告随后被告知其获取该商业秘密属于非法行为以后,其再使用或者披露该商业秘密时就应当承担侵权责任。对于此类情况,并不需要商业秘密权利人举证证明被告已经知道自己拥有该商业秘密的行为非法,只要证明被告应当知道即可。因此,如果当一个拥有正常思维的人处于被告的位置能够判断出自己拥有他人的商业秘密属于非法时,被告就应当对其随后的使用或者披露行为承担侵权责任。在现实中,基于类似的情形,只要法院认为根据已有的事实,凡是具有正常思维的人通过正常的思考和判断就能得出自己拥有他人的秘密信息属于非法时,法院都会判决被告随后实施的使用或者披露行为属于非法行为,被告应当为此承担侵权责任。

值得说明的是,故意回避获取商业秘密的途径的做法并不能必然地免除被告的侵权责任。

当审查被告是否应当对自己使用或者披露他人的商业秘密行为承担侵权责任时,可以综合地审查下列事项:①被告对商业秘密权利人所做的保密措施了解的程度;②被告对行业习惯或者行为方式熟悉的程度,以此可以帮助判断当第三方向被告披露该商业秘密时,被告自己能否判断出这一披露行为事先是否已经获得了商业秘密权利人的授权;③被告对商业秘密权利人与向其披露该商业秘密的第三方之间的关系的认识;④商业秘密权利人给被告的任何直接信息;⑤被告对第三方与该商业秘密权利人之间相互信任程度了解的情况;⑥第三方向被告出具的自己是该商业秘密的合法拥有者的各类保证。

综合分析以上各项内容,只有当被告信任第三方是该商业秘密的权利人或者合法授权者的资料具有合理性时,才能免除被告的侵权责任。

如果在商业秘密诞生之初,被告就知悉了该商业秘密的归属情况,以及哪些行为是否合法的情况,那么,该被告随后非法使用或者披露该商业秘密时就应当承担侵权责任。如果在商业秘密诞生之后的一段期限内,被告才知悉了该商业秘密的归属及其相关合法行为的情况,那么,对于其知悉之前所实施的使用或者披露行为不承担侵权责任,但是,在其知悉之后再使用或者披露时就应当承担侵权责任。

然而,虽然被告在已经知悉了哪些行为属于违法行为的情况下仍然继续非法地使用或者披露该商业秘密,因此应当承担侵权责任,但是,在有些情况下,被告实际应当承担的侵权责任可能会受到公平合理原则的制约。例如,如果被告在获知该商业秘密处于被侵害状态之前,善意地以公平合理的价格购买了该商业秘密,并且对涉及该商业秘密的相关设备或者研究项目进行了重大投资,或者由此已经获得了有别于该商业秘密的新的有益的信息,在这种情况下,即使是被告知悉其所购买的商业秘密在其购买时已经处于被侵害的状态,对其后续使用或者披露该商业秘密的行为追究全部的侵权责任就不够公平。

五、意外披露

商业秘密权利人、被告或者第三方的意外或者差错,都可能导致偶然或者错误地披露商业秘密。

如果被告知道或者应当知道其获得的某一信息是商业秘密,并且是由于意外或者错误的原因才使其获得的,那么,当其使用或者披露这一商业秘密时就应当承担侵权责任。但是,如果出现这种结果是由于该商业秘密权利人自己未对商业秘密采取合理的保密措施所导致的,那么将免除被告的侵权责任。

如果被告在获知该商业秘密处于被侵害状态之前,已经善意地实质性地停止利用该商业秘密,那么被告对商业秘密权利人承担的侵权责任就应当适当地受到限制。

第 41 条 保密责任

当一个人获取了一件商业秘密时,如果存在下列之一的情形,他就应当对该商业秘密权利人承担保密责任。

1. 在获取商业秘密之前,他已经作出了保密的承诺;

2. 基于披露者与接受者之间的关系,或者当时所处的情形,在披露时存在下列情形:

(1)接受披露的人当时知道或者应当知道是基于彼此间的信任才向其披露的;

(2)当其他人向接受者披露时,披露者有合理的理由作出判断接受者同意遵守保密的义务。

对第 41 条的诠释

一、适用范围

本条讨论商业秘密的接受者受到保密义务限制的问题,下一条则要讨论存在雇佣关系的主体之间的商业秘密的披露问题。

二、存在信任关系的披露

当接受商业秘密的人承诺对该商业秘密进行保密时,双方就建立起了一项保密义务。同样,也可以通过对披露者与接受者之间的相互关系以及当时的情形推断出他们双方之间已经建立起了一项保密义务。但是,只有当接受者知道被披露的信息具有秘密性时才能推断建立起这一类保密义务。

虽然对如何告知接受者的具体方式没有特别要求,但是,具体的情形必须能够明确地指示出接受者知道或者应当知道其接受的信息是保密的信息;另外,当时的情形还必须使得其他人相信接受者已经愿意承担保密的义务。因此,如果一个接受者已经表示不愿意接受秘密信息,或者在接受秘密信息之前没有机会拒绝这种接受,那么该接受者就不承担保密的义务。但是,在有些情况下,基于一些特殊的商业或者行业习惯,可以认为接受者已经同意承担保密义务。

同时值得注意的是,非商业目的的信息披露与基于商业目的的信息披露是不同的。例如,把一件商业秘密披露给一个工业公司时可能会促进其开发研究,并进一步促进其获取利益;如果把同样的商业秘密披露给一家非盈利的研究机构时,其所产生的社会效果可能是不同的。

商业秘密权利人采取了保密措施以后,如果有证据证明接受者已经知道商业秘密权利人采取的这种保密措施,那么这一证据就能够证明接受者知道或者应当知道商业秘密权利人希望进行保密。如果接收人唆使他人披露该信息,那么可以推断其知道该信息处于保密状态;如果披露行为是由于接收人的误导或者其他不正当的行为引起的,更能证明其知道该信息处于保密状态。在有些情况下,当事人之间对特定信息签订了明确的保密协议,这种协议可能是双方希望对有些并不属于该协议范围内的其他信息也进行保密的一种证据。如果商业秘密的权利人在向他人披露该商业秘密时规定了使用的目的,接受者接受该商业秘密时如果知悉该规定,他就应当接受这种约束,除非接受者明确表示不同意这种附加额外条件的接受。

在与潜在的购买者、客户或者被许可人进行谈判的时候,有时候需要向他们披露商业秘密的内容以便他们衡量是否值得对这一商业秘密进行交易,对此,保护商业秘密的法律规定这种披露只能限于在这种交易中使用,并且为此提供法律保护。在没有相反协议的情况下,销售包含商业秘密产品的行为一般不被视为披露该商业秘密的行为。合法购买商品的人也可以通过拆解和分析产品从中获取各类有用的信息,然后自由地加以利用。

然而,在有些情况下,如果双方当事人把财产的移交限于特定的目的以内,而不是一般的产品买卖,例如,财产的租赁或者财产的信托,在这些行为中一般认为接受者应当对这些财产中包含的商业秘密承担保密责任。同样,基于维修的目的把机器移交给接受者以后,一般认为接受者无权使用或者披露该机器中包含的商业秘密。法院认为未经授权使用或者披露他人商业秘密的行为往往发生在存在保密关系的当事人之中。在一些商业性的关系中,诸如雇主与雇员的关系、许可使用人与被许可使用人的关系等,都是典型的这类保密关系。

实际上,对于存在这种保密关系的商业秘密的接受方来说,如果他擅自对外披露该商业秘密,往往承担泄露商业秘密的侵权责任;然而,并不是在这种情形下擅自实施的所有披露行为都构成侵权。即使在双方存在着保密关系的情况下,对于接受者披露商业秘密的行为,在确定其责任时,也需要综合地考虑其披露的目的、他们过去的工作习惯、整个行业的惯例,以及披露时的其他情况。因而,虽然当把商业秘密许可给被许可人使用时,被许可人应当对该商业秘密承担保密责任,但是,当再把另一件信息也许可给该被许可人使用时,如果没有明确规定对该新的信息也应当进行保密,则该被许可人对这一新的信息就不承担保密责任,这一特殊的规定适用于雇佣关系当中。

三、违背保密协议构成单独的侵权行为

一些法院发现未经授权披露他人商业秘密的行为应当承担侵权责任,但是,有些商业性的秘密信息自身并不符合商业秘密的要求。在有些案件中,由于不能作为非法披露商业秘密的行为,这种披露行为就被称为"违反保密协议的行为",而在另一些案件中则被视为"不正当的竞争行为"。值得说明的是,在许多这类案件中法院通常采用的是一种狭义的商业秘密概念,在这种概念中排除了那些非技术性的信息,如客户的名单等,以及那些不能连续地长期适用的信息。本法中采用的是宽泛的商业秘密的概念,被上述狭义概念排除在外的一些信息也被包含在宽泛的商业秘密概念中。

在其他一些案件中,责令违反保密协议的一方承担法律责任,其原因可能主要出于对某些利益的保护,而不是为了保护有价值的秘密信息本身。例如,这类利益包括通过促使雇员认识到对雇主应当承担的一般性的忠诚义务,从而使得雇主的相关合法利益能够有所保障;以及在特殊关系中,例如,律师与委托人之间、医生与病人之间、律师和医生应当承担的特别的保密责任,从而保护客户和病人的合法权益。然而,如果缺失能够被法院认可和支持的应当受到保护的特殊利益,则只能对信息本身进行保护,此时原告需要证明该秘密信息符合商业秘密的条件。

显然,利用禁止使用和披露的方式对商业信息保护的范围越宽,就越有可能使公众对那些本应属于公共领域的信息的正常使用受限。

四、商业秘密的合同保护

商业秘密权利人可以通过合同的方式与接受者约定禁止使用该商业秘密的具体事项,从而保护该商业秘密。这类合同可以包含下列几种内容:①接受者承诺保护商业秘密,并且不与该商业秘密权利人进行商业竞争;②承诺不披露或者使用在特定关系或特定交易范围内获得的任何机密信息;③承诺不使用或者披露协议中规定的其他特定信息。

违反此类协议,使用或者披露协议中所约定的商业秘密之外的其他信息将承担违反合同的违约责任。

然而,由于这类合同能够减少或者排除潜在的竞争行为,因此,它们应当遵

从利用合同限制商业活动的传统规则,而且只能在合理的条件下对合法的交易活动产生效力。基于公平原则,在下列情形下的限制行为就是不合理的:①限制行为所排除的利益范围已经远远大于基于承诺所应当排除的范围;②由于过多地保护被承诺人的利益,有可能伤害承诺人或者公共的利益。

许多法院都承认合理的竞业禁止合同对承诺者的效力。在有些情况下,有关商业秘密保护的规则有助于人们判断竞业禁止合同的合理性。

如果雇员承诺在雇佣合同终止后不与雇主进行商业竞争,或者销售者许诺在购买者购买了其特定商品或者服务以后不与其进行商业竞争,这些许诺将被视为保护秘密信息的合理行为,在不损害许诺者(承诺者)合法利益的合适期限和范围内产生效力。

当法院承认这类竞业禁止合同的效力时,有关商业秘密的保护规则虽然不能在竞业禁止合同中起到决定性的作用,但是可以有助于推断竞业禁止合同中应当保护的合法利益,以及应当保护的合理的期限和范围。

判断只禁止使用或者披露特定信息的协议是否具有合理性,其主要依据在于审查协议中所保护的信息自身是否符合商业秘密的要求。如果该信息自身符合商业秘密的要求,那么禁止使用或者披露该信息的合同就属于有效合同。虽然在有些案件中,法院强制执行保密协议时将一些不符合保护条件的信息作为商业秘密进行保护,但一般来说,在这些决定中主要采用的还是狭义的商业秘密的概念,因此,一些形式上不属于商业秘密的秘密信息,如果按照宽泛的商业秘密的概念进行审查,可能就应当属于商业秘密的范畴,由此可见,法院的一些做法具有内在的正当性。

但是,在有些保密协议中,协议保护的信息自身可能已经是众所周知的内容,或者是对被承诺人没有实际的可被保护的利益的信息,例如,前雇员承诺不使用的信息可能只是一部分雇员所掌握的基本工作技能和专业知识内容,这样的保密协议自身就属于不合理的限制正常商业活动的行为,因此缺失合法有效性。

但是,并不是所有在保密协议中约定禁止使用处于公共领域中的某类信息的条款都属于无效条款,在有些情况下,这类约定仍然是合法有效的条款。如果在保密协议中禁止承诺人使用处于公共领域中的信息,当对这一保密协议进行强制执行时,实际上是为了保护协议中的一些利益,而不是保护这种信息本身。一些法院指出,这类保密协议在保护期限和地域范围上应当与传统的竞业禁止协议保持一致,然而,即使在保密协议中没有明确规定地域范围,该协议仍然可以合法有效。

众所周知的事实是,秘密信息一旦被披露,秘密信息的内容往往就难以被控制在一定的区域内,因此,未经授权的披露能够在任何地域内给商业秘密权利人造成危害。同样,未经授权的使用也能够在任何地域内剥夺商业秘密权利人所享有的对潜在的被许可使用人进行授权许可的机会。

虽然竞业禁止和对非法使用与披露的禁止都是"禁止"行为,但是两者存在着本质的差别。出于公平合理地保护被竞业禁止者(通常是前雇员)的合法利益的目的,通常情况下,对于竞业禁止行为的强制执行需要限制在合理的地域范围以内,因此,这种禁止行为属于一种有限的禁止行为。而对非法使用或者披露商业秘密行为的禁止则是一种绝对的禁止行为,它是基于有效地保护商业秘密权利人的合法利益而设立的,这种禁止行为没有地域限制。

对于合理的保密期限的问题,在约定不使用或者不披露商业秘密的协议中,即使没有明确约定保密的期限,只要该商业秘密自身一直合法有效,该保密协议就属于能够被强制执行的有效协议,因为在没有明确提出相反目的的情况下,签署保密协议的目的就是约定和履行对商业秘密的保密义务。

然而,如果保密协议中规定即使所保护的商业秘密进入公共领域之后,承诺人仍然不得使用该信息,在这种情况下,该保密协议仍然可以属于有效的协议,并且仍然可以进行强制执行。此时,维护协议的有效性,已经不是为了继续保护构成原商业秘密的信息本身,而是在于保护该协议中包含的其他合法利益。

例如,如果在商业秘密许可使用协议中约定,即使该商业秘密已经进入了公共领域,被许可使用人仍然需要支付许可使用费,对于这样的约定内容,通常可以进行强制执行。这种情况有时是合理的,特别是对于商业秘密第一次被许可使用时,双方基于对该商业秘密价值的评估最终约定了比较合理的支付方式和支付期限。而且在客观上也能够制止被许可使用人故意或者过失地公开披露该商业秘密,借以提前终止支付许可使用费的行为。

同样,在某些情况下,在协议中约定不得使用处于公共领域中的信息,这种约定可能是为了有效地保护被承诺人的声誉和信誉等合法的利益。

在这里陈述的规则并不要求所有的法院都应当支持和接受,有些法院可能更赞同那些只保护未处于公共领域中的信息的协议。然而,这些规则有助于确定能够获得强制执行的保密协议的范围,被承诺人往往希望借助这些保密协议对某些是否属于商业秘密存在争议,但是具有一定价值的特定秘密信息给予类似于商业秘密的保护。

第 42 条 雇员违反保密协议

一个雇员(或前雇员)违反保密义务擅自使用或者披露雇主(前雇主)的商业秘密须承担侵权责任。

对第 42 条的诠释

一、适用范围

本条的内容专门用于禁止在违反保密协议的情况下使用或者披露商业秘密的行为。

本法讨论的问题主要涉及那些与商业秘密权利人之间存在着隶属关系的雇员或者"佣人"侵害商业秘密的问题,不涉及与商业秘密权利人在法律地位上处于平等关系的"合同相对人"。

对于雇员来说,涉及当前的雇员以及前雇员使用或者披露商业秘密的行为。对于当前的雇员来说,除了基于商业秘密法律应当承担保密义务以外,他们还应当基于忠诚的一般原则对雇主承担更广泛的忠诚义务和职责。

那些与商业秘密权利人拥有平等的法律地位,但是又需要对商业秘密承担保密义务的人,例如,律师、财务顾问、商务顾问等,追究他们的保密责任问题适用本法第 41 条的相关规定。

然而,在有些情况下,本法中有关雇员关系下的保密义务处理规则也有利于处理那些与商业秘密权利人拥有平等法律地位关系的保密义务问题。

除了维护公平竞争以外,对一些专业人士来说,如律师和医生,他们也应当承担来自商业秘密法的保密义务。

二、雇员和前雇员的义务

在雇佣关系存续期间,雇员应当在所有的工作中对雇主履行忠诚的义务。

在这些忠诚义务中,基本的义务就是不得在从事雇主安排的工作的同时再开展与雇主的业务存在竞争关系的工作,包括不能利用在工作中获悉的属于雇主的秘密信息来开展与雇主竞争的商业性活动。因此,只要在职的雇员实施了与雇主竞争的商业性活动,无论是否侵害了雇主的商业秘密,其都应当承担法律责任。

除了不得实施竞争行为以外,在忠诚的义务中还包括不能向其他人披露雇主的秘密信息的义务。

在职雇员一旦把自己在工作中获悉的有价值的信息向第三方进行披露,审查的重点应当首先在于这一行为是否已经违反了该雇员应当遵守的忠诚义务,而不在于该信息自身的特征。然而,在通常情况下,如果该信息只是一般的常识,或者该雇员没有合理的理由认为该信息应当属于秘密信息,该雇员的披露行为就不属于违反忠诚义务的行为。

虽然在职雇员如果侵害了商业秘密应当承担侵权责任,但是,如果在职雇员只是未经授权使用或者披露了有价值的信息,而不是商业秘密,那么他承担法律责任的依据就主要来自他应当对雇主承担的忠诚义务。但是,在雇佣关系结束以后,责令侵害前雇主商业秘密的前雇员承担侵权责任的法律依据则是商业秘密法。一旦雇佣关系终结,如果双方没有签署可以强制执行的竞业禁止协议,那么,前雇员就有权利开展与前雇主竞争的商业活动。

如果双方签署了可以强制执行的竞业禁止协议,该协议也只能在合理的禁止范围内进行强制执行。然而,即使没有签署这类竞业禁止协议,前雇员也不得违背保密义务非法使用或者披露原雇主的商业秘密,因为对商业秘密的保密义务是一种法定义务,不受竞业禁止协议所约定的合同义务的影响。

当案件同时涉及违反商业秘密保护和前雇员的竞业禁止协议时,需要仔细衡量多种利益。对于前雇员来说,为了生计而向他人提供自己的才智和经验是其应当享有的基本权利。而且从社会的角度来看,雇员的正常流动也有利于通过扩散有用的技术和信息来促进行业的发展和竞争。

然而,在许多情况下,雇主如果不把有价值的商业秘密使雇员获悉及使用,其就难以有效地进行生产经营。但是,如果对雇员未经授权使用或者披露这些有价值的商业秘密缺乏合理有效的应对措施,雇主们又不得不花费高昂的代价,采取实际上难以充分有效地限制措施来防止雇员接触到这些商业秘密。同样地,如果商业秘密权利人的竞争者能够比较容易地从商业秘密权利人的雇员那里获得商业秘密权利人的商业秘密,那么,无论是商业秘密权利人还是其竞争对手,都不会再愿意对研发活动投入大量的资金,显然这也不利于社会的发展和公共利益。因此,必须根据具体案件的情况充分地权衡前雇主和前雇员双方的合理利益,以确保既能充分地保护商业秘密,又不会不当地限制雇员的合理流动性和应有的合法权益。

三、雇佣关系属于一种保密关系

根据雇佣关系的性质,总体上可以推断出雇员同意承担对自己在工作中获得的,自己认为或者有理由认为属于秘密的信息进行保密的义务,而且一般应当知道在雇佣关系终结以后,自己也不应当擅自使用或者披露这些秘密信息。

然而,有些信息是在雇佣关系存续期间主要由雇员研发出来的,它们更应该归属于雇员,而不是雇主。雇员有权利在自己的工作中不断地拓展和提高自己的一般技能、专业知识、工作能力和工作经验,即使开展这些活动需要利用雇主的一些资源也是合理的。虽然有些法院对缺乏保密协议的案件作出了有利于雇员的判决,但是,这些案件实际上更多的是由于雇主所主张的商业秘密自身不符合受保护的条件,或者是由于雇主没有对雇员合理地告知这些信息属于秘密信息,从而导致雇主未实施合理的保密措施所造成的。如果雇主明确地对商业秘密主张所有权,并且明确地告知雇员这些信息属于秘密信息,在这种情况下,这种雇佣关系将被视为包含着保密义务的雇佣关系。

四、一般技能、专业知识、工作能力和工作经验

对于那些构成雇员的一般工作技能、专业知识、工作能力和工作经验的信息,即使这些信息直接来源于前雇主投资的资源,前雇主也不能对这些信息主张享有商业秘密。早在 1562 年,英国就颁布了《学徒法令》,授权对于同一雇主可具有 7 年的学徒期,在此期间,雇员享有获得雇主对其进行技能培训的权利。这一法令的目的在于平衡雇主因为出资对雇员进行专业技能培训所应当获取的利益,以及雇员在竞争的市场中基于提供自己的劳动所应当获得的利益。

　　在现代法律中,雇主与雇员的利益平衡主要采用以下措施:①雇员承诺在雇佣关系存续期间对雇主负有忠诚的义务;②在多数情况下,双方可以通过合同约定,在雇佣关系终止以后合理地限制雇员不与原雇主开展竞业竞争;③雇员承认雇主对符合商业秘密条件的特别信息享有商业秘密权利。

　　因此,如果双方未签署有效的竞业禁止协议,那么雇佣关系终止以后,原雇员就可以利用在原雇主那里掌握的一般技能、专业知识、工作能力和工作经验与原雇主展开竞争活动,但是,该雇员仍然负有义务不能擅自使用或者披露原雇主的商业秘密。

　　当判断某一特定信息到底应当属于原雇主的商业秘密,还是应当属于原雇员的一般技能、专业知识、工作能力和工作经验时,要基于案件的具体事实和具体情况来确定。当雇主对该特定信息主张享有商业秘密权利时,他就必须首先提供证据证明该特定信息本身符合商业秘密的构成条件;其次,他还需要证明自己是这一商业秘密的合法权利人。构成商业秘密的信息通常被认为是那些只存在于雇主企业里的专门信息,而不是在整个行业里已经被普遍知悉的信息,或者是从同一行业雇员们普遍掌握的技巧里衍生出来的信息。

　　在有些情况下,雇主和雇员都会对某一特定信息的诞生作出贡献。如果竞争者进行独立研发后没能成功地获得这一特定信息,那么这一事实就能有力地证明该特定信息符合商业秘密的条件。另外,如果在雇佣关系终止以后,原雇员把记载着公式、蓝图、计划或者客户名单的物质载体据为己有,那么法院就很可能把这些信息认定为商业秘密。然而,对于那些留在雇员记忆里的信息,由于缺乏证据证明雇员是故意地保留在记忆里的,因此,这些信息就难以被认定为商业秘密,当然,在有些情况下,法院可能会作出相应的判断和决定。

　　在具体案件中,有时需要把商业秘密与一般技能、专业知识、工作能力和工作经验进行区分,这样做的目的在于在保护商业秘密与保护具有流动性的雇员的利益之间寻找合理的平衡。如果某一特定信息与雇员的整体工作经验密切相关,而且把这一信息作为雇主的商业秘密进行保护就将剥夺该雇员获得与其工作经验和工作能力相匹配的工作机会,在这种情况下,这一信息通常就不应当被作为雇主的商业秘密进行保护。

五、雇主与雇员之间的所有权分配

对于在雇佣关系存续期间,由雇员创造的有价值的信息的所有权归属问题,在代理法中已经作出规定,即在没有相反约定的情况下,发明或者创意的所有权归属于创造它的人。但是,即使是主要依靠雇员个人的知识或者技巧创造完成的有价值的信息,只要雇员完成这一工作属于下列履行本职工作的行为,或者是与本职工作相关的行为,这一信息的所有权归属问题就需要分别讨论。

（一）完成本职工作时获得的技术成果

如果雇员的本职工作就是为了创造发明开展试验（实验）工作,那么通常情况下人们会认为即使没有获得该雇员的特别同意,其通过试验（实验）所取得的可申请专利的发明应当归属于雇主所有,如果当雇员利用这种发明最终完成了雇主所期望获得的产品,由此更能说明雇员通过试验（实验）所获得的技术创新只是实现最终产品的中间过程和中间手段,因此这种发明本身应当归属于雇主。

然而,有所不同的是,如果一位被雇主雇佣的专家只是被要求完成某一环节中的具体工作,当他在工作中作出新的发明时,这一发明应当归属于该专家,而不是雇主。

（二）超越本职工作范围获得的技术成果

通常情况下,雇员对自己在本职工作之外开发创造的成果享有专利权或者商业秘密权,即使在这一过程中利用了雇主的时间、人员、设备和其他便利条件,雇员仍然能够对自己的创造成果享有所有权。但是,一旦利用了雇主的上述条件,对于这些创造成果雇主就享有一种"特殊的使用权",即一种不可撤销的、非独占的、免费的被许可使用权。与此同时,雇员对凡是构成他们的一般技能、专业知识、工作能力和工作经验的信息都享有所有权。当然,对于雇员完成的上述创造成果的所有权归属,雇员与雇主之间也可以通过合同进行约定和处分。

（三）雇员的技术成果处于不同归属时的法律责任

雇员开发完成的商业秘密,如果所有权归属于雇主,则雇员就必须按照法律规定承担保护该商业秘密的责任,不得擅自使用或者披露该商业秘密;如果所有权归属于雇员,当雇佣关系终止后,雇员就可以自由地使用或者对其他人披露该商业秘密,即使此时原雇主对该商业秘密仍然享有"特殊的使用权"。

（四）雇员完成的经营性信息的权利归属

上述对雇员在本职工作中完成的技术发明的权利归属所确立的规则，同样适用于诸如客户名单、经营计划和其他有价值的商业信息等经营性信息的权利归属。如果雇员完成这些工作时属于履行自己的本职工作，则这些信息的所有权归属于雇主，如果这些信息又构成了商业秘密，则雇员必须按照法律规定承担保护这些商业秘密的责任。

六、客户名单

保护商业秘密的一般规则同样适用于对"客户身份"和"客户需求"这类信息的保护。客户身份及相关的客户信息往往是公司最有价值的资产和重要的投资资源。虽然保护客户名单可能会涉及多种问题，但是绝大多数案件都是涉及前雇员利用其在雇佣关系存续期间获得的原雇主的客户名单进行非法利用的问题。从合理地保护公共利益和客户私人利益的角度来看，综合利用传统的保护商业秘密的措施，竞业禁止的措施，以及在职的雇员履行忠诚义务的措施是最有效的应对办法。

并不是所有的客户名单都能成为商业秘密，只有那些自身具有一定的价值和秘密性，又能为权利人创造一定的经济优势的客户名单才能被视为商业秘密。因此，对于一些特殊的产品或者服务来说，如果它们的潜在客户是容易识别的，那么这种客户信息本身就不属于商业秘密；相反，那些需要商业性清洁服务的家庭主人的信息，以及对一些单个客户特殊信息的汇总，这类信息如果能够满足价值和秘密性的要求则可以作为商业秘密。在现实中，如果一位雇员在雇佣关系终止前抄袭客户名单，或者企图努力地记住客户名单，这些证据能够证明这一客户名单是有价值的而且是用正当手段难以获取的，因此，这一客户名单可以被视为商业秘密。

然而，如果不同的竞争对手都在搜集相同的客户信息，显然这些客户信息已经是广泛知悉和容易被获取的，因此不能属于商业秘密；在有些案件中，客户的信息来自于送货时的客户名单，在绝大多数这类案件中，通过观察送货使用的交通工具就能比较容易地获取这些客户的名单和信息，因此，通过这些方式获取的客户名单也不属于商业秘密。

但是，如果是关于一些单个客户特殊需求的信息，这些信息的内容不容易被获知并且具有一定的价值,或者具有长期的需求。一旦有关客户身份和需求的信息符合商业秘密的条件,那么就可以参照本条诠释"五、雇主与雇员之间的所有权分配"的规则来确定该商业秘密在雇主与雇员之间的权利归属问题。

如果雇主基于工作需要把客户名单披露给雇员,或者雇主专门安排雇员找出潜在的客户,在这种情况下,这些客户名单的所有权一般都属于雇主。另一方面,在缺少竞业禁止协议的前提下,如果雇员在被雇用之前就已经获取了一定的客户信息,那么,在该雇佣关系终结后,他就可以自由地利用这些客户信息与原雇主开展竞争。

如果原雇主的客户名单构不成商业秘密,双方又无相反的有效约定,那么原雇员就有权利在雇佣关系终结后利用这些客户信息与原雇主展开竞争。只有很少的法院,特别是在涉及通过送货获取客户信息的案件中,即使前雇员已经与客户建立起了固定的个人关系,仍然禁止前雇员利用这种客户信息。显然,这种禁止是不公平的,它阻碍了雇员合理的流动性。

另外,通常情况下,如果这些客户名单和客户信息构不成商业秘密,那么,原雇主如果想要继续保护这些信息,他就应当采取与雇员签署合理的竞业禁止协议来实施。

七、利用合同进行保护

一般情况下,雇主和雇员之间对于商业秘密的保护和权利归属等问题可以通过合同进行协商和约定,通过合理的竞业禁止协议,雇主还可以排除前雇员对那些不能构成商业秘密的信息进行竞争性使用。同样,双方之间通过签署禁止披露的协议也可以禁止前雇员披露或者使用前雇主的特别信息。很显然,通过这些协议可以界定和扩大雇主的权利范围。

由于有关商业秘密的各项规则的合理性和科学性也都处于被不断地评估和完善之中,因此,有关商业秘密的相关合同的强制性效力也应当受到一定的限制。对于由雇员创造的发明或者发现,只有当这是雇员在本职工作中创造的成果时,依据普通法的规定,这些发明和发现才能归属于雇主。

另外,由于缺乏合理规范这方面问题的详细的法律规定,导致对于雇员在雇佣关系存续期间完成的发明和发现的归属问题只能主要地由雇主和雇员通过合同进行约定,而一般的雇佣合同中通常又规定,在雇佣关系存续期间,雇创造完成的所有发明和发现,其所有权都归属于雇主。显然,对于雇员来说,这种状况应当是不公平的。

与此相反的是,有时候又很难证明一项特别的发明是在什么时候完成的,雇员可能故意地把发明拖延到雇佣合同终止以后才公开,以便避开雇主依据普通法或者雇佣合同对该发明主张所有权。

除此之外,有时候审查确认一项由雇员完成的职务发明是否不正当地源自于其前雇主的商业秘密也是一件比较困难的事情。为了应对这一难题,在有些雇佣合同中就规定与雇员在前雇佣合同中的工作内容相关的发明和发现,即使是在前雇佣合同终止以后又由该雇员完成的,这些发明和发现的所有权仍然属于前雇主。

当然,这种合同规定自身也存在一些问题,甚至存在着不公平的因素。这种规定首先限制了该雇员提高和完善自己工作技能和工作水平的机会,同时又使其不能为新雇主提供更高水平的服务,不仅损害了雇员的合法利益,也损害了新雇主的合法利益。因此,这样也就在一定程度上限制了行业竞争,并且制约了雇员的合理流动。

基于上述种种原因,法院把这类具有"超期效力"的合同视为一种竞业禁止协议。这种协议的有效期限一旦超越合理的时间,或者前雇员完成的发明或发现完全是基于自己的一般技能和经验创造的,那么这种"超期效力"的合同就不得产生法律效力。

第43条　利用不正当手段获取商业秘密

本法第40条中所说的获取他人商业秘密的"不正当手段"主要包括:①盗窃他人的商业秘密;②利用欺诈手段获取他人的商业秘密;③通过非法窃听或者截取他人的通讯内容获取他人的商业秘密;④引诱别人泄密来获取他人的商业秘密;⑤故意参与泄密活动获取他人的商业秘密;⑥由于商业秘密权利人,以及其他合法的持有人自己的过错,或者由于环境的错误所导致的非法行为致使他人非法地获取了该商业秘密。

通过对公开合法地获得的产品或者信息进行独立分析和研究,并由此获得了他人商业秘密的行为属于合法行为。

对第 43 条的诠释

一、商业秘密保护的范围

由于商业秘密权利人对于占有或者使用该商业秘密信息并不具有排他性的权利,因此,对商业秘密的保护只限于禁止对商业秘密的非法获取、使用或者披露。对于非法使用或者披露商业秘密的问题已经在本法第 41 条和 42 条中进行了讨论,本条重点讨论通过非法手段获取商业秘密的问题。

二、获取商业秘密的正当手段

除非特殊情况,在正常情况下,凡是合法地获取商业秘密的人都应当承担保密的义务。另外,在正常的范围内,通过合法手段获取商业秘密的人都可以自由地使用或者披露该商业秘密而无须承担任何法律责任。与专利权人不同的是,商业秘密权利人对通过独立研发获得相同商业秘密的人无权主张禁止使用或者构成侵权的权利。除此之外,其他人还可以对商业秘密权利人公开销售的产品进行自由地拆解和分析,如果没有相应的专利权或者版权的保护,其他人就可以自由地利用通过反向工程从产品中获取的任何信息。另外,人们还可以通过分析发表的材料,观察或者以正当的方式接触那些处于公众视野中的物体或者事物来获取商业秘密,这些都是获取商业秘密的正当途径,因此都是合法行为。

三、不正当的获取行为

显然,要想把获取商业秘密的所有的不正当行为都列举出来是很难实现的。但是,下列行为应当都属于本法中所说的不正当行为:

(1)所有以侵权方式获取商业秘密的行为;

(2)所有以犯罪方式获取商业秘密的行为;

(3)到竞争对手的办公区域,通过入门盗窃的方式获取对方商业秘密的行为;

(4)雇员通过窃听雇主的电话,或者通过虚假的陈述诱导雇主披露商业秘密的行为;

(5)通过诱导或者故意地从第三方处获取商业秘密,而该第三方又是通过非法手段获取了该商业秘密的情形;

（6）通过诱导或者故意地从第三方处获取该商业秘密，而该第三方又是通过违反对商业秘密权利人承担的保密义务泄露该商业秘密的情形。

在有些情况下，获取商业秘密的具体方式本身可能并不违法，但是，整个获取行为却是违法的，这就需要对获取行为进行综合的考虑和评价。判断正当的获取行为时也应当综合考虑相关的所有问题，包括获取行为是否与公共政策相一致，是否有利于采取合理的预防措施防止秘密信息被泄露等。

对于商业秘密权利人能够采取的合理预防措施来说，主要涉及以下几种因素：①对不正当获取行为的预见能力；②预防措施的可行性；③以该商业秘密的价值为评价基础，采取该预防措施所需的有效成本额。

四、商业秘密的存在

侵害其他信息的法律责任与侵害商业秘密的法律责任不同。因此，虽然侵害其他合法利益的行为基于相关法律的规定应当承担相应的侵权责任，但是，只要不涉及商业秘密就不承担侵害商业秘密的法律责任，例如，只要该信息不属于商业秘密，无论获取该信息的手段是否合法，都不承担以不正当手段获取商业秘密的法律责任。

与此同时，如果利用正当的方式能够比较容易地确定某一信息的内容，那么该信息就不属于商业秘密。在此情况下，即使采用不正当的手段获取该信息也不构成侵害商业秘密的法律责任。然而，由于"采取正当手段比较容易地获知信息"这一条件直接决定着该信息是否属于商业秘密的范畴，也就是决定着信息的法律属性，因此，在具体的案件中应当慎重地对此作出判断，至少应当对采用正当手段获取该信息时所必须支付的成本和困难程度进行合理的评估。

在有些情况下，行为人决定采取不正当的手段获取该信息，他的这种行为本身就是难以通过正当手段获取该信息的一种证据，可以作为认定该信息属于商业秘密的证据。由于公共利益反对以不正当的手段获取商业秘密，因此，当有人明显地以不正当的手段获取某一信息时，反而有利于把该信息确认为商业秘密，并由此受到商业秘密法律的保护。

第 44 条　对侵害商业秘密行为的禁令措施

1. 对于本条第 2 项中侵害商业秘密的行为，应当采取禁令措施以阻止正在实施或者存在实施威胁的侵权行为。

2. 对侵权行为采取禁令措施时应当综合地评估案件的各种因素,通常情况下,应当综合地考虑下列基本因素:

(1)被保护的利益的性质;

(2)侵权的性质和程度;

(3)实施禁令措施和采取其他救济措施相比,实施禁令措施的合理性程度;

(4)实施禁令措施以后可能给被告的合法利益造成的损害,不实施禁令措施又可能给原告的合法利益造成的损害,两种损害的程度大小和总的社会后果;

(5)从第三方利益和社会公共利益的角度衡量采取禁令措施的合理性;

(6)原告在提起诉讼或者采取其他维权手段方面可能存在的不合理的拖延情况;

(7)原告可能存在的任何其他不当行为;

(8)颁布和实施禁令措施以后,在本案中可能产生的实际效果。

3. 在商业秘密案件中,禁令措施的有效期间应当能够使得禁令措施实现下列两个目的:①保护原告不再受任何侵权行为的侵害;②消除被告基于侵权行为所获取的全部经济优势。

对第 44 条的诠释

一、适用范围

本条适用于在商业秘密侵权纠纷案件中采用禁令措施的一般性规定。有关在侵权诉讼中采取禁令措施的一般性原则在《侵权法重述》的第 48 章中做了规定,这一原则同样适用于商业秘密侵权行为。本条中只侧重讨论那些在商业秘密侵权案件中与禁令措施相关的重要事项。本条的规定主要借鉴了《侵权法重述》第 936 条、第 933 至 935 条、第 937 至 943 条中的相关内容。主要涉及颁布禁令措施应当考虑的一般因素、适于颁布禁令措施的侵权行为的一般标准、禁止侵权行为所应当采取的具体法律措施等事项。另外,其他因素的考虑可能会影响对初步禁令措施的颁布实施。

侵害商业秘密的行为与侵害有形财产的财产权的行为比较类似,而与侵害商标和欺诈销售有所不同,商标侵权和销售欺诈行为主要影响到潜在的客户不再购买他们的产品。在《侵权法重述》第933至943条中对禁令措施所规定的一般原则可以直接适用于商业秘密侵权案件,而不宜直接适用于其他不公平竞争的行为。

值得说明的是,《侵权法重述》中规定的原则不适用于在办理商业秘密侵权案件时,为了保护商业秘密自身的秘密性不在司法程序中遭受泄露,而由法院等司法机关所采取的保密措施,例如,颁布和执行保护令,采取秘密审理程序,对记录材料进行签字和密封等措施(参见《统一商业秘密保护法》第5条)。

二、其他相关的救济措施

通常情况下,主要采用损害赔偿的方式对侵权行为造成的危害进行救济,只有当损害赔偿不能公平地弥补侵权危害时才适用禁令措施。出于维护法律和公正的需要,法院一般会自由地选择救济方式,或者把几种救济方式结合使用以便能够最有效地弥补侵权行为造成的危害。在商业秘密案件中,原告最主要的利益在于保护商业秘密的秘密性不被泄露和禁止对商业秘密的非法使用。但是,如同其他不正当竞争行为造成的危害一样,对于商业秘密侵权行为造成的实际危害,如果想要只借助经济赔偿的方式来实现全部补偿是十分困难的,因为一方面,想要证明全部的实际损失是比较困难的;另一方面,想要证明这些损失与被告的侵权行为之间的因果关系也是十分困难的。因此,对于被告可能继续实施的侵权行为或者实施侵权行为的威胁采取禁令措施是比较公正的。

在许多商业秘密案件中,经济赔偿和禁令措施被综合地适用,经济赔偿主要用来补偿原告已经遭受的损失,而禁令措施可以通过制止被告进一步地使用或者披露该商业秘密给原告所造成的新的损害。然而,在有些案件中则只需要采取禁令措施,例如,当被告通过不正当的手段获取商业秘密后还未使用或者披露该商业秘密时,或者当被告通过合法的方式获取商业秘密后威胁要违反保密协议对外披露该商业秘密而未披露时。而在有些案件中实施禁令措施反而不适当,例如,被告善意地对使用商业秘密已经进行了重大的投资,在其获得可以替换该商业秘密的知识以便维持其生产经营活动之前,不适宜对其采取禁令措施。

三、对侵权行为采取禁令措施

禁令措施通常适用于商业秘密案件,其目的在于一方面通过禁止被告进一步非法地使用该商业秘密给原告造成新的危害;另一方面剥夺被告基于侵权行为所获得的额外收益。该商业秘密如果还未被公开披露,禁令措施则可以保护该商业秘密的秘密性;该商业秘密如果已经被非法地公开,禁令措施则可以通过消除被告基于侵权行为所获得的领先优势和其他不公正的优势来弥补原告的损失。

当然,如果被告虽然非法公开了商业秘密,但是并未从侵权行为中获取任何优势,那么,此时对被告实施禁令措施就是对其实施侵权行为的惩罚和震慑。但是,由于促进竞争更符合公共利益,因此,在商业秘密案件中一般不适用这种惩罚性的禁令措施。

有时禁令措施可以阻止对商业秘密的威胁使用或者公开,但是对这类禁令的合理适用范围应当进行仔细地考虑和衡量,不能过度地限制合法竞争行为。例如,对于一位了解其前雇主商业秘密的雇员来说,如果其与前雇主之间未签署有效的竞业禁止协议,也没有明确的证据能够证明该雇员在从事新的相关工作时就必然地导致泄露前雇主的商业秘密,在这种情况下,即使该雇员到前雇主的特定竞争对手处工作,而且从事特殊的岗位,法院一般也不会禁止该雇员的这种就业行为。但是,对于这类情况,如果存在着重大的披露风险,就应当颁布禁止披露的禁令,或者禁止该雇员参与新雇主的具有特别泄露风险的特殊项目的禁令。

虽然禁令措施是商业秘密案件中比较常见的一种救济措施,但是,它也一直遵从着公正的原则,包括本条第 2 款对具体需要考量的因素做了具体的规定。

颁布禁令措施应当综合地衡量双方当事人的利益和社会的公共利益,对于原告来说,需要保护其基于商业秘密获得的商业优势;对于被告来说,需要保护其正当的商业交易机会避免受到不合理的干涉;对于社会公共利益来说,需要保护鼓励创新和促进竞争。例如,雇主有权保护他们的商业秘密免受雇员们的侵害,在双方缺少有效的包含禁止性条款的合同的情况下,雇员也有权利出售他们的技能和对其他人进行技术性培训。对于这些相互竞争的利益,不仅在审查确认信息本身是否属于商业秘密时值得考虑,而且在衡量合适的侵权责任时也应当考量。此外,在商业秘密侵权纠纷案件中同样适用传统衡平原则中的懈怠原则、禁止反言原则和不洁之手原则(译者注:在诉讼中提出主张的人自身应当无不当行为,否则该主张不应当被支持)。

依据本法第 40 条的规定,无辜使用他人商业秘密的人不应当承担侵权责任。只有当被告在已经获取了明确的消息,或者从已经获取的消息中可以推断出他所了解的信息属于别人的商业秘密的情况下,他仍然非法地使用时才承担侵权责任。一个基本的原则在于,如果某人善意地花费合理的金额购买了一项商业秘密,或者对善意地获得的一项商业秘密已经进行了重大投资,那么,当他接到该商业秘密处于被侵害状态的通知以后,他可以不停止使用该商业秘密。在这类案件中,可以通过采取其他救济措施,而不是采取禁止被告继续使用商业秘密的方式来合理地平衡各方的合法利益。

在许多情况下,当被告已经被告知其构成侵权后,如果再允许其继续使用该商业秘密显然是不公平的。在这种情况下,可以考虑通过额外增加补偿费的方式来进行解决。例如,可以规定被告必须再额外地另外支付一笔合理的许可使用费以后,其才能够在禁令存在的情况下继续有条件地使用该商业秘密(参见《统一商业秘密法》第 2 条第 2 款)。

在商业秘密案件中,当法院准备采取禁令措施时,还必须考虑制定和执行禁令的能力,以便既能保护商业秘密权利人的合法利益,又不至于过度影响被告的合法权益。例如,在禁令中应当准确地告知被告其应当知道的全部信息。

四、决定禁令措施范围的因素

对于确定禁令的范围及其合理性时应当考虑的具体因素已经在本条第 2 款中进行了列举,禁令措施一般只用于禁止使用或者披露商业秘密,以及实质上来自于商业秘密的特定信息。

然而,在现实中,禁令措施的颁布和执行有时还会涉及更多的问题。例如,在有些案件中,由于难以明确地区分哪些行为是利用原告的商业秘密继续非法地使用或者披露的行为,哪些行为是被告在使用或者披露自己独立研发出来的秘密信息的行为,从而导致保护原告商业秘密及其派生物的禁令措施难以执行。

有些禁令措施是基于被告已经掌握了原告的某些商业秘密,因而禁止被告参加特定的项目或者商业工作,这种禁令措施是合理的。在有些案件中,虽然侵权责任是明确的,但是,准确地确定商业秘密的界限却是困难的。为了在保护原告的权益与禁止被告的行为之间建立起合理的平衡,法院就需要为了有效地实施禁令措施而综合地衡量相关的各种因素。

当某一商业秘密的内容比较专一,并且又与公共领域中的有用信息密切相关时,颁布禁令时就应当严格规定商业秘密的界限,以免侵害到公有领域的信息。然而,如果商业秘密涉及一个大的工艺流程或者产品的主要组成部分,而其他方面又都属于公共领域中的内容,对于这种情况,在有些案件中,能够采取的唯一有效的保护方式可能就是通过颁布禁令来禁止使用这一工艺流程,或者制造这一产品。

在商业秘密案件中,禁令措施的法律效力没有地域上的限制。在法律有效的整个地域范围内,被告都将依据禁令的规定被禁止实施相关的行为。作出这种规定的合理性在于被告在任何地域中对商业秘密的非法使用都在增加泄露该商业秘密的风险性,同时也在剥夺原告在这一区域潜在的许可使用费用。即使被告在某些区域的非法使用没有给原告造成直接的损失,但是在法律有效的全部地域范围内禁止被告的使用行为可以剥夺被告利用侵害商业秘密进一步地非法获益。

在有些情况下,并非为了商业目的而非法披露他人商业秘密的行为可能是一种特殊的权利。虽然这类案例很少,但是在这种情况下颁布禁令必须要综合地考虑对原告商业秘密的保护、言论自由以及这种特殊的权利所代表的利益。

五、交出物品和转让专利

为了保证全面有效地补偿商业秘密权利人的损失和剥夺被告的全部非法收益,法院可以责令被告向商业秘密权利人返还包含商业秘密的全部资料、蓝图、客户名单,或者其他有形的物品(参见《统一商业秘密法》第 2 条第 3 款)。如果被告获得了发明,而该发明的技术又源自于该商业秘密,或者覆盖该商业秘密的内容,那么法院可以责令被告把该专利转让给商业秘密权利人。

六、禁令措施的有效期限

在商业秘密案件中设立禁令措施,目的是保护原告避免遭受被告进一步地使用或者披露该商业秘密所带来的危害,同时也在于剥夺被告基于侵权行为所获取的非法收益。但是,由于禁令措施在制止侵权行为或潜在的侵权行为的同时,可能还会制约被告的其他商业交易行为,而这些行为则不属于禁令措施所应当规范的范围,因此,在充分保护原告的合法权益的前提下,为了不损害被告的合法权益,就应当对商业秘密案件中的禁令措施设立一个合理的有效期限。

从理论上推断,为了避免被告再侵害被保护的商业秘密,禁令的合理期间应当一直持续到被告能够通过合法的手段获得该信息为止。因为当被告通过合法的手段获得了该商业秘密时,其再使用该商业秘密时就不属于侵权行为了。一般情况下,只有为了消除被告基于侵权行为所获得的领先使用优势或者其他非法优势时才可以再延长禁令措施的有效期限(参见《统一商业秘密法》第 2 条第 1 款)。在缺乏合理理由的情况下,如果继续延长禁令措施就可能不合理地损害了被告的合法利益,限制了合法的竞争,客观上损害了公共利益。

通过发布专利或者使用其他方式公开披露商业秘密所包含的信息时都会导致该商业秘密的秘密性丧失,从而使其不再属于商业秘密。

然而,对于公开披露对禁令措施所能产生的法律作用方面,不同的法院有不同的观点。有些法院在这种公开披露发生以后,仍然会签署禁令或者维持已经颁布的禁令以制止被告在该商业秘密未被公开以前实施的侵权行为;但是,另一些法院则主张公开披露以后就不应当再签署禁令,而且以前的禁令在公开披露之日也应当终止。

被告实施侵权行为以后,如果由原告或者其他第三人公开披露了该商业秘密,那么,在这种公开披露以后,判断是否还需要利用禁令措施来保护原告免遭进一步的侵害,或者消除被告已经获取的非法优势以及剥夺其进一步的非法收益,应当审查和衡量在该商业秘密披露之前被告所实施的侵权行为的情况。

总之,对于商业秘密被公开以后是否还需要颁布实施新的禁令措施或者继续维持已有禁令措施的效力的问题,具体到某一案件时,就应当依据这一案件的具体情况来决定。例如,被告在非法获取了他人的商业秘密以后,一方面利用该商业秘密通过生产经营活动获取非法的收益;另一方面又利用该商业秘密的内容申请专利,通过专利发布的方式公开了该商业秘密的内容,从而破坏了该商业秘密的秘密性,使其不能再作为商业秘密进行保护。而此时,被告可能成为专利权人,然后利用专利权进一步地获取更多的非法收益。在此情况下,在商业秘密被公开以后,显然有必要颁布实施新的禁令以禁止被告的非法行为,或者维持已有禁令的效力以禁止被告的非法行为。

另外,如前所述,虽然从理论上推断,如果公开披露来自被告的非法行为,那么禁令应当保持到被告通过合法手段能够比较容易地获取该商业秘密为止。然而,如果被告的泄露行为已经导致其他人大量地使用该商业秘密,那么,此时再对被告实施禁令措施就可能难以给原告带来有效的益处,并且对禁令应当持续的合理期限也难以作出准确的判断。从另一个方面来看,被告对于自己破坏原告商业秘密的行为应当承担侵权责任,而且通过侵权行为所获得的非法收益也应当属于原告的损失,基于这类情况,在有些案件中,有些法院就认为可以主要采用经济赔偿的方式来弥补原告的损失,而无须再采用禁令措施。

一般情况下,禁令的合理期限不应超过被告通过反向工程或者独立研发获取该商业秘密的时间,被告随后的使用也不应该再被视为侵权行为。在一些案件中,可以参照同一行业中的普通技术人员通过自己的独立研发最终获取这一商业秘密的时间,或者通过对购买于公开市场中的产品进行反向工程最终获取这一商业秘密的时间来衡量这一合理的期限;另外,熟悉这一行业领域的专家的观点也可以作为参考意见;其他竞争对手通过独立研发或者反向工程等正当手段获取这一商业秘密的时间也可以作为参考意见。这一期间就应当作为被告在没有侵权的情况下通过正当方式获取该商业秘密时应当花费的合理时间,也是禁令应当持续的有效时间。当然,这只是一般情况下禁令应当持续有效的最短时间,具体到每一个案件,具体的合理时间应当进行具体分析。

被告也可以向法院说明,由于自身拥有的与侵权无关的竞争优势,使得自身合法的发展速度比同行业的其他竞争者更快,因此,禁令的期限应当比一般情况要短。然而,应当明确的是,立法中建立禁令措施的基本原则是要能够完全地消除和剥夺被告基于侵权行为所获得的任何领先使用带来的优势和其他非法优势。因此,在具体的案件中,具体禁令措施的合理存续期限并不是简单地依据被告的发展速度来决定的。

在有些案件中,针对被告可能已经通过合法的方式获得了该商业秘密的情况,法院发布了具有特定期限的禁令。在另一些案件中,法院发布无固定期限的禁令,从而使被告在基于侵权行为所获得的商业优势全部消除以后,可以请求法院修订禁令的期限。当然,如果能够提前准确地判断出被告应当承担侵权责任的合理期限,那就容易确定禁令的有效期限。

除此之外,在任何情况下,如果被告由于实施侵权行为从而节省了其开展反向工程或者独立研发该商业秘密所需要的成本,那么这些节省的成本都是原告遭受的损失。

七、临时救济

本条讨论的内容主要是关于作为最终救济措施的禁令问题,但是在本法中也讨论了临时救济的问题。虽然不同法院对于这一问题的陈述不同,但是,几乎所有的法院都认识到是否给予临时救济,应当综合地考虑下列三种问题:①在缺失临时救济的情况下,原告将遭受无法挽回的损失的可能性;②原告胜诉的可能性;③实施临时救济措施在当事人之间,以及社会公共利益之间的公正合理性。

对于无法挽回损失的评估问题,法院普遍地认为,一旦被告非法地使用或者披露他人的商业秘密以后,即使责令被告通过经济手段进行赔偿,实际上也难以真正弥补给商业秘密权利人造成的全部损失,因此这种情形构成了无法挽回的损失。

第45条　对侵害商业秘密的经济补偿

1.计算商业秘密的侵权者应当对受害者承担的经济赔偿数额时,以受害者的损失额或者侵权者的非法收益额中数额较大的金额为准,除非这种赔偿方式在下列第2款中属于不合适的情形。

2.当判断一项具体的经济赔偿是否合适时,以及当确定作出这种判断所依据的方法本身是否合适时,应当综合考虑这一案件的所有因素,其中,应当考虑下列主要因素:

(1)原告对自己所遭受的经济损失或者被告因为侵权所获得的非法收益能够用证据加以证明的程度;

（2）侵权行为的性质和程度；

（3）原告获得其他补偿的可能性；

（4）侵权者实施侵权的意图，其自身所具备的知识情况，其能善意地信赖的事项以及所能信任的程度；

（5）原告在提起诉讼或者以其他方式进行维权方面所可能存在的任何不合理的拖延情况；

（6）原告的任何相关不当行为。

对第 45 条的诠释

一、适用范围

本条是关于在商业秘密侵权纠纷案件中获得经济补偿的规定，经济补偿数额的测算可以依据原告遭受的损失数额，或者被告获取的非法收益的数额进行估算，本条的测算规则同时包括这两种类型。

侵权诉讼中有关损害赔偿的一般性原则同样适用于商业秘密侵权案件。本条只涉及在商业秘密案件中有关损害赔偿比较重要的几个问题，主要涉及《侵权法重述》第二部分的下列内容：①第 902 和 903 条有关"损害"和"损害赔偿"的定义；②第 907 条有关恢复名义的规定；③第 908 和 909 条有关惩罚性赔偿的规定；④第 912 条有关"确定性"的规定；⑤第 435 条第 1 款和第 2 款中对故意侵权行为和非故意侵权行为的不同责任的规定。

有关因侵权获得的非法收益返还给原权利人的一般性规定也同样适用于商业秘密侵权案件［参见《返还请求权法重述》（1937 年）第 136 条］。

二、侵权行为的经济救济

由于被告实施的非法使用或者非法披露原告商业秘密的行为，使得原告从中遭受经济损失，并使被告从中获取非法收益。法院已经认识到有必要采取灵活的措施以便使得原告的损失获得补偿，同时使得被告的非法收益归还给原告。

一般情况下，只要有证据证明是由于商业秘密侵权行为所造成的经济损失，原告都有权利获得补偿。同时，原告还必须提供证据证明其所遭受损失的事实，以及这些损失与侵权行为之间的因果关系，而且通常情况下还会要求原告尽可能具体地确定合理的损失数额。另外,如果适当的话,原告还可以主张把被告因侵权所获得的非法收益都归还给原告,当前,原告主张赔偿自己遭受的全部损失与要求被告归还所有的非法收益之间,主要的界限就是原告不得获得双份的补偿。

在判断被告应当承担的赔偿损失数额时,被告的知识和实施侵权的目的也是值得考虑的因素。如果被告无辜地实施了侵害商业秘密的侵权行为,可以免除其赔偿责任。只有当其在实际知道或者应当知道使用或者披露他人商业秘密属于非法行为的情况下,才对其所实施的侵权行为承担赔偿责任。显然,如果被告无辜地使用了原告的商业秘密,并且在得知自己的行为属于非法行为之前已经对该商业秘密进行了投资,在这种情况下,对于被告自知道自己的行为属于非法行为开始,如果法院全部追回其随后基于使用该商业秘密所获得的所有收益也是不公平的。对于这种情况,一般情况下法院可以责令被告自收到侵权通知之日起向原告缴纳合理的许可使用费,同时,再缴纳在禁令条件下继续使用该商业秘密时应当缴纳的特别许可使用费,以此作为对原告的合理补偿。

另外,原告自身的行为也会影响对经济赔偿数额的判断,一些传统的衡平法原则,如懈怠原则、禁止反言原则、不洁之手原则等都会影响到商业秘密侵权案件中有关经济赔偿和禁令措施的认定。

三、法定救济和公平救济的关系

规范商业秘密侵权损害赔偿所遵循的一般原则是公平原则和合法原则。传统的损害赔偿数额主要是依据原告所遭受的具体损失额来计算,但是,由于市场本身的竞争特性,往往使原告很难明确地证明自己实际遭受的损失额和其他损失。与此同时,由于被告公开披露而遭到破坏的商业秘密自身的价值也只能通过推测来判断,很难有一个具体的准确的数额。由此决定了在商业秘密案件中采用归还原主的赔偿方式是一种比较重要的赔偿手段,即被告基于侵权行为所获取的非法收益就应该全部归还给原告。被告的非法收益体现在两个方面:一是被告通过销售使用了该商业秘密的产品所获取的非法收入;二是被告通过使用该商业秘密在生产经营中所节省的成本。

在有些案件中,测算原告所遭受损失的方式与测算被告非法收益的方式会产生重合。例如,通过测算被告通过销售收入获得的非法收益时,这些收益反过来也是原告的销售市场被被告夺占以后所遭受的损失。同样地,在正常情况下,被告使用该商业秘密所应当缴纳的合理的许可使用费,在遭受侵权的情况下就是被告非法节省的成本,也是原告损失的许可使用费。因此,在许多案件中,并没有明确地区分损害赔偿和返还原主赔偿。

虽然在少数案件中要求原告从损害赔偿和返还原主赔偿中选择其中一种进行主张,但是,在其他案件中,只要两种方式没有重合,则允许原告同时使用两种方式进行主张。但是比较合理的规则是允许原告根据具体的案件需要决定选择一种或者同时使用两种补偿方式来进行举证,因为在许多情况下,两种赔偿金额并不完全一致。

通常情况下,同时采用损害赔偿和返还原主赔偿是比较合适的。然而,如果只允许原告选择一种赔偿方式,物归原主的赔偿方式主要在于剥夺被告基于侵权所获得的非法收益,同时也能在一定程度上弥补原告由此遭受的损失;与此相似的是,根据原告遭受损害的赔偿方式也在一定程度上剥夺了被告的非法收益。相比较而言,在同一案件中,在两种赔偿方式中选择赔偿数额较高的方式作为整个案件统一的赔偿方式比较合适,这样也可以免除发生重复赔偿的可能性。

四、经济救济的测算方法

法院已经认识到至少有下列四种方法可以用来测算经济赔偿的数额。

(1)测算原告遭受的损失。原告遭受的损失一般包括下列四部分:①原告销售利润的减少;②许可使用费的减少或者丧失;③因侵权行为导致的其他收入的减少;④因被告公开商业秘密导致的商业秘密价值的损失。

(2)被告通过销售侵权产品所获得的非法利润。

(3)测算被告的成本差额。这种方法借鉴于专利侵权案件,就是利用"标准比较法"来测算被告由于侵权所节省的成本。具体做法是测算被告在侵权情况下和在未侵权情况下达到相同的生产经营状态时所支出的成本差异,这种差异就是通过侵权行为所节省的费用,应该归还给原告。

(4)确定合理的许可使用费。这种方法是对涉案的商业秘密测算出一个合理的许可使用费价格,测算的方法是基于市场上公平合理的原则,在买方和卖方都自愿的前提下由双方自由地进行协商所确定的许可使用费的价格,以此作为被告应当支付的许可使用费的参考价格。

最后,在具体案件中,究竟应当选择和使用哪一种测算方法要根据具体的案情和事实来确定。

五、以原告损失为依据的赔偿

通常情况下,体现原告经济损失的一种常见的指标就是原告预期销售收益的丧失。对此,原告可以提供证据证明自被告开始非法使用原告的商业秘密以后,自己的一些特定客户被被告夺走,或者自己正常的销售收入开始下降,或者自己的利润增长开始下降。虽然在市场中还会存在其他影响因素,而且这些影响因素会在一定程度上制约着原告上述证据的效力,但是这些证据对于支持原告遭受的损失是有利的。

当有证据能够证明如果被告未销售侵权产品,原告将会持续地销售包含自己商业秘密的产品时,原告可以依据自己产品的利润率以及被告的销售收入来主张自己遭受的损失。另外,在有充分证据的情况下,原告还可以把损失的范围扩展到配件产品、销售服务、耗材供应,以及正常情况下客户需要从原始供应商处购买的其他物品和服务上。在有些案件中,通过测算对销售的许可使用费也可以比较合理地估算出原告的损失。

原告也有权获得补偿那些能够用证据证明的,因为被告的侵权行为所带来的其他经济损失。法院也已经支持原告获得补偿那些为了挽回损失所支出的合理成本,例如,为了夺回因为被告的侵权行为而失去的客户所采取的宣传和促销的成本。另外,原告也有权利获得补偿那些由于侵权行为所导致的原告的产品必须降价所造成的损失。

在商业秘密案件中,非法泄露商业秘密所造成的损失比非法使用所造成的损失要难测算得多。如在一些案件中,当被告把商业秘密泄露给原告的一个竞争对手时,这一商业秘密可能会被很快地传遍其他竞争对手,甚至被公开披露,从而破坏了该商业秘密的价值。此时,原告所遭受的损失应当公平地以侵权行为发生时该商业秘密合理的市场价格为依据来进行确定。当然,采用测算方法时需要综合地考虑多种因素,包括在没有侵权行为的情况下该商业秘密被披露的可能性。如果被破坏的商业秘密属于原告企业的核心资产,那么,在有些案件中,原告可以用自己企业总的资本价值的减少量作为所遭受的损失进行主张。

六、以被告的非法收益为依据的赔偿

在商业秘密侵权案件中,归还原主赔偿方式的传统做法是测算被告涉及侵犯商业秘密的非法销售利润,有关会计利润的一般规则同样适用于商业秘密案件,原告可以对被告的净利润提出归还主张。

原告应当举证证明被告的销售额。被告应当举证证明在销售额中哪些部分不涉及商业秘密,以及在计算净利润时应当考虑哪些成本。关于成本的扣减和管理费用的分摊适用一般的会计规则,也可以参照商标侵权纠纷案中相关的计算方法。被告不仅必须提供销售含有商业秘密产品的利润,还要提供与侵权相关的其他利润。例如,销售包含商业秘密的机器的消耗品的利润、配件的利润、提供相关有偿服务的利润等,这些利润都与被告最初销售侵权机器产品时的侵权行为相关,因此都应当属于非法利润的范围。

如果在被告销售的产品中,原告的商业秘密只涉及该产品的一部分销售额,那么在此情况下,把被告销售该产品的整体利润都作为原告的损失显然不公平。此时,在公平合理的情况下,如果在原告和被告之间能够就该商业秘密约定一种许可使用费,这一许可使用费就可以作为被告获取非法利润数额的参考。

如果被告的利润主要体现在所节约的成本上,如所侵害的商业秘密是一种提高生产效率的方法,此时采用"标准比较法"来衡量和确定被告的非法收益就是比较合适的方法。比较的内容就是被告实际花费的成本,与被告如果未非法使用该商业秘密而达到当前相同的生产经营状态时所应当花费的成本进行比较,两者的差额就是原告的损失。

如果被告能够通过反向工程或者独立研发等合法手段获取该商业秘密,那么就应当利用被告通过合法手段获取该商业秘密时的成本与非法使用该商业秘密时的成本进行比较。在测算被告合法获取的成本时,应当考虑原告开发该商业秘密的成本,如果可能,还应当参考第三方通过独立研发或者反向工程获取该商业秘密的成本。

当通过合法的手段难以获取该商业秘密时,就应当把被告使用该商业秘密的成本,与被告为了寻找能够替代该商业秘密又能达到相同效果的方法所需要支出的成本进行比较。

基于本法第 44 条第 6 款中对禁令期间规定的原则,通常情况下,应当对被告颁布一项专门的禁令,即禁止被告在通过合法手段获得该商业秘密之前再使用该商业秘密,这样就逼迫被告对合法获取商业秘密的成本负责。然而,在这类案件中,虽然被告承担着合法获取商业秘密成本的责任,但是,这一被被告节省下来的成本往往不被列为被告的非法利润,从而不能合理地赔偿给原告,因此,在实际案件中,应当注意被告的这一非法利润。

七、参照合理的许可使用费进行赔偿

利用合理的许可使用费补偿原告的损失时,比较合理的许可使用费价格应当是买卖双方在自愿的基础上,以市场价格为基础经过双方讨价还价的结果。但是在商业秘密侵权案件中,往往需要法院对许可使用费的价格进行认定,这种认定越合理,也就越能更好地弥补原告的实际损失。但是,许可使用费并不能剥夺被告基于侵权行为所获得的全部非法收益。另外,由于支付合理的许可使用费的责任只是追究被告应当在使用之前通过讨价还价以后需要向原告支付的合理的使用费用,因此,这种责任方式并不能遏制被告实施侵权行为。因此,在一般情况下,不能单独地利用合理的许可使用费来赔偿原告的损失。

但是,在有些特殊的案件中,单独地利用合理的许可使用费却能够比较合理地弥补原告的损失。在实际的案件中,至少有下列三种情形比较适合于适用合理的许可使用费来进行赔偿。

(1)如果被告在收到原告告知侵权的通知之前,已经善意地对该商业秘密进行了重大的投资,对于被告接到通知之后所获得的全部收益如果都归属于原告显然是不公平的。在此情况下,接到原告的侵权通知以后,被告应当通过支付合理的许可使用费的方式来作为对原告的经济赔偿,同时,还应当另外支付新的合理使用费以便在禁令存在的情况下,有条件地继续使用该商业秘密,被告以此行为来表示认可该商业秘密的市场价值,同时也保护了被告的诚实信用。

(2)对于原告的损失,即使难以准确地计算,但是也明显高于被告获得的非法收益,此时,采用合理的许可使用费标准进行赔偿就是比较合理的方式。例如,由于被告生产经营的低效率导致被告虽然非法使用了原告的商业秘密,但是其获得的利润却很低,甚至无利润。而此时,原告的实际损失又难以估算,在这种情况下,采用合理的许可使用费的赔偿方式就是一种比较公正的选择。

（3）在有些情况下，被告的非法收益虽然难以准确地计算，但是明显高于原告的损失，此时，采用合理的许可使用费的方式也是比较合适的。

在侵权纠纷案件中"合理许可使用费"所能够发挥的作用，以及在具体案件中应当关注的公平合理的因素，这些都会影响法院对合理许可使用费数额的认定。对于那些故意侵害他人商业秘密的被告，为了确保赔偿措施能够真正地起到威慑和阻止进一步侵权的行为，法院可以调整和确认许可使用费的最终数额。

八、对经济救济的限制

无论是以原告的损失还是以被告的非法收益来计算经济赔偿的数额，被告承担经济赔偿的合法期限应当只限于被告通过合法手段获得该商业秘密之前的时期。合法获得商业秘密的手段诸如反向工程或者独立研发。

另外，由原告或者其他第三方通过申请专利或者其他方式公开后，该商业秘密由于失去了秘密性而不再属于商业秘密。有时，在商业秘密被公开以后，被告使用该商业秘密时仍然需要支付经济赔偿金，这是由于在该商业秘密被公开之前，被告已经利用了该商业秘密，并且已经获得了在先使用优势或者其他不公平的优势，由于这些不合法的优势的存在，使得被告对该商业秘密被公开以后的使用应当继续承担经济赔偿的责任。然而，这种经济赔偿也有期限的限制，一般延续到完全消除被告所有的非法优势为止，具体内容可以参考本法第44 条第 6 款中有关禁令期限限制的陈述。

值得说明的是，在商业秘密侵权纠纷中有关经济赔偿期限的规定不一定适用于有关违反商业秘密使用和保密合同的纠纷案件。有关违反商业秘密合同的义务通常是由合同条款约定的，例如，对于商业秘密许可使用合同来说，许可使用费覆盖的期限可以由双方在合同中约定，这一期限可以在该商业秘密被公开之前结束，也可以在被公开之后结束。但是，有时合同的条款不一定具有实际履行的可行性。例如，如果双方在签署的保密协议中约定在该秘密被公开以后仍然需要继续履行保护义务，则该项约定由于不合理地限制了被约定保密的一方正当的生产经营权利而属于无效条款；当然，双方可以约定在该秘密被披露之前终止合同关系，这一约定则是合法有效的条款。

然而，违反有效的保密协议擅自使用他人商业秘密的行为，不但构成了违反合同的责任,同时也构成了侵害商业秘密的责任。双方在合同中约定的时间限制对于侵权纠纷中涉及的经济赔偿具有一定的影响,但是不产生决定性的作用。

九、惩罚性赔偿

对于那些在侵权诉讼中适用惩罚性赔偿措施的法院,如果原告适用普通法能够在商业秘密侵权诉讼中争取到使法院判决被告承担惩罚性赔偿则是比较理想的诉讼结果。惩罚性赔偿的目的在于威慑和惩罚恶劣的侵权行为,通常需要证明被告存在"故意"或"恶意"的非法行为。《统一商业秘密法》中规定惩罚性赔偿的数额不能超过损害赔偿和返还原主赔偿的两倍。

十、律师费用

在美国的大多数州中都不会根据普通法的规定就律师费用的承担作出裁决。但是,根据《统一商业秘密法》的规定,对方合理的律师费用由下列方承担:①如果侵权行为是"故意和恶意的",由侵权人承担;②如果原告恶意地提起侵权诉讼,由原告承担;③如果恶意地申请终止禁令或者恶意地抵制禁令,由申请人和行为人承担。

（侯仰坤翻译,2018 年 4 月于北京）

本章附录:《反不正当竞争法重述》(节选)原文

Restatement Third, Unfair Competition
RESTATEMENT(THIRD) OF UNFAIR COMPETITION
CURRENT THROUGH JUNE 2009

CHAPTER 4. APPROPRIATION OF TRADE VALUES

TOPIC 2. TRADE SECRETS

§ 39. Definition of Trade Secret

A trade secret is any information that can be used in the operation of a business or other enterprise and that is sufficiently valuable and secret to afford an actual or potential economic advantage over others.

Comment:

a. Rationale for protection.

The protection of confidential business information dates at least to Roman law, which afforded relief against a person who induced another's employee to divulge secrets relating to the master's commercial affairs. The modern law of trade secrets evolved in England in the early 19th century, apparently in response to the growing accumulation of technical know-how and the increased mobility of employees during the industrial revolution. In the United States the protection of trade secrets was recognized at common law by the middle of the 19th century, and by the end of the century the principal features of contemporary trade secret law were well established.

The protection of trade secrets advances several interests. Early cases emphasized the unfairness inherent in obtaining a competitive advantage through a breach of confidence. The imposition of liability for the appropriation of a trade secret protects the plaintiff from unfair competition and deprives the defendant of unjust enrichment attributable to bad faith. The development of rules protecting trade secrets formed part of a more general attempt to articulate standards of fair competition. More recently, the protection of trade secrets has been justified as a means to encourage investment in research by providing an opportunity to capture the returns from successful innovations. The rules protecting trade secrets also promote the efficient exploitation of knowledge by discouraging the unproductive hoarding of useful information and facilitating disclosure to employees, agents, licensees, and others who can assist in its productive use. Finally, the protection afforded under the law of trade secrets against breaches of confidence and improper physical intrusions furthers the interest in personal privacy.

The subject matter and scope of trade secret protection is necessarily limited by the public and private interest in access to valuable information. The freedom to compete in the marketplace includes, in the absence of patent, copyright, or trademark protection (see §§ 16 and 17), the freedom to copy the goods, methods, processes, and ideas of others. The freedom to copy, however, does not extend to information that is inaccessible by proper means. Liability for the appropriation of a trade secret thus rests on a breach of confidence or other wrongful conduct in acquiring, using, or disclosing secret information.

b. Doctrinal development.

Early trade secret cases, responding to requests for injunctive relief against breaches of confidence, frequently supported the exercise of equity jurisdiction by describing the plaintiff's interest in the trade secret as a property right, often said to derive from the discovery of valuable information. Similar characterizations sometimes appear in the modern case law. The property rationale emphasizes the nature of the appropriated information, especially its value and secrecy. Even the earliest cases, however, also include an examination of the propriety of the defendant's conduct. The plaintiff's property right was effective only against defendants who used or acquired the information improperly. No exclusive rights were recognized against those who acquired the information by proper means. Other cases, choosing to begin their analysis with an examination of the defendant's behavior, concluded that the essence of a trade secret action is a breach of confidence or other improper conduct, sometimes explicitly disavowing any property dimension to a trade secret. The influential formulation in § 757 of the Restatement of Torts(1939), reporting that the property conception "has been frequently advanced and rejected," concluded that the prevailing theory of liability rests on "a general duty of good faith." Id., Comment a. Both the former Restatement and the supporting case law, however, also require that the information qualify for protection as a trade secret, thus incorporating the elements of secrecy and value that underlie the property rationale.

The dispute over the nature of trade secret rights has had little practical effect on the rules governing civil liability for the appropriation of a trade secret. The cases generally require that the plaintiff establish both the existence of a trade secret under the principles described in this Section and the fact of misconduct by the defendant under the rules stated in § 40. Many cases acknowledge that the primary issue is the propriety of the defendant's conduct as a means of competition. The substantive scope of the rights recognized under the law of trade secrets thus reflects the accommodation of numerous interests, including the trade secret owner's claim to protection against the defendant's bad faith or improper conduct, the right of competitors and others to exploit information and skills in the public domain, and the interest of the public in encouraging innovation and in securing the benefits of vigorous competition.

In 1979, the National Conference of Commissioners on Uniform State Laws promulgated the Uniform Trade Secrets Act. The Prefatory Note states that the "Uniform Act codifies the basic principles of common law trade secret protection." The original Act or its 1985 revision has been adopted in a majority of the states. (See the Statutory Note following this Section.) Except as otherwise noted, the principles of trade secret law described in this Restatement are applicable to actions under the Uniform Trade Secrets Act as well as to actions at common law. The concept of a trade secret as defined in this Section is intended to be consistent with the definition of "trade secret" in § 1(4) of the Act.

Some states have adopted criminal statutes specifically addressed to the appropriation of trade secrets. In other states, more general criminal statutes have been interpreted to reach such appropriations. In some circumstances the appropriation of a trade secret may also violate the federal wire and mail fraud statutes(18 U. S. C. A. § § 1341, 1343) and the National Stolen Property Act(18 U. S. C. A. § 2314). The definition of a trade secret contained in this Section, however, is directly applicable only to the imposition of civil liability under the rules stated in § 40. It does not apply, other than by analogy, in actions under criminal statutes or in other circumstances not involving civil liability for the appropriation of a trade secret, such as the protection of trade secrets from disclosure under the Freedom of Information Act(5 U. S. C. § 552).

c. Relation to patent and copyright law.

Federal patent law offers protection to "any new and useful process, machine, manufacture, or composition of matter," 35 U. S. C. A. § 101, unless the invention "would have been obvious at the time the invention was made to a person having ordinary skill in the art to which said subject matter pertains." 35 U. S. C. A. § 103. Federal design patents protect "any new, original and ornamental design for an article of manufacture," again subject to the requirement of non-obviousness. 35 U. S. C. A. § 135. Unlike the limited protection against improper acquisition, disclosure, and use accorded to the owner of a trade secret under the rules stated in § 40, the holder of a patent enjoys a general right to exclude others from making, using, or selling the patented invention, 35 U. S. C. A. § 271, enforceable even against persons relying on independent discovery or reverse engineering. An application for a patent must include a specification containing "a written description of the invention, and of the manner and process of making and using it," and "the best mode contemplated by the inventor of carrying out" the invention. 35 U. S. C. A. § § 111 and 112. Upon issuance of a patent, the specification and other materials comprising the patent file become available for public inspection. 37 C. F. R. § 1. 11. Thus, for matter disclosed in the patent, issuance terminates the secrecy required for continued protection as a trade secret, even if the patent is subsequently declared invalid. See Comment f. Pending, denied, and abandoned patent applications, however, are not generally open to public inspection. 35 U. S. C. A. § 122; 37 C. F. R. § 1. 14. Thus, the filing of a patent application does not in itself preclude continued protection of the invention as a trade secret.

The United States Supreme Court in *Kewanee Oil Co. v. Bicron Corp.*, 416 U. S. 470, 94 S. Ct. 1879, 40 L. Ed. 2d 315(1974), held that federal patent law does not preempt the protection of inventions and other information under state trade secret law. The Court concluded that the requirement of secrecy fundamental to the protection of trade secrets(see Comment f) avoids interference with the federal patent policy of access to information in the public domain. It also concluded that the limitations on the scope of state trade secret protection(see § 40) make it unlikely that the federal policy of inducing public disclosure in exchange for the protection of a patent will be significantly undermined by reliance on trade secret protection for patentable inventions. In a subsequent decision, however, the Supreme Court emphasized that any rule of state law that substantially interferes with the use of information that has already been disclosed to the public or that is readily ascertainable from public sources is preempted. *Bonito Boats, Inc. v. Thunder Craft Boats, Inc.*, 489 U. S. 141, 109 S. Ct. 971, 103 L. Ed. 2d 118(1989).

Federal copyright law protects "original works of authorship fixed in any tangible medium of expression," 17 U. S. C. A. § 102(a), against unauthorized reproduction, use in the preparation of derivative works, distribution, public performance, or public display. 17 U. S. C. A. § 106. Protection is limited, however, to the manner in which the authorship is expressed and does not extend to "any idea, procedure, process, system, method of operation, concept, principle, or discovery" embodied in the work. 17 U. S. C. A. § 102 (b). Copyright protection subsists from the creation of a work and is not contingent upon public dissemination. See 17 U. S. C. A. § 302. A claim of federal copyright is thus not in itself inconsistent with a claim to trade secret protection for information contained in the work. Although § 301 of the Copyright Act preempts the recognition under state law of "rights that are equivalent to any of the exclusive rights" of copyright in works "within the subject matter" of the statute, the protection afforded to trade secrets under the rules stated in § 40 has been held to lie outside the preemptive scope of the Copyright Act.

Registration of a copyright is not a condition of copyright protection. 17 U. S. C. A. § 408. The registration of a copyright claim in an unpublished work ordinarily requires the deposit of a complete copy of the work, 17 U. S. C. A. § 408 (b) (1), which is then open to public inspection. 17 U. S. C. A. § 705. However, the regulations of the Copyright Office permit the deletion of material constituting trade secrets from deposits made in connection with computer programs and also authorize the granting of special relief from the normal deposit requirements in other cases. The status as a trade secret of information contained in a work that is the subject of a copyright registration is determined under the general principles governing secrecy and accessibility described in Comment f.

d. Subject matter.

A trade secret can consist of a formula, pattern, compilation of data, computer program, device, method, technique, process, or other form or embodiment of economically valuable information. A trade secret can relate to technical matters such as the composition or design of a product, a method of manufacture, or the know-how necessary to perform a particular operation or service. A trade secret can also relate to other aspects of business operations such as pricing and marketing techniques or the identity and requirements of customers (see § 42, Comment f). Although rights in trade secrets are normally asserted by businesses and other commercial enterprises, nonprofit entities such as charitable, educational, governmental, fraternal, and religious organizations can also claim trade secret protection for economically valuable information such as lists of prospective members or donors.

The prior Restatement of this topic limited the subject matter of trade secret law to information capable of "continuous use in the operation of a business," thus excluding information relating to single events such as secret bids and impending business announcements or information whose secrecy is quickly destroyed by commercial exploitation. See Restatement of Torts § 757, Comment b (1939). Both the case law and the prior Restatement, however, offered protection against the "improper" acquisition of such short-term information under rules virtually identical to those applicable to trade secrets. See id. § 759, Comment c. The Restatement, Second, of Agency in § 396 similarly protects both trade secrets and "other similar confidential matters" from unauthorized use or disclosure following the termination of an agency relationship. The definition of "trade secret" adopted in the Uniform Trade Secrets Act does not include any requirement relating to the duration of the information's economic value. See Uniform Trade Secrets Act § 1 (4) and the accompanying Comment. The definition adopted in this Section similarly contains no requirement that the information afford a continuous or long-term advantage.

A person claiming rights in a trade secret bears the burden of defining the information for which protection is sought with sufficient definiteness to permit a court to apply the criteria for protection described in this Section and to determine the fact of an appropriation. In the case of technical information, a physical embodiment of the information in the form of a specific product, process, or working model often provides the requisite definition. However, there is no requirement that the information be incorporated or embodied in a tangible form if it is otherwise sufficiently delineated. The degree of definiteness required in a particular case is also properly influenced by the legitimate interests of the defendant. Thus, a court may require greater specificity when the plaintiff's claim involves information that is closely integrated with the general skill and knowledge that is properly retained by former employees. See § 42, Comment d.

An agreement between the parties that characterizes specific information as a "trade secret" can be an important although not necessarily conclusive factor in determining whether the information qualifies for protection as a trade secret under this Section. As a precaution against disclosure, such an agreement is evidence of the value and secrecy of the information, see Comments e and f, and can also supply or contribute to the definiteness required in delineating the trade secret. The agreement can also be important in establishing a duty of confidence. See § 41. However, because of the public interest in preserving access to information that is in the public domain, such an agreement will not ordinarily estop a defendant from contesting the existence of a trade secret. (On the protection of information by contract, see § 41, Comment d.)

It is not possible to state precise criteria for determining the existence of a trade secret. The status of information claimed as a trade secret must be ascertained through a comparative evaluation of all the relevant factors, including the value, secrecy, and definiteness of the information as well as the nature of the defendant's misconduct.

e. Requirement of value.

A trade secret must be of sufficient value in the operation of a business or other enterprise to provide an actual or potential economic advantage over others who do not possess the information. The advantage, however, need not be great. It is sufficient if the secret provides an advantage that is more than trivial. Although a trade secret can consist of a patentable invention, there is no requirement that the trade secret meet the standard of inventiveness applicable under federal patent law.

The value of information claimed as a trade secret may be established by direct or circumstantial evidence. Direct evidence relating to the content of the secret and its impact on business operations is clearly relevant. Circumstantial evidence of value is also relevant, including the amount of resources invested by the plaintiff in the production of the information, the precautions taken by the plaintiff to protect the secrecy of the information (see Comment g), and the willingness of others to pay for access to the information.

The plaintiff's use of the trade secret in the operation of its business is itself some evidence of the information's value. Identifiable benefits realized by the trade secret owner through use of the information are also evidence of value. Some early cases elevated use by the trade secret owner to independent significance by establishing such use as an element of the cause of action for the appropriation of a trade secret. Such a "use" requirement, however, imposes unjustified limitations on the scope of trade secret protection. The requirement can deny protection during periods of research and development and is particularly burdensome for innovators who do not possess the capability to exploit their innovations. See Comment h. The requirement also places in doubt protection for so-called "negative" information that teaches conduct to be avoided, such as knowledge that a particular process or technique is unsuitable for commercial use. Cases in many jurisdictions expressly renounce any requirement of use by the trade secret owner. It is also rejected under the Uniform Trade Secrets Act. See the Comment to § 1 of the Act. Use by the person asserting rights in the information is not a prerequisite to protection under the rule stated in this Section.

f. Requirement of secrecy.

To qualify as a trade secret, the information must be secret. The secrecy, however, need not be absolute. The rule stated in this Section requires only secrecy sufficient to confer an actual or potential economic advantage on one who possesses the information. Thus, the requirement of secrecy is satisfied if it would be difficult or costly for others who could exploit the information to acquire it without resort to the wrongful conduct proscribed under § 40. Novelty in the patent law sense is not required. Although trade secret cases sometimes announce a "novelty" requirement, the requirement is synonymous with the concepts of secrecy and value as described in this Section and the correlative exclusion of self-evident variants of the known art.

Information known by persons in addition to the trade secret owner can retain its status as a trade secret if it remains secret from others to whom it has potential economic value. Independent discovery by another who maintains the secrecy of the information, for example, will not preclude relief against an appropriation by a third person. Similarly, confidential disclosures to employees, licensees, or others will not destroy the information's status as a trade secret. Even limited non-confidential disclosure will not necessarily terminate protection if the recipients of the disclosure maintain the secrecy of the information.

Information that is generally known or readily ascertainable through proper means (see § 43) by others to whom it has potential economic value is not protectable as a trade secret. Thus, information that is disclosed in a patent or contained in published materials reasonably accessible to competitors does not qualify for protection under this Section. Similarly, information readily ascertainable from an examination of a product on public sale or display is not a trade secret. Self-evident variations or modifications of known processes, procedures, or methods also lack the secrecy necessary for protection as a trade secret. However, it is the secrecy of the claimed trade secret as a whole that is determinative. The fact that some or all of the components of the trade secret are well-known does not preclude protection for a secret combination, compilation, or integration of the individual elements.

The theoretical ability of others to ascertain the information through proper means does not necessarily preclude protection as a trade secret. Trade secret protection remains available unless the information is readily ascertainable by such means. Thus, if acquisition of the information through an examination of a competitor's product would be difficult, costly, or time-consuming, the trade secret owner retains protection against an improper acquisition, disclosure, or use prohibited under the rules stated in § 40. However, any person who actually acquires the information through an examination of a publicly available product has obtained the information by proper means and is thus not subject to liability. See § 43. Similarly, the theoretical possibility of reconstructing the secret from published materials containing scattered references to portions of the information or of extracting it from public materials unlikely to come to the attention of the appropriator will not preclude relief against the wrongful conduct proscribed under § 40, although one who actually acquires the secret from such sources is not subject to liability.

Circumstantial evidence is admissible to establish that information is not readily ascertainable through proper means and hence is eligible for protection as a trade secret. Precautions taken by the claimant to preserve the secrecy of the information(see Comment g), the willingness of licensees to pay for disclosure of the secret, unsuccessful attempts by the defendant or others to duplicate the information by proper means, and resort by a defendant to improper means of acquisition are all probative of the relative accessibility of the information. When a defendant has engaged in egregious misconduct in order to acquire the information, the inference that the information is sufficiently inaccessible to qualify for protection as a trade secret is particularly strong. See § 43, Comment d.

Although courts have recognized that trade secret rights may not be asserted in information that is in the public domain, the cases disagree on the consequences of a loss of secrecy that occurs between the time of a defendant's confidential receipt of the trade secret and the defendant's subsequent unauthorized use or disclosure. Some decisions refuse to consider the availability of the information from public domain sources at the time of the alleged appropriation, at least when the defendant's knowledge derives from the confidential disclosure rather than from the public sources. Other decisions, more narrowly construing the obligations attendant upon a confidential disclosure, hold that protection against unauthorized use or disclosure is not available after the information has ceased to be a secret.

（On the remedial consequences of a loss of secrecy occurring after a defendant's appropriation, see § 44, Comment f; § 45, Comment h.）However, in many of the cases that refuse as a matter of law to take into account a loss of secrecy, the information was in fact only theoretically rather than readily ascertainable from the public domain at the time of the defendant's use or disclosure, thus justifying relief under either rule.

When information is no longer sufficiently secret to qualify for protection as a trade secret, its use should not serve as a basis for the imposition of liability under the rules stated in § 40. If the information has become readily ascertainable from public sources so that no significant benefit accrues to a person who relies instead on other means of acquisition, the information is in the public domain and no longer protectable under the law of trade secrets. Even those courts that decline to take into account a loss of secrecy following a confidential disclosure to the defendant often assert in dicta that no liability attaches if the defendant actually extracts the information from public sources. When the information is readily ascertainable from such sources, however, actual resort to the public domain is a formality that should not determine liability. The public interest in avoiding unnecessary restraints on the exploitation of valuable information supports the conclusion that protection as a trade secret terminates when the information is no longer secret. The defendant remains liable, however, for any unauthorized use or disclosure that occurred prior to the loss of secrecy. This position is consistent with the language and policy of the Uniform Trade Secrets Act. Section 1(2) of the Act defines "misappropriation" as the improper acquisition, disclosure, or use of a "trade secret," and § 1(4) excludes from the definition of "trade secret" information "generally known or readily ascertainable by proper means." Termination of trade secret rights upon a loss of secrecy is also consistent with the limitations on injunctive and monetary relief in §§ 2 and 3 of the Act(and in §§ 44 and 45 of this Restatement) applicable to appropriations occurring prior to the loss of secrecy.

g. Precautions to maintain secrecy.

Precautions taken to maintain the secrecy of information are relevant in determining whether the information qualifies for protection as a trade secret. Precautions to maintain secrecy may take many forms, including physical security designed to prevent unauthorized access, procedures intended to limit disclosure based upon the "need to know," and measures that emphasize to recipients the confidential nature of the information such as nondisclosure agreements, signs, and restrictive legends. Such precautions can be evidence of the information's value(see Comment e) and secrecy(see Comment f). The prior Restatement of this topic included the precautions taken to maintain the secrecy of the information as one of a number of factors relevant in determining the existence of a trade secret. See Restatement of Torts § 757, Comment b(1939). The Uniform Trade Secrets Act requires a trade secret to be "the subject of efforts that are reasonable under the circumstances to maintain its secrecy." Section 1(4)(ii). Whether viewed as an independent requirement or as an element to be considered with other factors relevant to the existence of a trade secret, the owner's precautions should be evaluated in light of the other available evidence relating to the value and secrecy of the information. Thus, if the value and secrecy of the information are clear, evidence of specific precautions taken by the trade secret owner may be unnecessary.

The precautions taken by the trade secret owner are also relevant to other potential issues in an action for the appropriation of a trade secret. They can signal to employees and other recipients that a disclosure of the information by the trade secret owner is intended to be in confidence. See § 41. They can also be relevant in determining whether a defendant possessed the knowledge necessary for the imposition of liability under the rules stated in § 40(see § 40, Comment d), whether particular means of acquisition are improper under the rule stated in § 43 (see § 43, Comment c), and whether an accidental disclosure results in the loss of trade secret rights(see § 40, Comment e).

h. "Law of ideas."

Cases involving the submission of ideas by employees, customers, inventors, and others to businesses capable of reducing the idea to practice are sometimes analyzed under separate rules referred to as the "law of ideas." Idea submission cases often arise in the context of suggestions for new or improved products submitted to manufacturers, or in connection with programming and other ideas submitted to the entertainment industries. Plaintiffs seeking compensation for their ideas typically rely on contract claims alleging an express or implied-in-fact promise by the recipient to pay for the submitted idea. In some cases, however, compensation is sought through tort or restitutionary claims. These non-contractual claims are generally resolved through an analysis of the nature of the information and the circumstances of the submission that is fundamentally indistinguishable from the rules governing trade secrets. Some decisions explicitly incorporate such claims within the scope of trade secret law.

To sustain a claim in tort for the appropriation of an idea, most courts require the submitted idea to be "novel" in the sense of not being generally known (cf. Comment f) and sufficiently "concrete" to permit an assessment of its value and the fact of its use by the recipient (cf. Comment d). The courts also examine the circumstances of the disclosure to determine whether the recipient is bound by an obligation of confidentiality. Factors such as the relationship between the submitter and recipient, prior dealings between the parties, the customs of the industry, and the recipient's solicitation or opportunity to refuse the disclosure are relevant in determining the recipient's obligations. Cf. § 41.

With the rejection under the Uniform Trade Secrets Act and under this Section of any requirement of use by the owner of a trade secret, see Comment e, there is no longer a formal distinction between trade secrets and the ideas that form the subject matter of the idea submission cases. The developing rules governing the rights of submitters and recipients of ideas in the absence of an express or implied-in-fact contract can thus be understood as specific applications of the general rules stated here. The rules in this Restatement relating to the protection of trade secrets are therefore applicable, either directly or by analogy, to claims in tort alleging the appropriation of ideas.

Since the public and private interests favoring access to information that is in the public domain are also relevant in analyzing contractual claims, many jurisdictions require proof of novelty and concreteness for the enforcement of express or implied-in-fact contracts to pay for submitted ideas. Thus, the rules stated here may also be helpful in analyzing contractual liability in idea submission cases.

§ 40. Appropriation of Trade Secrets

One is subject to liability for the appropriation of another's trade secret if:

(a) the actor acquires by means that are improper under the rule stated in § 43 information that the actor knows or has reason to know is the other's trade secret; or

(b) the actor uses or discloses the other's trade secret without the other's consent and, at the time of the use or disclosure,

(1) the actor knows or has reason to know that the information is a trade secret that the actor acquired under circumstances creating a duty of confidence owed by the actor to the other under the rule stated in § 41; or

(2) the actor knows or has reason to know that the information is a trade secret that the actor acquired by means that are improper under the rule stated in § 43; or

(3) the actor knows or has reason to know that the information is a trade secret that the actor acquired from or through a person who acquired it by means that are improper under the rule stated in § 43 or whose disclosure of the trade secret constituted a breach of a duty of confidence owed to the other under the rule stated in § 41; or

(4) the actor knows or has reason to know that the information is a trade

secret that the actor acquired through an accident or mistake, unless the acquisition was the result of the other's failure to take reasonable precautions to maintain the secrecy of the information.

Comment:

a. Scope.

The rules stated in this Section are applicable to common law actions in tort or restitution for the appropriation of another's trade secret, however denominated, including actions for "misappropriation," "infringement," or "conversion" of a trade secret, actions for "unjust enrichment" based on the unauthorized use of a trade secret, and actions for "breach of confidence" in which the subject matter of the confidence is a trade secret. Except as otherwise noted, the rules governing trade secrets as stated in this Restatement are also intended to be consistent with and applicable to actions under the Uniform Trade Secrets Act. This Section does not govern the imposition of liability for conduct that infringes other protected interests such as interference with contractual relations[see Restatement, Second, Torts §§ 766 – 774A (1979)], breach of the duty of loyalty owed by an employee or other agent [see Restatement, Second, Agency §§ 387 – 398 (1958)], or a breach of confidence not involving a trade secret (see § 41, Comment c).

The rules stated in this Section are not applicable to actions for breach of contract, including breach of a promise not to use or disclose a trade secret or a promise not to compete with the owner of a trade secret. Such agreements are governed by the rules generally applicable to the formation and enforcement of contracts, including the limitations on the enforcement of contracts in restraint of trade stated in Restatement, Second, Contracts §§ 186 – 188 (1981). The rules stated in this Chapter, however, can be useful in interpreting and implementing the principles embodied in those limitations. See § 41, Comment d. The existence of an express or implied-in-fact contract protecting trade secrets does not preclude a separate cause of action in tort under the rules in this Section. The terms of the contract may be relevant to a number of issues in such an action, including the existence of a protectable trade secret(see § 39, Comment d)and the creation of a duty of confidence(see § 41, Comment b).

In an action for the appropriation of a trade secret, the plaintiff bears the burden of proving both a proprietary interest in information that qualifies for protection as a trade secret under the rule stated in § 39 and an acquisition, use, or disclosure of the information by the defendant in violation of the rules stated here. A proprietary interest sufficient for relief under this Section can arise through the discovery of a trade secret or through the acquisition of rights in a trade secret discovered by another. On the rights of an employer in trade secrets discovered by an employee, see § 42, Comment e. Since neither novelty nor absolute secrecy is a prerequisite for protection as a trade secret, see § 39, Comment f, each of several independent discoverers can have a proprietary interest in the same information.

b. Improper acquisition.

The prior Restatement of this topic imposed liability only for the wrongful use or disclosure of another's trade secret. Improper acquisition of a trade secret was not independently actionable. See Restatement of Torts § 757(1939). Wrongful use or disclosure is also frequently recited in the case law as an element of the cause of action for trade secret appropriation. The cases requiring proof of wrongful use or disclosure, however, typically involve information that has been acquired by the defendant through a confidential disclosure from the trade secret owner. In such cases the acquisition of the secret is not improper; only a subsequent use or disclosure in breach of the defendant's duty of confidence is wrongful. Even in these circumstances the courts have recognized a plaintiff's right to obtain relief prior to any wrongful use or disclosure if such misconduct by the defendant is sufficiently likely. See § 44, Comment c. A defendant's willingness to resort to improper means in order to acquire a trade secret is itself evidence of a substantial risk of subsequent use or disclosure. Subsection (a) of this Section follows the rule adopted in § 1 (2) (i) of the Uniform Trade Secrets Act, which imposes liability for the acquisition of a trade secret by improper means. Thus, a person who obtains a trade secret through a wiretap or who induces or knowingly accepts a disclosure of the secret in breach of confidence is subject to liability. See § 43, Comment c. Subsequent use or disclosure of a trade secret that has been improperly acquired constitutes a further appropriation under the rule stated in Subsection (b) (2) of this Section. The relief available to the trade secret owner in such circumstances, however, may be more extensive than that available prior to any use or disclosure of the secret by the defendant.

c. Improper use or disclosure.

There are no technical limitations on the nature of the conduct that constitutes "use" of a trade secret for purposes of the rules stated in Subsection (b). As a general matter, any exploitation of the trade secret that is likely to result in injury to the trade secret owner or enrichment to the defendant is a "use" under this Section. Thus, marketing goods that embody the trade secret, employing the trade secret in manufacturing or production, relying on the trade secret to assist or accelerate research or development, or soliciting customers through the use of information that is a trade secret(see § 42, Comment f) all constitute "use." The nature of the unauthorized use, however, is relevant in determining appropriate relief. See § § 44 and 45.

The unauthorized use need not extend to every aspect or feature of the trade secret; use of any substantial portion of the secret is sufficient to subject the actor to liability. Similarly, the actor need not use the trade secret in its original form. Thus, an actor is liable for using the trade secret with independently created improvements or modifications if the result is substantially derived from the trade secret. The extent to which the actor's sales or other benefits are attributable to such independent improvements or modifications, however, can affect the computation of monetary relief. See § 45, Comment f. However, if the contribution made by the trade secret is so slight that the actor's product or process can be said to derive from other sources of information or from independent creation, the trade secret has not been "used" for purposes of imposing liability under the rules stated in Subsection(b). Although the trade secret owner bears the burden of proving unauthorized use, proof of the defendant's knowledge of the trade secret together with substantial similarities between the parties' products or processes may justify an inference of use by the defendant.

The owner of a trade secret may be injured by unauthorized disclosure of a trade secret as well as by unauthorized use. A public disclosure injures the trade secret owner by destroying the secrecy necessary for continued protection of the information as a trade secret. See § 39, Comment f. A private disclosure can increase the likelihood of both unauthorized use and further disclosure. An actor may thus be subject to liability under the circumstances described in Subsection (b) in connection with either a public or private disclosure of a trade secret. To subject the actor to liability, the unauthorized disclosure need not be express. Any conduct by the actor that enables another to learn the trade secret, including the sale or transfer of goods or other tangible objects from which the trade secret can be obtained, is a "disclosure" of the secret under the rules stated in this Section.

The unauthorized disclosure of a trade secret ordinarily occurs as part of an attempt to exploit the commercial value of the secret through use in competition with the trade secret owner or through a sale of the information to other potential users. The scope of liability at common law and under the Uniform Trade Secrets Act for disclosures that do not involve commercial exploitation of the secret information is unclear. If the trade secret is disclosed primarily for the purpose of causing harm to the trade secret owner, a court may properly conclude that the actor is subject to liability despite an absence of commercial exploitation. Thus, a former employee who publicly discloses trade secrets of the former employer in retaliation for a termination of the employment is subject to liability under this Section. In other circumstances, however, the disclosure of another's trade secret for purposes other than commercial exploitation may implicate the interest in freedom of expression or advance another significant public interest. A witness who is compelled by law to disclose another's trade secret during the course of a judicial proceeding, for example, is not subject to liability. The existence of a privilege to disclose another's trade secret depends upon the circumstances of the particular case, including the nature of the information, the purpose of the disclosure, and the means by which the actor acquired the information. A privilege is likely to be recognized, for example, in connection with the disclosure of information that is relevant to public health or safety, or to the commission of a crime or tort, or to other matters of substantial public concern.

d. Knowledge of wrongful possession.

The owner of a trade secret is protected under Subsection(b) of this Section only against a use or disclosure of the trade secret that the actor knows or has reason to know is wrongful. If the actor has not acquired the information through a confidential disclosure from the trade secret owner, see Subsection(b) (1), use or disclosure of the information will not subject the actor to liability unless the actor knew or had reason to know that the use or disclosure was wrongful due to the manner in which the actor acquired the trade secret. See Subsection(b) (2) – (4). Thus, if an actor acquires a trade secret by improper means, such as by inducing or knowingly accepting a disclosure of the information from a third person that is in breach of a duty of confidence, the actor is subject to liability for any subsequent use or disclosure of the secret. See Subsection(b) (2). However, an actor who acquires a trade secret from a third person without notice of that person's breach of confidence has not acquired the information by improper means and is not subject to liability for use or disclosure unless the actor subsequently receives notice that its possession of the information is wrongful. See Subsection(b) (3).

To subject an actor to liability under the rules stated in Subsection(b) (2) – (4), the owner need not prove that the actor knew that its possession of the trade secret was wrongful; it is sufficient if the actor had reason to know. Thus, if a reasonable person in the position of the actor would have inferred that he or she was in wrongful possession of another's trade secret, the actor is subject to liability for any subsequent use or disclosure. A number of cases also subject an actor to liability if, based on the known facts, a reasonable person would have inquired further and learned that possession of the information was wrongful. Studious ignorance of the circumstances surrounding the acquisition of the information thus will not necessarily avoid liability under this Section. Among the facts relevant in establishing the actor's actual or constructive knowledge are the actor's knowledge of any precautions against disclosure taken by the trade secret owner, the actor's familiarity with industry customs or practices that would justify an assumption that a disclosure to the actor by a third person was unauthorized, information known to the actor regarding the nature of the relationship between the trade secret owner and the person from whom the actor acquired the secret, and any direct communications to the actor from the trade secret owner. The actor's reliance on claims of ownership or other assurances given by the person from whom the actor acquired the information is sufficient to avoid liability only if the actor's reliance is reasonable under the circumstances.

If an actor possesses the actual or constructive knowledge required under Subsection(b)(2) – (4) of this Section at the time of the initial acquisition of the secret, the actor is subject to liability for all use or disclosure of the trade secret. If the actor obtains such knowledge after acquisition of the trade secret, the actor is subject to liability for any use or disclosure occurring subsequent to receipt of the requisite knowledge, but is not liable for prior use or disclosure. However, although receipt of the requisite knowledge is sufficient to subject the actor to liability for subsequent conduct, the relief available to the trade secret owner may be limited by the equities of the case. Thus, if before receiving the required knowledge the actor has in good faith paid value for the trade secret, undertaken significant investment in equipment or research relating to the secret, or otherwise substantially changed its position in reliance on the information, the imposition of

particular remedies for subsequent use or disclosure may be inappropriate. See §
44, Comment b; § 45, Comment b.

e. Accidental disclosure.

An accidental or mistaken disclosure of the trade secret to the actor under the
rule stated in Subsection(b)(4) of this Section may result from a mistake by the
owner of the trade secret, the actor, or a third person. If the disclosure to the
actor is not the result of the owner's failure to take reasonable precautions to
protect the trade secret, an actor who knows or has reason to know that the
information is a trade secret that has been disclosed to the actor through an
accident or mistake is subject to liability for subsequent use or disclosure. If the
actor in good faith has substantially changed its position in reliance on the
information prior to acquiring the requisite knowledge, however, the relief
available to the trade secret owner may be appropriately limited. See § 44,
Comment b; § 45, Comment b.

§ 41. Duty of Confidence

A person to whom a trade secret has been disclosed owes a duty of confidence
to the owner of the trade secret for purposes of the rule stated in § 40 if:

(a) the person made an express promise of confidentiality prior to the
disclosure of the trade secret; or

(b) the trade secret was disclosed to the person under circumstances in which
the relationship between the parties to the disclosure or the other facts surrounding
the disclosure justify the conclusions that, at the time of the disclosure,

(1) the person knew or had reason to know that the disclosure was intended
to be in confidence, and

(2) the other party to the disclosure was reasonable in inferring that the
person consented to an obligation of confidentiality.

Comment:

a. Scope.

This Section describes when the recipient of a trade secret disclosure is bound by a duty of confidence. Section 42 treats the special considerations that influence the application of the principles discussed in this Section when the disclosure occurs within an employment relationship.

b. Confidential disclosures.

A duty of confidence enforceable under the rules stated in § 40 can be created by an express promise of confidentiality made by the recipient of the disclosure. A duty of confidence may also be inferred from the relationship between the parties and the circumstances surrounding the disclosure. However, no duty of confidence will be inferred unless the recipient has notice of the confidential nature of the disclosure. Although no specific form of notice is required, the circumstances must indicate that the recipient knew or had reason to know that the disclosure was intended as confidential. In addition, the circumstances must justify the other party's belief that the recipient has consented to the duty of confidence. Thus, a disclosure to one who has indicated an unwillingness to accept the confidence or who has no opportunity prior to the disclosure to object to the imposition of the confidence will not create an obligation of confidentiality in the recipient.

In some cases the customs of the particular business or industry may be sufficient to indicate to the recipient that a particular disclosure is intended as confidential. The customary expectations surrounding the disclosure of information in noncommercial settings may differ from those arising in connection with disclosures in commercial contexts. The customary expectations regarding the confidentiality of information disclosed within the research facilities of an industrial firm, for example, may differ from those regarding disclosures in a nonprofit research laboratory. Precautions undertaken by the trade secret owner to maintain the secrecy of the information, if known to the recipient, can be evidence that the recipient knew or had reason to know of the owner's expectation of confidentiality. Solicitation of the disclosure by the recipient can also contribute to an inference of confidentiality, particularly if the disclosure is prompted by a misrepresentation or other improper conduct on the part of the recipient. In some cases an express agreement regarding the confidentiality of particular information may be evidence of the parties' expectations regarding the confidentiality of other information not within the scope of the agreement.

If the owner of a trade secret discloses information for a limited purpose that is known to the recipient at the time of the disclosure, the recipient is ordinarily bound by the limitation unless the recipient has indicated an unwillingness to accept the disclosure on such terms. During negotiations with prospective buyers, customers, or licensees, for example, it is sometimes necessary to disclose trade secrets in order to permit the other party to evaluate the merits of the proposed transaction. The law of trade secrets provides the necessary assurance that the limited purpose of such disclosures will be respected.

In the absence of an agreement to the contrary, the sale of a product embodying a trade secret is not ordinarily regarded as a confidential disclosure. The purchaser is thus free to exploit any information acquired through an examination or analysis of the product. However, a transaction such as a lease or a bailment may be more likely to support an inference of confidentiality if the parties understand the transfer to be for a limited purpose. The transfer of a machine embodying trade secrets for the purpose of repair, for example, does not ordinarily authorize the transferee to use or disclose trade secrets learned as a result of the transaction.

Courts frequently recognize an obligation to refrain from the unauthorized use or disclosure of information that is communicated between parties in a so-called "confidential relationship." Certain business relationships such as employer-employee and licensor-licensee are sometimes characterized as "confidential." The fact that the parties are engaged in such an on-going relationship is relevant in determining whether a specific disclosure creates a duty of confidence, but not every disclosure made in the context of a particular relationship is properly treated as confidential. Even within a relationship generally characterized as "confidential," the purpose of the disclosure, the past practice of the parties, the customs of the industry, and the other circumstances of the disclosure remain relevant in determining the recipient's obligations. Thus, although the disclosure to a licensee of a secret formula that is the subject of a license is normally regarded as confidential, a disclosure of other information to a licensee with no indication that the information is confidential may not give rise to a duty of confidence. The special considerations applicable to disclosures within an employment relationship are considered in § 42.

c. Breach of confidence as a separate tort.

Some courts have recognized liability in tort for the unauthorized disclosure of confidential business information found to be ineligible for protection as a trade secret. In some cases the claim is designated as one for "breach of confidence," while in others it is described as one for "unfair competition." Many of these cases rest on a narrow definition of "trade secret" that excludes non-technical information such as customer identities or information that is not subject to continuous, long-term use. Such information is now subsumed under the broader definition of "trade secret" adopted in § 39. In other cases the imposition of liability for breach of confidence may be justified by interests other than the protection of valuable commercial information, such as the interests that prompt recognition of the general duty of loyalty owed by an employee to an employer, see § 42, Comment b, or the special duties of confidence owed in particular relationships such as attorney and client or doctor and patient. However, in the absence of interests justifying broader duties, the plaintiff should be required to demonstrate that the information qualifies for protection as a trade secret under the rule stated in § 39. The recognition of more extensive rights against the use or disclosure of commercial information can restrict access to knowledge that is properly regarded as part of the public domain. Cf. § 39, Comment f.

d. Contractual protection of trade secrets.

The owner of a trade secret may seek protection against unauthorized use or disclosure through a contract with the recipient of a disclosure. Such contracts may take several forms, including a promise by the recipient not to compete with the trade secret owner, a general promise to refrain from disclosing or using any confidential information acquired within the context of a particular relationship or transaction, or a promise to refrain from using or disclosing particular information specified in the agreement. Use or disclosure in violation of such agreements can result in liability for breach of contract under the rules stated in the Restatement, Second, of Contracts. However, since such agreements can reduce or eliminate potential competition, they are subject to the traditional rules governing contracts in restraint of trade and are accordingly enforceable only when ancillary to a valid transaction and otherwise reasonable. See Restatement, Second, Contracts §§ 186 – 188. As a general matter, a restraint is unreasonable if it is greater than necessary to protect the legitimate interests of the promisee or if the promisee's interest in protection is outweighed by the likely harm to the promisor or to the public. Id. § 188, Comment a.

In many jurisdictions a reasonable covenant not to compete is enforceable against the promisor. The rules governing the protection of trade secrets as stated in this Restatement can sometimes be helpful in evaluating the reasonableness of such a covenant. A promise by an employee not to compete with the employer after the termination of the employment or by a seller of a business not to compete with the buyer after the sale may be justified as a reasonable attempt to protect confidential information, provided that the duration and geographic scope of the covenant are appropriately related to the promisee's legitimate interests. When this justification is offered to support the enforcement of a covenant not to compete, the rules governing trade secrets, although not determinative, can be useful in identifying both the legitimate interests served by the covenant and the appropriate limitations on the scope of protection.

The reasonableness of an agreement that merely prohibits the use or disclosure of particular information depends primarily upon whether the information protected by the agreement qualifies as a trade secret. If the information qualifies for protection under the rule stated in § 39, a contract prohibiting its use or disclosure is generally enforceable according to its terms. Although in some cases courts have enforced nondisclosure agreements directed at information found ineligible for protection as a trade secret, many of these decisions merely reflect a more narrow definition of trade secret than that adopted in § 39. However, a nondisclosure agreement that encompasses information that is generally known or in which the promisee has no protectable interest, such as a former employee's promise not to use information that is part of the employee's general skill and training(see § 42, Comment d), may be unenforceable as an unreasonable restraint of trade. Agreements that deny the promisor the right to use information that is in the public domain are ordinarily enforceable only if justified on the basis of interests other than the protection of confidential information.

Some courts have indicated that nondisclosure agreements are subject to the same durational and geographic limitations traditionally applied to covenants not to compete. However, a nondisclosure agreement can be reasonable even if the agreement is not limited to a specific geographic area. Once a secret is disclosed, knowledge of the information cannot normally be confined to a particular area. Unauthorized disclosure in any geographic area can therefore result in harm to the trade secret owner. Similarly, unauthorized use in any area may deprive the trade secret owner of potential licensing opportunities. Thus, although the more onerous burden of a covenant not to compete is normally enforceable only if confined within appropriate geographic limits, an absolute prohibition against the use or disclosure of a trade secret is ordinarily justified by the legitimate interests of the trade secret owner. The absence of an express duration on a promise not to use or disclose a trade secret should also not in itself render the agreement unenforceable since in the absence of a clear intention to the contrary a nondisclosure agreement is ordinarily interpreted as imposing an obligation of confidentiality only until the information becomes generally known or readily ascertainable by proper means. However, enforcement of an agreement that is interpreted to prohibit the promisor from using information even after it has entered the public domain cannot be justified by the interest in protecting confidential information, although it may be justified on some other basis. For example, licensing agreements that require the continuation of royalty payments for the use of a trade secret even after the secret becomes generally known are ordinarily enforceable. Such agreements may be justified as a reasonable attempt by the parties to measure the value of the head start obtained by the licensee through the initial disclosure of the trade secret. Similarly, in some circumstances an agreement not to use information that is in the public domain may be justified by a legitimate interest in protecting the reputation or good will of the promisee. The rules stated here do not purport to encompass the full range of justifications that may support the enforcement of an agreement not to use or disclose particular information. These rules may be helpful, however, in determining the appropriate limits on the enforceability of an agreement that the promisee seeks to justify on the basis of interests analogous to those protected under the law of trade secrets.

§ 42. Breach of Confidence By Employees

An employee or former employee who uses or discloses a trade secret owned by the employer or former employer in breach of a duty of confidence is subject to liability for appropriation of the trade secret under the rule stated in § 40.

Comment：

a. Scope.

This Section is a specific application of the general rules stated in § § 40 and 41 prohibiting the use or disclosure of a trade secret in violation of a duty of confidence. The issues discussed in this Section are primarily applicable to persons who are regarded under the law of agency as employees or "servants" of the trade secret owner as distinguished from "independent contractors." See Restatement, Second, Agency § § 2, 220. The Section applies to the use or disclosure of trade secrets by both current and former employees. Current employees, however, are also subject to a general duty of loyalty that is broader than the specific obligations arising under the law of trade secrets. See Comment b. The obligations imposed by trade secret law on persons who provide services to the trade secret owner as independent contractors such as attorneys, financial advisors, or consultants are determined according to the general principles governing duties of confidence as stated in § 41. In some circumstances, however, the rules relating to employees as stated in this Section may be useful by analogy in cases involving independent contractors. To advance interests other than the maintenance of fair competition, some professionals such as attorneys and physicians are also subject to obligations of confidentiality apart from those arising under the law of trade secrets.

b. Duties of employees and former employees.

During the duration of an employment relationship, an employee is subject to a duty of loyalty applicable to all conduct within the scope of the employment. See Restatement, Second, Agency § 387. The duty of loyalty encompasses a general duty not to compete with the employer in the subject matter of the employment, id. § 393, including a duty to refrain from using confidential information acquired through the employment in competition with the employer. Id. § 395. Thus, if a current employee enters into competition with the employer, liability may be imposed without regard to the existence or appropriation of trade secrets. The duty of loyalty also includes a duty not to disclose the employer's confidential information to others. Id. When it is alleged that a current employee has disclosed to third persons valuable information acquired in the course of the employment, the emphasis is properly on whether there has been a breach of loyalty by the employee and not on the character of the particular information. However, it is not ordinarily regarded as a breach of loyalty to "disclose" information that is common knowledge or that the employee has no reason to believe is confidential. Id. , Comment b. Although a current employee can be subject to liability for the appropriation of a trade secret under the rules stated in this Chapter, the liability of current employees for the unauthorized use or disclosure of valuable information is more typically determined under the rules governing the general duty of loyalty owed by an employee to the employer.

The rules governing liability for the appropriation of trade secrets play a more central role in regulating the behavior of employees after the termination of the employment relationship. Once the employment has ended, the former employee has the right to compete with the former employer absent an enforceable agreement to the contrary. Restrictive covenants limiting competition by former employees are enforceable only if the restriction is reasonable. See § 41, Comment d. However, even in the absence of an enforceable covenant a former employee remains subject to the general rules prohibiting use or disclosure of another's trade secrets in breach of a duty of confidence.

Application of the rules protecting trade secrets in cases involving competition by former employees requires a careful balancing of interests. There is a strong public interest in preserving the freedom of employees to market their talents and experience in order to earn a livelihood. The mobility of employees also promotes competition through the dissemination of useful skills and information. In many instances, however, employers cannot conduct business efficiently without disclosing valuable trade secrets to their employees. Absent reasonable protection against the unauthorized use or disclosure of such information by former employees, employers would be forced to adopt expensive and inefficient restrictions on access to information. Businesses would also be less likely to invest in research and development if competitors could easily appropriate the gains from such investments through disclosures by former employees. Thus, the interests of both the former employer and the former employee must be weighed in light of the circumstances of the particular case in order to insure sufficient protection for trade secrets without unduly restraining the mobility of employees.

c. Employment as a confidential relationship.

The employment relationship by its nature ordinarily justifies an inference that the employee consents to a duty of confidence with respect to any information acquired through the employment that the employee knows or has reason to know is confidential. See § 41, Comment b. The duty to refrain from unauthorized use or disclosure of confidential information continues after termination of the employment relationship. However, some information developed during the employment relationship may belong to the employee rather than the employer. See Comment e. Former employees are also entitled to exploit their general skill, knowledge, training, and experience, even when acquired or enhanced through the resources of the former employer. See Comment d. Although some courts have justified particular decisions in favor of employees on the absence of a confidential relationship, these cases are often better understood as resting on the absence of a protectable trade secret owned by the employer or on a lack of adequate notice to the employee of the confidential nature of the information. If an employer establishes ownership of a trade secret and circumstances sufficient to put the employee on notice that the information is confidential, the employment relationship will ordinarily justify the recognition of a duty of confidence.

d. General skill, knowledge, training, and experience.

Information that forms the general skill, knowledge, training, and experience of an employee cannot be claimed as a trade secret by a former employer even when the information is directly attributable to an investment of resources by the employer in the employee. The Statute of Apprentices enacted in England in 1562, 5 Eliz. I, ch. 4, which mandated a seven-year period of apprenticeship to a master, was in part an early attempt to reconcile the interest of employers in capturing the benefits of their investment in the training of employees and the interest of employees in a competitive market for their services. The modern balance relies primarily on the recognition of a duty of loyalty during the period of employment, see Comment b, the ability of employers and employees in most states to contract for reasonable restrictions on the employee's freedom to compete with the employer after termination of the employment, see § 41, Comment d, and the recognition of rights in specific information that is eligible for protection as a trade secret. Thus, absent an enforceable covenant not to compete, a former employee may utilize in competition with the former employer the general skills, knowledge, training, and experience acquired during the employment, but the employee remains obligated to refrain from using or disclosing the employer's trade secrets.

Whether particular information is properly regarded as a trade secret of the former employer or as part of the general skill, knowledge, training, and experience of the former employee depends on the facts and circumstances of the particular case. An employer who is asserting rights in information against a former employee bears the burden of proving the existence and ownership of a trade secret. Trade secret rights are more likely to be recognized in specialized information unique to the employer's business than in information more widely known in the industry or derived from skills generally possessed by persons employed in the industry. The relative contribution of the employer and employee to the development of the information can also be relevant. The fact that other competitors have been unsuccessful in independent attempts to develop the information may suggest that the information qualifies for protection as a trade secret. Courts are also more likely to conclude that particular information is a trade secret if the employee on termination of the employment appropriates some physical embodiment of the information such as written formulas, blueprints, plans, or lists of customers. However, although information that is retained in the employee's memory may be less likely to be regarded as a trade secret absent evidence of intentional memorization, the inference is not conclusive.

The distinction between trade secrets and general skill, knowledge, training, and experience is intended to achieve a reasonable balance between the protection of confidential information and the mobility of employees. If the information is so closely integrated with the employee's overall employment experience that protection would deprive the employee of the ability to obtain employment commensurate with the employee's general qualifications, it will not ordinarily be protected as a trade secret of the former employer.

e. Allocation of ownership between employers and employees.

The law of agency has established rules governing the ownership of valuable information created by employees during the course of an employment relationship. See Restatement, Second, Agency § 397. In the absence of a contrary agreement, the law ordinarily assigns ownership of an invention or idea to the person who conceives it. However, valuable information that is the product of an employee's assigned duties is owned by the employer, even when the information results from the application of the employee's personal knowledge or skill:

If, however, one is employed to do experimental work for inventive purposes, it is inferred ordinarily, although not so specifically agreed, that patentable ideas arrived at through the experimentation are to be owned by the employer. This is even more clear where one is employed to achieve a particular result which the invention accomplishes. On the other hand, if one is employed merely to do work in a particular line in which he is an expert, there is no inference that inventions which he makes while so working belong to the employer.

Restatement, Second, Agency § 397, Comment a.

An employee is ordinarily entitled to claim ownership of patents and trade secrets developed outside the scope of the employee's assigned duties, even if the invention or idea relates to the employer's business and was developed using the employer's time, personnel, facilities, or equipment. In the latter circumstances, however, the employer is entitled to a "shop right"— an irrevocable, nonexclusive, royalty-free license to use the innovation. Similarly, employees retain ownership of information comprising their general skill, knowledge, training, and experience. See Comment d. The allocation of ownership between employers and employees is also subject to alteration by contract. See Comment g.

If a trade secret developed by an employee is owned by the employer, the employee is subject to liability under the rule stated in § 40 for any unauthorized use or disclosure. If the trade secret is owned by the employee, the employee is free, when no longer subject to the duty of loyalty owed by current employees, to use the information or to disclose it to others even if the former employer retains a "shop right" in the trade secret.

Although the rules governing ownership of valuable information created during an employment relationship are most frequently applied to inventions, the rules are also applicable to information such as customer lists, marketing ideas, and other valuable business information. If an employee collects or develops such information as part of the assigned duties of the employment, the information is owned by the employer. Thus, if the information qualifies for protection as a trade secret, unauthorized use or disclosure will subject the employee to liability under the rule stated in § 40.

f. Customer lists.

The general rules that govern trade secrets are applicable to the protection of information relating to the identity and requirements of customers. Customer identities and related customer information can be a company's most valuable asset and may represent a considerable investment of resources. Although issues relating to the protection of customer lists may arise in a variety of contexts, most cases involve the solicitation of a company's customers by a former employee who acquired information about the customers in the course of the former employment. The public and private interests that are implicated in the protection of customer information are best accommodated through application of the traditional rules governing trade secrets, covenants not to compete, and the duty of loyalty owed to an employer by a current employee.

A customer list is not protectable as a trade secret under the rule stated in § 39 unless it is sufficiently valuable and secret to afford an economic advantage to a person who has access to the list. Thus, if the potential customers for a particular product or service are readily identifiable, their identities do not constitute a trade secret. On the other hand, specialized customer information that cannot easily be duplicated, such as a list of homeowners who employ commercial cleaning services or a compilation of specific information about individual customers, may be sufficiently valuable and secret to qualify as a trade secret. The fact that an employee has appropriated a written list or has made an attempt to memorize customer information prior to terminating the employment may justify an inference that the information is valuable and not readily ascertainable by proper means. However, solicitation of the same customers by a number of competitors is evidence that the customer identities are generally known or readily ascertainable in the trade. Some of the customer list cases involve the identities of customers on delivery routes. In most cases the identities of such customers are readily ascertainable by observing the delivery vehicle. Information concerning the particular requirements of individual customers may be eligible for protection as a trade secret if such knowledge is difficult to obtain and valuable in gaining or retaining patronage.

When information relating to the identities or requirements of customers qualifies for protection as a trade secret, the rules described in Comment e are applicable in determining ownership. If the employer discloses the list of customers to the employee, or if the employee specifically assigned to identify potential customers, the employer is ordinarily the owner of the information. On the other hand, in the absence of an enforceable covenant not to compete, a employee who possessed the relevant customer information prior to the former employment is free to use the information in competition with the former employer after termination of the employment relationship.

If the identities of the former employer's customers are not protectable as a trade secret former employee is entitled, absent an enforceable agreement to the contrary, to solicit the customers in competition with the former employer once the employment has ended. A few courts, particularly in delivery route cases, have nevertheless enjoined such solicitation when former employee had developed substantial personal relationships with the customers. However such a prohibition can unfairly limit employee mobility. If the customer list or related information does not qualify for protection as a trade secret, the former employer should ordinarily be limit to the protection available through a reasonable covenant not to compete. See § 41, Commond.

g. Contractual protection.

The rules governing the protection and ownership of trade secrets are generally subject to reasonable modification by the parties. By means of a reasonable covenant not to compete, an employer may achieve protection against the competitive use by a former employee of information not technically protectable as a trade secret. See § 41, Comment d. Similarly, a nondisclosure agreement prohibiting the use or disclosure of particular information can clarify and extend the scope of an employer's rights. 1d. However, the rules governing trade secrets remain relevant in assessing the reasonableness hence the enforceability of such contractual restrictions. 1d.

The common law accords to an employer ownership of inventions and discoveries made by an employee only when the information is the product of the employee's assigned duties. See Comment e. However, absent an applicable statutory prohibition, agreements relating to the ownership of inventions and discoveries made by employees during the term of the employment are generally enforceable according to their terms. Employment agreements sometimes include provisions granting the employer ownership of all inventions and discoveries conceived by the employee during the term of the employment. In some situations, however, it may be difficult prove when a particular invention was conceived. The employee may have an incentive to delay disclosure of the invention until after the employment is terminated in order to avoid the contractual or common law claims of the employer. It may also be difficult to establish whether post-employment invention was improperly derived from the trade secrets of the former employer. Some employment agreements respond to this uncertainty through provisions granting the former employer ownership of inventions and discoveries relating to the subject matter of the former employment that are developed by the employee even after the termination of the employment. Such agreements can restrict the former employee's ability to exploit the skills and training desired by other employers and may thus restrain competition and limit employee mobility. The courts have therefore subjected such "holdover" agreements to scrutiny analogous to that applied to covenants not to compete. Thus, the agreement may be unenforceable if it extends beyond a reasonable period of time or to inventions or discoveries resulting solely from the general skill and experience of the former employee.

§ 43. Improper Acquisition of Trade Secrets

"Improper" means of acquiring another's trade secret under the rule stated in § 40 include theft, fraud, unauthorized interception of communications, inducement of or knowing participation in a breach of confidence, and other means either wrongful in themselves or wrongful under the circumstances of the case. Independent discovery and analysis of publicly available products or information are not improper means of acquisition.

Comment:

a. Scope of protection.

The owner of a trade secret does not have an exclusive right to possession or use of the secret information. Protection is available only against a wrongful acquisition, use, or disclosure of the trade secret. See § 40. Use or disclosure of a trade secret in breach of a duty of confidence is treated in §§ 41 and 42. This Section considers the acquisition, use, and disclosure of trade secrets by persons who have not obtained the secret through a confidential disclosure.

b. Proper means of acquisition.

Unless a trade secret has been acquired under circumstances giving rise to a duty of confidence, a person who obtains the trade secret by proper means is free to use or disclose the information without liability. Unlike the holder of a patent, the owner of a trade secret has no claim against another who independently discovers the secret. Similarly, others remain free to analyze products publicly marketed by the trade secret owner and, absent protection under a patent or copyright, to exploit any information acquired through such "reverse engineering." A person may also acquire a trade secret through an analysis of published materials or through observation of objects or events that are in public view or otherwise accessible by proper means.

c. Improper means of acquisition.

It is not possible to formulate a comprehensive list of the conduct that constitutes "improper" means of acquiring a trade secret. If a trade secret is acquired through conduct that is itself a tortious or criminal invasion of the trade secret owner's rights, the acquisition ordinarily will be regarded as improper. Thus, a person who obtains a trade secret by burglarizing the offices of a competitor acquires the secret by improper means. So also does one who obtains a trade secret by wiretapping the owner's telephone or by employing fraudulent representations to induce the owner to disclose the trade secret. A person who obtains a trade secret by inducing or knowingly accepting a disclosure from a third person who has acquired the secret by improper means, or who induces or knowingly accepts a disclosure from a third person that is in breach of a duty of confidence owed by the third person to the trade secret owner, also acquires the secret by improper means.

The acquisition of a trade secret can be improper even if the means of acquisition are not independently wrongful. The propriety of the acquisition must be evaluated in light of all the circumstances of the case, including whether the means of acquisition are inconsistent with accepted principles of public policy and the extent to which the acquisition was facilitated by the trade secret owner's failure to take reasonable precautions against discovery of the secret by the means in question. Among the factors relevant to the reasonableness of the trade secret owner's precautions are the foresee ability of the conduct through which the secret was acquired and the availability and cost of effective precautions against such an acquisition, evaluated in light of the economic value of the trade secret.

d. Existence of a trade secret.

A person is not subject to liability for an appropriation of information under the rules stated in § 40 unless the information qualifies for protection as a trade secret under the rule stated in § 39. Thus, although an actor may be subject to liability under other rules for conduct that is actionable as an invasion of other protected interests, the acquisition of information that is not a trade secret will not subject the actor to liability under § 40 regardless of the means of acquisition. Information that is readily ascertainable by proper means is not protectable as a trade secret, see § 39, Comment f, and the acquisition of such information even by improper means is therefore not actionable under § 40. However, the accessibility of information, and hence its status as a trade secret, is evaluated in light of the difficulty and cost of acquiring the information by proper means. See § 39, Comment f. In some circumstances the actor's decision to employ improper means of acquisition is itself evidence that the information is not readily ascertainable through proper means and is thus protectable as a trade secret. Because of the public interest in deterring the acquisition of information by improper means, doubts regarding the status of information as a trade secret are likely to be resolved in favor of protection when the means of acquisition are clearly improper.

§ 44. Injunctions: Appropriation of Trade Secrets

(1)If appropriate under the rule stated in Subsection (2), injunctive relief may be awarded to prevent a continuing or threatened appropriation of another's trade secret by one who is subject to liability under the rule stated in § 40.

(2) The appropriateness and scope of injunctive relief depend upon a comparative appraisal of all the factors of the case, including the following

primary factors:

(a) the nature of the interest to be protected;

(b) the nature and extent of the appropriation;

(c) the relative adequacy to the plaintiff of an injunction and of other remedies;

(d) the relative harm likely to result to the legitimate interests of the defendant if an injunction is granted and to the legitimate interests of the plaintiff if an injunction is denied;

(e) the interests of third persons and of the public;

(f) any unreasonable delay by the plaintiff in bringing suit or otherwise asserting its rights;

(g) any related misconduct on the part of the plaintiff; and

(h) the practicality of framing and enforcing the injunction.

(3) The duration of injunctive relief in trade secret actions should be limited to the time necessary to protect the plaintiff from any harm attributable to the appropriation and to deprive the defendant of any economic advantage attributable to the appropriation.

Comment:

a. Scope.

This Section states the principles governing injunctive relief in actions for the appropriation of a trade secret. The general rules relating to injunctive relief in tort actions stated in Chapter 48 of the Restatement, Second, of Torts apply in actions for the appropriation of trade secrets. Only those rules that have particular significance to injunctions in trade secret cases are considered here. This Section is derived from Restatement, Second, Torts § 936, which sets forth the general factors relating to the appropriateness of injunctions in tort actions. See also § § 933 – 935, stating the standard of "appropriateness" for injunctive relief, and § § 937 – 943, describing in detail the factors relevant in determining appropriateness.

Additional considerations may influence the award of preliminary injunctive relief. See Comment g.

The appropriation of a trade secret is more closely analogous to tortious interference with rights in tangible property than is trademark infringement or deceptive marketing, which depend on the perceptions of prospective purchasers. The general rules on injunctions in tort actions stated in Restatement, Second, Torts § § 933 – 943 are thus more likely to be directly applicable in trade secret cases than in other unfair competition actions.

This Restatement does not treat the rules governing the various techniques available to preserve the secrecy of trade secrets during litigation, such as protective orders, in camera proceedings, and the sealing of records. See Uniform Trade Secrets Act § 5.

b. Relation to other remedies.

The usual remedy in tort actions is an award of damages, and the equitable remedy of an injunction was traditionally available only when the remedy of damages was inadequate. With the merger of law and equity, courts are generally free to select the remedy or combination of remedies that most effectively protects the interests threatened by the defendant's misconduct. See Restatement, Second, Torts § 938, Comment c. In trade secret cases, the primary interest of the plaintiff is in the secrecy and exclusive use of the appropriated information. As in the case of other forms of unfair competition, the harm caused by the appropriation of a trade secret may not be fully reparable through an award of monetary relief due to the difficulty of proving the amount of loss and the causal connection with the defendant's misconduct. Thus, a defendant's continuing or threatened use or disclosure of a trade secret normally justifies an award of injunctive relief.

In many trade secret cases, both injunctive and monetary relief are appropriate: monetary relief to compensate the plaintiff for existing losses and injunctive relief to prevent future loss through further use or disclosure of the trade secret. In some cases, however, an injunction may be the only appropriate remedy, as when the defendant has not yet disclosed or used a trade secret acquired by improper means or when a defendant threatens to breach a duty of confidence arising from a confidential disclosure of the trade secret. In other cases, unqualified injunctive relief may be inappropriate, as when the defendant in good faith makes a substantial investment in reliance on the trade secret prior to receiving knowledge sufficient to subject the defendant to liability for further use. See § 45, Comment b.

c. Appropriateness of injunctive relief.

Injunctive relief is often appropriate in trade secret cases to insure against additional harm from further unauthorized use of the trade secret and to deprive the defendant of additional benefits from the appropriation. If the information has not become generally known, an injunction may also be appropriate to preserve the plaintiff's rights in the trade secret by preventing a public disclosure. If the trade secret has already entered the public domain, an injunction may be appropriate to remedy any head start or other unfair advantage acquired by the defendant as a result of the appropriation. However, if the defendant retains no unfair advantage from the appropriation, an injunction against the use of information that is no longer secret can be justified only on a rationale of punishment and deterrence. Because of the public interest in promoting competition, such punitive injunctions are ordinarily inappropriate in trade secret actions.

An injunction may sometimes be appropriate to prevent a threatened use or disclosure of a trade secret. The scope of such an injunction should be carefully framed to avoid undue restraint on legitimate competition. For example, a court will not ordinarily enjoin an employee who has knowledge of a former employer's trade secret from engaging in a particular occupation or working for a particular competitor in the absence of an enforceable covenant not to compete or clear evidence that the contemplated employment will result in disclosure of the secret.

However, if there is a substantial risk of disclosure, an injunction prohibiting the disclosure or prohibiting participation in a particular project that presents a special risk of disclosure may be appropriate.

Although injunctive relief is routinely granted in trade secret cases, the remedy remains subject to equitable principles, including the factors stated in Subsection(2) of this Section. The appropriateness of injunctive relief must be determined in light of the interests of both the parties and the public, including the interest of the plaintiff in preserving the commercial advantage inherent in the trade secret, the interest of the defendant in avoiding interference with legitimate business transactions, and the interest of the public in fostering innovation and promoting vigorous competition. For example, although employers are entitled to protection against appropriations of trade secrets by employees, employees are entitled, absent an enforceable contractual restraint, to market their skills and training to others. These competing interests are properly considered not only in defining the subject matter eligible for protection as a trade secret, see § 42, Comment d, but also in fashioning appropriate relief. The traditional equitable principles of laches, estoppel, and unclean hands are also applicable in trade secret cases.

Under the rules stated in § 40, innocent use of another's trade secret is not actionable. A defendant is subject to liability only for use occurring after the defendant acquires actual or constructive knowledge that the information is the trade secret of another. See § 40, Comment d. There is some authority for the rule that a good faith user who pays value for the secret or otherwise invests in its use before receiving notice of the appropriation is not subject to liability for continued use after notice. A more appropriate balance of interests can be achieved in such cases, however, by limiting the remedy rather than precluding liability for subsequent use. Although it may sometimes be inequitable to prohibit the defendant from continued use of the secret after notice, it may be appropriate to impose other remedies such as an injunction conditioning further use on the payment of a reasonable royalty. See Uniform Trade Secrets Act § 2(b).

A court contemplating injunctive relief in a trade secret case must also consider its ability to fashion and enforce the injunction so as to protect the legitimate interests of the trade secret owner without unduly interfering with legitimate competition by the defendant. For example, an injunction should be sufficiently precise to give the defendant fair notice of the information that is encompassed within the terms of the injunction.

d. Factors determining the scope of injunctive relief.

The factors listed in Subsection(2) of this Section are relevant in determining the scope as well as the appropriateness of injunctive relief. An injunction ordinarily prohibits only use or disclosure of the trade secret and information substantially derived from the trade secret. Practical considerations, however, may sometimes justify broader relief. In some cases, for example, an injunction limited to the trade secret and its derivatives may be impossible to enforce due to the difficulty of distinguishing further improper use or disclosure of the trade secret from independent discovery. An injunction against participation in a particular project or business may then be appropriate. Similarly, in some cases, although liability may be clear, the exact boundaries of the trade secret may be difficult to define. The proper balance between the plaintiff's right to protection and the defendant's right to fair notice of prohibited conduct may then require the court to include a somewhat broader or somewhat narrower field of information within the scope of the injunction.

When the trade secret is narrow in scope and closely related to publicly available information, the injunction should be carefully restricted to the contours of the trade secret in order to avoid encroachment on the public domain. Nevertheless, if the trade secret is an essential component of a larger process or product, other aspects of which are in the public domain, in some cases the only effective means of protecting the trade secret may be an injunction against use of the process or manufacture of the product.

Geographic limitations on the scope of injunctive relief in trade secret cases are ordinarily inappropriate. A defendant will normally be enjoined from disclosing or using the trade secret even outside the geographic market of the trade secret owner. The defendant's use of the secret in any market may increase the risk of disclosure to the public and may deprive the plaintiff of potential licensing revenues. Even when direct injury to the plaintiff is unlikely, an injunction unlimited in geographic scope is ordinarily appropriate to deprive the defendant of further unjust enrichment from the appropriation of the trade secret.

In some circumstances the unauthorized disclosure of another's trade secret for a purpose other than commercial exploitation may be privileged. See § 40, Comment c. Although there is little case law, any injunctive relief issued in such situations must accommodate protection of the plaintiff's trade secret with the free speech or other interests underlying the privilege.

e. Surrender of objects and assignment of patents.

In order to insure full compensation to the trade secret owner and to deprive the defendant of all unjust gains, a court may properly require a defendant to return to the trade secret owner documents, blueprints, customer lists, or other tangible embodiments of the trade secret. See Uniform Trade Secrets Act § 2(c). If the defendant has obtained a patent covering either the trade secret or an invention derived from the trade secret, a court may also require the defendant to assign the patent to the owner of the trade secret.

f. Duration of injunctive relief.

Injunctions are appropriate in trade secret cases to protect the plaintiff from further harm caused by the use or disclosure of the trade secret and to deprive the defendant of further unjust gain. However, the law of trade secrets does not afford protection against losses or gains that are not attributable to the defendant's appropriation. This principle establishes the appropriate duration of injunctive relief in trade secret cases. Thus, injunctive relief should ordinarily continue only until the defendant could have acquired the information by proper means. Injunctions extending beyond this period are justified only when necessary to deprive the defendant of a head start or other unjust advantage that is attributable to the appropriation. See Uniform Trade Secrets Act § 2 (a). More extensive injunctive relief undermines the public interest by restraining legitimate competition.

The issuance of a patent or other public disclosure renders the disclosed information ineligible for continued protection as a trade secret. See § 39, Comment f. Some courts, however, have issued or continued injunctions after public disclosure of the trade secret against defendants who appropriated the information while it was still secret. Other courts hold that public disclosure precludes the subsequent issuance of an injunction and justifies termination of an injunction previously granted. When the trade secret is publicly disclosed by the plaintiff or a third person after the defendant's appropriation, the proper inquiry is whether injunctive relief remains necessary to protect against future injury to the plaintiff or future unjust enrichment to the defendant that is attributable to the defendant's wrongful actions prior to the public disclosure. Whether an injunction remains appropriate thus depends on the facts of the particular case. For example, early access to information subsequently disclosed in a patent may allow the defendant to bring to market or reduce to practice the teachings of the patent more quickly than otherwise possible. Similarly, the public disclosure may not encompass all aspects of the information appropriated by the defendant. Limited injunctive relief may thus remain appropriate to eliminate an improper economic advantage that would otherwise be retained by the defendant after the public disclosure of the trade secret. If the public disclosure results from the defendant's own unauthorized conduct, injunctive relief may remain appropriate until the information would have become readily ascertainable to the defendant through proper means. However, if the defendant's public disclosure results in extensive use of the information by others, a continuing injunction against the defendant may yield little benefit to the plaintiff. It may also be difficult to determine the appropriate duration of such an injunction. Since the defendant is subject to liability for the pecuniary loss to the plaintiff resulting from the destruction of the trade secret and for its own pecuniary gain derived from the unauthorized disclosure, see § 45, in some cases a court may properly conclude that monetary relief is a sufficient remedy.

An injunction also should not ordinarily extend beyond the time when the defendant could have properly acquired and implemented the information through reverse engineering or independent discovery. Subsequent use by the defendant does not subject the plaintiff to harm that is attributable to the appropriation of the trade secret. In some cases this duration may be measured by the time it would take a person of ordinary skill in the industry to discover the trade secret by independent means or to obtain the trade secret through the reverse engineering of publicly marketed products. The opinions of experts familiar with the particular industry are thus relevant in determining an appropriate duration. The experience of other competitors in attempting to acquire the information by proper means is also relevant in determining the time it would have taken the defendant to acquire the information in the absence of the appropriation. The defendant may also show that because of a comparative advantage unrelated to the appropriation, the period of lawful development would have been shorter than that for others in the industry. The duration of the injunction, however, should be sufficient to deprive the defendant of any head start or other economic advantage attributable to the appropriation. In some cases courts have issued injunctions for a specific period reflecting the time when the defendant could have acquired the information by proper means. In other cases courts have awarded unlimited injunctions, with the burden on the defendant to seek a modification of the injunction when the commercial advantage from the appropriation has ended. The most efficient procedure depends on the ease and certainty with which the appropriate duration of relief can be determined in advance. In either case the defendant remains liable for any expenses of reverse engineering or independent development that the defendant has saved as a result of the appropriation. See § 45, Comment f.

g. Preliminary relief.

The rule stated in this Section deals primarily with injunctions granted as final relief, but the factors stated in Subsection(2) are also relevant to the imposition of provisional remedies. Although courts differ on the precise formulation, all courts recognize that the appropriateness of preliminary relief depends upon the likelihood that the plaintiff will suffer irreparable harm in the absence of preliminary relief, the plaintiff's likelihood of success on the merits, the balance of equities between the parties, and the interest of the public. In evaluating the possibility of irreparable harm in trade secret cases, the courts have recognized that the loss to a trade secret owner from the unauthorized use or disclosure of a trade secret is often difficult to remedy through a subsequent award of monetary relief.

§ 45. Monetary Relief: Appropriation of Trade Secrets

(1) One who is liable to another for an appropriation of the other's trade secret under the rule stated in § 40 is liable for the pecuniary loss to the other caused by the appropriation or for the actor's own pecuniary gain resulting from the appropriation, whichever is greater, unless such relief is inappropriate under the rule stated in Subsection(2).

(2) Whether an award of monetary relief is appropriate and the appropriate method of measuring such relief depend upon a comparative appraisal of all the factors of the case, including the following primary factors:

(a) the degree of certainty with which the plaintiff has established the fact and extent of the pecuniary loss or the actor's pecuniary gain resulting from the appropriation;

(b) the nature and extent of the appropriation;

(c) the relative adequacy to the plaintiff of other remedies;

(d) the intent and knowledge of the actor and the nature and extent of any good faith reliance by the actor;

(e) any unreasonable delay by the plaintiff in bringing suit or otherwise asserting its rights; and

(f) any related misconduct on the part of the plaintiff.

Comment:

a. Scope.

This Section states the rules governing the recovery of monetary relief in actions for the appropriation of a trade secret. Monetary relief may consist of compensatory damages measured by the loss to the plaintiff or restitutionary relief measured by the unjust gain to the defendant. This Section states the rules applicable to both measures of monetary relief.

The general rules relating to the recovery of compensatory damages in tort actions apply in actions for the appropriation of trade secrets. This Section addresses only issues that have particular significance to the recovery of damages in trade secret actions. The following sections of the Restatement, Second, of Torts are also relevant: § § 902 and 903 defining "damages" and "compensatory damages"; § 907 stating the rule for recovery of nominal damages; § § 908 and 909 stating the rules for recovery of punitive damages; § 912 stating the requirement of "certainty"; and § § 435A and 435B stating rules relating to intended and unintended consequences of tortious conduct.

The general rules relating to the restitution of benefits tortiously acquired are also applicable in actions for the appropriation of trade secrets. See Restatement of Restitution § 136(1937).

b. Appropriateness of monetary relief.

Loss to the plaintiff or gain to the defendant can result from either unauthorized use or unauthorized disclosure of a trade secret. The courts have recognized the need for flexibility in formulating monetary remedies in order to achieve both compensatory and restitutionary objectives.

The plaintiff is generally entitled to recover any proven pecuniary loss attributable to the appropriation of the trade secret. The plaintiff bears the burden of proving the fact and cause of any loss for which recovery is sought. However, the plaintiff is required to prove the amount of such loss with only as much certainty as is reasonable under the circumstances. See Restatement, Second, Torts § 912. If otherwise appropriate, the plaintiff may also recover any gain acquired by the defendant as a result of the appropriation, subject to the limitation on double recovery. See Comment c.

The knowledge and intent of the defendant are relevant in determining appropriate relief. A defendant is not subject to liability under the rules stated in § 40 until the defendant has actual or constructive knowledge that the use or disclosure of the trade secret is wrongful. See § 40, Comment d. If the defendant has invested in the trade secret prior to acquiring such knowledge, it may be inequitable to deprive the defendant of all gains attributable to subsequent use of the trade secret. The award of a reasonable royalty for use made after notice and an injunction conditioning further use upon payment of a reasonable royalty may be an appropriate remedy. See Comment g.

The conduct of the plaintiff may also affect the appropriateness of monetary relief. The traditional equitable doctrines of laches, estoppel, and unclean hands are applicable to the award of monetary as well as injunctive relief in trade secret actions. Cf. § § 31 and 32.

c. Relationship of legal and equitable remedies.

The rules governing the award of monetary relief for the appropriation of a trade secret derive from both legal and equitable principles. Cf. § 36, Comment b. The traditional measure of damages awards relief measured by the loss to the plaintiff resulting from the appropriation. The nature of a competitive marketplace, however, often makes it difficult for a plaintiff to prove lost sales or other losses attributable to the appropriation of a trade secret. Similarly, the value of a trade secret that has been destroyed through public disclosure is often speculative. The remedy of restitution is thus an important form of monetary relief in trade secret cases. The restitution remedy awards to the plaintiff the enrichment unjustly acquired by the defendant as a result of the appropriation of the plaintiff's trade secret. In some situations the defendant's enrichment is represented by profits from sales made possible by the appropriation; in others, by savings achieved through the use of the trade secret in the defendant's business. In some cases the measure of the plaintiff's compensatory damages and the measure of the defendant's unjust enrichment may converge. For example, relief based on the defendant's profits on sales can measure either the gain derived by the defendant or the loss to the plaintiff from diverted business. Similarly, relief based on a reasonable royalty for the defendant's use may measure either the defendant's savings or the plaintiff's lost revenue. Thus, many cases do not maintain a sharp distinction between compensatory and restitutionary remedies.

Although a few cases have required the plaintiff to elect between compensatory damages and restitution, others permit the plaintiff to pursue both measures provided that there is no double recovery. The better rule permits the plaintiff to prove either or both measures since in many circumstances the loss to the plaintiff and the gain to the defendant do not fully overlap. Both compensatory and restitutionary objectives are ordinarily satisfied, however, if the plaintiff is permitted to recover only the greater of the two measures. The restitutionary remedy serves to deprive the defendant of unjust gains, but it also has the effect of compensating the plaintiff to the extent of the award for any losses resulting from the appropriation. Similarly, an award of the plaintiff's proven losses also has the effect of reducing the defendant's unjust enrichment by the amount of the award. An award of the greater of the two remedies thus ordinarily serves the objectives of both forms of relief and best prevents double recovery. See also § 36, Comment c.

d. Measures of monetary relief.

Courts have recognized at least four methods of measuring monetary relief in trade secret cases. The first method measures the loss to the plaintiff caused by the appropriation. The plaintiff's loss usually consists of profits lost on sales diverted from the plaintiff by the appropriation, loss of royalties or other income that would have been earned by the plaintiff but for the appropriation, or the value of the trade secret if it has been destroyed through a public disclosure by the defendant. The second measure awards to the plaintiff the defendant's profits earned on sales that are attributable to the trade secret. A third method, the "standard of comparison" measure, is derived from patent infringement cases and measures the savings to the defendant that are attributable to the use of the trade secret. This method compares the costs to the defendant of achieving the same result with and without the improper use of the trade secret and awards the difference to the plaintiff. The fourth method awards to the plaintiff a reasonable royalty for the defendant's use of the trade secret. A reasonable royalty is the price that would be agreed upon by a willing buyer and a willing seller for the use made of the trade secret by the defendant. The method is not limited to a percentage of the defendant's sales or profits and may instead rely on any appropriate measure of the fair market value of the defendant's use. Selection of the appropriate method of measuring monetary relief depends on the facts and circumstances of the particular case. See Comments e – g.

e. Relief measured by plaintiff's loss.

A frequent element of loss resulting from the appropriation of a trade secret is the lost profit that the plaintiff would have earned in the absence of the use by the defendant. The plaintiff may prove lost profits by identifying specific customers diverted to the defendant. The plaintiff may also prove lost profits through proof of a general decline in sales or a disruption of business growth following the commencement of use by the defendant, although the presence of other market factors that may affect the plaintiff's sales bears on the sufficiency of the plaintiff's proof. If the evidence justifies the conclusion that the sales made by the defendant would have instead been made by the plaintiff in the absence of the appropriation, the plaintiff may establish its lost profits by applying its own profit margin to the defendant's sales. Upon sufficient proof, the plaintiff may also recover lost profits on sales of spare parts, service, supplies, or other items normally purchased from the original seller. In some cases it may be appropriate to measure the plaintiff's loss by a reasonable royalty on the sales made by the defendant. See Comment g.

A plaintiff may also recover any other proven pecuniary loss attributable to the appropriation. Courts have permitted recovery of the costs of remedial efforts such as promotional expenses undertaken to recapture customers lost as a result of the defendant's appropriation. The plaintiff is also entitled to recover losses associated with sales of its own goods at reduced prices resulting from the wrongful competition of the defendant.

Damages resulting from the unauthorized disclosure of a trade secret are frequently more difficult to measure than damages caused by unauthorized use. For example, in some cases a defendant's unauthorized disclosure to one competitor of the plaintiff may cause the trade secret to become known to other competitors or to enter the public domain, thus destroying the value of the secret. The appropriate measure of relief may then be the fair market value of the trade secret at the time of the appropriation. This measure can depend upon a variety of factors, including the likelihood that the trade secret would have become known in the absence of the defendant's appropriation. See Comment h. If the destroyed trade secret is a central asset of the plaintiff's business, the plaintiff can in some cases measure damages by the reduction in the capital value of the business caused by the appropriation.

f. Relief measured by defendant's gain.

The traditional form of restitutionary relief in an action for the appropriation of a trade secret is an accounting of the defendant's profits on sales attributable to the use of the trade secret. The general rules governing accountings of profits are applicable in trade secret actions. The plaintiff is entitled to recover the defendant's net profits. The plaintiff has the burden of establishing the defendant's sales; the defendant has the burden of establishing any portion of the sales not attributable to the trade secret and any expenses to be deducted in determining net profits. The rules governing the deductibility of expenses and the allocation of overhead are analogous to those stated in § 37, Comments g and h, on accountings in actions for trademark infringement. The defendant must account not only for profits earned on sales of products incorporating the trade secret, but also on other sales dependent on the appropriation. For example, profits on the sale of consumable supplies used in a machine embodying the trade secret or profits on spare parts and service may be included in the accounting to the extent that such profits were made possible by the defendant's sale of the original product.

If the trade secret accounts for only a portion of the profits earned on the defendant's sales, such as when the trade secret relates to a single component of a product marketable without the secret, an award to the plaintiff of defendant's entire profit may be unjust. The royalty that the plaintiff and defendant would have agreed to for the use of the trade secret made by the defendant may be one measure of the approximate portion of the defendant's profits attributable to the use. See Comment g.

If the benefit derived by the defendant consists primarily of cost savings, such as when the trade secret is a more efficient method of production, the "standard of comparison" measure that determines relief based on the savings achieved through the use of the trade secret may be the most appropriate measure of relief. The standard of comparison measure determines the defendant's gain by comparing the defendant's actual costs with the costs that the defendant would have incurred to achieve the same result without the use of the appropriated trade secret. When it would have been possible for the defendant to acquire the trade secret by proper means such as reverse engineering or independent development, the appropriate comparison may be between the costs of such acquisition and the cost of using the appropriated information. In determining the costs of proper acquisition, the court may consider the actual development costs of the plaintiff and, if available, the development or reverse engineering costs of third persons. When acquisition of the trade secret by proper means is unlikely, the appropriate comparison may be between the costs of using the trade secret and the costs of alternative methods available to the defendant to achieve the same result.

Under the principles discussed in § 44, Comment f, it is often appropriate to enjoin the defendant's use of a trade secret only for the period of time that would have been required for the defendant to acquire the information by proper means. In such cases, however, the defendant remains liable for any development or reverse engineering costs saved as a result of the appropriation that are not otherwise accounted for through an award of the defendant's profits or other monetary relief.

g. Reasonable royalty.

A reasonable royalty measure of relief awards to the plaintiff the price that would be set by a willing buyer and a willing seller for the use of the trade secret made by the defendant. However, the royalty agreed to in an actual market transaction reflects a price at which both parties gain from the transaction. To the extent that a court-awarded reasonable royalty accurately reflects the marketplace, the royalty may compensate the plaintiff for loss but it does not necessarily deprive the defendant of the full gain attributable to the appropriation. Since the imposition of a reasonable royalty requires the defendant to pay only the amount it would have paid had it fairly bargained for use of the plaintiff's secret, it may not adequately discourage the appropriation of trade secrets.

There are at least three situations in which the reasonable royalty measure of relief has been applied. First, when the defendant has made a substantial good faith investment in the trade secret prior to receiving notice of the plaintiff's claim, it may be inequitable to require the relinquishment of all profits earned by the defendant after notice. An award of damages measured by a reasonable royalty for use subsequent to the notice and an injunction conditioning future use on the payment of a reasonable royalty gives the plaintiff the market value of the trade secret but protects the defendant's good faith reliance. Second, when the plaintiff's loss, although difficult to measure, is apparently greater than any gain acquired by the defendant, a reasonable royalty may be the most appropriate measure of relief. For example, if the defendant's inefficiency results in little or no profit from the exploitation of the trade secret and the loss to the plaintiff cannot otherwise be established, a reasonable royalty may be the best available approximation of the plaintiff's loss. Third, in cases in which the defendant's gain from the trade secret is difficult to measure but apparently exceeds the plaintiff's loss, a reasonable royalty may be the best means of approximating the defendant's unjust enrichment.

The purpose for which the reasonable royalty measure is invoked and the equities of the particular case may properly influence the calculation of the appropriate royalty. To insure adequate deterrence and to prevent unjust enrichment, a court may resolve issues relating to the amount of the royalty against a defendant who has willfully appropriated the trade secret.

h. Limitation on monetary relief.

Monetary remedies, whether measured by the loss to the plaintiff or the gain to the defendant, are appropriate only for the period of time that the information would have remained unavailable to the defendant in the absence of the appropriation. This period may be measured by the time it would have taken the defendant to obtain the information by proper means such as reverse engineering or independent development. Similarly, the issuance of a patent or other public disclosure of the information by the plaintiff or a third person terminates the secrecy necessary to the protection of the trade secret. Monetary relief based on the defendant's use of the information after the loss of secrecy is therefore appropriate only to the extent necessary to remedy a head start or other unfair advantage attributable to the defendant's prior access to the information. The limitations on the appropriate duration of injunctive relief as stated in § 44, Comment f, are thus also generally applicable to the calculation of monetary relief.

The rules governing the appropriate period of liability for monetary relief in actions in tort for the appropriation of a trade secret are not necessarily applicable in actions in contract for breach of agreements relating to the use or disclosure of trade secrets. Remedies for breach of contracts relating to trade secrets are ordinarily measured by the terms of the obligations imposed under the agreement. Licensing agreements, for example, can ordinarily provide for royalty payments covering a period that ends before or after any public disclosure of the trade secret. See § 41, Comment d. Similarly, although a nondisclosure agreement that is interpreted to extend beyond a public disclosure of the trade secret may be unenforceable as an unreasonable restraint of trade, id. , obligations under a nondisclosure agreement may terminate according to its terms prior to any public disclosure. The use of a trade secret in breach of an enforceable agreement, however, can give rise to both a claim for breach of contract and a claim for appropriation in tort under the rules stated in § 40. Durational limits contained in the agreement may influence but do not necessarily determine the appropriate duration of monetary relief awarded in a tort action pursuant to the rules stated here.

i. Punitive damages.

A successful plaintiff in an action at common law for the appropriation of a trade secret may recover punitive damages under the rules generally applicable in the jurisdiction to the award of punitive damages in tort actions. See Restatement, Second, Torts § 908. The purpose of punitive damages is to deter and punish egregious conduct, and normally proof of malice or willful misconduct is required. Section 3(b) of the Uniform Trade Secrets Act provides for an award of punitive damages not exceeding twice the amount of compensatory and restitutionary damages in cases of "willful and malicious misappropriation. "

j. Attorney's fees.

Most states do not provide for an award of attorney's fees in actions at common law. In actions under the Uniform Trade Secrets Act, reasonable attorney's fees may be awarded if the appropriation is "willful and malicious," if the claim of appropriation is made in bad faith, or if a motion to terminate an injunction is made or resisted in bad faith. Id. § 4.

第四篇

美国国会在审议的
主要商业秘密立法草案

第一章　美国国会当前审议的主要商业秘密立法法案

第一节　美国国会对商业秘密法案的审议

笔者研究发现,从1995年以来,在这二十多年的时间内,美国国会审议了一批有关商业秘密保护的重要法案,至今已经批准和颁布实施了四件。这四件联邦法律,就是前文已经介绍过的保护商业秘密的专门性联邦法律,即《1996经济间谍法》《2012盗窃商业秘密罪扩大适用范围法》《2012外国经济间谍罪加重处罚法》和《2016商业秘密保护法》。

除了上述四部联邦法律以外,还有十余部比较重要的法案处于国会的审查之中。当然,从立法的角度来说,这些在审查中的法案有可能成为联邦法律,也有可能不能成为联邦法律,或者只有部分法案能够成为联邦法律,甚至最终都不能成为联邦法律,几种可能性都存在。

但是,从现有的这些法案中可以看出美国当前有关商业秘密保护的基本观点、基本政策和想要采取的基本措施,这对我们认识和了解美国的商业秘密立法和政策具有一定的参考价值。

从全面了解和掌握美国商业秘密法律的角度来说,不仅要了解和掌握已经颁布实施的法律,还应当进一步地了解和掌握已经列入立法计划中的主要法案的内容,只有这样,才能全面认识和把握美国商业秘密保护联邦法律的整体状况和发展趋势。

正如在本书第一篇第一章中介绍过的那样,从立法程序上来说,一项立法法案可以由总统建议提出,也可以分别由众议院或者参议院提出,但是都必须先后经过众议院和参议院进行投票表决通过,然后再提交总统批准,只有当总统批准以后其才能生效成为美国联邦的法律。

当然,正如本书在第一篇第一章第二节的第二个问题即"二、美国《宪法》中涉及权力分立的重要事项"中所介绍的那样,如果总统否决了国会通过的法案,国会的参众两院如果都能够以三分之二的多数票再次表决通过该法案,那么,该法案就直接成为生效的联邦法律,无须再经过总统批准,而且总统也无权再对该法案行使否决权。

第二节　国会审议中的专门保护商业秘密的重要法案

下列法案都是截至 2018 年美国国会官方网站公布的法案,当然,随着时间的推移,一定还会不断地增加新的重要的专门保护商业秘密的法案,而且这些法案最终能否成为联邦法律还需要经历比较漫长的审议程序。

这些法案是从已经查询到的保护商业秘密的法案中选出的部分重要内容,其他有些法案虽然也比较重要,但是在内容上与已经颁布实施的上述四部商业秘密法律比较接近,再单独立法的可能性应该不大,在此就不再单独列出。

当然,由于受到查询方式等原因的制约,而且从 1995 年以来,处于国会审查之中的法案数量又比较多,不能完全排除还有其他个别重要的有关商业秘密保护的方案没有查询到,不过在此列出下列方案的目的只是为了研究当前美国商业秘密立法的基本趋势和特点,并不是完全地列举出所有的与商业秘密相关的法案。

1.《1996 工业间谍法案》(法案)

(1)原文名称:*Industrial Espionage Act of 1996*;

(2)在国会中的法案编号:S. 1556—104th Congress(1995—1996);

(3)法律状态:在国会审查中;

(4)主要立法目的和内容:要求通过修改联邦刑法典以禁止对他人拥有的价值在 10 万美元以上的经济信息的侵害行为。

2.《软件商业秘密保护法案》(法案)

(1)原文名称:*Software Trade Secrets Protection Act*;

(2)在国会中的法案编号:S. 1692—105th Congress(1997—1998);

（3）法律状态：国会审查中；

（4）主要立法目的和内容：这是 1998 年美国国会众议院财政委员会提交的法案，当前处于审议中。还有一个《1997 年软件商业秘密保护法案》（*Software Trade Secrets Protection Act of 1997*），法案编号是 H. R. 2657—105th Congress（1997—1998），这是由国会参议院提交的法案，两个法案的名称相同，内容都与税收和软件保护相关，但是又有所区别，也在国会审查中。由此可见，对于同一类型的社会问题，众议院和参议院可能会分别提出自己的法案，最终通过的法律只能是双方相互妥协和协商的法案。其主要内容是要求通过修订联邦国内税法典以禁止对计算机软件源代码进行非法测试和破解的活动。

3.《2001 年刑法技术修正法案》（法案）

（1）原文名称：*Criminal Law Technical Amendments Act of 2001*；

（2）在国会中的法案编号：S. 1235—107th Congress（2001—2002）；

（3）法律状态：国会审查中；

（4）主要立法目的和内容：主要内容是要求对联邦刑法典以及相关的刑法如《1996 经济间谍法》等的相关法律定义和技术问题进行修订和完善。

4.《2010 年间谍罪立法现代化法》（法案）

（1）原文名称：*Espionage Statutes Modernization Act of 2010*；

（2）在国会中的法案编号：S. 4051—111th Congress（2009—2010）；

（3）法律状态：国会审查中；

（4）主要立法目的和内容：要求通过修订联邦刑法典加重对通过各种手段侵害机密信息的违法行为的处罚力度，包括延长刑期、增加罚款、扩大刑法覆盖的涉案人员范围。

5.《网络经济间谍责任法》（法案）

（1）原文名称：*Cyber Economic Espionage Accountability Act*；

（2）在国会中的法案编号：H. R. 2281—113th Congress（2013—2014）；

（3）法律状态：国会审查中；

（4）主要立法目的和内容：对于网络经济间谍行为，要求美国政府通过外交途径先与中国、俄罗斯等相关国家进行谈判处理。另外，建议美国总统向国会提交一份可靠的可能涉嫌网络经济间谍的人员名单,采取法律手段禁止名单中的人员获得签证进入美国,并对这些人员的财产进行冻结或者禁止交易。同时要求总统批准设立"国际紧急经济权力法案",以加大处罚力度。

6.《2014 年阻止网络盗窃法》(法案)

(1)原文名称:*Deter Cyber Theft Act of 2014*;

(2)在国会中的法案编号:S. 2384—113th Congress(2013—2014);

(3)法律状态:国会审查中;

(4)主要立法目的和内容:与此相似的法案是《阻止网络盗窃法案》(*Deter Cyber Theft Act*),法案号是 S. 884—113th Congress(2013—2014)。它们都在审查中。主要内容分别是要求总统或者美国国家情报局局长每年要向国会专门委员会报告哪些国家是借助网络,通过经济间谍手段侵害美国商业秘密和专有信息的重点国家,同时要求总统通过贸易制裁手段保护美国的知识产权和美国国防的安全供应链。

第二章　美国联邦商业秘密立法的基本特点分析

第一节　联邦商业秘密立法的特点

一、经济间谍罪成为突出的立法关注点

从世界范围来看,美国对于商业秘密的立法,最大的特点就是把侵害商业秘密的犯罪行为区分为"经济间谍罪"和"盗窃商业秘密罪"。也就是在商业秘密保护中创造性地增加了"经济间谍罪"的罪名和专门的刑事责任,这是目前除了美国之外,世界上其他国家都没有的一种立法类型和立法内容,因此,这是属于最具特色的立法特点。

当然,对于这一立法特点,本书第二篇第一章第四节"对《1996 经济间谍法》的评析"中从法学理论的角度对"经济间谍罪"这一问题进行了分析和讨论,实际上,除了从法学的角度进行分析以外,还可以从社会的角度对这一问题进行讨论,以便加深对这一问题的认识和理解。

（一）政府的社会定位和自己应有的社会责任担当

在当今社会中,世界上不同的国家分别选择和实施着不同的社会制度,采取着不同的社会管理方式和管理理念。政府作为管理整个国家的主体,在不同的发展历史和社会制度中,其自身产生的方式,内部的组织构造,整体权力的设计和运行,不同权力机构之间的权力分配和制衡,国家权力所涉及社会利益的大小及界限,政府能够为社会公众承担的基本责任和义务这些事项都可能有所不同,或者部分地存在不同。这些因素会直接影响着社会公众所实际享有的权利的大小和利益的多少,也会直接影响着一个国家整体的发展水平、发展质量、发展速度,以及可持续发展的程度。

因此,不同的国家之间,或者同一个国家的不同政府之间,对于整个国家和社会利益的占有和控制的程度可能不同,对本国公众所实际担负的责任和义务也会不同,这就是不同政府,不同国家,不同社会制度的基本区别和差异。

(二)美国联邦政府利用"经济间谍罪"保护商业秘密的宪法性依据

众所周知,美国是一个联邦制的国家,它由 50 个州组成,而且它的总统是由全国的公民通过公开选举产生的。如前所述,就整个国家的公共权力来说,首先是划分为两部分,一部分由中央政府享有,另一部分由各个州政府享有。另外,从中央政府到各个州政府,在每个政府中,再把公共权力划分为三部分,即立法权、行政权和司法权,这是美国政府的基本权力结构和构造。

那么美国政府的工作宗旨和基本目的是什么? 对于这一问题,可能不同的专家学者和不同的国家的法律制定者会有不同的感受和认识,也会提出各自不同的观点,在此只围绕设计和实施"经济间谍罪"所可能涉及的主要原因进行讨论,其他诸如可能涉及的社会文化、政治、经济、宗教、生活传统等方面的原因都不做讨论。

当然,从理论上来说,一个国家政府的宗旨和目的到底是什么,不能光看它说了什么,主张了什么,重要的还是要看它实际在做什么,在朝哪个方向努力。因为在当今社会,任何一个国家的政府为了自身能够获得民众的支持,至少是为了减缓民众对自己的不支持或者反对,在正常情况下,都会声称自己是为民众谋福利的,是为社会公众和国家服务的,这一现象在最近几十年内许多国家不断发生的政府更迭中就表现得比较明显,几乎任何一个新上任的政府都会作出上述的宣示和宣言。但是,对于一些政府来说,它们实际实施的政策和具体实施的行政行为则可能他们与宣扬的口号完全不同,甚至完全相反。由此可以得出,认识一个国家的制度,不能只停留在其宣传的口号上,或者说,有些口号和宣言只能作为一种参考。

设立"经济间谍罪"以及加重对侵害商业秘密行为的处罚力度,这既是一种法律性活动,也是一种国家公权力的实施行为,这里不仅涉及国家的立法权、司法权和行政权的实施问题,同时也彰显着国家权力的价值选择和价值趋向问题。另外,需要注意的是,这里所要保护的"商业秘密"都是属于美国企业的商业秘密,其中,除了少数企业属于政府以外,多数企业都是民营企业,也就是私营企业,这样,这些商业秘密实际上多数都是私营企业的私有财产,而不是由国家拥有的"全社会共有的公共财产"或者"州政府的财产"。很显然,政府这样做更多地体现出利用"公权力"对美国民营企业私有利益的重视和保护。

当然,基于美国社会的特点,拥有和控制民营企业的人员毕竟只是少数,因此,美国民营企业的"私有利益"与美国普通民众的"私有利益"并不相同,对于美国民营企业"私有利益"的重视和充分保护并不等于是对美国普通民众"私有利益"的重视和充分保护。

另外,由于"经济间谍罪"涉及外国政府受益的问题,因此,把该类犯罪行为列为"间谍罪",其中也内含着保卫国家安全的合理成分,并不完全是基于对美国企业利益的保护。

最后,美国政府是基于美国《宪法》诞生的,这一政府的宗旨在《宪法》中做了明确的宣示:"我们美国人民,为了建立一个能够维护公平正义,确保国家安全和国内安宁,不断提高人民福利,确保我们自己以及子孙后代都能够享有自由和幸福的更加美好的联邦共和国,创建这部美国《宪法》。"

也许,这一宣示能够从社会的角度来解释为什么美国要在商业秘密保护中突出地建立"经济间谍罪",这是因为:第一,他们要维护公平正义,制止和打击不择手段地获取财富,以及各类不劳而获的扭曲理念和行为,维护社会的正常秩序,这就需要最大可能地制止侵害他人商业秘密的非法行为;第二,他们要确保国家的安全和国内的安宁,由于侵害他人商业秘密的行为是为了让外国政府受益,外国的强大就在客观上增强了国际竞争的实力,以及增大了对美国的潜在威胁,因此,破坏了美国的国家安全和国内安宁;第三,他们要确保他们的民众能够世代享受到自由和幸福,这就要求他们民众的财富不能被别人侵害,更不能被外国政府所侵害。

(三) 美国企业的商业秘密中可能涉及一定的美国国家秘密

国家秘密涉及国家的利益和安全,任何通过非法手段获取他国国家秘密的行为通常都被视为"间谍行为",对于"间谍行为",各个国家都会进行严厉的防范和积极的打击。

值得注意的一个社会现象在于,美国的许多企业,特别是一些高科技的公司和企业集团,都会或多或少地承担来自美国政府,甚至是美国军方的科研生产任务,这样,对于这些企业来说,其中的很多商业秘密本身可能就是美国的国家秘密,因此,盗窃这一类"商业秘密"的行为,也就自然地被视为窃取"国家秘密"的间谍行为。

但是,值得注意的是,在《1996 经济间谍法》中,并没有把商业秘密区分为一般的商业秘密和国家秘密两类,而是把经济间谍罪直接界定在了侵害商业秘密上,只是依据对所盗窃的商业秘密的使用目的来区分是否构成经济间谍罪。

这样,在客观上就存在着下列情况:

(1)本身应该归属于"国家秘密"的那一部分秘密信息,由于仍然属于"商业秘密",当被盗窃了以后,如果不是用于外国政府的利益或者与外国政府相关的利益,则就不属于"经济间谍罪",只属于"盗窃商业秘密罪"。这样就可能使得实际上盗窃了"国家秘密"的行为没有构成"经济间谍罪",从而受到相对较轻的刑事处罚。

从形式上来看,这种立法设计方式似乎使得美国的部分"国家秘密"被降低为一般的商业秘密进行保护,似乎国家的利益可能会因此受到侵害。实际上,这部分"国家秘密",其中应当主要涉及先进的科学技术信息,如果这些先进的技术不被外国政府所使用,也就不能直接被外国的国防工业和军方所利用,而被国外的民营企业使用时,也只能利用这种先进的科学技术生产销售民用产品,这种状况对于美国的国家安全和国家利益也就难以构成实质性的危害和威胁。因此,从这里也就可以看出,美国在《1996 经济间谍法》中的立法设计还是比较科学合理的。

(2)可能把一部分本身就应当属于商业秘密的秘密信息,由于被盗窃以后用在了外国政府的利益或者与外国政府相关的利益上,从而盗用者构成了"经济间谍罪"。在这种情况下,实际上在利用"经济间谍罪"保护一般的商业秘密。

显然,由于"经济间谍罪"的处罚力度比"盗窃商业秘密罪"重,而且"经济间谍罪"完全是以国家公权力的侦查方式进行立案、侦查、批捕和审判的,这在很大程度上替代了该商业秘密权利人进行维权的工作,并且节省了维权的成本,而且还能获得和完成商业秘密权利人自己和法院都可能难以获取的证据材料,这一切都表明对于"商业秘密"这类知识产权,在这种情况下,国家完全是在利用公权力为商业秘密权利人服务。此时,在法律上,实际上是国家公权力在保护商业秘密权利人基于商业秘密所应当获取的私有利益。

从这个角度上来说,在《1996 经济间谍法》中设计"经济间谍罪",对于那些本质上就是商业秘密而不是国家秘密,但是又被认为属于"经济间谍罪"保护对象的商业秘密来说,显然是一种超越民事权利的特殊性保护。

（四）为美国企业保护商业秘密开辟了一条捷径

根据《1996 经济间谍法》的规定,当某一美国企业发现自己的商业秘密被盗窃以后,摆在他面前的维权道路有两条,一条是追究盗窃者的"盗窃商业秘密罪",另一条是追究盗窃者的"经济间谍罪"。

但是,如前所述,两种不同罪的立案调查、法律责任和法律程序都不同,如果对于某一商业秘密的盗窃行为,被盗窃的美国企业难以确认盗窃者是否用于与外国政府相关的利益之中,或者对于盗窃行为本身自己也难以调查取证从而获取确凿的证据时,如果他向政府有关部门控告盗窃嫌疑人涉嫌构成"经济间谍罪",一旦政府有关部门受理这一控告,则这一案件就由联邦司法部所属的有关部门动用国家的公权力进行侦查和取证,甚至逮捕嫌疑人,从而获取更多的证据材料。

由此可见,这样就在客观上为商业秘密的权利人提供了一条维权的捷径,从而借助"经济间谍罪"能够更加有效和快捷地获取相关的犯罪证据,惩治盗窃嫌疑人,保护自己的商业秘密。

但是,在这种情况下,从维护社会公平正义的角度来说,就应当对于"经济间谍罪"的立案条件和立案标准在立法中进行明确的规定。否则,就可能把一些本来属于"盗窃商业秘密罪"的一般刑事案件作为"经济间谍罪"办理,这样就可能损害犯罪嫌疑人的合法利益,甚至使一些无罪的人,因为受到怀疑,便可能受到无辜的侦查和审查,甚至无辜的审判,从而受到公权力侵害。

最后,需要说明的是,对于保护国家秘密,美国有专门的涉及国家安全的政治性的间谍法律,与保护商业秘密的法律不再是一类法律,在此不再讨论。

二、有关商业秘密的立法内容丰富

当前，在世界范围内，只有美国一个国家在保护商业秘密立法方面进行了比较全面的专门性立法，已经远远地走在了世界各国的前列。美国的这种立法，并不仅仅局限于利用现有的保护知识产权的途径和方法来比较全面地保护商业秘密，而是结合商业秘密自身的特征，在已有的保护知识产权理念和方式的基础上，又创造性地设立了"经济间谍罪"，从而开创了保护知识产权的另一种新的理念和新的途径。

如果对美国这种立法模式和保护思路进行分析就不难发现，美国在保护商业秘密的立法中，并不以所谓的现有的保护知识产权的理论、方式、规定、原则来束缚自己立法的手脚，而是与此相反，他们完全是基于社会现实情况和现实需要，大胆地创造和设立"经济间谍罪"，并且使其与"盗窃商业秘密罪"并列，从而从多个层次来有效地保护商业秘密。虽然他们现有的立法内容并不一定已经达到十分科学和完善的状态，但是这种立法理念和立法做法本身就是一种科学的选择和探索，它打破了各种所谓的理论和原则的条条框框的制约和限制，而这些所谓的理论和原则有的已经明显地与现实社会脱节了，已经过时了，甚至有的已经成为阻碍知识产权法律制度发展和进步的障碍，这就首先需要一种实事求是和勇于探索的精神和勇气，在这方面，美国的立法走在了世界各国的前列；其次，在完成这种探索性立法的过程中，还需要找出能够解决具体问题的办法，这也是一种智慧和行动。

如前所述，在保护商业秘密方面，截至 2018 年 5 月，美国现在已经颁布实施的专门性的联邦法律，共有下列四部有效的法律：①《1996 经济间谍法》；②《2012 盗窃商业秘密罪扩大适用范围法》；③《2012 外国经济间谍罪加重处罚法》；④《2016 商业秘密保护法》。

其中，《1996 经济间谍法》《2012 盗窃商业秘密罪扩大适用范围法》和《2012 外国经济间谍罪加重处罚法》这三部联邦法律都是关于商业秘密刑事保护的法律，而且《2012 盗窃商业秘密罪扩大适用范围法》和《2012 外国经济间谍罪加重处罚法》都是对《1996 经济间谍法》相关条款的修改和补充。因此，在本质上，这三部法律属于同一部法律，即保护商业秘密的联邦刑事法律。而《2016 商业秘密保护法》主要是保护商业秘密的联邦民事法律,其中,也包含部分对《1996 经济间谍法》相关条款进行修改和补充的内容,即《2016 商业秘密保护法》主要是一部保护商业秘密的民事法律,同时也包含着部分刑事内容。

值得特别说明的是,上述四部法律都是保护商业秘密的"联邦"法律。如前文所述,在美国,除了上述四部联邦法律以外,还存在着保护商业秘密的各个州的州法律,而各个州的州法律也同样包含保护商业秘密的刑事法律和民事法律。当前,由于 50 个州的州法律都已经采用了《侵权法重述》中有关保护商业秘密的内容,而且绝大多数州也已经采用了《统一商业秘密法》的内容,从而使得各个州的州法律在保护商业秘密的民事法律方面已经基本接近一致,具有比较大的统一性,但是,在刑事保护方面还存在着比较大的差异。

这样,概括起来就可以说,美国保护商业秘密的法律包括联邦法律和州法律两种类型,每一种类型中又都包含着各自的民事法律和刑事法律,对于各个州的州法律来说,当前各个州在保护商业秘密的民事法律方面已经基本统一和趋于一致,但是在保护商业秘密的刑事法律方面还是由各个州单独立法来确定,或者直接适用其本州的刑法处理,因此,在刑事保护方面还很不一致,甚至存在较大的差异。

另外,在美国现有的立法中,除了上述专门保护商业秘密的法律以外,在其他一些法律中也会涉及商业秘密,以及设立保护商业秘密的规定和条款,但是,与这些专门性的保护商业秘密的法律相比,在其他法律中设立的保护商业秘密的条款更多地是对保护商业秘密的一种延伸应用,在此就不再进行专门的介绍和讨论。

如果用一个图示来表示上述专门保护商业秘密的联邦和州法律,其基本关系就如图 4 所示:

保护商业秘密的联邦法律			保护商业秘密的各州法律	
民事法律	一般性 刑事法律 (盗窃罪)	政治性 刑事法律 (间谍罪)	刑事法律 各州不统一	民事法律 各州基本一致

图 4　美国保护商业秘密的专门性法律

三、侵害商业秘密的救济措施多样化

在美国现行的四部联邦性商业秘密专门法律中规定了多种保护措施,这些措施归纳起来可以分为刑事措施和民事措施两大类,而在民事措施中又包括多种具体的措施。

（一）刑事救济和惩罚措施

在刑事措施中,主要包括逮捕、羁押和审判犯罪嫌疑人,一旦判刑之后,对罪犯进行监禁和罚款,并且没收其非法收入和财产。

（二）民事救济和惩罚措施

立法中所规定的民事措施,可以概括地分为在民事诉讼中的民事救济措施和对发生在美国境外的侵害行为的报告制度两部分。

1. 法院采取的主要民事措施

在民事诉讼中,法院采取的救济和惩罚措施主要包括下列行为:①颁布实施扣押令,扣押嫌疑人的财产和犯罪证据;②颁布实施各类禁令,包括对侵害人、相关人员实施禁令,以及对雇员实施禁令;③判决被告赔偿损害,包括实施惩罚性赔偿;④判令被告承担原告合理的律师费用。

除此之外,在民事诉讼程序中还规定了下列具体的保护措施:①在诉讼程序中颁布保密令;②设置专门的保密负责人;③对涉及商业秘密的扣押物采取加密措施,对提交涉及商业秘密的材料要求密封。

2. 对美国境外侵害美国企业商业秘密的报告制度

对于发生在境外侵害美国企业商业秘密的行为,立法中设立了专门的"司法部长向美国国会提交并在司法部网站公开报告的制度",借以维护美国企业在国外遭遇商业秘密侵害时的利益。

需要说明的是,这里的报告制度只是一种措施和手段,其并不影响美国企业依据上述保护商业秘密的联邦性刑事和民事法律在美国联邦法院起诉追究国外侵害人的法律责任的行动,也不影响美国司法部根据《1996 经济间谍法》对境外的侵害人进行立案侦查,并采取灵活的措施实施抓捕境外犯罪嫌疑人的行动。

四、重视打击通过网络侵害商业秘密的行为

虽然在现行的四部联邦性商业秘密保护法中没有专门设立通过网络侵害商业秘密行为的特别法律规定和具体措施,但是,在美国国会当前审议的有关保护商业秘密的法案中,不但具有专门的这类法案,而且占有比较多的比例。由此可见,美国政府对于通过网络侵害商业秘密的问题已经十分关注和重视,具体的此类法案包括:

(1)《软件商业秘密保护法案》(*Software Trade Secrets Protection Act*),在国会中的法案编号:S. 1692—105th Congress(1997—1998)。

(2)《网络经济间谍责任法》(*Cyber Economic Espionage Accountability Act*),在国会中的法案编号:H. R. 2281—113th Congress(2013—2014)。

(3)《2014年阻止网络盗窃法》(*Deter Cyber Theft Act of 2014*),在国会中的法案编号:S. 2384—113th Congress(2013—2014)。

可以想到,随着网络技术的不断创新和发展,利用网络侵害商业秘密的方式和方法也会不断地发生着变化,与此相对应,相关的立法内容和应对措施也会相应地发生着更新和变化。

如果进行分析就能发现,通过网络进行侵权主要影响的是侵害商业秘密的途径和方法,以及造成的危害程度,在立法中这就涉及对具体侵害行为类型的扩展,以及救济措施类型的变化,还有如何评估损失的问题,同时也间接地涉及对"合理保密措施"的界定问题。

五、不断加重侵害商业秘密的刑事责任

我国《刑法》第219条中明确规定了"商业秘密罪",规定给商业秘密的权利人造成重大损失的,处3年以下有期徒刑或者拘役,并处或者单处罚金;造成特别严重后果的,处3年以上7年以下有期徒刑,并处罚金。在第220条中规定,单位犯此罪的,对单位判处罚金,并对其直接负责的主管人员和其他直接责任人员,依照第219条的规定处罚。

与我国上述规定不同的是,美国有关侵害商业秘密的刑事责任不但增加了"经济间谍罪",而且在刑罚的力度上也大于我国的规定,并且刑罚的力度还在

不断地加重,通过下列的对比就能发现这一趋势。

(一)《1996 经济间谍法》中对于"经济间谍罪"和"盗窃商业秘密罪"的刑罚规定

1. 对"经济间谍罪"的刑事处罚

个人犯罪的,最高处罚 50 万美元,或者最高监禁 15 年,或者两者同时执行;单位犯罪的,最高处罚 1000 万美元。

2. 对"盗窃商业秘密罪"的刑事处罚

个人犯罪的,按照本法的规定处罚,或者最高监禁 10 年,或者同时实施罚款和监禁;单位犯罪的,最高罚款 500 万美元。

(二)《2012 外国经济间谍罪加重处罚法》属于第一次修订并加重了对"经济间谍罪"的刑事处罚

1. 对"经济间谍罪"的刑事处罚

个人犯罪的,最高处罚 500 万美元,或者最高监禁 15 年,或者两者同时执行。单位犯罪的,最高 1000 万美元,或者被侵害商业秘密价值的 3 倍,其中包括该单位因利用间谍行为所节省的用于研发的费用和正当地使用该商业秘密所应当支出的成本费用。

通过修改,把对个人的处罚数额由原来的"最高 50 万美元"增加为"最高 500 万美元";把对单位的处罚数额由原来的单纯的"最高 1000 万美元"修改为"最高 1000 万美元;或者被侵害商业秘密价值的 3 倍,其中包括该单位因利用间谍行为所节省的用于研发的费用和正当地使用该商业秘密所应当支出的成本费用"。

2. 对"盗窃商业秘密罪"的刑事处罚

个人犯罪的,按照本法的规定处罚,或者最高监禁 10 年,或者同时实施罚款和监禁;单位犯罪的,最高罚款 500 万美元。

(三)《2016 商业秘密保护法》属于第二次修订并加重了对"盗窃商业秘密罪"的刑事处罚

1. 对"经济间谍罪"的刑事处罚

个人犯罪的,最高处罚 500 万美元,或者最高监禁 15 年,或者两者同时处罚。单位犯罪的,最高处罚 1000 万美元;或者被侵害商业秘密价值的 3 倍,其中包括被告单位因利用间谍行为所节省的用于研发的费用和正当地使用该商业秘密所应当支出的成本费用。

2. 对"盗窃商业秘密罪"的刑事处罚

个人犯罪的,按照本法的规定处罚,或者最高监禁 10 年,或者同时处罚。单位犯罪的,最高处罚 500 万美元,或者被侵害商业秘密价值的 3 倍,其中包括被告单位因利用间谍行为所节省的用于研发的费用和正当地使用该商业秘密所应当支出的成本费用。

通过修改,把对单位的处罚数额由"最高处罚 500 万美元",修改为"最高处罚 500 万美元,或者被侵害商业秘密价值的 3 倍,其中包括被告单位因利用间谍行为所节省的用于研发的费用和正当地使用该商业秘密所应当支出的成本费用"。

由此可知,通过修订《2012 外国经济间谍罪加重处罚法》和《2016 商业秘密保护法》分别对《1996 经济间谍法》的"经济间谍罪"和"盗窃商业秘密罪"进行了修改,都增加了刑事处罚的力度。

与我国的《刑法》规定相比,《1996 经济间谍法》在刑事没收方面的规定也有所不同。在《1996 经济间谍法》中对于需要没收的财产范围进行了规定:对于实施本法犯罪的被告,法院在作出判决时,除了判处应有的刑罚以外,还应当罚没被告的下列财产:①任何直接或者间接地借助犯罪行为所得的财产;②任何人的财产,只要被用来或者企图被用来实施犯罪,或者为犯罪提供便利,无论被使用的方式和方法如何,法院在慎重考虑这些财产在犯罪中的性质,被使用的范围和比例以后决定没收的程度。显然,其比我国《刑法》中的规定要具体明确,便于实际实施和操作。

六、"经济间谍罪"缺乏明确的立案标准和立案条件

通过《1996 经济间谍法》中有关"经济间谍罪"的规定可以发现,对于犯有"经济间谍罪"的被告,包括个人和单位进行刑事处罚都是比较重的,如前所述,个人犯罪的,最高处罚 500 万美元,或者最高监禁 15 年,或者两者同时处罚。单位犯罪的,最高处罚 1000 万美元,或者被侵害商业秘密价值的 3 倍,其中包括被告单位因利用间谍行为所节省的用于研发的费用和正当地使用该商业秘密所应当支出的成本费用。

另外,除了判处应有的刑罚以外,法院还应当罚没被告的下列财产:①任何直接或者间接地借助犯罪行为所得的财产;②任何人的财产,只要被用来或者企图被用来实施犯罪,或者为犯罪提供便利,无论被使用的方式和方法如何,法院在慎重考虑这些财产在犯罪中的性质,被使用的范围和比例以后决定没收的程度。

由此可见,对于"经济间谍罪"的刑事处罚是比较重的。但是,对于这样的刑事犯罪,却在立法中没有规定具体的刑事立案标准,这是值得关注和讨论的问题。

在这里之所以要求应当明确建立"经济间谍罪"的立案标准,并对这一问题进行专门的讨论,是由于"经济间谍罪"具有与其他刑事犯罪完全不同的独特的特点,这一独特的特点就在于它是基于"商业秘密"所诞生的一种罪行,而商业秘密又是一类没有事先经过具有公信力的政府机关审查,并且经过社会公众质疑,并最终经过政府机关确认的一类事物(经过这类公示、审查和确认的知识产权如专利权、商标权、植物新品种权等),这样就在客观上存在着如下的问题:

(1)被指控侵害的"商业秘密"的秘密信息是否真正的存在。

(2)被指控侵害的"商业秘密"本身是否符合商业秘密的条件,即是否能够构成商业秘密。

(3)被指控侵害的"商业秘密"本身是否具有合法性,即是否涉嫌在先侵害了他人的商业秘密、专门技术或者其他合法权益,从而使该商业秘密自身不具有合法性。

(4)在商业秘密刑事案件中,特别是涉及"经济间谍罪"的案件中,确立进行立案并开始侦查的最低标准是什么,这一标准应当包含哪些具体的事项,以及每一事项应当达到什么样的具体条件和要求。

(5)禁止和防范商业秘密权利人在商业秘密刑事案件中调换商业秘密的措施是什么? 即由于商业秘密的秘密性,以及事先未被政府机关审查和确认的特点,在现实中就可能存在下列的情形:商业秘密权利人为了顺利获得政府机关的立案,商业秘密权利人知道应当不存在侵犯商业秘密 A 的犯罪问题,实际怀疑可能侵犯了商业秘密 B,但是,商业秘密 A 比较符合作为商业秘密的条件,商业秘密 B 自身作为商业秘密可能会被他人产生质疑,所以,先利用商业秘密 A 获得立案,然后再添加商业秘密 B 也涉嫌被侵害的内容,或者利用商业秘密 B 更换出商业秘密 A,从而实现把对方列入打击对象的目的。提供了便于审查确认的商业秘密 A,但是,立案以后,即使嫌疑人最终被判决无罪,这一逮捕和审判经过也足以严重地破坏和损害对方的声望和信誉,实现了打击对方的目的。

(6)怎么杜绝"经济间谍罪"被作为一项法律手段和工具,甚至被作为一种政治手段和工具的问题。在当前的立法内容中,在被指控的商业秘密或侵权行为自身都难以客观地、科学合理地确认的情况下,更多地基于"政治因素"的考虑而对被指控的嫌疑人直接采取刑事立案、侦查、逮捕、审判活动,显然,这些法律措施都应当在立法中加以明确的规定。

由此可见,由于"经济间谍罪"是一项比较特殊的"刑事 + 经济 + 政治"的三位一体的犯罪,因此,人们应该更多地关注这一犯罪,特别是中国的公民和企业,更需要关注、重视、了解和研究这一类犯罪。在条件合适时,也可以考虑通过合适的途径和方式向美国国会提交立法建议,请求他们从科学合理的角度不断地修改完善这一类犯罪的相关规定,避免错案的发生以及无辜者受害。

第二节　美国重视商业秘密立法的内在原因分析

当前,在世界范围内,虽然对于"商业秘密"这一事物的法律属性的认识和定性有所不同,不同的国家基于本国的立法特点和本国对于商业秘密的认识,以及本国的社会需要所选择的商业秘密立法方式和保护模式存在差异,但是,这些因素都无法解释为什么美国对于商业秘密建立了这么多内容丰富的专门性立法。其立法和保护商业秘密的积极性是世界上其他国家都无法比拟的。很显然,出现这种状况的内在原因绝对不可能只是单纯的法学研究、法学观点和立法特点所导致的,而一定存在着内在的重大的社会需求,应当是由这种重大的社会内在需求所决定的。

通过分析和研究,笔者发现以下三种原因对于美国积极地建立和完善商业秘密保护制度至关重要,当然,这只是一种理论研究和讨论,不免存在着遗漏或者偏颇,对于这一方面的问题有待于人们进行更进一步的分析和研究。

一、先进科学技术构成美国社会发展和进步的坚定基础

(一)美国社会的基本特征

众所周知,自第二次世界大战结束以来,美国和苏联就是世界上的两个超级大国,1991 年 12 月 25 日苏联解体后,美国成为世界上唯一的超级大国。

在地理位置上,美国位于北美洲,由 50 个州 1 个特区及海外领土和领地组成。在 50 个州中,48 个州位于美国本土,另外 2 个州位于美国本土之外,一个是阿拉斯加州,它位于北美洲最西北部,东与加拿大接壤,另外三面分别与北冰洋、白令海峡和北太平洋相接;另一个是夏威夷州,它是位于亚洲太平洋中的一个群岛。而海外领土和领地主要包括波多黎各、关岛和美属维尔京群岛。

美国本土东临大西洋,西临太平洋,北邻加拿大,南部与墨西哥接壤,总人口约 3.3 亿。

美国的自然资源十分丰富,具有丰富的植物、矿产、水产等资源,特别是矿产资源的探明总量居于世界首位,铁矿石、煤炭、天然气、石油等资源的储量都居于世界前列;森林覆盖率也非常高,农业的种植面积大,粮食产量高。

美国作为一个国家诞生于 1776 年 7 月 4 日,到 2018 年只有 242 年的建国历史,与世界上的其他许多国家相比,美国的这一建国历史比较短暂。

但是,美国却在这么短暂的 242 年的历史中创造性地成为世界上唯一的超级大国,这种状况的产生也可以称为是一种奇迹,当然,任何奇迹的发生都应当有其内在的原因,甚至内在的必然性。作为一个国家能够发生这种奇迹,并且能够长期地保持这种奇迹,还能进一步地不断向前发展,显然不是偶然的,其中必有其内在的原因。

美国成为世界强国和超级大国主要依靠的是自身强大的先进技术的研发力量和先进产品的制造能力。

(二)先进技术构成美国成为世界唯一超级大国的重要依托

作为世界上唯一的超级大国,其作为"强大国家"的具体特征主要表现在以下方面。

1. 世界第一的强大的军事力量

当前,在世界范围内,军事力量最强的国家无疑是美国,虽然俄罗斯拥有

许多先进的军事武器装备,特别是拥有数量众多的威力无穷的核武器,但是,无论就核武器的数量还是威力来说,美国拥有的核武器一点也不逊色,两者基本可以保持一种力量对比的平衡,从而也形成了一种长期的力量制衡和制约。除此之外,两者都拥有强大的空军和陆军部队,都拥有世界上最先进的飞机、坦克、导弹和其他常规武器,并且军队的训练方式、作战理念和作战组织方式等比较先进和超前,这一切综合起来使得他们的军队和国防力量处于世界的领先地位。在上述这些方面,两个国家的总体力量和总体水平也能够基本保持平衡。

但是,与俄罗斯相比,美国拥有着强大的航母舰队和海军力量,这是美国当前比俄罗斯突出的地方。

由此可见,俄罗斯作为原世界另一个超级大国苏联的主要继承者,虽然继承了苏联的主要军事装备和军事力量,但是,现在总体上只能与美国抗衡,还没有超越和领先美国,这就使美国在军事的总体上基本处于领先的状态。

除了俄罗斯以外,世界上其他国家的军事力量,与美国就有比较大的差距,这种差距主要体现在先进武器的装备上,更突出地体现在对先进武器的开拓性和创新性的持续性研发、制造、装备、使用、维护和后勤保障上。在这一整套相互衔接的军事技术和装备的发展过程中,内在的灵魂就是持续不断地向前发展和不断地提高。

2. 世界领先的众多的高科技产品

对于美国这个世界上唯一的超级大国来说,除了其显赫的军事力量以外,另一个重要的特征就应当属于其不断创造出来的引领和改善人们工作和生活的丰富多彩的新的科技产品。在我们当今生活和工作中所使用的众多先进的科技产品中,许多产品都是由美国的科学家研究发明的,而且极大地提高和改善了人们的工作和生活质量。例如,现在人们常用的电脑和智能手机,主要就是由美国的科学家研究发明的,至今我国绝大部分电脑用户所使用的电脑中的CPU 主要是由美国英特尔公司研发制造的,而且自 1971 年研究推出第一款微处理器——4004 芯片以后,英特尔公司一直都在不断地研究和推出微处理器的新型号和新产品,实现着新技术和新产品的更新换代,从而利用技术优势占领着世界上的市场。同样,当前我国绝大多数电脑用户使用的电脑操作系统是由美国微软公司研究推出的 Windows 系统,并且微软公司自 1985 年 11 月 20

日发布第一款"Windows 1.0"版本的操作系统后,平均一到两年发布一款更新的版本,截至 2015 年,已经发布了"Windows10"版本。微软公司凭借这些先进的技术优势和良好的产品性能,其产品也占据着世界市场。

除了这些日常所见的电脑产品以外,我国人民在日常生活中普遍使用的导航系统就是美国的 GPS 卫星定位系统。当然,近年来,我国的卫星定位系统——北斗星系统也已经初步建立起来,这是非常值得中国人民骄傲的重大的技术进步! 但是,应该看到的是,卫星导航定位系统这一技术在美国多年前就已经研发出来并且已经被广泛地使用了很多年,这说明在这一领域他们确实走在了我们的前面。

除此之外,在其他领域,诸如医学研究和医药研发领域、航空和航天科学领域、海洋和航海科学领域、工业产品制造领域、生物科学和育种技术领域、生命科学和转基因工程技术领域、人工智能领域、高等教育和体育发展领域等诸多方面,美国也都拥有世界领先的众多的先进技术和突出的研究成果。

(三)国家的内在精神支柱是推动先进技术诞生和发展的原动力

当然,至于为什么美国的科学家和美国的公司能够长期坚持不懈地进行积极探索,勇于奋进,不断地研究和获取新的重大的科技成果和科学突破,这就是另外一种问题了。当然,想要完整深入地研究和回答这一问题,应当涉及美国社会的众多方面,在这里就不做深入的讨论了。

不过,纵观人类社会发展的历史,一个国家如果能够在某一个历史阶段出现一种社会民众,或者说社会主流都能够普遍地奋发向上的状态时,一定有内在的崇高的精神在召唤和支撑,这一局面在我国现代历史中也曾经出现过。中国共产党从领导全国人民团结抗日,到经历三年解放战争建立中华人民共和国,再到中华人民共和国成立之后的社会主义建设,在这一历史阶段中,勤劳智慧的中华民族在中国共产党的坚强领导下,万众一心,团结奋进,积极奉献,在短短的几十年间,就把我国从一个一穷二白,连火柴(当时被称为洋火)都制造不出来的落后的国家很快地建设成为一个工业门类基本齐全,成功研制原子弹和氢弹,发射了人造地球卫星,制造了飞机、坦克、导弹、火箭、火炮、汽车、火车、军舰和潜艇,实力强劲,后劲无穷的军事强国。在这一期间,中国人民解放军不但在朝鲜打败了以美国为首的所谓的联合国军队,又帮助越南人民打败了美国对越南北部的侵略,这些事实都足以说明当时的中国在世界上已经是一个军事力量比较强大的国家。

这一社会发展的基本原理,不仅适用于中国,也适用于其他国家。

概括起来讲,这种充满着社会公平正义、积极进取、无私奉献,以及民族自豪感的内在精神力量,其精髓和内涵至少应该包含下列事项:①为了祖国的利益,为了社会大众的幸福,为了整个人类社会的进步,甘愿奉献自己的时间、精力、财物和聪明才智,甚至贡献出自己的一切! ②认识到推动人类社会进步的重要力量是创造和拥有先进的科学技术和先进的文化,因此,为了自己的理想和信念,应当积极主动地坚持学习和思考,应当勤奋努力地工作和探索,应当不断地进取和提高,应当百折不挠,坚持不懈,无怨无悔! ③坚信人的生命的真正的价值在于为人类社会创造出了多少财富,作出了多少实际的贡献,而不在于向社会索取和占有了多少财富及利益! ④坚信人生的最高境界就是在智慧和贡献上不断地超越前人,超越常人,超越自己,让自己的生命之火在人类历史的长河中闪耀着光芒!

一个国家,一个民族,只有当他们的社会主旋律具有这种意识和信念,并且已经转化为社会公众的普遍的内在精神时,这个国家和这个民族才可能始终保持着旺盛的进取精神,并且不断地取得优异的成果!

因此,当一个国家能够在比较长的时期内一直保持着强劲的发展势头和快速的发展脚步时,这个国家一定内含着一种内在的精神力量,无论其表面的管理方式如何变化和多样化,最终起决定作用的一定是这种内在的精神力量。

通过以上的分析可见,作为当今世界上唯一的超级大国,美国主要依靠的是其强大的科学技术研究能力,以及凭借这些先进的科学技术所制造和生产出来的各类先进的产品和先进的武器,这些因素是使其称雄于世界的中坚力量。而在此背后,实际上存在着一种内在的精神力量,这种力量使得美国的民众能够长期地保持着积极进取的信念和状态。

二、先进科学技术一直是美国处理国际政治关系的重要武器

如果进行深入的分析就能发现,科学技术是人类脑力劳动创造的产物,虽然对于人类社会来说,它也属于一种社会财富,但是它却是一类特殊的社会财富,它与来自自然界中的天然财富,如黄金、白银、钻石、石油、煤炭、天然气、森

林等财富不同,也与人们主要通过体力劳动建造的房屋、桥梁、大坝、家具、衣物等物质性财富不相同,科学技术自身是无形的,可以同时在不同的地方被不同的人们加以利用并创造财富。因此,在一定程度上可以说,科学技术是一类能够用来创造财富的财富!

不仅如此,随着人类科学研究活动的积累,伴随着时间的延续,科学技术正在沿着很多的方向不断地向前延伸,其所包含的内容也正在以几何级数的增长方式进行拓展,这些特征都是其他物质性财富所不具备的。

基于以上的认识,我们可以看到,对于科学技术来说,如果只是单纯地把它看作一种"财产",或者一种"科学研究成果",或是种"法律保护的对象",这些认识都是片面的,都没有包含和体现出它实际包含的全部内容,以及它对一个国家、一个民族和整个人类社会所能产生的作用和影响。

人是由精神和躯体两部分组成的,国家和社会又主要是由人所组成的,因此,对于一个正常的国家和社会来说,它们也应当是由精神财富和物质财富两部分组成的。

与物质财富相比,科学技术应当属于人类社会精神财富的范畴,因此,对于一个正常的国家和社会来说,要想获得健康的发展和进步,科学技术是不可缺少的重要内容。

在人类历史上,美国对于科学技术的认识和运用更加与众不同,他们不仅非常重视科学技术的商业性价值,而且更加重视科学技术能够发挥的政治作用,并且把这两种不同的作用都发挥到了极致。

(一)美国促成了人类历史上第一部知识产权国际公约的诞生

1.《巴黎公约》的基本内容和状况

在世界范围内,第一部知识产权国际公约是《巴黎公约》,该公约于 1883 年 3 月 20 日在巴黎外交会议上,分别由比利时、巴西、法国、危地马拉、意大利、荷兰、葡萄牙、萨尔瓦多、塞尔维亚、西班牙和瑞士 11 个国家的代表签署,于 1884 年 7 月 7 日生效。

《巴黎公约》的内容涉及专利、商标、工业品外观设计、实用新型、服务标志、商品名称、地理标志和反不正当竞争。自 1883 年缔结以后,又先后于 1900 年在布鲁塞尔,1911 年在华盛顿,1925 年在海牙,1934 年在伦敦,1958 年在里斯本和 1967 年在斯德哥尔摩修订,1979 年又进行了修订。

截至 2018 年,该公约共有成员方 177 个,我国于 1985 年 3 月 19 日成为该公约成员方。

2.《巴黎公约》诞生简史

在 1883 年《巴黎公约》诞生以前,美国和一些欧洲国家已经在各自的国内颁布实施了本国的《专利法》,但是,在国际上还没有一部能够协调各国法律的统一的知识产权国际公约。

在 19 世纪后期,随着发达国家工业的快速增长,国际货物贸易以及国际技术交流也都有了快速发展。在这种背景下,许多国家也都需要在国际范围内建立一个能够统一规范专利、商标、原产地名称和企业名称等与国际贸易及技术交流密切相关的国际公约,这是当时的一种客观需要。

当时的奥匈帝国计划于 1873 年在其首都维也纳召开一次国际博览会,但是,美国的发明家和制造商却提出了一项特殊的要求,要求举办方奥匈帝国要为这次国际博览会专门修改一次其本国的《专利法》(1852 年),在修订的条文中应当规定对于在这次国际博览会上展出的外国的技术发明给予合适的法律保护,美国的发明家和制造商特别提出这些技术发明一旦被奥匈帝国授予专利权,自专利权授权之日起,在一年的期限内这些专利必须在奥匈帝国进行生产和实施。美方代表声明,如果举办方奥匈帝国不能满足他们的上述要求,他们将联合抵制这次维也纳国际博览会。

美国政府使节约翰杰伊与奥匈帝国的外交部部长专门就这些要求在维也纳进行了讨论,由于修改《专利法》的程序复杂,考虑到奥匈帝国政府机关中的官僚作风和工作效率,最后商定参照英国政府于 1851 年和 1862 年在伦敦举办国际博览会期间,以及法国政府于 1855 年和 1867 年在巴黎举办国际博览会期间,专门颁布过临时性保护法令的做法,决定在这次维也纳国际博览会上颁布一项"临时保护的特别法",以此来满足美国一方的要求。最后,奥匈帝国政府颁布了一项"临时保护的特别法"①。

在这次国际博览会期间,应奥匈帝国政府邀请,一些国家的政府代表出席

---

① WIPO, The International Protection of Industrial Property: From The Paris Convention to The TRIPs Agreement, http://www. wipo. int/meetings/en/fulltext_mdocs. jsp? q = Paris + Convention + for + the + Protec,访问日期:2018 年 4 月 11 日。

了专门讨论共同建立一项知识产权国际公约的会议,这应当也是世界上第一次共同讨论筹建知识产权国际公约的会议,会议中确立了一个知识产权国际公约筹备委员会,筹备委员会向参加会议的代表们提出了一系列需要讨论和解决的具体问题,包括发明者能够享有的国际性权利;这些国际性专利权的界限,即这种专利权的权利有效范围应该是国际的,还是限于本国范围内的;有关专利权的授予费用问题,其成本无效和有效期限问题;国际专利局的管理以及国际性事物的安排等事项。大会就这些问题请各国代表们进行讨论,并要求准备出各自的建议和方案。然后在 1873 年 8 月 4 日至 8 日又基于上述问题专门举行了一次大会,共同讨论了相关的规定,并且提出了"国民待遇"和"国家主权独立"的基本原则①。

随后,各国又先后于 1878 年、1880 年和 1883 年围绕建立知识产权国际公约的问题召开了国际外交会议。

1878 年 9 月 18 日和 19 日各国又召开了专门的建立知识产权国际公约的专门性外交会议,会议的重要任务是确立建立知识产权国际公约应由各国政府支持和确认,并且决定成立一个"常设委员会"作为常设的工作机构。在会议上还审议了由瑞士成员博登海默(Bodenheimer)编写的知识产权国际条约草案②。

在 1878 年会议的基础上,1880 年在巴黎又召开了一次专门讨论建立知识产权国际公约事宜的国际外交会议。来自 21 个国家的 35 位代表出席了这一外交会议,这些国家包括阿根廷、奥地利、比利时、巴西、法国、危地马拉、匈牙利、意大利、卢森堡、荷兰、挪威、葡萄牙、俄罗斯、萨尔瓦多、瑞典、瑞士、土耳其、英国、乌拉圭、美国、委内瑞拉。在这次会议上,各国代表投票否决了在 1878 年会议上初步审议的由瑞士成员博登海默编写的公约草案文本,接纳了由法国外交部的查尔斯 – 贾格施密特(Charles Jagerschmidt)编写的国际公约草案,并对一些相关事项进行了商议。由于参加这次国际外交会议的外交代表们事先都

---

① WIPO, The International Protection of Industrial Property: From the Paris Convention to the TRIPs Agreement, http://www. wipo. int/meetings/en/fulltext_mdocs. jsp? q = Paris + Convention + for + the + Protec, 访问日期:2018 年 4 月 11 日。

② 同上。

没有获得签署国际公约的授权,因此,与会代表们都在会议记录上签了字,并且同意将公约草案提交给各自的政府进行审议和批准①。

1883 年 3 月,法国外交部部长又召开了第二次建立知识产权国际公约的外交会议,认为各国政府已经有足够的时间研究和审议在 1880 年外交会议上提供给各国外交代表的国际公约草案。因此,1883 年大会决定不再对 1880 年草案文本作任何实质性的修正,而是允许将不同的要求和建议列在最后议定书中。在此基础上,1883 年 3 月 20 日,由比利时、巴西、法国、危地马拉、意大利、荷兰、葡萄牙、萨尔瓦多、塞尔维亚、西班牙和瑞士 11 个国家的代表共同签署同意《巴黎公约》的条款,从而诞生了世界上第一部知识产权国际公约——《巴黎公约》②。

3. 美国加入《巴黎公约》的曲折程序

美国政府在加入《巴黎公约》时遇到了美国《宪法》和最高联邦法院的影响和制约。

在美国《宪法》中,对于知识产权保护的问题作出了下列规定:"为了促进科学和有用艺术的进步,应当基于作者创作的作品,以及发明者创造的发明,分别授予作者和发明人一类专有的权利,这类权利都应当具有明确的有效期限。"

基于上述规定,由于其中没有包含"商标"的内容,美国联邦最高法院认为美国联邦政府没有权力颁布实施涉及"商标"内容的法律,也无权签署涉及"商标"内容的国际公约。

由于《巴黎公约》中涉及商标的内容,因此,美国外交代表无权在《巴黎公约》上签字,因此,也没有出席 1883 年的巴黎会议。但是,1887 年 3 月 18 日美国通知瑞士联邦委员会,美国政府加入《巴黎公约》,但是《巴黎公约》中有关商标的内容美国需要单独安排,《巴黎公约》自 1887 年 5 月 30 日起对美国生效③。

---

①　WIPO,The International Protection of Industrial Property:From The Paris Convention to The TRIPs Agreement,http://www. wipo. int/meetings/en/fulltext_mdocs. jsp？q = Paris + Convention + for + the + Protec,访问日期:2018 年 4 月 11 日。

②　同上。

③　同上

由此可见,由于美国对于科学技术等知识产权问题的重视,最终引起和促成了第一部知识产权国际公约的诞生,从这个角度来说,也是为国际知识产权的建立和发展起到了一定的积极作用。

从另一个方面来说,对于科学技术问题的重视和对保护科学技术的坚持,也有其历史的根源、传统和特点。

(二)美国建立起世界上第一个抵制社会主义的科学技术组织

美国对于"科学技术"所能产生的社会作用和社会效果的认识并没有停留在建立知识产权国际公约上,他们早就发现和认识到"科学技术"在处理国际政治关系上也具有独特的作用,能够产生独特的社会效果。为此,在第二次世界大战结束以后,美国就筹划建立了利用"战略物资"和"科学技术"作为武器来封锁、遏制和打击社会主义国家发展的专门性国际组织——巴黎统筹委员会。

巴黎统筹委员会的全称为"对共产党国家出口管制统筹委员会"(CO－COM),是美国专门在世界范围内用于对付社会主义国家的一种手段和工具,采取的措施主要是在重要物资和先进科学技术上对社会主义国家进行禁止贸易或者限制贸易,以达到遏制社会主义国家的发展,或者颠覆社会主义国家制度的目的。

早在俄国发生"十月革命"以后,美国就宣布《对敌国贸易法》适用于苏俄,对苏俄实行贸易禁运,这一遏制政策一直延续到第二次世界大战爆发。在第二次世界大战期间,由于需要共同对付德国纳粹的侵略,美苏作为盟国,双方开始进行合作和相互支援。

第二次世界大战以后,随着美苏意识形态的差异和对全球发展趋势的不同主张,美国又开始对苏联采取其惯用的制裁手段。1947 年 12 月 17 日,美国国家安全委员会作出决定,立即无限期地停止向苏联及其附庸国出口所有美国短缺的物资和有助于增强原苏联军事潜力的物资。1948 年 3 月 1 日,美国政府开始实行新的贸易管制制度,禁止向苏联、东欧国家出口美国贸易管制清单内的各种物资。1949 年 2 月,美国国会制定了战后第一个《出口管制法》,将对共产党国家的贸易管制制度确定下来①。

除了自己采取制裁措施以外，为了扩大制裁力量，美国最初曾经设想与北约组织一起采取制裁行动，把经济安全作为西方政治和军事战略的组成部分，并且进一步提出建立一个国际贸易管制组织，与《共同防卫援助协定》联系起来。令美国没有想到的是，这些方案都遭到西欧国家的抵制。在这种情况下，1949 年 11 月 23 日，美国提议建立一个由有关国家政府高级官员组成的非政府性的"协商团体"（CG），下设由事务级官员组成的技术专家处和秘书处。1950 年 1 月 9 日，正式将该协商团体的执行机构定名为"对共产党国家出口管制统筹委员会"（CO – COM），总部设在美国驻巴黎大使馆，因此，该机构又简称"巴统"。美国、英国、法国、意大利、比利时、荷兰是巴统组织的创始国。在朝鲜战争结束以前，卢森堡、挪威、丹麦、加拿大、西德、葡萄牙、日本、希腊、土耳其先后加入。1985—1989 年，西班牙和澳大利亚加入巴统。至此，巴统一共有 17 个正式成员方。北约成员方当中，只有冰岛这一个国家不是巴统成员方②。

从 19 世纪 60 年代起，巴黎统筹委员会遏制社会主义国家的政策逐渐发生调整，由禁运战略物资转向限制高新技术转让，加强了对高新技术的控制和禁运。

1976 年，美国国防部国防科学局研究小组提出了《对先进技术输出管制的分析》报告，系统论证了东西方贸易管制政策的重点从战略物资禁运转向限制高新技术转让的必要性和涉及的一系列政策问题。1979 年，美国《出口管制法》正式将限制高新技术转让作为出口管制的"特殊重点"，并将"军事方面重要技术清单"作为美国商品管制清单的组成部分。其中包括计算机网络技术、大型计算机系统技术、软件技术、瞬时处理信息自动控制技术、集成材料、防务材料处理和制造技术、能源开采技术、大型积集和特大型积集设计制造技术、军事仪器技术、电子通信技术、诱导和控制技术、超短波构成技术、军用车辆引擎技术、高级光学（光纤）技术、传感技术、海底系统技术等③。

---

① 崔丕："美国的遏制战略与巴黎统筹委员会、中国委员会论纲"，载《东北师大学报（哲学社会科学版）》2000 年第 2 期，第 48 ~ 49 页。

② 崔丕："美国的遏制战略与巴黎统筹委员会、中国委员会论纲"，载《东北师大学报（哲学社会科学版）》2000 年第 2 期，第 48 ~ 49 页。

③ 崔丕："美国的遏制战略与巴黎统筹委员会、中国委员会论纲"，载《东北师大学报（哲学社会科学版）》2000 年第 2 期，第 54 页。

随着苏联的解体,国际社会形势发生重大变化,1994 年 3 月 31 日,巴黎统筹委员会、中国委员会宣布解散①。

(三)美国建立了世界上第一个控制科学技术交易的组织

1994 年 3 月,由美国的主导下于荷兰瓦森纳举行的高层会议上进一步确认了解散"巴统"的决定。1994 年 3 月 31 日,"巴统"正式解散。参加国同意在新的机制建立之前,继续采用"巴统"的控制清单作为全球出口管制的基础。原来与"巴统"合作的奥地利、芬兰、爱尔兰、新西兰、瑞典和瑞士等国被纳入"新论坛"。1995 年,美国联合一些盟国先在荷兰的瓦森纳召开会议,决定加快建立常规武器和双用途物资及技术的出口控制机制,弥补现行大规模杀伤性武器及其运载工具控制机制的不足。1996 年,在奥地利维也纳签署了《瓦森纳协定》,决定从 1996 年 11 月 1 日起实施新的控制清单和信息交换规则②。成员包括原"巴统"的全部 17 个成员以外,还增加了俄罗斯等其他国家,1996 年成立时共有 33 个成员方,至今已经增加到 40 多个国家,但是把中国、伊朗等国家排除在外③。

《瓦森纳协定》有两份清单,一份是军品清单;另一份是军民两用商品和技术清单。军品清单中涵盖了各类武器弹药、设备及作战平台等共 22 类;军民两用商品和技术清单中涵盖了先进材料、材料处理、电子器件、计算机、电信与信息安全、传感与激光、导航与航空电子仪器、船舶与海事设备、推进系统等九大类,每一类的限制内容又具体划分为 5 个小类别,即设备、组件与部件,测试、检验与生产设备,材料,软件,技术④。

2007 年 6 月 19 日,美国商务部正式公布了《对中华人民共和国出口和再出口管制政策的修改和阐释;新的经验证最终用户制度;进口证明与中国最终用户说明要求的修改》,扩大了对我国出口物品和技术的管制范围,虽然在某

---

① 崔丕:"美国的遏制战略与巴黎统筹委员会、中国委员会论纲",载《东北师大学报(哲学社会科学版)》2000 年第 2 期,第 55 页。
② 科工力量:"听习主席博鳌演讲:是要翻翻美国对中国技术封锁的账了",http://user. guancha. cn/main/content? id = 11952&page = 0,访问日期:2018 年 4 月 11 日。
③ 王丽丽:"'对华禁令'下的创新方向",载《装备制造》2009 年第 8 期,第 88 页。
④ 科工力量:"听习主席博鳌演讲:是要翻翻美国对中国技术封锁的账了",http://user. guancha. cn/main/content? id = 11952&page = 0,访问日期:2018 年 4 月 11 日。

些程序上有所修改,但是实质上更加严格了管控措施①。

(四)颁布《1996 经济间谍法》是美国长期奉行的治国政策在法律中的体现

通过上述分析和讨论可以进一步看出,对于涉及高新技术的美国企业的商业秘密来说,如果被盗窃以后使得外国政府受益,通过上述的介绍和分析可以看出,按照美国政府长期以来处理国际关系的观点和判断标准来说,很自然地会把这种盗窃行为列为间谍行为,只是由于商业秘密具有财产的属性,因此界定为“经济间谍罪”。这里似乎体现着一种思维的惯性和做法上的传统性,从而使得美国在处理国际关系的方式和方法上基本保持不变。同时这也能够说明,美国政府对于当前国际关系的评价和判断与过去没有实质性的变化和改变。

有了这种分析和认识以后,也许可以在一定程度上解释为什么在美国的商业秘密立法中专门设立“经济间谍罪”这一带有明显政治色彩的罪名和刑事处罚措施了。

当然,如果想从理论上对于这一问题再进行比较全面的考证和分析,还可以从政治、经济等多个方面进行讨论,在此就不再过多地进行讨论。

三、现有的专利法等其他知识产权法律自身存在着缺陷和不足

由于商业秘密包含着技术秘密和经营秘密两类有价值的秘密信息,对于先进的技术秘密来说,除了利用商业秘密法律进行保护以外,还可以借助专利法、植物新品种保护法、集成电路布图设计保护法等相关法律来进行保护。但是,在现实中,仍然有不少企业选择利用商业秘密法律来保护自己的先进科学技术,如果对这种现象进行分析就能发现,这里面主要存在着如下几方面的原因。

(一)专利技术的公开和保护期限的限制是高精技术的一大障碍

由于受到《巴黎公约》以及《TRIPs 协议》的影响和制约,在这些公约和协定的所有成员方的专利法中,申请和授予专利权的基本条件和基本程序都是相似的,保护的期限也基本接近或者一致。

---

① 商务部新闻办公室:“商务部产业司负责人就美对华出口管制新规定接受记者采访”,http://www. mofcom. gov. cn/article/ae/ai/200706/20070604822694. shtml,访问日期:2018 年 4 月 24 日。

而在现有的专利法中,以发明专利为例,首先都必须经过向全世界公开全部专利技术的程序。这样,对于花费较大投资获得的高精的技术来说,客观上就必须承担被世界各国的不同企业免费使用的巨大风险。对于任何一个公司来说,当它已经花费了巨额资金研发出某一尖端的科学技术以后,即使它再花费较多的投资在世界各国申请专利,一方面难以保证在不同的国家都能及时地获得专利权;另一方面,即使在某一个国家获得了专利权,但是,一旦在该国发生了专利侵权以后,如果再到这个国家去开展维权活动,无论从人力、物力和财力上来说,都将是一笔不小的开支。而且,在当今社会,在不同的国家进行知识产权诉讼,即使案情基本相同或者相似,也可能会产生不同甚至相反的判决结果,具有很大的不可预知性,这样都增加了维权的实际风险和困难。另外,以我国为例,即使在诉讼中打赢了官司,还有一个执行的问题,也就是不得不面对"执行难"的问题。可以想象,对于一个国外的高科技公司来说,这些工作都是额外发生的,也都是他们不擅长的工作,因此,都是他们不愿意面对的工作。而在现有的法律体系下,如果不采用专利法等上述几种可供选择的法律,也只能选择和利用商业秘密的法律来保护自己的高精技术。

除此之外,专利权都有保护期限的限制,对于一些尖端技术来说,它们在生产经营中所能实际发挥作用的期限可能长于专利权的保护期限,在这种情况下,过早地公开这一尖端技术,并且在这一技术还在发挥重要作用的期间就已经失去了法律的保护,这种状况对于这一尖端技术的权利人来说显然都是比较大的损失,这些因素都在客观上影响和制约着利用专利法等现有的其他知识产权法律来保护尖端技术的积极性。

(二)尖端技术难以被他人破解

按照现有的法律规定,通过合法的反向工程方式破解他人的商业秘密属于合法行为,除此之外,未经商业秘密权利人的许可,获取、披露或者使用他人的商业秘密的行为都是非法行为。

在这种情况下,只要某一尖端的技术在正常使用下难以被他人利用反向工程的方式进行破解,而且能够采取合理有效的保密措施进行长期的保护,那么在现实中就能长期的使用,而且被他人侵权的机会也会很少。从这个角度来说,选择利用商业秘密的方式来保护这一尖端技术要比利用专利法进行保护更加合理,当然,前提是商业秘密保护的法律要完善和有效。

　　在当今世界范围内,美国作为世界上科技最发达的国家,美国企业拥有许多世界顶级的尖端技术,从总体上来说,对这些技术使用有效的商业秘密法律进行保护要比使用专利制度进行保护更加合理。因此,这也在一定程度上促使美国比其他国家更加重视商业秘密法律的立法和保护工作,以及不断加强对各类商业秘密侵害行为的打击力度,只有这样才能更好地保护美国企业大量的商业秘密和尖端技术。

后　记

　　虽然在出国之前,笔者已经对我国、美国、德国、法国、日本、俄罗斯等一些国家的商业秘密保护立法情况进行过多年的研究,但是,2015年我在美国斯坦福大学法学院做访问学者时查阅和分析了一些资料以后,还是对美国有关商业秘密保护的立法和研究情况感到惊讶。当时,我非常明显地感受到我国与美国在商业秘密保护立法和学术研究方面存在很大的差距,这种差距既有立法技术方面的差异,更有立法理念和对商业秘密这一事物整体认识上的差别。对于商业秘密,我国整体上的认识和观念显得比较狭窄,明显地带有受国外,特别是以德国立法为代表的大陆法系立法理念和立法体系的影响,而且明显地体现着我国知识产权立法中普遍存在的受国外立法影响的制约性和被动性,似乎不敢擅自越雷池一步,这些特点从我国有关商业秘密的立法上就能表现出来。

　　为此,我当时就想把美国现有的商业秘密法律翻译介绍给国内的同行和读者。美国整个商业秘密法律体系包括联邦法律和各个州法律两部分。联邦法律比较集中,但是,各个州的法律却各不相同,对于商业秘密保护的刑事责任都由各个州的刑法规定,难以逐一整理。比较有利的是在民事保护方面,美国有50个州都已经基本在适用《统一商业秘密法》和《侵权法重述》两部示范法,这样,通过介绍这两部示范法就能够基本涵盖美国各个州保护商业秘密的民事责任的基本状况。

　　另外,我注意到,对于我国广大的具有涉外学习和工作背景的读者来说,最大的危险是涉及"经济间谍罪",而且这种风险似乎正在增大。这一犯罪属于联邦性商业秘密法律的范畴,不仅美国已经有了 4 部相关的法律规定,而且美国国会也正在加强这方面的立法,一批新的相关法律也已经处于国会的审议之中。因此,我把"经济间谍罪"作为研究的重点。

这样,从 2015 年开始,我就一直在关注和整理分析有关这方面的材料。在 2017 年冬季到 2018 年上半年,我集中了半年多的时间终于完成了这一书稿,期望这一本书能够为我国的商业秘密保护学术研究和立法工作,特别是对于具有涉外背景的读者们有所帮助。

在本书的调查、研究、写作和出版过程中,得到过许多亲朋好友的真诚的支持和帮助,在此一并感谢!

侯仰坤

2018 年 8 月 16 日于北京